BOOKS BY
GILBERT CHINARD

●··●··●··●··●

THOMAS JEFFERSON : *The Apostle of Americanism*

HONEST JOHN ADAMS

HONEST JOHN ADAMS

HONEST JOHN ADAMS

BY

GILBERT CHINARD

LITTLE, BROWN AND COMPANY · BOSTON · TORONTO

GILBERT CHINARD'S *HONEST JOHN ADAMS*

AN APPRECIATION

IF one goes to the *Harvard Guide to American History* (1955) in search of the best one-volume biography of John Adams, he will find listed there Gilbert Chinard's *Honest John Adams*. Checking further in the authoritative Library of Congress *Guide to the Study of the United States* (1960), he will find the same listing. Yet when these guides were published the Chinard life was out of print, and secondhand copies could be purchased only with difficulty.

Professor Chinard's biography of John Adams was first published in 1933, four years after his biography of Thomas Jefferson. The two books showed the same care in research and skill in writing; each has been highly praised as the most readable one-volume life of its subject. While one went through several reprintings and was published in a revised second edition, the other fell stillborn from the press and soon went out of print. So disproportionate was the popularity of the Jefferson image during the early years of the New Deal that John Adams stood in the shadows, nobody's favorite.

The status of our American heroes is constantly shifting. In the 1940's we found new stature in James Madison; in the 1950's we at last rediscovered John Adams. Famous without being truly known even in his own lifetime, Adams became during the nineteenth and early twentieth centuries a half-forgotten man of American history. Then with suddenness the spotlight veered, and in the past twelve years Adams has had more study devoted to him, more books written about him, than in the hundred and twenty-five years previous to 1950.

Among recent Adams books are important documentary publications: the six volumes of diaries, autobiographies and early letters superbly edited by L. H. Butterfield; two Adams "dialogues" — the magnificent exchange of letters between Adams and Jefferson in their old age, and the Adams debate (written in the margins of his books) with the *philosophes* and theorists of the French Revolution. Two new Adams biographies have appeared: the charming fictionalized portrait of the young Adams by Catherine Drinker Bowen, and the prize-winning, two-volume biography by Page Smith, which will be the definitive study for our generation. Important new monographs deal with Adams's presidency and the tortuous politics-cum-diplomacy of the 1790's. Adams even emerges as the hero of a novel, which pretends that a secret mission from George III offered to make him the Duke of Braintree if he would stop the Revolution. Besides this small library of books centering on Adams published since 1950, there have been scores of essays and articles. The late President Kennedy shortly after his election reviewed the early Butterfield volumes, thus giving John Adams an exceptional kudos.

What special qualities distinguish Chinard's *Honest John Adams* to justify its reprinting?

First, in the great French tradition of popular scholarship, Chinard writes in order to make his reader share his pleasure and wonder in the greatness and rich humanity of John Adams. He succeeds in making us feel the intensity of this passionate New England moralist and puritan turned revolutionary statesman; he makes us recognize the vanity, inflexibility, contrariness joined in Adams with courage, wisdom and integrity. "Always an honest man, sometimes a great one, but sometimes absolutely mad" — thus Jefferson paraphrases a comment of Franklin's about Adams. It is Chinard's chief virtue that his readers understand why John Adams's colleagues would reach such colorful judgments on him.

Secondly, Chinard's portrait remains a true likeness of John Adams. Readers will certainly ask, Has Butterfield's more complete edition of the Adams manuscripts not changed the earlier estimate of the man? Chinard based his study on the ten-volume collection of John Adams's writing which the grandson, C. F. Adams, published in 1850-56. In Butterfield's judgment, C. F. Adams was "the ablest historical editor of his time," and one who was scrupulous both in not holding back any key manuscripts and in achieving "textual fidelity." His only error of judgment was in printing more public and official letters than ones to the family and private friends, thereby exaggerating the formal and pompous traits in the personality of Adams, and minimizing, though not hiding, his warmth, humor, and incurable playfulness. Chinard's readers will not find these latter traits missing in his portrait.

Thirdly, the viewpoint from which Chinard examines his subject makes *Honest John Adams* of special relevance to alert readers today. A major figure of the early republic, John Adams was closely connected with every political crisis in America from 1765 to 1801, and in some of these he was the key figure. Naturally Chinard deals with the history Adams helped to make, but the biographer's deepest interest is less in the public activities of Adams than in his character and in the principles and ideas that informed his politics. It is Chinard's judgment, reached after his sympathetic study of Jefferson, that John Adams was "the most realistic statesman of his generation in America." In particular Chinard stresses his criticism of eighteenth-century doctrines of progress and his dubiety whether simple democracy is the panacea for all political ills. These embarrassing questions with which Adams challenges our pioneer optimism help explain why he has not been a popular figure during so much of our history.

As Chinard makes clear, however, it is wrong to call Adams anti-democratic. He believed that the people ought to be sovereign, but he also recognized that they are on occasion unwise, unjust, even brutal. His strictures on democracy therefore became a series of questions asking us, the sovereign people of the United States, how we can make ourselves more wise, more just, and more faithful in serving the common good. Chinard's Adams, then, is not merely a great and delightful personality that each of us is the richer for knowing; he is also a man who speaks seriously to us about enduring issues of our own time.

These are the reasons why I am so pleased to see this biography back in print, at a price that will make it available to the wide audience it deserves. Hopefully it will introduce John Adams to many who know him hardly at all, and I suspect that, in the words of his great compatriot Thomas Jefferson, they will find him "so amiable, that I pronounce you will love him if ever you became acquainted with him."

DOUGLASS ADAIR
Professor of American History
Claremont Graduate School

INTRODUCTION

It is a strange reflection on the attitude of democracies towards their great men that America should have exalted two born aristocrats from Virginia and failed to recognize in John Adams, the descendant of humble and honest folk, a striking illustration of the principle of "equal opportunities", and the symbol of a new social order. More than a century after his death, the second President of the United States remains unsung, a distant and lonely figure in American history. Between Washington, who saved and made the country, and Jefferson, who heralded in the New World the advent of democracy, John Adams stands in a chiaroscuro as a man of fundamental honesty and real courage, to whose memory is attached no great historical achievement. Mount Vernon and Monticello have become national shrines, but the stone church at Quincy, in which the "old chief" sleeps his last sleep "till the trump shall sound", receives only a casual glance from the hurried tourist. The man who had wished to be buried alone on a rocky hill under a slab of granite would be the last one to protest against this neglect, for all his life he was haunted by a feeling of frustration and unfulfillment.

Born in New England and buried in New England, he seems to belong to New England more than to the country. During his life he failed to appeal to the imagination of his contemporaries, and to posterity he bequeathed no sharply coined motto, no political maxims to be quoted on patriotic occasions and used in electoral campaigns. Never yearning for popular applause, he was refused popular recognition after his death and no legend has formed around him. In a country where hero worship may be considered a national trait, he seems to have been excluded from the Pantheon of great Americans.

To the student of international psychology, however, the

"fortune" of John Adams and the story of his destiny offer a fascinating field of research. Granting that Washington, who will always remain a somewhat mysterious and puzzling figure, stands by himself, that Benjamin Franklin was the first to explain his country to Europe and to make American traits acceptable to the sophisticated peoples of the Old World, that Jefferson exemplifies a unique and striking combination of pioneer vision, classical learning and eighteenth-century optimism, John Adams has appeared to many historians as the personification of all that is stanch, honest, stubborn and somewhat narrow in his native province. Americans as well as foreigners have been so prone to overemphasize the democratic aspects of American civilization and the American mirage has lured so many adventurous spirits in their quest of happiness, that we have a traditional and well-rooted tendency to underestimate or ignore the continuous efforts made during the last century and a half on the new continent to select an élite from among the people and to balance the ship on an even keel. Having very few born aristocrats, and apparently frowning on aristocracies, America has offered splendid opportunities for men of energy and talent to become self-made aristocrats. Such was the case of John Adams, whose ascent was only possible in a democracy.

Born on a farm, educated at first in the village public school, the boy Adams did the usual chores, — cutting wood for the stove, making hay in the summer, and reluctantly digging ditches in the marshy meadows. Like his father, he would have become in time a deacon in the church and an officer in the militia, had not the family decided to send him to Harvard and to have him study for the ministry. An impecunious and hardworking student during his college years, he soon discovered that for all the social prestige he enjoyed, the New England minister, subject to constant watching and to the criticism of village theologians, had a very unenviable lot. Dreading the ordeal, fearing to be unequal to the task, unwilling to profess doctrines in which he did not believe and conscious that he could not repress his ebullient disposition, the young man, to the great distress of his family, decided to give up the ministry.

In another land, in other times, he would have become a

writer and found in the production of literary work.
of self-expression for which he always yearned. He
of the English moralists and essayists; he had real ta.
observation, caustic delineation of characters; he re
against social evil and social injustice and he was not devoid of
courage. Studious, learned, at times pedantic, an omnivorous
reader with a distinct preference for history, politics and
philosophy, he would have made a name for himself in London
or Paris. In Boston he could only be a lawyer and through his
legal practice hope to acquire enough leisure to indulge in his
literary hobbies. Mixing freely with sea captains, fishermen
and good country people, he felt a naïve and almost childish
pleasure when invited to the houses of the Boston gentry.
Simple in his ways, but not democratic in the current sense of
the word, he abominated the rabble, the blind anger of the
mob, and did not hesitate to appear before the court for Captain
Preston of Boston Massacre fame. Had not the Revolution
come, he would have lived in Boston for the rest of his days,
as a successful lawyer, slowly gathering a comfortable com-
petency, at times writing letters to the newspapers, joining
literary clubs, a good father and a respectable member of the
bar. Such a slow ascent would have raised him noticeably above
the social level of his forebears, but would have been in no way
different from the ascent of a typical European bourgeois.

The Revolution took him out of his provincial surroundings
when he was forty, already portly and "hippy", and made of
him a national figure. Unlike Franklin, who foresaw the westward development of the United States, and unlike Jefferson,
who, being born on the fringe of the frontier, was an expan-
sionist, John Adams had no great vision of the future of America. He did not go to Paris to preach a new political gospel, to
represent his country as the "example and the hope of the
world." He was too well versed in ancient and modern history,
he had studied too well and too long the works of Cicero,
Polybius, Bolingbroke and Montesquieu to believe that there
was any possibility of setting up anywhere on earth a new form
of government. The political history of Europe from the
ancient times was a long recital of the rise and fall of societies

and states; everywhere and ineluctably, at a certain time, the best constituted government degenerated. To imagine that America, making an exception to the rule, would enjoy an uninterrupted and continuous progress was a dangerous illusion. Externally the country would encounter animosities and jealousies, just as the other nations of the world; internally it would be subjected to the same convulsions and revolutions which had torn the old empires. To avoid external dangers without suppressing them entirely, the new republic had to avoid all possible entanglements and foreign alliances and give the impression that it could pursue its course without foreign help. To insure some sort of stability to the internal government, a system based not upon a political ideal but upon the moral constitution of man had to be established.

John Adams' puritanical training, his study of the ancient moralists, his own observations and temperament, had led him early to the conclusion that men in all times and in all climes are led by selfish motives and selfish considerations, often disguised under high-sounding names. Human nature cannot be reformed, but it can be corrected, and above all it must be held in check. Men everywhere strive to rise above their own level, they covet more power, more influence, more prestige, more riches, and when in power always try to keep what they have acquired. There were, in his opinion, no special virtues and no special wisdom in the people, not any more than in the aristocratic or ruling classes. Both were formed of the same clay, both were subject to the same weaknesses and appetites, and any government which gave undue influence to the many or to the few was equally unstable and tyrannical. Political wisdom, then, consists in opposing these two forces, which pull in contrary directions, so as to obtain a certain equilibrium, at best precarious, but preferable to the alternate rules of the mob and the aristocracy of which history offers so many examples. A good constitution of government should essentially be based on an elaborate system of checks and balances, so as to prevent usurpation of powers by men in office and to preserve the rights of the people, as well as to make impossible ochlocracy or mob rule and the subjection of society to the whims of the mass.

Equally critical of the few and the many, refusing to grant an exclusive right to rule to either, equally misunderstood by both, Adams was abandoned by the aristocrats, who considered him as unreliable and almost as a traitor, and was fiercely insulted by the democrats. Had he been a thinker writing in his study, or a professor of government with a chair at Harvard, he would probably be considered as one of the most original and penetrating writers of his generation. He was, at any rate, the most consistent and systematic critic of the theory of infinite progress so dear to Condorcet, which corresponded so exactly to the aspirations and ambitions of a young country. The pitiless dissection of democracy, the pessimistic analysis of society, found in Adams' writings could not appeal to a nation of builders and pioneers.

To a young people who had recently drunk of the strong wine of liberty and was preparing to write a new page in the history of the world, Adams proposed a philosophy of life and government based on the experience of past civilizations. Eighteenth-century theories had failed in Europe with the French Revolution but many believed that they could succeed in a new country unfettered by traditions and historical fatality, with a God-chosen people convinced of its manifest destiny.

That such a faith and such an *élan vital* singularly favored the growth of America at the beginning of her national history cannot be denied. For almost a century and a half it had been the country where the dreams of the French philosophers came true, a land of limitless opportunities opened to all, where life had run more generous and faster, where the horizon had widened with each generation, and where the future seemed always secure.

American democracy, however, from its very beginning, has been restricted and limited by the very checks and balances praised and defined by John Adams in his "Defence of the American Constitutions of Government." The Constitution of 1787 was far from being the complete and accurate expression of the principles proclaimed by Jefferson in the Declaration of

Independence. It was a compromise which pleased Adams more than Jefferson. It established a conservative body, chosen by the legislatures to counteract the power of the popular assembly directly elected by the voters, and in the words of Madison, the Senate was admirably organized to protect the minority of the opulent against the majority. It gave to the chief executive more power than any constitutional monarch of Europe ever had, and through an elaborate system provided this equilibrium, which seemed to Adams the only possible means to avoid the disasters which had befallen the republics of the ancient and modern world.

For a hundred and fifty years the political philosophies of Adams and Jefferson have ruled alternately the destinies of America, and eighteenth-century optimism has contended against historical pessimism. Whether America can continue to have a development of her own and become the home of a new race of men preserved from the weaknesses and faults of the rest of mankind, or whether the country, now "come of age", will follow the same course and will encounter the same obstacles and difficulties as the older nations, is a question for the political prophets to decide.

A careful study of John Adams' writings would enable them at any rate to throw a singularly vivid light on the most perplexing problems of the present. As much as Jefferson he contributed to the formulation of the puzzling and often contradictory theories which may be called the doctrine of Americanism. The author of the Declaration of Independence and the writer of the "Defence of the American Constitutions of Government" are the two extreme points between which the American system has oscillated since its beginning. Never were the two doctrines satisfactorily reconciled and never will they be, for both of them are the expressions of radically opposed philosophies of life.

Through an unique good fortune the two men who had been the chief exponents of these radically opposed doctrines spent the last twelve years of their lives discussing freely the underlying principles of their philosophies. Without being hampered by the fear of having their letters published and used as campaign material, they wrestled with the fundamental problems of government and society. Always "protestant and never reformed", Adams appears in this correspondence with Jefferson true to himself, full of apparent contradictions and intensely human. An American, he had all the faults, prejudices and traditions of the man of the Old World. A pessimist who did not believe in the goodness of human nature and who thought that men had, after all, the kind of government they deserved, he was to his last day ready to sacrifice his personal interest and to fight for the rights of his fellow beings. A self-made aristocrat, he led a simple life, never gathered a fortune, and never thought of building a palace for his old days. A regular and orderly citizen who never broke a law, he never hesitated to speak his mind and to criticize unreservedly the institutions of his country. An irascible man, subject to uncontrollable fits of temper, he was a devoted and faithful husband, a friend and a guide for his children and a loving grandfather.

At all times he was himself and intensely honest. A son of New England, where reticence, reserve and self-control are held essential virtues, he was irrepressible and unguarded in his speech and writings. To the end of his days he remained as much of an *enfant terrible* as Clemenceau, and belongs to the same intellectual family as the old "Tiger." Keeping his feet squarely on the ground, refusing to be carried away by theories, even by his own, this philosopher and moralist was the most realistic statesman of his generation in America.

He loved his country passionately and jealously, with the love of the farmer for the mother earth, for the soil tilled by his forbears in which he will be buried. In Paris, more concerned with the security than the growth of the United States, he fought for American rights against friend and foe.

During his Presidency, he entertained no imperialistic designs and sacrificed his popularity to keep out of the war. In a land where the pioneer spirit dominated, he exemplified a type of patriotism more often associated with Europe than with America. In a nation often compared to an army on the march, he stands as the best representative of the people who stayed at home, plodding and ploughing the ancestral acres. This isolationist who wanted to protect his country against all foreign entanglements was more conscious than any of his contemporaries of the cultural bonds which connected America with Europe, and of her intellectual and moral kinship with the nations of the Old World.

GILBERT CHINARD

CONTENTS

CONTENTS

BOOK ONE

THE PROGRESS OF JOHN ADAMS

CHAPTER I

A NEW ENGLAND BOYHOOD

ON October 19, 1735, John Adams, the son of a modest land-owner, was born in a typical New England farmhouse, built of clapboards and brick, covered with shingles, and widened by a lean-to, added as an afterthought. It had been put together by his paternal grandfather in 1681, and was in no way different from the other unpretentious structures scattered a short distance from the shore, which then constituted the town of Brain-tree, not far from Boston. Yet the place had its originality and character; it also had its memories. There Captain Wollaston, steering for the "high mountain of Massachusit" (the summit of the Blue Hills) had landed in 1625, and there he had left a settlement under the headship of a certain Thomas Morton, whose name was to become anathema around New England.

To Morton and his gay companions, the newly settled land was not to become a New Jerusalem, but a land where care-free, joyous and independent vagabonds could carouse far from the restraining hand of custom and give free play to their exuberant spirits. Frowned upon by the Plymouth authorities, but left undisturbed for almost two years, the adventurers became an insufferable thorn in the side of the Pilgrims after their grand carouse of May Day, 1627. Not only had they erected a Maypole, but they started the beating of drums, discharging of muskets, and dancing with ribald songs:

> Drink and be merry, merry, merry boyes;
> Let all your delight be in the Hymens joyes
> To the Hymen, now the day is come,
> About the merry Maypole take a Roome.

For several days the festivity lasted; with "lasses in beaver coats" they "frisked like so many fairies, or furies rather."

There was a Renaissance and Rabelaisian rejoicing in the wilderness of Mare Mount, or Merry Mount, as Morton had called the inviting spot between the shore and the first slopes of the Blue Hills, a few miles away. The scene was shocking enough, but Morton became intolerable when he was suspected of having sold arms and spirits to the dreaded Indians. The settlement had become a public danger for the neighboring communities and, with characteristic ruthlessness, the Plymouth magistrates undertook to eradicate the evil. The story is well known. Morton was arrested by Captain Miles Standish and sent back to England. A few months later John Endicott crossed the Bay from Salem, hewed down the Maypole, and warned the remaining roisterers that "ther should be better walking." Thus the first attempt to establish a colony of "gallant vagabonds" in the New Canaan had failed, and of their settlement nothing remained but the name Merry Mount as a sort of defiance to the sterner spirit of New England.[1]

Four years later a company of immigrants of a very different character, fleeing from Braintree, Essex, arrived during the summer and settled at the Mount. Hardly an hour's ride from Boston, it was at first considered an extension of the larger group, and the land, owned by Bostonians, was not really settled until the end of the decade. The town of Braintree, however, had obtained its charter in 1640; a meetinghouse had been built, magistrates elected, and the typical system of local government — the town meeting — established.[2]

Among the grantees of these lands was one Henry Adams,

[1] The most picturesque account of Merry Mount will be found in Thomas Morton's "New Canaan", Amsterdam, 1637, reprinted in Force's "American Tracts", and in the "Publications of the Prince Society" (1883). See also Charles Francis Adams, "Three Episodes of Massachusetts History", 2 vols., Boston, 1892, and Samuel Eliot Morison, "Builders of the Bay Colony", Boston, 1930.

[2] On the history of Braintree see, "Some Account of the Early History and Present State of the Town of Quincy", by George Whitney, *Christian Register's* office, 1827; Charles Francis Adams, "History of Braintree, Massachusetts (1639–1708)", "The North Precinct of Braintree (1708–1792)", Cambridge, 1891, and "Three Episodes of Massachusetts History", Boston, 1892; also "Three Hundred Years of Quincy", by Daniel Munro Wilson, Quincy, 1926.

the American progenitor of a most remarkable family, who probably had recently come over from England. He received, on the twenty-fourth day of the twelfth month, 1640, forty acres, at three shillings per acre. Very little is known of this early pioneer, who may or may not have been a brother of a certain Thomas Adams of London, a person of importance, one of the grantees of the first charter of the Colony of Massachusetts Bay, but who never left England. In 1646 he became lord mayor of London.

Whatever may have been the remote origins of the family, its history begins with the immigrant who broke ground at Braintree and put up a shelter for his wife, his eight sons, and his daughter Ursula. He had little time in which to improve his land, and when he died, in 1646, his estate amounted to seventy-five pounds, thirteen shillings, the land and personal property being of equal value. He had built a house of two rooms — the bedroom and parlor, in a corner of which were treasured some old books, and as a remnant of Old World luxuries "one silver spoon." In the stable were a cow, a heifer and swine. A farmer he was, in the true American sense of the word, standing foursquare on the land he had bought and owned, paying no rent, and calling no man his master. He was a pioneer undertaking to reclaim the wilderness, but, as the early settlers of New England, he remained within sight of the sea, which could afford a refuge, an escape, a means of returning to the old country in case of danger or ruin. Consciously or unconsciously, they were loath to establish themselves far from the coast. The true pioneers were those who penetrated the howling wilderness and cut their paths through the virgin forest; remote as were these early immigrants from their mother country, they had not severed all connection with civilization; in them appeared no eremitic or Rousseauistic leanings.

Of Henry Adams' large number of children, only two, Peter and Joseph, settled for life at Braintree. Joseph (1626–1694), probably the youngest son of the family, married Abigail Baxter, the 26th of November, 1650. Emulating his father, he had no less than twelve children, and added to his farm a malt house and a brewery. A useful member of the town, he took his share of the duties incumbent upon each inhabitant. When a young man, he had served as a drummer in the military organization in which three of his elder brothers served as sergeants. Later he was chosen as selectman and surveyor of highways, the latter being a hard task as well as an honor. But although the social standing of the family was slowly rising, the American Adamses had not yet attained social recognition; theirs was the lot of the hard-working, modest country folks, very different from the *haute bourgeoisie* already established in Boston. That they were ambitious to rise above the ordinary level of farmers appeared in the third generation.

The respect of the early New Englanders for such knowledge as could be obtained in the colony was perhaps one of their most characteristic traits. As early as 1636, the General Court had appropriated "four hundred pounds towards a school or college", to which was added, two years later, the bequest by John Harvard of his library and half his fortune. The infant seminary had grown throughout the seventeenth century and had rapidly become the center of all intellectual life in the colony. Limited as the scope of the curriculum may have been in the early days, and in spite of its theological emphasis, it presented the great advantage of enabling the colonists to educate their sons at home, under the guidance of professors and tutors selected from among the residents. To a certain extent, Harvard contributed to the establishment of a spiritual and intellectual independence long before any real signs of political independence could be discerned. It also helped toward the formation of a certain moral unity, for from the graduates of the young institution were to be recruited the clergymen and magistrates, leaders of the colony. Associations were formed among the young men coming from different settlements. To be educated at Harvard was at once to rise above the common level.

This was keenly felt by Joseph Adams, Junior (1654–1737). Materially his position was not much superior to his father's, but he had married into a good family when he took as his wife Hannah Bass, granddaughter of Deacon Bass, and great-granddaughter of John and Priscilla Alden, of Plymouth and of Mayflower fame. He consequently decided to send to Harvard the first-born of his eleven children, Joseph, the third of the name, who received a college education in lieu of his share in the paternal inheritance. This resulted, however, in removing him from Braintree, and the care of continuing the family tradition fell upon the second son, John (1691–1761).

On the 31st of October, 1734, the first John Adams was married to Susanna Boylston, daughter of Peter Boylston of Brookline. They established themselves in the frame house built in 1681 by the Plymouth highway, and there were born John (October 19, 1735), Peter Boylston (October 16, 1738), and Elihu (May 29, 1741).

The family had grown with the village. Braintree, at the beginning of the eighteenth century, could proudly show an old meetinghouse built of granite, to which was added in 1732 a wooden church and a stone garrison house, to afford refuge and protection against the hostile Indians. It was already noted for its free school, and before the end of the seventeenth century it had sent forty-nine young men to Harvard. Since the raid made by the Indians in 1675, the natives had given little trouble. No great industry had as yet developed, but the farms, with their salt meadows, arable lands and wood extending to the slopes of the Blue Hills, were fairly prosperous. The granite that was later to make the town famous was outcropping everywhere in the fields, but the soil was fairly fertile and yielded abundant crops. The sea generously gave of its fish, which constituted one of the main staples of the first colonists. And above all, in spite of its proximity to Boston, the town had developed a strong local feeling of independence. It could no longer be considered as an extension of Boston, with absentee landowners; it already had its traditions, its old families and, to a certain extent, its aristocracy, with the Quincy family, who, later, were to give their name to the North Precinct.

If not of the very best people, the Adamses occupied a very honorable place in the social life of the village. They were not unlike many New England farmers, slowly and laboriously improving their condition, and placing all their hopes of further fulfillment in their eldest son. In 1722, being by occupation a "cordwainer" or maker of shoes, the first John Adams was chosen a "sealer of leather." In 1724 he was tithingman, in 1727 constable, in 1734 ensign in the militia, and a little later lieutenant; chosen several times as selectman, he finally took his place among the deacons of the church in May, 1747.[3] He died of a current epidemic, probably influenza, in 1761, and many years later his son could truly write of him, on the back of a draft of his will: he had "a good education, though not at college, and was a very capable and useful man. In his early life he was an officer of militia, afterward a deacon of the church, and a selectman of the town; almost all of the business of the town being managed by him in that department for twenty years together; a man of strict piety, and great integrity; much esteemed and beloved, wherever he was known, which was not far, his sphere of life being not very extensive."[4]

This very meager and very general information gives but little insight into the true character of John Adams' father, and even less is known of his mother. In a place where servants were almost nonexistent and slaves could not be had, every inhabitant was of necessity a very practical farmer and a Jack-of-all-trades. Life in Braintree, as in all the rural communities of Massachusetts, was at the same time slow and laborious, for each farm was largely self-supporting. During the long winters, when work in the fields was interrupted for at least five months, implements for the farm were made, all sorts of ingenious contraptions devised for the kitchen and fireplace, furniture made or repaired, and shoes for the family sewed and nailed, while the mother looked after the children and spun by the window. This picture of New England farm life probably needs no re-drawing here, and yet the character and spirit of the New Englanders were molded by these very circumstances. With no slaves and few servants, unlike the Virginians, manual labor was an integral part of their existence. Struggling against an untamed nature, short-handed and with hard work to perform, they made their own tools, perfecting the curve of a handle,

---

[3] Charles Francis Adams, "Three Episodes of Massachusetts History", Vol. II, p. 715.

[4] "Writings of John Adams", Vol. I, p. 12.

the edge of an ax, the shape of a yoke or the traces of a harness. Every good man had to be, in turn, a butcher, a cobbler, a smith, a carpenter and a bricklayer; and the mistress of the house was confronted with endless and most varied tasks. Thus probably was developed Yankee inventiveness and handiness which have permeated the whole country and become true American traits.

But more remarkable perhaps was the eagerness of these people to attain and develop some sort of intellectual culture. Books were few, and the Bible remained the essential and constant guide of life; but the pastor generally had a good enough library so that books could be borrowed, which were slowly read and meditated upon during the winter months; and many were the farmers who, like John Adams' father, without ever going to college, had acquired "a good education." In this respect also the New England farmers, at least those who had settled along the seacoast, were very different not only from the European farmers, but from the Southern mountaineers.

Of the childhood of John Adams very little is known; the few bare facts available to the biographer hardly permit any picture to be drawn. His father had not forgotten that his older brother Joseph had been sent to college — no doubt at a sacrifice — and had thus been enabled to take his place among the New England clergy. The precedent was to be followed, and from his early days the child John was intended for the ministry. Hardly "out of petticoats", as he wrote later, he was sent to school. He was first entrusted to the care of Mrs. Belcher, whose schoolhouse stood on Penn Hill, by a big white-oak tree; and more than once, so the legend goes, the boy helped the old woman carry her corn to the mill, receiving as his reward three coppers, which she commanded him to keep "to buy land with." [5] A few years later he was sent to the Latin school, where he was to go through the frightful ordeal of Greek and Latin grammars. There, for a few years, he sat with John Hancock, son of the pastor of the Congregational Church, until at the death of his father, in 1774, the young Hancock was

[5] Peter Whitney, "Early History and Present State of the Town of Quincy", 1827, p. 43.

adopted by an uncle and sent to Boston. They were to meet again at Harvard, from which Hancock graduated a year ahead of John Adams. His studies did not, however, take all of his time, and it is not likely that the young scholar was excused from the usual chores that would befall the children of any New England farmer. He knew the hard work of the farm, but he also enjoyed the pleasures that a normal child would naturally find in the country, — the long rambles through meadows and woods; perhaps the shooting of birds, for game was plentiful in the forests and on the salt marshes; horseback riding; and the simple festivities of corn-husking, nut-gathering and story-telling. The New England people were not a highly imaginative race, and no fairy stories were told at evening, but the Indians, the *"coureurs des bois"*, the Jesuitical machinations of the black-cassocked priests who lived in New France, and the last sermon of the pastor provided inexhaustible themes for conversation.

Life on a New England farm in the middle of the eighteenth century must have been very dreary, and the long winter an ordeal that inhabitants of more fortunate climes can hardly visualize. Yet it was not quite so bare and desolate as the scenes described by Whittier in "Snowbound", and when Charles Francis Adams drew his well-known picture of life in Braintree, he looked at it as a refined traveler and city dweller, and put into it touches that the old inhabitants would hardly have noticed. It was monotonous and uncomfortable, but not without charms, for, highly intellectual as he seems to have been, and as he really was, John Adams was never reconciled to city life. Whether in Boston, Philadelphia, Paris or London, he always looked back with regret to the days when he roamed through the meadows and woods of Braintree. Able as he was to do his share on the farm, and precisely because on more than one occasion he had to lend a hand, he did not relish physical exertion. In his old days he used to retell an incident which he considered the turning point of his career. It is not as picturesque and dramatic as the apocryphal anecdote of Washington and the cherry tree, but it may well serve to illustrate the characters of both the boy and his father.

"When I was a boy," he used to relate, "I had to study the Latin-grammar; but it was dull and I hated it. My father was anxious to send me to College, and therefore I studied the grammar till I could bear with it no longer; and going to my father, I told him I did not like study, and asked for some other employment. It was opposing his wishes, and he was quick in his answer. 'Well, John,' said he, 'if Latin-grammar does not so suit you, you may try ditching, perhaps that will; my meadow yonder needs a ditch, and you may put by Latin and try that.'

"This seemed a delightful change, and to the meadow I went — But I soon found ditching harder than Latin, and the first forenoon was the longest I ever experienced. That day I ate the bread of labor, and glad was I when night came on. That night I made comparison between Latin-grammar and ditching, but said not a word about it. I dug the next forenoon, and wanted to return to Latin at dinner, but it was humiliating, and I could not do it. At night toil conquered pride, and I told my father, one of the severest trials of my life, that, if he chose, I would go back to Latin-grammar. He was glad of it; and if I have since gained any distinction, it has been owing to the two days' labor in that abominable ditch." [6]

The backbone of his pride once broken, the boy went back to his studies, but the humiliation felt on the occasion was not soon to be forgotten and still appears in the words of the old man. He had to forgo the ramblings in the woods and the marshes, keep to his books, and prepare in earnest for Harvard.

The entrance requirements of the college would seem both limited and exacting to our undergraduates. Nothing was said about history or the sciences, but the candidate had to give evidence of a thorough foundation in Latin, and even in Greek. He had to be of "past blameless behaviour", and in the examination given by the president and at least two tutors, to prove that he was able, "extempore to read, construe, and parse Tully, Virgil or such like common classical Latin authors, and to write true Latin in prose, and to be skilled in making Latin verse, or at least in the rules of the Prosodia, and to read, con-

[6] George Whitney, "Some Account of the Early History of the Town of Quincy", *Christian Register* office, 1827, p. 52.

strue, and parse ordinary Greek, as in the New Testament, Isocrates, or such like, and decline the paradigms of Greek nouns and verbs." [7]

John Adams was only fifteen when, in August, 1751, he entered Harvard College. What these four years were for him can only be surmised, for in his later years he was singularly reticent about his experience as a student. We may venture to say that his Harvard memories were not particularly pleasant. The proud, sensitive boy who, as the eldest of the family and a prospective candidate for the ministry, enjoyed a modicum of prestige and consideration, both at home and in his rural community, had to become the servant of the upper classmen, do errands for them, and submit to their petty and tyrannical requests. For such was the rule that all freshmen had to obey. Worst of all, after roaming at will in the fields, taking his Latin grammar to the hayloft and being for the most part master of his time, he was shut in, not only behind the fence of the college, but even in his room. The rule was, in fact, that the scholars "should keep in their chambers and diligently follow their studies; except half an hour at breakfast; at dinner from twelve to two; and after evening prayers till nine of the clock." Four days a month those who lived within ten miles of the college could visit their friends and family, and those who lived from ten to fifty miles were granted ten days in each quarter for "the aforesaid purpose." During the summer a six-weeks' vacation afforded a longer respite, but the rest of the year was spent under the supervision of the tutors, and mulcts or fines fell heavily on the heads of delinquents.

Curricula have always been deceiving and disappointing documents from which no real view of the work done or benefit acquired by the students may be gathered. The most objectionable feature of the system then in use at Harvard was, perhaps, that each class was placed in charge of a tutor, who kept the direction of it during the four years of the college course, and was supposed to be informed *de omni re scibili*, from geography to metaphysics. Not until 1766 was it proposed that "one tutor shall teach Latin; another, Greek; another Logic, Meta-

[7] Benjamin Peirce, "History of Harvard University", Boston (1831). Appendix, p. 125.

physics, Ethics, and the other Natural Philosophy, Geography, Astronomy, and the Elements of the Mathematics." [8] The unavoidable result was that a large part of the exercises consisted in copying, memorizing from books and reciting, and thus was developed in the students the habit so general in the eighteenth century of keeping a commonplace book. No translating of the Greek and Latin texts was required; the scholars, like parrots, recited from memory a certain number of lines. No examinations were held, and it seems that in most cases the students had simply to show that they had faithfully copied the contents of their textbooks. The minutes of the Board of Overseers are singularly revealing in this respect. On October 6, 1761, a committee reported that they "find upon inquiry that the Students are not required to translate English into Latin nor Latin into English, neither in verse nor prose." On May 4, 1762, "The Board finds that the Tutors have not conformed to the vote passed the last meeting relating to the translations and the introducing of more classical authors; and thereupon, voted, that it be recommended to the President and Tutors to conform to the said vote as soon as may be." [9]

Some of the tutors were superannuated. Tutor Flynt, familiarly called "Father" Flynt by generations of undergraduates, taught at Harvard through sixty-five years, and although the old man endeared himself to the students by his dry wit, his picturesque appearance, and his readiness to mitigate punishment meted out to them, we may well question the value of his teaching.

Philosophy was a very formal affair, but towards the middle of the century enthusiasm for science had reached the colonies, and through generous benefactors the college had been provided with "a machine for experiments of falling bodies, thermometers, barometers, mirrors, lenses, prisms, a telescope of 24 feet, a brass quadrant, 'a curious telescope,' two skeletons of different sexes and anatomical cuts." [10]

That John Adams had a chance to acquire at least some no-

[8] Peirce, *op. cit.*, p. 245.
[9] *Ibid.*, p. 239.
[10] Josiah Quincy, "History of Harvard University", Boston (1840). Vol. II, p. 481.

tions of astronomy will appear later in the meditation on the starry heavens consigned to his Diary. He followed the lectures and demonstrations of John Winthrop, who exhibited "experiments in Natural Philosophy"; but he had no real taste for science, and the reflective youth was more attracted by belles-lettres. From contemporary accounts, we may suspect that even in the subjects which then formed the foundation of a liberal education, the teaching of literature was not altogether extensive. Fluent as the scholars may have been in the use of the Latin language, they had read very little besides Cicero and Virgil,[11] and it was only in 1763 that Stephen Sewall presented a plan to promote classical learning, recommending that Horace be studied and that "Cæsar's Commentaries or some other approved classical author be recited." It was urged in the same plan that "Homer's Odyssey, or some other approved Greek poet be learned . . . that Xenophon's Cyropædia, Demosthenes' Select Orations, or some other approved Greek prose composition (besides the New Testament) be recited, in view of carrying the knowledge of that noble language to a greater length." [12]

The library, however, was rather considerable, at least in the number of volumes, for in 1764 it contained over five thousand, most of them on religion: the Holy Scriptures in almost all the languages, all the Fathers, Greek and Latin, a great number of tracts on revealed religion, sermons of English divines, the Greek and Latin classics, presented by Bishop Berkeley, historical and biographical tracts, the translations of the Royal Society of the Academy of Sciences of France, the works of Boyle and Newton, the Acta Eruditorum, and a collection of the most approved medical authors.[13]

In those days, even more than in ours, colleges were reluctant to pay much attention to the literature of the times; but a few undergraduates, during John Adams' last two years of college,

---

[11] See the account of Timothy Pickering, admitted to the Freshman class in 1759, "Life of Timothy Pickering", by his son, Octavius Pickering. Boston (1867). Vol. I, p. 9.

[12] Josiah Quincy, op. cit., Vol. II, p. 497.

[13] Peirce, op. cit., p. 284.

formed a club and planned "to spend their evenings together in reading any new publications, or any poetry or dramatic composition that might fall in their way." John Adams was invited to join, and soon proved to have a real talent in reading tragedies; he put so much fire in his declamation, that it was rumored among his friends that "he should make a better lawyer than divine." [14]

No list of the books read and discussed in the club has been preserved, but as even at night the students were subject to the constant supervision of the tutors, the reading programs could not be very bold or very extensive; in fact, we shall see that John Adams was practically ignorant of contemporary English writers when he graduated. On the other hand, the echoes of the religious controversies then raging in New England, and particularly in Boston, could not be excluded from the college. On the whole, the Harvard authorities were remarkably liberal for the time, and because of this had been denounced by the famous John Whitefield for the laxity of their doctrines. The charges were indignantly denied by Doctor Wigglesworth, but the professors had to use great skill to avoid being entangled in theological discussions with outsiders. [15] Only a few years before Adams entered college, a young Harvard graduate, the Reverend Mr. Mayhew, had succeeded over the opposition of the Boston ministers in being ordained pastor of the West Church and, in 1749, he had published a series of sermons in which he canvassed freely the doctrines of Calvinism. His theories, although not officially countenanced by the college authorities, were at least singularly consonant with their own views, and their friendship for Mr. Mayhew was a well-known fact. Preaching on "Salvation by Grace", he did not hesitate to condemn unreservedly the overscrupulous and zealous bigots as unchristian: "The divisions and contentions that have hitherto happened and still subsist in the Christian Church, are all, in a manner, owing to the unchristian temper and conduct of those, who could not content themselves with *scripture orthodoxy*, with the simple, spiritual worship of the Father, enjoined by

[14] "Autobiography" in the "Life of John Adams", Vol. I, p. 42.
[15] Josiah Quincy, *op. cit.*, Vol. II, p. 41.

our Saviour, and with the *platform* of church discipline enjoined in the New Testament." [16]

Yet all the students were not intended for the ministry; many sons of rich merchants and of officials also received their education in the "Cambridge of New England", and they did not submit willingly to the strict discipline of the college. Changes that took place in New England during the middle of the century affected Harvard. Profane cursing and swearing, "habits of frequenting taverns and alehouses, practice of using wine, beer and distilled liquors by undergraduates in their rooms" greatly increased. Tutors were insulted, unlawful acts were perpetrated. Wealthy students indulged in extravagance: laws were passed by the Overseers in October, 1754, forbidding the scholars on any occasion to wear any gold or silver lace, any gold or silver brocades, in the town of Cambridge or in the town college. On Commencement Day every candidate should appear "in dark or gray clothes." [17]

The son of the Braintree farmer needed no such regulations to govern his conduct. The obligation to take their meals in the commons, where the fare was abundant but far from refined, to live in the college buildings, was hard to enforce on the sons of the gentry, but the over-serious and earnest young man probably accepted uncomplainingly the régime which made his more fortunate fellow students fret and revolt.

In 1755, the very year in which John Adams graduated, two students were expelled for having offered "indignities and personal insults" to some of the tutors of the college. Disorderly tendencies increased during commencement week. In spite of the efforts of the Overseers, commencement took very early the character of a country fair rather than an academic function. Many of the inhabitants of Boston visited the college town on this occasion. Booths were erected to accommodate the populace; "gambling, rioting, and dissipation of all kinds prevailed", students received guests in their rooms and offered them punch, many even indulged in the practice of addressing "the female

---

[16] "Seven Sermons preached at a lecture in the West Meetinghouse, in Boston", Boston (1749) and Josiah Quincy, *op. cit.*, Vol. II, p. 69.

[17] Josiah Quincy, *op. cit.*, Vol. II, pp. 90, 91.

sex."[18] This is at least one American tradition against which legislation has proved powerless. It is more than likely that by choice, as well as out of necessity, Adams abstained from these more or less excusable pranks and weaknesses. College for him was a solemn business, and his "Diary", begun shortly after he graduated, offers much evidence that he took his studies with unusual seriousness.

In July, 1755, he received his bachelor's degree. He was only twenty and could have stayed in college as a graduate student to pursue his work towards a Master of Arts and ultimately qualify for the ministry; but this he was very reluctant to do, and for some reasons that can be ascertained and some that can be surmised, he postponed taking such a decisive step at once. It is very likely that the young man was impelled to some extent by financial considerations. To maintain him at Harvard for four years had been a heavy drain on the family resources, and he probably felt that the time had come when he should support himself. It may also be that he confusedly felt that he needed a change of scene. He knew little of the outside world — Braintree, Boston, and the college buildings bounded his narrow horizon, and he was too much of an individualist to have accepted meekly the discipline of the college and the constant supervision of the tutors and professors. It must also be said that the call of his vocation was not very imperious. Religion was not so simple a matter as the lad had been led to believe when at Braintree. The life of a pastor under the close scrutiny of his fellow ministers, constantly watched by his congregation, called to account for the slightest departure from orthodoxy, was an everyday trial. In Cambridge and Boston, John Adams had witnessed the attacks against Mr. Mayhew, and his own native village was not free from theological quarrels and from what a contemporary called "the exquisite rancor of theological hate." Even during his stay at Harvard, the peaceful life of Braintree had been deeply disturbed by the controversies that raged around Mr. Lemuel Briant, the young pastor of the Congregational Church. A man ahead of his time, very highly strung, feeling the effects of a

[18] Josiah Quincy, *op. cit.*, Vol. II, p. 95.

sickness which was to cause his early death, Mr. Briant had a boldness of view and a power of invective rare even in New England. In one of his first sermons he had undertaken to attack vigorously the absurdities of conventional religion, taking as his text Isaiah lxiv, 6: "All our righteousnesses are as filthy rags." Taken to task by his brethren, he had referred to the Reverend Mr. Foxcroft of Boston as "a verbose, dark, Jesuitical writer", who returned the compliment in kind, accusing Mr. Briant of being not merely an Arminian, but even a Socinian.

Although some members of the congregation sustained the views of their pastor, an Ecclesiastical Council was called and sat in Deacon Adams' house. Committees of the parish headed by John Quincy took up the matter, but the controversy was not settled until October, 1753, when Mr. Lemuel Briant, although vindicated on many points and particularly on the ground of immorality, presented his resignation, which was accepted. The unfortunate pastor, whose health was already failing, died in the early autumn of the following year.[19]

During the whole procedure John Adams read feverishly the pamphlets pro and con, and soon found himself involved in difficulties which he could not solve. It was one thing to consult the Church authorities at leisure in one's study at Harvard, to defend a certain thesis before his professors and fellow students, but it was an entirely different thing to stand before accusers, to have to answer irrelevant questions, to wrangle with ill-intentioned people, and to fight to keep one's position. To be a minister procured no *otium* and many indignities. Well enough, if on these points of doctrine one had been able to form a firm conviction, but no such certainty had been reached by the young man who shrank from blind and passive orthodoxy and had not been able to find his way in the theological maze.

And yet, when commencement week came, no other alterna-

[19] Charles Francis Adams, "History of Braintree", pp. 49–54, and fragment from "Autobiography" in the "Life of John Adams", Works, Vol. I, p. 41. On Mr. Briant see also, "Two Discourses delivered on the occasion of the Two Hundredth anniversary of the First Congregational Church, with an appendix." Boston, 1850. Pp. 131–143.

tive had presented itself. Fortunately for the young man, he had acquired in college a certain poise and some ability to speak. It was then the custom to hold at commencement a "Syllogistic Disputation in Latin, in which four or five or more of those who were distinguished as good scholars in the class were appointed by the President as Respondents to whom were assigned certain questions. This was conducted wholly in Latin, and in the form of syllogisms and theses." [20] John Adams was appointed one of the respondents, and was noticed by the Reverend Mr. Maccarty of Worcester, who had been empowered by the selectmen of the town to procure a Latin master for the grammar school. The emoluments were more than moderate, the task did not appeal in any particular way to the young man, and there was no future in the job. Such as it was, it was a respite, however, a chance to live away from his family, his native surroundings, to think over matters, and to find himself. The new graduate accepted at once and went to Braintree for a short vacation. Three weeks later a horse was sent to him from Worcester, with a man to attend him. John Adams made the journey of sixty miles in one day, which would be no mean feat for a modern student of theology, and he entered at once upon his duties as a schoolmaster.

[20] Judge Wingate, in Peirce, *op. cit.*, p. 308.

CHAPTER II

THE EDUCATION OF JOHN ADAMS

EIGHTEENTH-CENTURY schoolmasters were not better paid than in our day; they received hardly as much as a common laborer and were not even free to live where they pleased. They boarded, at the expense of the town, with persons of sound and honorable character, and often went from one family to another in the course of a very few months. Their social standing, however, was much higher than their comparatively low economic situation. A Harvard graduate, chosen by the pastor, was immediately made welcome by the inhabitants, and at Worcester John Adams found them "sociable, generous and hospitable people." His school duties, to be sure, were very boresome. Being young, he had to keep a stiff, "frowning" attitude, and "as a haughty monarch ascends his throne, the pedagogue mounts his awful *great chair*, and dispenses right and justice through his whole empire." His vanity found some satisfaction in walking out "in awful solemnity, through a cringing multitude", and even in the manifold occupations which require the pedagogue's attention, "sometimes paper, sometimes his penknife, now birch, now arithmetic, now a ferule, then A B C, then scolding, then flattering, then thwacking." [1]

When school was dismissed he still had much time to walk in the country, to read in his room, and to spend evenings at the house of Mr. Maccarty, with Doctor Willard and his vivacious wife, or at the house of Major Gardiner. In Worcester he found a wider choice of books than had been available at Harvard. At the house of "one Green", with whom he boarded at first, he discovered Morgan's "Moral Philosopher", which circu-

[1] To Richard Cranch, September 2, 1755. Works, Vol. I, p. 27.

lated with some freedom in the town, and he spent whole days reading Thomas Gordon's "Independent Whigs", Hutcheson's "Introduction to Moral Philosophy" and, a few months later, Bolingbroke. He had come away from Harvard in a troubled state of mind, and readings as well as conversation and long discussions with his friends increased both his distress and his anxiety to see clearly his way through the theological fogs. Mr. Maccarty had engaged, a few years before, in a fierce controversy with Mr. Mayhew, and was leaning towards Whitefield, while some of his parishioners visibly inclined towards a moral Christianity whose purpose would be to make men not "good riddle-solvers, or good mystery-mongers, but good men, good magistrates, and good subjects, good husbands and good wives, good parents and good children, good masters and good servants." Such was true religion and not the Ecclesiastical Synods, Convocations, Councils, Decrees, Creeds, Confessions, Oaths, Subscriptions, "and whole cart-loads of other trumpery." [2]

Truly Deism had made "considerable progress" in Worcester, since such theories could be maintained not quite openly, but among friends, at night, around the fireplace, while smoking pipes filled with strong tobacco, and drinking cider or punch. It was after such conversations that the young man started dreaming of a nation in which the precepts of the Bible would be faithfully followed: "What a Utopia; what a Paradise would this region be!" [3] Thus little by little he built up for himself an ideal of society far different from the government of New England, the dream of a nation where the people would be good almost without effort and "obliged, in conscience, to temperance and frugality and industry." This would have been the true New Jerusalem that the Pilgrims had failed to establish in New England, where "no man would impair his health by gluttony, drunkenness, or lust; no man would sacrifice his most precious time to cards or any other trifling and mean amusement; no man would steal, or lie, or in any way defraud his neighbor." At the very moment when the young schoolteacher found himself unable to follow the accepted tenets of

[2] Diary, February 18, 1756. Works, Vol. II, pp. 5–6.
[3] Diary, February 22, 1756. Works, Vol. II, pp. 6–7.

Calvinism, he formulated again the ideal of the true Puritan — an ideal in comparison to which modern society seemed petty, corrupted and spineless. This naturally led him to morose introspection. "Constantly forming but never executing good resolutions," he exclaimed in despair. "Oh! that I could wear out of my mind any mean and base affectation; conquer my natural pride and self-conceit; expect no more deference from my fellows than I deserve; . . . subdue every unworthy passion, and treat all men as I wish to be treated by all."

This realization of his own weaknesses kept the young man from falling into the usual fault of enthusiastic reformers. It even helped him to take some interest in his students, and to realize that "human nature is more easily wrought upon and governed by promises, and encouragement, and praise, than by punishment, and threatening, and blame . . . corporal as well as disgraceful punishments depress the spirits, but commendation enlivens and stimulates them to a noble ardor and emulation." We do not know whether he gave up entirely the use of the "birch and the ferule" in his class, but there is at least some indication that he no longer found it necessary to maintain with his scholars the haughty and threatening attitude which he had assumed at the beginning. Soon he even became interested in the microcosm over which he was ruling, and in describing it showed clear indications of that sarcastic power of observation which makes him so akin to La Bruyère, Voltaire, or Addison:

In this little state I can discover all the great geniuses, all the surprising actions and revolutions of the great world, in miniature. I have several renowned generals but three feet high, and several deep projecting politicians in petticoats. I have others catching and dissecting flies, accumulating remarkable pebbles, cockle shells, &c., with as ardent curiosity as any virtuoso in the Royal Society. . . . At one table sits Mr. Insipid, foppling and fluttering, spinning his whirligig, or playing with his fingers, as gaily and wittily as any Frenchified coxcomb brandishes his cane or rattles his snuff-box. . . . In sort, my little school, like the great world, is made up of kings, politicians, divines, L.D.'s, fops, buffoons, fiddlers, sycophants, fools, coxcombs, chimney sweepers, and every other character drawn in history, or seen in the world. Is it not, then, the highest pleasure, my friend, to preside in this little world, to bestow the proper applause upon virtuous and generous actions, to blame and punish every vicious and contracted trick. . . . I had rather sit in school and consider which of my pupils will turn out in his future life a hero, and which a rake, which a philosopher, and which a parasite, than change breasts with them, though possessed of twenty laced waistcoats and a thousand pounds a year.[4]

Had he been born in Paris, the boy who at twenty could write with such "verve" would have been hailed as a wit of the first class, and would have been encouraged to develop his rare talent; but neither Worcester nor Boston constituted a favorable milieu in which literary geniuses could grow and receive appreciation and applause, and Adams himself employed all possible effort to suppress and subdue his too ready disposition to ridicule, to mock and to satirize. Fortunately for us, he was never able entirely to suppress his "righteous indignation", and whenever occasion presented itself gave vent to his feelings, often much to his damage, but most of the time for our great enjoyment. One occasion of such violent talk was simply that "four months since, a poor girl in this neighborhood, walking by the meeting-house upon some occasion in the evening, met a fine gentleman with laced hat and waistcoat, and a sword, who solicited her to turn aside with him into the horse stable. The girl relucted a little, upon which he gave her three guineas, and wished he might be damned if he did not have her in three months. Into the horse stable they went. The three guineas proved three farthings, and the girl proved with child, without a friend upon earth that will own her, or knowing the father of her three-farthing bastard."[5]

At other times the young schoolmaster "turned politician." This was the year 1755, — a year "never to be forgotten in America." The war between France and Great Britain was not formally declared until May, 1756, but it had already been carried on for many months in America by "the turbulent Gallicks." — "Braddock, the commander of the forces destined against Du Quesne, and six or seven hundred of his men, were

[4] Diary, March 15, 1756. Works, Vol. II, pp. 9–10.
[5] Ibid., p. 10.

butchered in a manner unexampled in history . . . Monckton
and Winslow, at Nova Scotia, gained their point, took the
fortresses, and sent off the inhabitants into these provinces"
(an allusion to the episode made famous by Longfellow in
"Evangeline"): finally an earthquake had destroyed Lisbon,
and the strength of the tremendous arm of God Almighty had
been felt even in America. "Very expensive and very formidable
preparations" had been made by England, and "the gathering of the clouds seems to forebode very tempestuous weather."
The repercussions of these momentous events could not but be
felt in Worcester; they were discussed at great length at evening, and the young man, having put things together, indulged
in reflections of his own, by which the English statesmen of the
time might have profited. He sent them to his friend and kinsman Nathan Webb, in a letter too long to be reproduced in
full, but the following paragraph at least must be quoted:

Soon after the Reformation, a few people came over into this new
world for conscience' sake. Perhaps this apparently trivial incident may
transfer the great seat of empire into America. It looks likely to me:
for if we can remove the turbulent Gallicks, our people, according to
the exactest computations, will in another century become more
numerous than England itself. Should this be the case, since we have,
I may say, all the naval stores of the nation in our hands, it will be easy
to obtain the mastery of the seas; and then the united force of all Europe
will not be able to subdue us. The only way to keep us from setting up
for ourselves is to disunite us. *Divide et impera*. Keep us in distinct
colonies, and then, some great men in each colony desiring the monarchy
of the whole, they will destroy each other's influence and keep the
country *in equilibrio*.[6]

Although the prophecy that ultimately the colonies would
separate from Great Britain was no doubt frequently made at
times, and the idea must have presented itself to many Anglo-
Americans, the young man evidently saw in it only a fascinating
subject for philosophical disquisition. Much more curious, however, was the declaration that to achieve and to keep their independence from the mother country the different colonies

[6] October 12, 1755. Works, Vol. I, pp. 23–24.

must renounce their separate entities, for it contains the germ of the political system that John Adams was to advocate and to fight for during his whole public career.

All the while he was studiously abstracting Tillotson, and wondering whether it would not be good for a candidate to the ministry to *transcribe* the complete works of the reverend doctor. Spring was coming and, much to his surprise and disgust, the young Puritan found himself unable to apply his mind to scholarly pursuits:

> I am dull and inactive, and all my resolutions, all the spirits I can muster are insufficient to rouse me from this senseless torpitude. My brains seem constantly in as great confusion and wild disorder as Milton's chaos; they are numb, dead. I have never any bright, refulgent ideas. Every thing appears in my mind dim and obscure, like objects seen through a dirty glass or roiled water.[7]

More than once he had to enter in his Diary, "dreamed away the afternoon", or "rambled about all day, gaping and gazing." Had he been in England or France, he would have written poetry or fallen in love, or both. In Worcester he could only despair at his lack of courage and persistency, occasionally get up at two, "write" Bolingbroke, St. James, the endless Tillotson, or make a new and pitiless survey of his faults and failings. Less than ever he felt attracted to the ministry; it was probably the best of the three learned professions, since the divine "will be able to do more good to his fellow-men, and make better provision for his own future happiness in this profession than in another", but he had already decided not to "very suddenly become a preacher."[8] Never had the call been less imperious. Since meeting Mr. Putnam, a Worcester lawyer, taking long walks and going shooting with him, visiting his farm or spending the evenings at his house, he had been introduced to a new school of thought. Mr. Putnam had been intimate with "one Peasley Collins, the son of a Quaker in Boston, who had been to Europe, and came back a disbeliever of every thing; fully satisfied that religion was a cheat, a cunning invention of priests

---

[7] April 23, 1756. Works, Vol. II, p. 13.
[8] Letter to Charles Cushing, April 1, 1756. Works, Vol. I, pp. 29, 30.

and politicians; that there would be no future state, any more than there is at present any moral government." [9]

Putnam refused to go the whole length with him, and John Adams neither at that time nor later could accept the theory that death was an endless sleep. These objections, however, had to be met; faith in the miracles, in the historicity of the New Testament, was severely shaken, for, after all, we have only the word of the apostles "to prove that they spoke with different tongues, raised the dead, and healed the sick." Unable to understand the inextricable and mysterious complication of causes which rule the universe, yet playing a part in this great drama, Adams tried to prove to his entire satisfaction that an intelligent and benevolent friend had the disposal and determination of these matters. But this was Deism, not Christianity, so word went around that the young schoolmaster was an Arminian.[10] If such an accusation was launched against him even before he entered the ministry, what difficulties would he not have to encounter later — for one thing he had already decided upon: to revere his own understanding more than "the decrees of councils or the sentiments of fathers."

At this juncture, the Court held its session at Worcester, and John Adams was introduced to a new realm of human activity. During a whole week he could neither read nor write, because of the noisy bustle of the public occasion. With his mind trained to long argumentations and subtleties by his theological reading, John Adams listened to the pleas of the lawyers. This was not an unscrupulous game to make black appear white, but a human effort to discover truth in spite of "passion, prejudice, interest, custom and fancy." Such an undertaking was worthy of the noblest efforts. More than ever he felt great apprehension when he considered his future career: "The frightful engines of ecclesiastical councils, of diabolical malice and Calvinistical good-nature never failed to terrify me exceedingly whenever I thought of preaching." [11]

[9] Diary. Works, Vol. II, p. 13 *note*.
[10] Postscript of letter to Charles Cushing, April 1, 1756. Works, Vol. I, p. 32.
[11] To Richard Cranch, August 29, 1756. Works, Vol. I, p. 35.

When the new school year opened, he had not come to a decision. While boarding at the house of Doctor Nahum Willard, he had read Doctor Cheyne's works, Sydenham and others, and Van Swieten's "Commentaries on Boerhaave", and for a time he had entertained the thought of becoming "a physician and a surgeon." He hesitated, for a few weeks, between divinity, medicine and law; then, after long conversations with Mr. Putnam, made up his mind and on the 22d of August, 1756, he entered in his Diary his momentous decision: "Yesterday I completed a contract with Mr. Putnam to study law, under his inspection, for two years." [12]

In taking this step against the advice of his best friends, Cranch and Cushing, and against the most cherished wishes of his family, he had not been impelled by vanity or ambition. In pre-revolutionary New England, lawyers occupied a social position far inferior to ministers. They were slowly coming into their own and, with the development of business and an increase of trade, law could, with much luck, open the way to some influence and provide more than a mere pittance. But in 1756 no prophet would have been bold enough to predict the part that men trained in the study of law were to play twenty years later in the making of a new nation. [13] With his friends and to his family he insisted that among the many reasons which had directed him in his choice, this was paramount: that he should have the liberty to think for himself without molesting others or being molested himself. For obvious reasons he could not give up his teaching, the only way he had of making a living. Mr. Putnam very kindly accepted to take him in his house for "no more than the town allowed" for his lodgings, with the understanding that he should pay one hundred dollars when convenient. [14]

Unfortunately we have very little information about the two years spent by the young man as an apprentice to the local lawyer, for he seems to have neglected to keep his Diary dur-

[12] Works, Vol. II, p. 30.
[13] See James Truslow Adams, "Revolutionary New England" (1923), pp. 39-40.
[14] Works, Vol. I, p. 43.

ing this period. Doubtless Coke's "Institutes" was substituted for Tillotson, and he entered in his commonplace book copious extracts from Horne, Brackton, Fleta, Thornton, Glanville and Fortescue. Law schools did not exist at that time, and no regular training was available to the students of law. The prospective lawyer learned from actual cases, from sessions of the court, from memorizing and abstracting the legal classics, and by a close study of the Yearbooks. John Adams did not even have the help that Blackstone was to provide for the students of the next generation; but Mr. Putnam was kind, he had most of the essential law books, and he sent to England for additional ones. To these must be added the complete works of Lord Bacon, Lord Bolingbroke's "Study and Use of History", his "Patriot King", and his posthumous works recently published in five volumes.[15] As when a student of theology, he read more for profit than for pleasure, but neither the time nor the atmosphere of the town was very propitious for close application. His school duties must have become more and more irksome; the young men of Worcester were training in the militia and leaving for the war against the "turbulent Gallicks." On some occasions great alarm was felt that finally the French would master the country. This was no time to study law and collect precedents, so Adams, eager to participate in some way in the general agitation, took dispatches to the Governor of Rhode Island. Probably more than once the young man regretted that lack of patronage should prevent him from enlisting in the army. "Could I have obtained a troop of horse or a company of foot, I should infallibly have been a soldier."[16] His bellicose ardor evidently was not strong enough to decide him to enlist in the ranks. Thus two years were spent, not altogether profitably employed; Adams was still dissatisfied with himself, with his progress in the law, and with his future prospects.

In the summer of 1758 he had finished his apprenticeship. Several courses, none of them satisfactory, were open to him. He could have remained in Worcester and come up at the next

---

[15] Works, Vol. I, p. 43. See also the program of readings he mapped out for Jonathan Mason, August 21, 1776. Works, Vol. IX, p. 433.

[16] To Mr. Cushing, March 13, 1817. Works, Vol. I, p. 38 *note*.

election for the position of Register of Deeds, which would have procured him "something handsome for the present" and a possibility of gradually building up a law practice. By doing so, however, he would have entered a field which he could rightly consider as belonging to Mr. Putnam. This he refused to do, in spite of the enticing offer made by two prominent gentlemen of the town. He could not seriously entertain the ambition of succeeding in Boston — lawyers were already too many, he was totally unacquainted with the tradesmen and judges of the city, and he would have had to bend the knee to too many people. Furthermore, he was really homesick and tired of city life; he "panted for want of the breezes from the sea, and the pure zephyrs from the rocky mountains" of his native town.[17] His father and mother had finally been reconciled to his new vocation. They invited him to return to Braintree and live with them. His prospects were very modest, but as there was no other lawyer in the county, all the business being transacted in Boston by Boston lawyers, he had at least a chance to make an honest living, if not to acquire wealth and reputation. This time he made up his mind quickly, and on October 5, 1758, came back to the ancestral farmhouse.

Practically unknown, without sponsors, he felt that he had to make his mark in some manner, and to stand out among the ordinary run of candidates to the bar. His knowledge of the fine points of law was very scanty, his practical experience rather short, but he had some hopes that his knowledge of Greek and Latin would make him shine in the eyes of the Boston lawyers. On his way home he had stopped in Cambridge and borrowed a few books from the Harvard library, and he undertook at once to translate Justinian, to examine "the laws of the province concerning roads, cattle, fences, etc., etc.", and to read in Gilbert's "Feudal Tenures." It was fine to be again in Braintree! To spend a whole day smoking, chatting, trifling, loitering away the time, or unloading a cart, cutting oven wood, eating victuals and apples, drinking tea and talking with the pretty wife of Doctor Savil, who lived in the next house, and to whom he had decided occasionally to read from Ovid's "Art

[17] Diary. Works, Vol. II, p. 35.

of Love." Sometimes, in the evening, he was invited to the house of Colonel Quincy, the local justice, to discuss at length the case of "Lambert's horse broke into Field's inclosure and lay there some time, *damage feasant.*"

Soon, however, he went to Boston, renewed acquaintance with his former classmates, some of them preparing for the bar, and became acquainted with a serious youth by the name of Peter Chardon, the son of a Huguenot exile, whom he greatly admired and took as his model, at least for a few weeks. "This fellow's thoughts are not employed on songs and girls, nor his time on flutes, fiddles, concerts, and card tables: he will make something." His other friends were far less inspiring. Robert Treat Paine complained of having "neither health enough for an active life nor knowledge enough for a sedentary one." Edmund Quincy "has not courage enough to harbor a thought of acquiring a great character." Several times Adams went to the courthouse, sitting at the lawyers' table, looking in awe at the luminaries of the Boston bar: Mr. Gridley, Mr. Pratt, Mr. Otis, Mr. Thatcher, who "were all present and looked sour." He eventually mustered his courage and went to Mr. Gridley, to ask what steps to take for an introduction to the practice of the bar. Kindly received by Mr. Gridley, rather rebuked by Mr. Pratt, John Adams was finally recommended to the court as a man in whose hands the interests of a client might be safely entrusted, and he was duly sworn in at the same time as Edmund Quincy, after which the court took a recess and the whole company adjourned to Stone's tavern "to drink some punch . . . and had a very cheerful chat."

None better than John Adams could realize the deficiency of his legal knowledge and training. Had he been left alone, he would have spent many months between Braintree and Boston, reading in legal treatises, attending the court, getting acquainted with people in Boston and carefully preparing for his début. He was not permitted to do so. Yielding to "the cruel reproaches" of his mother and the entreaties of his friends, he consented to take up a case hardly two weeks later, and lost it, as he lost the next.[18]

[18] Diary. Works, Vol. II, p. 53.

He grieved and fretted and complained in his Diary. Once more he searched his conscience, accused himself of levity, precipitation, ignorance, and found himself guilty — with extenuating circumstances, since he had been almost forced into this inconsiderate step. More than once during the following years he was to go through the same trial, each time making new resolutions soon broken, new schedules of work followed for one short day.

For the next two years he was to divide his time between Braintree and Boston, hesitating and irresolute, at times regretting not to have selected the ministry,[19] spurring himself to work, vainly attempting every morning to get his thoughts into a steady train, to raise his courage and inflame his ambition — for he was both irresolute and passionately ambitious. Not generally thought of as a romantic character, John Adams at twenty-three went through a romantic crisis. His imagination at that time was very vivid:

I can at pleasure revive in my thoughts the ideas and assemblages of ideas that have been before in my mind; can revive the scenes, diversions, sports of childhood, youth; can recall my youthful rambles to the farms, frolics, dalliances, my lonely walks through the groves, and swamps, and fields, and meadows at Worcester; can imagine myself with the wildest tribes of Indians in America, in their hunting, their wars, their tedious marches through wild swamps and mountains; can fly, by this faculty, to the moon, planets, fixed stars, unnumbered worlds; can cross the Atlantic and fancy myself in Westminster Hall, hearing causes in the courts of justice, or the debates in the House of Commons or Lords.[20]

With these flights of fancy he had a keen sense of observation and delighted in the picturesqueness of eighteenth-century Boston:

Who can study in Boston Streets? I am unable to observe the various objects that I meet, with sufficient precision. My eyes are so diverted with chimney-sweepers, sawyers of wood, merchants, ladies, priests, carts, horses, oxen, coaches, market-men and women, soldiers, sailors;

[19] Diary. Works, Vol. II, p. 83.
[20] *Ibid.*, p. 73.

and my ears with the rattle-gabble of them all, that I cannot think long enough in the street, upon any one thing, to start and pursue a thought. I cannot raise my mind above this mob crowd of men, women, beasts, and carriages, to think steadily. My attention is solicited every moment by some new object of sight, or some new sound. A coach, cart, a lady, or a priest, may at any time, by breaking a couplet, disconcert a whole page of excellent thoughts.[21]

No less remarkable was his talent for portraits. This is the landlady of Doctor Webb: "She is awkward, shamefaced, bashful, yet would fain seem sprightly, witty, &c. She is a squaddy, masculine creature, with a swarthy pale face, a great, staring, rolling eye, a rare collection of disagreeable qualities." [22] Whoever has lived in New England boarding houses can attest the scorching veracity of the picture; the old Weston woman must have had a large progeny.

Even keener was John Adams' characterization of moral traits. The conceited, pedantic, and somewhat awkward young lawyer was an easy target for men like Lambert and Robert Treat Paine, who once called him "a numskull and a blunderbuss" before all the superior judges. This was more than enough to arouse the ire of the young man who, in the silence of his room, drew a ferocious portrait of Bob Paine, "an impudent, ill-bred, conceited fellow"; as for the other, he was "like a little knurly, ill-natured horse, that kicks at every horse of his own size, and sheers off from every one that is larger." [23] He tried to be fair to Mr. Pratt, who had treated him at first rather contemptuously: "Pratt has a strong elastic spring, or what we call smartness, and strength in his mind . . ." Finally there was a two-line portrait of Otis: "Otis is extremely quick and elastic; his apprehension is as quick as his temper. He springs and twitches his muscles about in thinking." [24]

He had for the time a remarkably rich vocabulary, the result, it seems, of work and application, more than a native gift. "The names of things do not flow naturally into my mind when

[21] Diary. Works, Vol. II, p. 65.
[22] Ibid., p. 61.
[23] Ibid., p. 51.
[24] Ibid., p. 67.

I have occasion to use them," he complained one day, probably meaning that he had some difficulty in improvising. Never quite at ease, and always self-conscious in conversation, when he took his pen, reminiscences, terse formulas, copious enumerations came naturally to him; with his quill he seemed to pick out long strings of words from the inkstand. A simple, deluded creature is not simply unjustly sentenced, but "brought by the craft of others to brutal debauchery, sickness, cold, hunger, prison, whipping-post, pillory, or gallows." [25] Taverns are not just disorderly houses, but places where originate "quarrels, boxing, duels, oaths, curses, affrays, and riots", and the young fellows do not simply exercise, but improve their strength by "wrestling, running, leaping, lifting, and the like vigorous diversions." [26]

His vocabulary of invectives is even richer: "An old, withered, decrepit person eighty-seven years of age, with a head full of all the wiles and guile and artifice of the infernal serpent, is really a melancholy sight." The shyster lawyers, so numerous in Boston, become: "Myrmidons, bull dogs, hounds, creatures, tools." Probably he was responsible for the following, "an offspring of the passions of the moment", found in his diary:

′Recipe to make a Patriot

Take of the several species of malevolence, as revenge, malice, envy, equal quantities; of servility, fear, fury, vanity, profaneness, and ingratitude, equal quantities; and infuse this composition into the brains of an ugly, surly, brutal mortal, and you have the desideratum.[27]

To a large extent this style was original, though not uncommon by any means. It was good, strong and virile eighteenth-century English, the style of a man who had read the Bible, in Cicero placed the Speeches against Catiline above the more polished orations, and kept close at hand the *Spectator* and the works of Swift.

If he had developed this native talent for satire and em-

[25] Diary. Works, Vol. II, p. 121.
[26] *Ibid.*, p. 113.
[27] *Ibid.*, p. 143.

ployed it in drawing a picture of colonial society, Boston could have boasted in the eighteenth century of a writer of the first water, and we would not have to prize so highly the flaccid Hartford wits. John Adams' ambitions, however, were of an entirely different order. To write for the newspapers as Benjamin Franklin had done, or even to compose books, could not lead him anywhere. His powers of observation and talent for satire could not make friends for the son of the Braintree farmer. "Affecting wit and humor", shrugging his shoulders, moving and distorting the muscles of his face were "faults, defects, fopperies, and follies, and disadvantages" that had to be subdued. "Playing cards, drinking punch and wine, smoking tobacco and swearing" while hundreds of good books lie on the shelves is a "misspense of time." Girls were fascinating, particularly those of "a thinking mind", who had read, and asked in company such questions as "What do you think of Helen? What do you think of Hector, &c.? What character do you like best? Did you wish the plot had not been discovered in 'Venice Preserved'?" [28] Such persons proved irresistible, and John Adams came very near getting married at twenty-three, with one of these New England sirens:

Accidents, as we call them, govern a great part of the world, especially marriages. S—— and E—— broke in upon H—— and me, and interrupted a conversation that would have terminated in a courtship, which would have terminated in a marriage, which marriage might have depressed me to absolute poverty and obscurity, to the end of my life; but that accident separated us. . . .[29]

Law, not poetry, was to be the business of his life, and after escaping from this tight corner, the young man fled back to Braintree. He had remained a practical farmer, and his interest in "husbandry" was not a mere diversion:

My thoughts are running continually from the orchard to the pasture, and from thence to the swamp, and thence to the house and barn and land adjoining. Sometimes I am at the orchard ploughing up acre after acre, planting, pruning apple-trees, mending fences, carting dung;

[28] Diary. Works, Vol. II, p. 56.
[29] Ibid., p. 70.

sometimes in the pasture, digging stones, clearing bushes, pruning trees, building walls to redeem posts and rails; and sometimes removing button trees down to my house; sometimes I am at the old swamp, burning bushes, digging stumps and roots, cutting ditches across the meadows and against my uncle; and am sometimes at the other end of the town, buying posts and rails to fence against my uncle, and against the brook; and am sometimes ploughing the upland with six yoke of oxen, and planting corn, potatoes, &c., and digging up the meadows and sowing onions, planting cabbages, &c. &c. Sometimes I am at the homestead, running cross fences, and planting potatoes by the 'acre, and corn by the two acres, and running a ditch along the line between me and Field, and a fence along the brook against my brother, and another ditch in the middle from Field's line to the meadows. Sometimes am carting gravel from the neighboring hills, and sometimes dust from the streets upon the fresh meadows, and am sometimes ploughing, sometimes digging those meadows to introduce clover and other English grasses.[30]

This was not an unpleasant life with its combination of husbandry, reading, talking with friends, riding to Boston when tired of the country and to Braintree when tired of Boston, going to the Doctor's and even wasting one's time at mere trifles. After a time more cases came to the young lawyer, for Braintree was known as "the most litigious" town in New England. Every year a new field could be added to the farm. John Adams, had he walked in the footsteps of his American ancestors, would have become in time a substantial small-town lawyer, and would finally have taken place among the gentry of the town. He was not satisfied with the prospect of such a slow ascent. He panted for fame and social recognition. "Popularity," he wrote in his Diary, "next to virtue and wisdom, ought to be aimed at; for it is the dictate of wisdom, and is necessary to the practice of virtue in most." [31] He had more than his normal share of human vanity; he bristled when offered the slightest criticism and could not dismiss the memory of bad compliments or harsh words. But most of all he had to spread an opinion of himself as a lawyer of distinguished genius, learning and virtue. At Braintree the

[30] Diary. Works, Vol. II, pp. 137–138.
[31] Ibid., p. 57.

young man, vaguely conscious of his destiny, once more searched his heart. He had no taste for the slow, tedious and ineffectual ways employed by so many of his friends to push themselves into the world: "That is the question; — a bold push, a resolute attempt, a determined enterprise, or a slow, silent, imperceptible creeping; . . . In such a slow, gradual ascent to fame and fortune and business, the pleasure that they give will be imperceptible; but by a bold, sudden rise, I shall feel all the joys of each at once. Have I genius and resolution and health enough for such an achievement?" [32]

Perhaps the scene of his efforts was too small for such an achievement and, curiously enough, he began then to exhibit the spirit of restlessness, the thirst for something else, the longing for an older civilization which sometimes concealed, sometimes half admitted, has tormented so many Americans. Even if he had been a genius, what opportunity had he to become a great lawyer? Had he been born in a small city, Cicero himself would have lived an ignoble life, and his memory would be forgotten. Confessing himself to his friend Jonathan Sewall, Adams admitted that "I expect to be totally forgotten within seventy years from the present hour, unless the insertion of my name in the college catalogue should luckily preserve it longer." But he characteristically added: "Yet, though I have very few hopes, I am not ashamed to own that a prospect of an immortality in the memories of all the worthy, to the end of time, would be a high gratification to my wishes." [33]

Very slim were the chances that he would ever be able to renounce this semi-contemplative life. Without being able to see clearly the objects he was after, in a "whirlwind of dust, straws, atoms and feathers", nevertheless he continued to prepare for an unforeseen opportunity. First of all, he wanted to stand out among his fellow lawyers. To know law alone was not enough: one had to know the fundamentals of human nature, the broad general principles upon which it rested — to discard the compilers, abridgers and abstract makers, and draw science from its fountain in original authors, and also to perfect one's

[32] Diary. Works, Vol. II, pp. 63–64.
[33] To Jonathan Sewall, February, 1760. Works, Vol. I, p. 52.

literary education. In his rage to discover the depths of his ignorance, he even forgot the sacrifices made by his father to send him to Harvard. He fumed against "ignorance of parents, masters Cleverly, Marsh, tutors, Mayhew, &c. By constant dissipation among amusements in my childhood, and by the ignorance of my instructors in the more advanced years of my youth, my mind has laid uncultivated; so that, at twenty-five, I am obliged to study Horace and Homer! — *proh dolor!*" [34]

These deficiencies he courageously undertook to remedy. After Horace, he took up Homer, first in the translation of Pope, reading the six volumes in seven days, and he felt that in six months he would "be bound [to] conquer him in Greek"! [35] He was no less ashamed of his ignorance of French, the importance of which he recognized as early as 1760, and he went through Montesquieu's "Esprit des Lois", writing in the margin "a sort of index to every paragraph."

All the time he kept up his study of legal texts, longing for a copy of Blackstone, reading Hale's "History of the Common Law", the "Institutes" in Latin, Coke on Littleton, the volumes of Fitz-Gibbons and Salked's Reports, and numberless texts and abridgments. The list of his readings established when he entered upon the fifth year of his study of law looks formidable and would terrify a modern student, but Adams chided himself for not yet having read Pufendorf and Grotius, Justinian and Domat. He used the occasion to draw up another impressive plan of work, and discarded the law books, sat by his fire, read Bolingbroke, and once more felt discouraged, dissatisfied with himself.[36] Mr. Gridley had warned him before he took oath that "A lawyer in this country must study common law, and civil law, and natural law, and admiralty law; and must do the duty of a counsellor, a lawyer, an attorney, a solicitor, and even of a scrivener." [37] For so much work a successful lawyer could receive handsome fees but little consideration, and

[34] Diary, May 31, 1760. Works, Vol. II, p. 86.
[35] Diary. Works, Vol. II, p. 97.
[36] November, 1760. *Ibid.*, pp. 103, 105.
[37] October 25, 1758. *Ibid.*, p. 46.

could not enjoy the same social position as "a gentleman of the bar in England." The disrepute in which the profession was held came largely from the fact that "the practice of law was grasped into the hands of deputy sheriffs, pettifoggers, and even constables, who filled all the writs upon bonds, promissory notes, and accounts, received the fees established for lawyers, and stirred up many unnecessary suits." [38] This evil Adams undertook to attack with all the zeal of a born reformer. Year after year he made representations to the gentlemen in Boston, drafted speeches and articles; [39] many times rebuked and turned down by the older lawyers, arousing against him the "pettifoggers" of his town, he finally succeeded, in 1763, in having the bar agree on four rules, defining the duties of the attorney and stating definitely that "no attorney be allowed to practice here unless sworn in this court or the superior court." All these efforts came to naught, however, because of the opposition of James Otis, who was eager to keep "his retenue of pettifoggers, tools and myrmidons", under the pretense of speaking in behalf of the laws of the province and the laws of mankind.

Adams found some consolation in his fight against the taverns and licensed houses. Far from being a prohibitionist, either in practice or in theory, he was interested only in the social and political danger presented by places which "are become the eternal haunt of loose, disorderly people of the same town." [40] The worst effect of all was that "these houses are become in many places the nurseries of our legislators. An artful man, who has neither sense nor sentiment, may by gaining a little sway among the rabble of a town, multiply taverns and dram shops, and thereby secure the votes of taverner and retailer, and of all; and the multiplication of taverns will make many who may be induced by flip and rum to vote for any man whatever." [41] In Braintree there were no less than twelve taverns; several other small country towns had at least half a dozen taverns and retailers, every place dirty and filthy,

[38] Diary. Works, Vol. II, p. 58 *note*.
[39] Works. Vol. II, p. 122.
[40] On the use of intoxicants in New England, see Charles Francis Adams' "History of Quincy", p. 174.
[41] Diary. Works, Vol. II, p. 85.

filled in the evening with people drinking drams, flips, toddy, carousing, swearing, but especially plotting with the landlord to get him, at the next town meeting, an election either for selectman or representative. After campaigning energetically, Adams succeeded in bringing the matter before the town meeting. Resolutions were adopted limiting the number of taverns to three, one for each precinct. In his Diary, he entered the draft of the speech he made or intended to make on this occasion. It is a curious document, not without some cleverness, since he placed the onus of blame on the Boston justices, the importers of molasses and the distillers, rather than on the town government. Adams felt that he had done good work, although his reform was as short-lived as most reforms usually are and nothing was changed in the situation, either at Braintree or in the province. Still he had the impression that he was beginning to be taken seriously by the townspeople, that he had at least "advanced a few steps."

On October 14, 1761, he was sworn before the Superior Court, dressed in "gown, and bands, and tie wig." In March, 1761, he had been chosen "surveyor of highways", which made him at first "very wroth." It was less an honor than an irksome task, which could be, and often was, evaded by paying an assessment. After due consideration of the matter with Doctor Savil, who had nominated him for the office, Adams accepted it as a duty, and went to "ploughing, and ditching, and blowing rocks upon Penn's hill, and building another bridge of stone." These humble duties, however, did not quite satisfy him; he saw in them a new opportunity for reform and went into the principles of local taxation. He rode around to see what was done in Weymouth, Roxbury and Boston, and finally evolved a plan which was adopted by the town meeting, and under which roads were repaired for half a century. The death of his father, on May 25th of the same year, placed upon his shoulders new responsibilities. He soon succeeded in having his brother Boylston appointed deputy sheriff, much to the chagrin of the local pettifoggers. He had become a person of importance to be reckoned with and not without some satisfaction wrote in his Diary: "I am creating enemies in every quarter of the town. The Clerks hate; — Mother Hubbard, Thayer, Lamb, Tirrell, J. Brackett. This is multiplying and propagating enemies fast. I shall have the ill will of the whole town." [42]

Apparently he was now resigned to spend the rest of his life in Braintree, but he had evidently outgrown his native surroundings. While keeping up his legal reading, he was at this time able to disentangle himself from mere technicalities, to determine the broad principles of law and government. "Multitudes of needless matters, and some that are nonsensical, it must be confessed, have in the course of ages crept into the law. . . . But, if the grandeur and importance of a subject have any share in the pleasure it communicates, I am sure the law has by far the advantage of most other sciences." [43]

No man in eighteenth-century New England could hold very rosy views of man and human society, and lawyers see too much of the unpleasant side of human nature ever to become bleating optimists. Adams believed with many of his contemporaries that "In short, vice and folly are so interwoven in all human affairs, that they could not, possibly, be wholly separated from them without tearing and rending the whole system of human nature and state; nothing would remain as it is." [44]

But this social pessimism, from which Adams never recovered, was allied in him with a curious belief in the reliability and soundness of judgment of the common people, at least the common people of New England, and more particularly of Braintree. Thus spake the son of dissenter and the product of town meeting:

In Protestant countries, and especially in England and its colonies, freedom of inquiry is allowed to be not only the privilege, but the duty of every individual. We know it to be our duty to read, examine, and judge for ourselves, even of ourselves, what is right. No priest nor pope has any right to say what I shall believe, and I will not believe one word they say, if I think it is not founded in reason and in revelation. [45]

---

[42] Diary. Works, Vol. II, p. 130.
[43] To Peter Chardon. Works, Vol. II, pp. 114, 115.
[44] Diary. Works, Vol. II, p. 107.
[45] Ibid., p. 131.

Then, in the draft of a plea made in behalf of a poor apprentice whom his master had neglected to teach either to read, write, cipher or weave, he drew a picture of a moderately enlightened democracy which could not have been improved upon by Jefferson himself:

The English constitution is founded, it is bottomed and grounded, on the knowledge and good sense of the people. The very ground of our liberties is the freedom of elections. Every man has in politics as well as religion, a right to think and speak and act for himself. No man, either king or subject, clergyman or layman, has any right to dictate to me the person I shall choose for my legislator and ruler. I must judge for myself. But how can I judge, how can any man judge, unless his mind has been opened and enlarged by reading? A man who can read will find in his Bible, in his common sermon books that common people have by them, and even in the almanac, and the newspapers, rules and observations that will enlarge his range of thought, and enable him the better to judge who has, and who has not that integrity of heart and that compass of knowledge and understanding which forms the statesman.[46]

Similar opinions were not by any means infrequent in New England long before the Revolution; they could be delivered before a town justice without sounding unusual or extraordinary. It was not even necessary to resort to an abstract definition of the rights of man; these were commonplaces, commonsense truths, statements of facts, rather than declarations of principles. To some extent they may have been an echo of James Otis' speech against the writs of assistance, by virtue of which an inferior officer of the customs in Salem had petitioned the Superior Court in November, 1760, for the authorization to break open ships, shops, cellars, and houses, to search for prohibited goods. Adams took notes feverishly during Otis' oration. Years later he still remembered that "his argument, speech, discourse, oration, harangue — call it by which name you will — was the most impressive upon his crowded audience of any I ever heard before or since, excepting only many speeches by himself in Faneuil Hall and in the House of

[46] Diary. Works, Vol. II, p. 131.

Representatives, which he made from time to time for ten years afterwards." [47]

Whether the speech really was to "Mr. Adams like the oath of Hamilcar administered to Hannibal", as maintained by the grandson of John Adams, seems very doubtful. On reading George the Third's speech to his Parliament, Adams had been much impressed by the declaration of a king who showed himself to be "a man of piety and candor in religion, a friend of liberty and property in government, and a patron of merit. . . . These are sentiments worthy of a king; — a patriot king." [48]

This is a far cry from the Declaration of Independence. It is probable that in Otis' speech James Adams appreciated, as a connoisseur and a lawyer, the strength of the argumentation, the marshaling of texts and precedents, the logic and fire, and the masterly way in which the speaker had brought forward the most essential and fundamental principles of social law. But that he felt indignant, and that a revolutionary ardor inflamed his breast at that time, is more than doubtful. At twenty-five John Adams greatly admired the King of Great Britain, liked to think of himself as a "Britton" and not an American, and found only one fault with England. Her position as "the leading and most respectable power in the whole world" was very questionable. In his youthful and sensitive patriotism he wondered why Great Britain had a smaller army than France; why she did not seem to be followed by any one except Prussia. "Thus," he concluded, "we are the leading power without followers." "To determine the character of 'leading and respectable,' as Doctor Savil does, from a few victories and successes . . . is most ignorant and silly." He wondered how it came

---

[47] The notes taken by John Adams at the time will be found in his Works, Vol. II, p. 521; they are very dry and consist mainly of a list of the legal references quoted by Otis. They seem to have been used by Minot in his "History of Massachusetts Bay", in 1803. Fifty-seven years after the argument was delivered, Adams attempted to reconstruct from memory the main parts of the speech in a series of letters to William Tudor, Works, Vol. X, pp. 295–375. I cannot help feeling that Adams put in it much of his own theory, notwithstanding the contrary opinion of Charles Francis Adams.

[48] Diary, February, March, 1761. Works, Vol. II, pp. 117, 118.

that foreigners resorted to France "to learn their policy, military discipline, fortification, manufactures, language, letters, science, politeness, &c., so much more than to England?" [49] This was the language of a patriotic Briton, somewhat impatient that his country did not come up to his high expectations, zealous to see her obtain hegemony in every field. This ambitious and noble patriotism John Adams did in time transfer to the country of his birth, but at twenty-six he had not yet heard the call of America.

[49] Diary. Works, Vol. II, pp. 109, 110.

CHAPTER III

THE DAWN OF INDEPENDENCE

DURING the years 1763 and 1764 John Adams made no entry in his Diary, and, apparently, was little concerned with the political situation. He had always been of "amorous disposition", and at Braintree as well as in Boston, had spent many hours "in absolute idleness" or, much worse, in "gallanting the girls." At Braintree he found several of his old playmates, and read Ovid to the wife of Doctor Savil; at the house of Colonel Quincy he met a bevy of charming "young females" and discussed with "Esther", "Hannah", and "Olivia", Homer, Pope, Milton and Otway. There, also, he met Parson Smith of Weymouth, and talked to him "about despising gay dress, grand buildings and estates, fame, &c., and being contented with what will satisfy the real wants of nature." [1] The Reverend Mr. Smith had married the daughter of the old colonel, and as the small town of Weymouth, a few miles south of Braintree, had very little social life, he often visited the house of his father-in-law, with his wife and two young daughters, Polly and Abigail. Richard Cranch, at the time the most intimate friend of John Adams, soon fell in love with Polly and married her in November, 1761. Adams, for various reasons, hesitated several years and did not become engaged to Abigail until the early part of 1764.

In spite of his avowed "amorous disposition", John Adams was a very serious and well-behaved young man, who could write in his Diary: "No virgin or matron ever had cause to blush at the sight of me, or to regret her acquaintance with me. No father, brother, son, or friend, ever had cause of grief or resentment for any intercourse between me and any

[1] Diary, January 3, 1759. Works, Vol. II, p. 56.

daughter, sister, mother, or any other relation of the female sex. . . . I presume I am indebted for this blessing to my education." [2] He found in Abigail Smith an unusually serious and well-educated young person. She never had any schooling, but very early in life she had received invaluable lessons from her grandmother. She loved reading and had made ample use of the library of her father. She had memorized many excellent lines, never to be forgotten, from Pope and Young; she could occasionally quote Plato on virtue and Shakespeare on courage, recite Collins' Ode, "How sleep the brave. . . !", and during the long months of hibernal seclusion she had meditated, kept a diary, and written long letters full of highly moral and edifying thoughts to her friends. She probably had some "sparks" or admirers, but as she had very little money and wanted above all "justice, honesty, prudence and many other virtues", she had no hope of ever meeting her ideal. Such a rare combination she found in John Adams, and the young man, on his part, recognized in her a seriousness and sterling qualities far superior to the "pert, sprightly and gay" manners of her sister. [3] He seems to have hesitated a long time before proposing, for he had very little to offer the daughter of Parson Smith. From his father he had inherited the house formerly rented to Doctor Savil, and added a few fields to the farm; he had slowly built up a small local practice, but had no great prospects of ever becoming a rich man. He knew also that a small-town lawyer enjoyed very little social prestige; he had done his best to raise the standards of the profession, but in pre-revolutionary days, and particularly outside of Boston, no great difference was made between the real lawyer, sworn before the courts, and the pettifoggers and scriveners who swarmed around the sheriff's offices. The popular feeling in Weymouth was that Abigail Smith was marrying beneath her, and it seems that there was some difficulty on this account. Early in 1764 the two young people were engaged and very much in love. John was in Boston recovering from the effects of the "inoculation", Abigail was in Weymouth,

[2] Diary. Works, Vol. II, p. 145.
[3] *Ibid.*, p. 55.

writing every day, not caring whether he lighted his pipe
with her letters, sending him milk and bags filled with balm,
and "love, respects, regards, good wishes — a whole wagon
load of them." [4]

They were married in the fall (October 25, 1764) and settled in the Braintree house, next to the place where John
Adams was born. The two dwellings were very much alike,
typical New England farmhouses, but Adams had a room
where he could place his many books, for his library was growing rapidly. He at once resumed his regular routine, going to
Boston several times a week when not prevented by the
weather, keeping busy with his practice, and apparently making an effort to preserve a judicial composure of mind in the
prevailing excitement.

To remain completely aloof was not to be thought of.
Early in 1763 he had become acquainted with the work of
the Caucus Club, of which Samuel Adams, his distant relative,
was the soul. "There they smoke tobacco till you cannot see
from one end of the garret to the other. There they drink
flip, I suppose, and there they choose a moderator, who puts
questions to the vote regularly; and selectmen, assessors, collec-
tors, wardens, fire-wards, and representatives, are regularly
chosen before they are chosen in the town." [5] This was a most
efficient organization, too efficient, in fact, not to disturb somewhat our traditional admiration for the town meeting, to which
apparently was left very little initiative and hardly more than
a shadow of power.

It does not seem that Adams was invited to attend the meeting of this junto, but much more flattering was the invitation he received from Mr. Gridley to join the Sodalitas Club.
Gridley's expectation was "to see at the bar, in consequence of
his Sodality, a purity, an eloquence, and a spirit surpassing
any thing that ever appeared in America." [6] He picked, as the
most promising members of the bar, three young men, Adams,

---

[4] "Letters of Mrs. Adams, the wife of John Adams", with an introductory
Memoir by her grandson, Charles Francis Adams. Boston, 1840. P. 7.
[5] Diary. Works, Vol. II, p. 144.
[6] Works, Vol. I, p. 66.

Fitch and Dudley, whom he intended "to bring into practice, the first practice", by recommending them on every possible occasion. The members of the club were to meet every week, on Thursday night, "in order to read in concert the Feudal Law and Tully's Orations." For their first meetings they certainly had full programs, and the conversation rambled upon Hurd's "Dialogues", the Pandects, Lambard's "De Priscis Anglorum Legibus", Lord Kames, Mr. Blackstone and, finally, Tully's Oration for Milo. Rousseau's "Contrat Social" was quoted by John Adams and found "shallow" by Gridley.[7]

The main purpose of these meetings, as may easily be seen from the minute account written by Adams, was essentially to get at the principles of the law. With this in view, Adams prepared for the club a long paper, soon after published without title in the *Boston Gazette*, and later reprinted in England as a "Dissertation on the Canon and Feudal Law." It was not Adams' first production. He had already published a series of essays "On Private Revenge" in August and September, 1763. These were very timely. In a city where political passions were exacerbated, and frequent riots and brawls were occurring, where men had sharp tongues, impatient tempers, and were apt to use strong language, scenes of violence were bound to happen. Among the common people the business was settled by fisticuffs, but the gentry wore swords, and such smart sayings as these were very frequently heard: "If a man should insult me, by kicking my shins, and I had a sword by my side, I would make the sun shine through him." — "If any man, let him be as big as Goliath, should take me by the nose, I would let his bowels out with my sword, if I had one, and if I had none, I would beat his brains out with the first club I could find." [8] Adams eagerly seized the opportunity to display his knowledge of the law and to moralize at the same time. He wrote, not a lay sermon such as those so often found in the

[7] Diary, February 21, 1765. Works, Vol. II, p. 149. This is the earliest mention I know of Rousseau in any American author. The "Contrat Social", published in 1762, had been advertised in the *Boston Gazette*, December 17, 1764, according to J. T. Adams, "Revolutionary New England", p. 288 *note*. John Adams probably bought a copy at once.

[8] Works, Vol. III, p. 441.

papers of the time, but a "history of sentiments", which showed that he had long meditated upon the origin and functions of society. There was nothing Rousseauistic in his position, since "to exterminate among mankind such revengeful sentiments and tempers is one of the highest and most important strains of civil and humane society." There was no preaching of Christian forbearance, but an attempt to substitute legality for passion and social discipline for disorder. Both the Puritan and the student of law appear in his conclusion, in which he severely warned his contradictors "to have a care how they believe or practice his rule about 'passion and killing,' lest the halter and the gibbet should become their portion; for a killing that should happen by the hurry of passion would be much more likely to be adjudged murder than justifiable homicide only."[9]

The same qualities reappear in the "Dissertation on the Canon and Feudal Law." Certainly less fiery and eloquent than the speeches of Otis, it has a scholarly and judicial tone seldom found in similar productions of the age. First read and discussed before the Sodalitas, then elaborated upon at leisure during the spring of 1765, while the whole city of Boston was discussing the effect of the recently passed Stamp Act, the first long and sustained literary effort of John Adams was a remarkable production. Primarily it was an attempt to ascertain the existence of an American tradition, to define it, and to make his readers New England conscious. It started originally with a significant declaration, left out in the *Gazette*, but found in the draft:

I always consider the settlement of America with reverence and wonder, as the opening of a grand scene and design in Providence for the illumination of the ignorant, and the emancipation of the slavish part of mankind all over the earth.[10]

This passage, probably the only one ever quoted from the "Dissertation", fails to do justice to the real talent and great literary ability displayed by the young writer. In any other

[9] Works, Vol. III, p. 443.
[10] *Ibid.*, p. 452 *note*.

country it would have become a classic, to be memorized by schoolboys; in America a few specialists may have read it, but I am not aware that it has ever been discussed or analyzed. Yet it contains a very keen and, for the time, extraordinary analysis of the essentials of the New England character and history. There is in it no undue display of legal erudition, no great oratorical fling, but the subject was so near to the heart of the writer that he could not make it cold, judicial and dispassionate. His American patriotism, based upon reverence for the ancestors, was taking shape; his vision of America was not a sort of golden mirage held out before the eyes of sentimental, emotional and credulous people. For him America was not a new country, without a past; it was essentially heir to a great tradition, for it rested on the law of nature as formulated by the great men of Greece and Rome, it preserved the spirit of the British constitution and "of our own British ancestors, who have defended for us the inherent rights of mankind against kings and cruel priests, in short, against the gates of earth and hell." [11]

The trials of the Pilgrims have so often been depicted and their virtues extolled that one hesitates to quote further; but few pictures have the same authority as that drawn by one of their sons who knew whereof he was speaking, and who was paying tribute to the humble line of New England farmers and deacons from whom he was descended:

Let us read and recollect and impress upon our souls the views and ends of our own more immediate forefathers, in exchanging their native country for a dreary, inhospitable wilderness. Let us examine into the nature of that power, and the cruelty of that oppression, which drove them from their homes. Recollect their amazing fortitude, their bitter sufferings, — the hunger, the nakedness, the cold, which they patiently endured, — the severe labors of clearing their grounds, building their houses, raising their provisions, amidst dangers from wild beasts and savage men, before they had time or money or materials for commerce. Recollect the civil and religious principles and hopes and expectations which constantly supported and carried them through all hardships with patience and resignation. Let us recollect it was liberty,

[11] Works, Vol. III, p. 462.

the hope of liberty, for themselves and us and ours, which conquered all discouragements, dangers and trials.[12]

Then came a vehement and somewhat rhetorical appeal to the pulpit, the colleges and the bar to investigate and proclaim the true origin of the British constitution: "Let them search for the foundations of British laws and government in the frame of human nature, in the constitution of the intellectual and moral world." In the conclusion only, evidently added as an afterthought, and as the "dissertation" was sent to the printer, did he make a direct reference to recent events. The first danger he saw in the "prospect before him" rested in "the designs and labors of a certain society, to introduce the canon law into America" with the complicity of the ministry or parliament. This is an allusion to an old fear often expressed in the eighteenth century, of the establishment of an episcopate, and to the doings of the Society for the Propagation of the Gospel in Foreign Parts.[13] It was only at the end, and almost incidentally, that the Stamp Act was mentioned. Curiously enough, at that time Adams did not seem to be as shocked by the fact that the colonies had not been consulted, as by the nature of the tax.

It seems very manifest from the Stamp Act itself, that a design is formed to strip us in a great measure of the means of knowledge, by loading the press, the colleges, and even an almanack and a newspaper, with restraints and duties; and to introduce the inequalities and dependencies of the feudal system, by taking from the poorer sort of people all their little subsistence, and conferring it on a set of stamp officers, distributors, and their deputies.

At this stage it seems that Adams' objection to the Stamp Act was just as much a question of expediency as of principle, and his contention that the "poorer sort of people" would be especially affected by the enforcement of the new law smacks somewhat of demagogy and, perhaps, simply reflects some of the views of his distant cousin, Samuel Adams. The "poorer

[12] Works, Vol. III, p. 462.

[13] On this point see the very good essay of Mellen Chamberlain: "John Adams, the Statesman of the American Revolution." Boston, 1899.

sort of people" were not slow in taking the hint. On the morning of August 14th, a crowd gathered around a "Liberty Tree" upon which was hung in effigy Mr. Oliver, secretary of the province, who had solicited for the office of distribution of stamps when they should arrive. The ludicrous mannikin remained there all day, guarded by a crowd which succeeded in preventing the local deputy sheriff from cutting it down. At night the effigy was carried to the town house, then to Oliver's projected stamp office, which was leveled to the ground. Finally it was burned to ashes and, as Oliver's house was not far, the mob broke the fence and the windows and "destroyed part of the furniture." It was the first serious mob action that had occurred in Boston, and it was to be followed by even more serious disorders.[14]

John Adams was much perplexed by the occurrence. To approve of "the blind, undistinguishing rage of the rabble" was repellent to his legal training as well as to his natural disposition. He saw in it "a very atrocious violation of the peace, and of dangerous tendency and consequence." At the same time, he found some extenuating circumstances in the grasping, avaricious and ambitious disposition of his Honor the Lieutenant Governor, who had excited jealousy among the people. But the next day he had to leave Boston for Martha's Vineyard, and he was still away when, on the 26th of August, Hutchinson's house was entered and pillaged by a mob.

Shortly after his return, the stamps for the province arrived, and John Adams, still unwilling to enter the politics of Boston, circulated a petition among the inhabitants of Braintree and drew up the "Instructions of the Town of Braintree to Their Representative", which were adopted on September 24, 1765.[15] This time the tone had changed entirely. The famous principle "no taxation without representation" was strongly asserted:

We further apprehend this tax to be unconstitutional. We have always understood it to be a grand and fundamental principle of the

---

[14] Thomas Hutchinson, "The History of Massachusetts." 3 Vols. 1764–1767–1828. Vol. III, p. 121.
[15] Works, Vol. III, p. 464.

constitution, that no freeman should be subject to any tax to which he has not given his own consent, in person or by proxy.

Even stronger was the protestation against the new powers recently given to the judges of the Admiralty Courts to whom were to be referred violations of the Stamp Act. There the lawyer asserted himself, quoting from the "Great Charter itself", reaffirming the right of the freeholder not to be passed upon or condemned but "by lawful judgment of his peers, or by the law of the land." The conclusion rang as forcibly and vehemently as any declaration of Otis, Samuel Adams or Doctor Mayhew:

We further recommend the most clear and explicit assertion and vindication of our rights and liberties to be entered on the public records, that the world may know, in the present and all future generations, that we have a clear knowledge and a just sense of them, and, with submission to Divine Providence, that we never can be slaves.

It is no wonder that a Cambridge correspondent of the *Evening Post* picked out this paragraph as "worthy to be wrote in letters of gold."

This declaration, printed in the *Boston Gazette* on October 14, 1765, "rang through the State" and, according to Adams, was adopted by no less than forty towns as instructions to their representatives.

The opposition to the Stamp Act had created a very strange situation, to which Adams was particularly sensible. The operation of the Act was to commence on the 1st of November. An attempt was made to carry a vote in the General Court, authorizing the courts of justice and the customhouse to proceed in their business without the stamps; the motion was defeated, but business proceeded as usual, both in the customhouse and in all the counties except Suffolk, where Hutchinson, Chief Justice of the Superior Court and Judge of Probate for the county, refused to hold court.

So far Adams had carefully avoided any step which might compromise his position as a law practitioner; although well acquainted with the liberal and radical lawyers of Boston, he had carefully refrained from taking any active or conspicuous part in the agitation. After ten years of hard work he had finally succeeded in building up a respectable practice, and he now had family responsibilities. He was "just getting into his gears, just getting under sail", when an embargo was laid upon the ship. With the courts closed for an indefinite period of time, the situation looked very gloomy.

At this juncture he, with James Otis and Jeremiah Gridley, was chosen to appear as town counsel before the governor in support of a memorial praying that the courts of law in the province be opened. The memorial had no practical result, the governor refusing to act and leaving to the judges the responsibility of a decision, but, as Samuel Adams pointed out to his cousin, such an instance of respect from the Town of Boston could not fail to attract attention to him and would probably cause him to be chosen as representative from Braintree at the next election, in May. It would not be rash to believe that Samuel Adams, who sensed in John promising political material, had contrived to have him selected as town counsel.

The first immediate result was to place John Adams in direct contact with the members of the Monday Night Club: Otis, Cushing, Wells, Pemberton, Gray, Austin, Waldo, Inches, Doctor Parker — "politicians all", above whom Samuel Adams towered, not because of his understanding of law and constitution, but because of his "most thorough understanding of liberty and her resources in the temper and character of the people." Even more satisfactory to John's vanity was his introduction into the circle of rich Boston merchants. He was invited to dine at Mr. Nick Boylston's — "a seat it is for a nobleman, a prince", with furniture which had cost a thousand pounds sterling, "turkey carpets, painted hangings, marble tables, rich beds with crimson damask curtains and counterpanes." There, besides the two Boylstons, were the two Smiths, Mr. Hallowell, and their ladies — "an elegant dinner indeed!"

The Sons of Liberty, at Samuel Adams' request, had asked him to visit them. They were a different class of people. John Avery, distiller, John Smith, brazier, Thomas Craft, painter, Joseph Field, master of a vessel, and George Trott, jeweler, were present and treated him civilly and respectfully, while

making plans for great rejoicing when the repeal of the Stamp
Act should receive official confirmation.

But most of his time was spent in Braintree, going to Colonel
Quincy's for tea, driving his cattle through the snowdrifts
to the spring, reading at home on taxation without representation, searching in his law books for texts and precedents, delving
into history and literature for apt quotations, and memorizing
the lines of Shakespeare:

> . . . For upon these taxations,
> The clothiers all, not able to maintain
> The many of them 'longing, have put off
> The spinsters, carders, fullers, weavers, who,
> Unfit for other life, compell'd by hunger
> And lack of other means, in desperate manner
> Daring th' event to th' teeth, are all in uproar,
> And danger serves among them.
>
> *King Henry VIII, Act I, Sc. 2.*

Samuel Adams, who had taken to heart the political career
of his young cousin, had wisely advised him to try to get recognition from his native town. The March elections were approaching, and Adams reluctantly engaged in local politics.
He was now selectman, and had been elected by a pleasing
majority — a new honor and probably a new source of troubles,
for the church people would grow angry and hot and furious
at the defeat of their candidate. But Braintree was a very small
place, where no real glory could be acquired, and when Adams
was unable to join his friends in Boston to celebrate the repeal
of the Stamp Act because of a town meeting and the illness of
his wife and baby, he grew almost desperate and could not
remember having passed a "duller day."

He was still interested in his farm, pruning the trees, clearing away the bushes, felling without mercy pine, savin and
hemlock, but a change had taken place in his heart and in his
life as well. John Adams at thirty was no longer an inexperienced young lawyer. A new generation of law students was
swarming and multiplying; the older members of the bar —
Mr. Gridley, Mr. Davis — were between sixty and seventy,
and Otis, Dudley, Sewall, S. Quincy, and Adams were looked

upon as their worthy successors. Fees were still too low in Boston, whereas in Jamaica and New York a lawyer could make an independent fortune in ten years. Still, an industrious lawyer could make an honest and comfortable living. The repeal of the Stamp Act had hushed to silence almost every popular clamor; the province was in a state of peace, order and tranquillity, and the people were as quiet and submissive to the government as any people under the sun — so little inclined to tumult, riot, sedition, as they were ever known to be since the foundation of the government. John Adams could look forward to the resumption of business; but at this very time — and this was characteristic of him — he felt vaguely discontented with the prospect offered by the life of a successful lawyer. It meant before all that he would have no leisure, no tranquillity; that he would be tossed about from pillar to post, from Martha's Vineyard to Worcester, from court to court, without a moment for reading or reflection. Some of these exertions could at least be lessened by living in Boston, so in the spring of 1768, somewhat reluctantly, Adams, with his wife and their young child, left Braintree and settled down in the "white house" in Brattle Square.

Fortune at once seemed to smile upon him. His friend Jonathan Sewall, who was then Attorney-general, came one evening rather mysteriously to Brattle Square and invited himself to dinner. When Mrs. Adams had retired, leaving the two men together, smoking by the fireside, Sewall delivered his message. He had been asked by Governor Bernard to offer Adams the vacant office of Advocate General in the Court of Admiralty. It was an unexpected opportunity, the office was lucrative in itself and it was a first step in "the ladder of royal favor and promotion." On the other hand, Adams had already expressed strong disapproval of the Courts of Admiralty in the Braintree instructions which had been so admired in the province. He had protested against "the alarming extension of the power" of these courts, which, having a single judge and no jury, had opened "a vast number of sources of new crimes." The possibility of accepting did not even enter his mind; politely but firmly he refused the offer, and no insistence of Sewall could make him waver. This was a decisive step: without taking part in town politics, Adams had definitely chosen his side.

In the fall, while he was away on court business, two regiments arrived from Halifax and were quartered upon the town of Boston. When he returned, he found the town full of redcoats; all day long soldiers were drilling in Brattle Square, directly in front of Adams' house, and in the evening the Sons of Liberty paraded the streets, serenading him with sweet songs, violins and flutes. This time Great Britain's determination to subjugate the colonists was beyond doubt. The issue was joined and reconciliation seemed impossible. Adams made no new decision. He constantly refused to attend the town meetings, yet in 1768 and 1769 he was placed on a committee appointed to draw up instructions to the representatives. Once again he protested against the presence of troops in the city and the undue extension of the jurisdiction of the Admiralty Court.

When the sloop *Liberty*, belonging to Hancock, unloaded a cargo of wines without paying duty, and Hancock was threatened with penalties amounting to one hundred thousand pounds sterling, Adams was retained as counsel and advocate by the rich merchant. With Otis, he appeared in the Court of Admiralty in behalf of four sailors accused of killing Lieutenant Panton. Meanwhile he was "cooking up paragraphs, articles, occurrences" for the newspapers, or dining with three hundred and fifty Sons of Liberty in Dorchester. Undoubtedly Mr. Adams was already a very important person, running from court to court, attending club meetings, spending evenings with his colleagues of the bar, fretting and hardly bearing the fitful, nervous, eccentric ways of Otis, wasting a great deal of time, and dangled out of his house every morning by a tyrannical bell.

At times he longed for the peace of Braintree. Only too seldom could he escape from Boston, occasionally hearing a good sermon — and a more affecting and more rational entertainment he had not had on any Sabbath for many years. There only could he indulge in a bucolic mood:

Here is solitude and retirement. Still, calm, and serene, cool, tranquil, and peaceful, — the cell of the hermit; out at one window you see Mount Wollaston, the first seat of our ancestors, and beyond that, Stony Field Hill, covered over with corn and fruits; out at the other window, an orchard, and, beyond that, the large marsh called the broad meadow; from the east window of the opposite chamber, you see a fine plain covered with corn, and beyond that the whole harbor and all the islands; from the end window of the east chamber, you may see with a prospect-glass every ship, sloop, schooner, and brigantine, that comes in or goes out.[16]

His legal practice, however, left him little leisure for meditation; he now had a sulky in which to travel from court to court. In his Boston office were two clerks, or rather two apprentices, Jonathan William Austin and William Tudor. His only diversion was attending the meetings of his club. He was growing more and more irritated at the behavior of Otis, who was so filling up the time with "trash, obsceneness, profaneness, nonsense, and distraction", that none was left for "rational amusements or inquiries." Never had Adams seen "such an object of admiration, reverence, contempt, and compassion, all at once, as this." And the temper of the Boston populace was growing more and more irritable every day. When a former customhouse officer, Ebenezer Richardson, fired on the crowd attacking his house and killed a twelve-year-old boy, Adams witnessed with amazement the funeral procession extending "further than can well be imagined." He saw in this a sign that the ardor of the people was "not to be quelled by the slaughter of one child . . ."[17] Adams vaguely felt and apprehended that a sudden explosion was imminent, but he was too much a man of the town meeting and due process of law to believe that anything was to be gained by violence.

On the evening of the 5th of March he went to South Boston to attend the regular meeting of his club. About nine o'clock the members were alarmed by the ringing of bells. Supposing it a signal of fire, they ran out into the street and were informed that the British soldiers had fired on the inhabitants,

[16] Diary. Works, Vol. II, pp. 216–217.
[17] Ibid., p. 228.

killed some and wounded others, near the tower house. There, nothing was to be seen except a few soldiers drawn up in front of some fieldpieces. One could only mix with the angry crowd, rubbing elbows with the indignant citizenry, so Adams decided to go home, even before ascertaining what had taken place. Mrs. Adams, who was expecting a child,[18] was alone in the house, and her husband thought first of her and of his family. Brattle Square was occupied by the military and quiet enough; the house was still, but Adams had a restless night.

We cannot here go into the details of the affray, dignified at the time by the name of the "Boston Massacre." It started with an insignificant incident — a barber boy throwing snow-balls at a peaceful sentry, pacing his walk in front of the custom-house. When the boy, handled roughly by the soldier, screamed for help, a crowd soon gathered and the soldier called the guard. Six men arrived, under the command of Captain Preston. They were drawn up, facing an angry mob made up of the roughest elements in the town. The soldiers were threatened, insulted and pushed about, until the six men fired their muskets, every bullet taking effect. Five men fell mortally wounded and six more were slightly hurt. In a few minutes the street was filled with angry citizens, the townspeople turning out, and the whole regiment appearing. The situation was threatening and would soon have been beyond control had Lieutenant Governor Hutchinson not succeeded in calming the crowd by ordering the arrest of Preston and his men, and advising Lieutenant Colonel Carr to withdraw the troops to their barracks.

During this historic night, when Samuel Adams and his friends were surrounding Hutchinson, urging him to withdraw all the troops from the town, threatening and pleading with him, John Adams stayed at home, fearing that following this explosion "the poor tools" who for months had been encouraged "to excite quarrels, encounters, and combats" with the soldiers should gain the upper hand. They would be tried and the result would be "the perversion of law, and the corruption or partiality of juries", insensibly disgracing the jurisprudence of

---

[18] Charles Adams, born May 29, 1770.

the country and corrupting the morals of the people.[19] Perhaps a revolution was inevitable, but the whole people should "rise in their majesty", and not keep the town in a constant state of ferment.

The next morning Adams went as usual to his office and was sitting there when a friend of Captain Preston came in, with tears streaming from his eyes. Preston, upon his arrest, had vainly tried to secure the assistance of counsel. Even Mr. Auchmuty had refused and, in sheer desperation, Preston's friends decided to call on Quincy and Adams. It was an embarrassing request and an embarrassing position. That Adams was hostile to the new taxes and to garrisoning British mercenaries in the town, and that he sympathized with the party opposing Lieutenant Governor Hutchinson, was hardly to be doubted. On the other hand, he had some reason to believe that the explosion "had been intentionally wrought up by designing men, who knew what they were aiming at better than the instruments employed." If some of the participants in the riot were arrested and prosecuted, no one could tell what might be uncovered, and some of Adams' friends might be implicated. As a lawyer, his duty was simple. He could not promise to defend Captain Preston without knowing whether he was guilty or not, but he could not refuse to help gather the evidence and to see that the accused man should have a fair trial. This was all that Preston's friends were asking for. Adams received a "single guinea" as a retaining fee, and clamor went abroad that he had been bought by the friends of the government.[20] Such, at least, is the account given by him in his "Autobiography", written in his late years. He always maintained that single-handed and unaided he had chosen the more difficult path:

It was one of those cases, of which I could give you the history of many, in which my head or my heart, and perhaps a conspiracy of both, compelled me to differ in opinion from all my friends, to set at defiance all their advice, their remonstrances, their raillery, their ridicule,

[19] Diary. Works, Vol. II, pp. 229, 230.
[20] *Ibid.*, p. 231.

their censures, and their sarcasms, without acquiring one symptom of pity from my enemies.[21]

Against these affirmations of John Adams, we must quote here the biographer of Samuel Adams, according to whom Josiah Quincy and John Adams consented to become counsels for the prisoners "at the urgent solicitation of Samuel Adams and his associates." [22] The eagerness of Samuel Adams to secure a severe sentence against Preston, his dissatisfaction when only two soldiers were convicted and received light sentences, would rather seem to support John Adams' version. On the other hand, it must be admitted that John certainly exaggerated the resentment of his friends. A few weeks later, when a general election was held, the young lawyer, who had never attended a town meeting in Boston, was selected as representative to the General Court, a result which could hardly have been obtained without the engineering of the man who held the town in his hand.

The days which followed the "Massacre" were full of excitement: the town committee, headed by Hancock, going to the State House; Samuel Adams wrangling with Hutchinson for the withdrawal of the two regiments; the citizens arming themselves to preserve order, and John Adams himself doing his turn of duty, for, as he wrote, "I had the honor to be summoned in my turn, and attended at the State House with my musket and bayonet, my broadsword and my cartridge-box, under the command of the famous Paddock." All the while he had to collect evidence for the coming trial.

Under the physical and mental strain, John Adams almost broke down. He felt that a revolution was impending which would imperil his good name and perhaps his life. Just at the time when he had at last become a successful lawyer and had

[21] To James Lloyd, April 24, 1815. Works, Vol. X, p. 162.

[22] William V. Wells, "Life of Samuel Adams", Boston, 1865. Vol. I, p. 329; James K. Hosmer, "Samuel Adams", Boston, 1896, p. 182. The story seems to rest mainly on an equivocal passage in a letter of Quincy quoted by Charles F. Adams, according to which Quincy would have been urged by "an Adams" to undertake the defense of the prisoners. Works, Vol. I, p. 105 *note*.

more business at the bar than any other man in the province, he was to throw away these bright prospects to perform a thankless duty. But of his dire forebodings Mrs. Adams was the only confidant and before his friends and colleagues he kept a stiff upper lip.[23]

Whenever he could, during the session of the General Court, he escaped to his study, and all the time he kept his Diary. The only way to compose himself and collect his thoughts was to sit at a table and take his pen into his hand: "Pen, ink, and paper, and a sitting posture, are great helps to attention and thinking." His real calling was that of the man of letters, of the essayist and scholar; but few were the moments he could spend in the library of which he was so proud, enjoying his books and his pen. In preparation for the Preston case, he carefully went through the legal authorities on the common law, dull legal enumeration of precedents. Once, however, in a book by the Marquis de Beccaria, recently translated, he found a passage which so deeply thrilled him that he copied it to use as the introductory paragraph of the speech he was then writing:

If, by supporting the rights of mankind, and of invincible truth, I shall contribute to save from the agonies of death one unfortunate victim of tyranny, or of ignorance equally fatal, his blessing and tears of transport will be a sufficient consolation to me for the contempt of all mankind.

A close study of the testimonies had thoroughly convinced Adams of the innocence of Captain Preston and most of his men. Abominable as was the presence of British soldiers in Boston, there was no possible excuse for the conduct of the crowd. "Mobs will never do to govern States or command armies." His friends had more zeal than knowledge, and Adams felt it his duty "to lay open before our people the laws against riots, routs, and unlawful assemblies."[24] "The law and the testimony" was to be his maxim. The law and the testimony prevailed; Captain Preston and six of his men were acquitted,

[23] Diary. Works, Vol. II, p. 232.
[24] To Benjamin Hichborn, January 27, 1787. Works, Vol. IX, p. 551.

two were sentenced to be branded in the hand and then dismissed.

On many occasions in later years John Adams was to refer to the part he played in these "trials as important in the history of mankind as any that are recorded in the history of jurisprudence." His exertions, he thought, brought upon him "a load of indignation and unpopularity" which he knew "would never be forgotten, nor entirely forgiven." [25] However exaggerated this view may be, the fact remains that Samuel Adams and his followers deeply resented the verdict as a miscarriage of justice. In a series of articles signed "Vindex", published in the *Boston Gazette* from December 10, 1770, to January 28, 1771, Samuel Adams reviewed the whole case; he vehemently protested against the acquittal of Captain Preston, painted a pathetic description of the people who had fallen victims to the rage and cruelty of the soldiery, and called the murderers to the tribunal of God, since the human judges had shown themselves so weak and so fallible. Whether Samuel Adams was quite sincere or was trying to exploit the "Massacre" to the limit, he did not hold his young cousin responsible for the issue of the trial, and his friendship for him was not altered or diminished in the least degree. During the long session of the General Court, they sat on the same committees, worked together hand in glove, swapped stories, had good dinners and took pleasant trips around Boston. If, instead of resorting to letters written at a time when John Adams thought himself a victim of a long-standing conspiracy, we go back to the Diary, the story will appear very different. When, in the spring of 1771, John Adams, feeling absolutely exhausted, with "a pain in his breast and a complaint in his lungs", decided to leave Boston and return to "still, calm, happy Braintree", he expressed his appreciation of the innumerable civilities received from many of the inhabitants, and the many expressions of their good will, both of a public and private nature. "Of these," he added, "I have the most pleasing and grateful remembrances." In fact, Adams' courageous reaffirmation of the principles of law and order had placed him in good stead with the

[25] To Benjamin Rush, April 12, 1809. Works, Vol. IX, p. 617.

rich merchants of the town. He was a much invited-out young lawyer, had the best practice in Boston and, on the whole, life and men treated him fairly.

During the next eighteen months John Adams carefully avoided politics. The family was settled in Braintree, he had "a little farm, and stock, and cash", which he had acquired through work, and his health was rapidly improving. His was by no means a sedentary life; driving from Braintree to Boston several times a week, attending court in different towns of the province, and visiting friends kept him outdoors a large part of the time. He even decided in the spring of 1771 to take a journey to Stafford Springs in Connecticut, and on his way revisited Worcester and looked for his old haunts, spending days "riding through Paradise", enjoying the scenery, chatting with the people in the road houses and taverns, drinking in the "clear, dry, elastic air" of the hills. All the while he kept out of politics as much as he could, and when he returned to Boston, in November, 1772, he had decided to "remember temperance, exercise, and peace of mind; above all things, I must avoid politics, political clubs, town meetings, General Court, &c. &c. . . . and when in Boston, must spend my evenings in my office or with my family, and with as little company as possible." [26] He was now ready to enjoy life:

My father-in-law, Mr. Hall, and my mother are well settled in my farm at Braintree. The produce of my farm is all collected in; my own family is removed and well settled in Boston; my wood and stores are laid in for the winter; my workmen are nearly all paid; I am disengaged from public affairs, and now have nothing to do but to mind my office, my clerks, and my children. [27]

No wonder Otis "ranted" at him: "You will never learn military exercises. . . . You have a head for it, but not a heart; tired with one year's service, dancing from Boston to Braintree, and from Braintree to Boston; moping about the streets of this town as hipped as Father Flynt at ninety, and seemingly regardless of every thing, but to get money enough to carry you smoothly through this world."

[26] Diary. Works, Vol. II, p. 302.
[27] *Ibid.*, p. 304.

Needless to say, Adams fumed about it and back in his study wrote in his Diary what he might have answered to Mr. Otis. He suspected that two thirds of the town spoke of him in a similar way, and it hurt him deeply in his vanity, but did not make him change his resolution not to take part in political activities any more. His friends, however, and particularly Samuel Adams, knew him too well not to believe that he might be tempted. At the end of the year they called on him to deliver an oration on the evening of March 5th, in commemoration of the so-called Boston Massacre. One must admit that it was a strange request, which did little credit to Samuel Adams, who carried the invitation. The old politician saw in it a chance for his kinsman to come back into the fold, to define his position, to win back popular support and estranged friends. Quite sensibly John answered that he was "clearly, fully, absolutely and unalterably determined against it", but he attended the meeting held at the Old South Meetinghouse and listened to Doctor Benjamin Church's oration, which gave him a chance to reassert to himself his own righteousness:

It was . . . one of the most gallant, generous, manly, and disinterested actions of my whole life, and one of the best pieces of service I ever rendered my country. Judgment of death against those soldiers would have been as foul a stain upon this country as the executions of the quakers or witches anciently. As the evidence was, the verdict of the jury was exactly right.

This, however, is no reason why the town should not call the action of that night a massacre; nor is it any argument in favor of the Governor or Minister who caused them to be sent there. But it is the strongest proof of the danger of standing armies.[28]

In spite of these pious resolutions, he found that "the old warmth, heat, violence, acrimony, bitterness, sharpness of his temper and expression, was not departed." Occasionally he flared up and exploded, even among his family, as when, discussing the English Courts at "brother Cranch's", he exclaimed that "there was no more justice left in Britain than there was in hell; that I wished for war, and that the whole Bourbon

[28] Diary, March 5, 1773. Works, Vol. II, p. 317.

family was upon the back of Great Britain; avowed a thorough disaffection to that country; wished that any thing might happen to them, and, as the clergy prayed of our enemies in time of war, that they might be brought to reason or to ruin." [29] Back in his study among his books he scourged himself for his lack of self-control and flights of passion, but with such a temper how could he keep entirely out of politics, when politics could not be kept out of everyday life?

In January, 1773, Governor Hutchinson, irritated by constant references to the rights of the colonies made in speeches, newspaper articles and controversies, thought he could silence the opposition by entering into a long, elaborate and fully documented exposition of the rights of Parliament. He maintained and thought that he could prove that Parliament had a right to make laws for the colonies, to lay taxes on all things internal and external, and to regulate trade on land as well as on sea. A committee of the House, among whom were Hawley and Samuel Adams, was entrusted to draw up an answer to the governor. It is certain that John Adams was consulted by his kinsman and had a share in the preparation of the document which, on historical authorities, claimed for the colonies the right to make their laws and maintained that the General Court had in the province the same power and attributes as Parliament in England.[30]

When General Brattle, in a discussion on the independence of the judges, offered to dispute his point of view with any member of the bar, and particularly with "Mr. Otis, Mr. Adams and Mr. Josiah Quincy", John Adams forgot all his resolutions and decided "to enter the lists." In such controversies he was much more at home than in the feverish discussions of the town meetings. Armed with legal authorities, he poured over the head of the unfortunate Brattle an avalanche of texts and Latin

[29] Diary, December 31, 1772. Works, Vol. II, p. 308.
[30] New England historians have entered upon an animated controversy concerning the authorship of the document. See Tudor, "Life of Otis", p. 410; Charles Francis Adams, in "Life of John Adams", Works, Vol. I, p. 123 and Vol. II, p. 310 *note*; Wells, "Life of Samuel Adams", Vol. II, p. 31; Frothingham, "Life of Joseph Warren", p. 229. The text will be found in the "Works of Samuel Adams", Vol. II, p. 401.

quotations, called upon Lord Coke, Lord Holt, Chancellor Fortescue, Rapin, Hume and Blackstone to prove his point, and finally silenced his adversary.[31]

The controversy was hardly ended when Adams received communication of the famous secret letters written by Hutchinson, Oliver, Moffat, Paxton, and Rome, during the years 1767, 1768 and 1769. They had been sent from London by Benjamin Franklin and were first circulated among the patriots, before being published in June. In them appeared clearly the intention of the governor to abridge what some people called "English liberties", in order to preserve peace and "good order." Indignation ran high among the patriots, and apparently John Adams shared it; but, strong as were his feelings, he was even more interested in "the fine gentle rain" which fell during the night and would "lay a foundation for a crop of grass." His bucolic preoccupations were disturbed once more when he heard that he had been selected by the Friends of Liberty to go on the Council at the next general election.

Beset by dark forebodings, he spent the day before the election in fear and trembling. The "plots, plans, schemes and machinations" of which he was aware thoroughly sickened him. In all sincerity and humility he dreaded the perplexities, intricacies, difficulties and temptations to which he would be exposed. What would become of his sweet tranquillity, of his hope to give himself entirely to his private business, the education of his children, and the preservation of his health? He felt, however, that if elected this time, he could not refuse; his duty was clear, and his Puritan conscience had already told him that between two courses he must select "the more arduous and disagreeable." On the next day he was elected, but the governor interposed his negative because of the conspicuous part Mr. Adams had taken in the opposition, and for a time Adams felt relieved of further responsibility and thought that he would be left to his private and legal pursuits.

This is not the place to retrace the story of the legal and administrative tangle which resulted in the Tea Party of De-

[31] These articles, originally published in the *Boston Gazette*, will be found in Volume III of the Works.

cember, 1773. Duty on tea and wine had been maintained by the Townshend Revenue Act of 1767 and for several years no violent opposition had developed. Plenty of tea from Holland was smuggled in; some was legally, if somewhat surreptitiously, imported. But matters took a different turn when, in order to rescue the weakened East India Company, the British Government granted it a virtual monopoly. This measure, as has been often pointed out, as a first result coalesced the interests of the Boston merchants and the patriots.[32] So strong was the popular feeling aroused by Samuel Adams that the cargo could not be landed; and so great was the obstinacy of the governor that it could not obtain clearance to go back to England. After several weeks of wrangling and turmoil, matters came to a head, and on the night of December 16th a party of men disguised as Indians boarded the vessel, methodically broke open the chests of tea, dumped the contents into the harbor, and with fife and drum defiantly paraded the streets and serenaded Admiral Montague, who was lodging in the town.

The next morning John Adams wrote exultantly in his Diary: "Last night, three cargoes of Bohea tea were emptied into the sea. . . . This is the most magnificent movement of all. There is a dignity, a majesty, a sublimity, in this last effort of the patriots, that I greatly admire." [33] He was even more lyrical in a letter to James Warren: "The die is cast. The people have passed the river and cut away the bridge. Last night three cargoes of tea were emptied into the harbor. This is the grandest event which has ever yet happened since the controversy with Britain opened. The sublimity of it charms me!" [34] His enthusiasm ran so high as to condone the views of those who wished that "as many dead carcasses were floating in the harbor, as there are chests of tea", and he dryly added, "a much less number of lives, however, would remove the causes of all our calamities." This, of course, was an allusion to the much hated Hutchinson and "that brother-in-law of

[32] See J. T. Adams, "Revolutionary New England", p. 389, and A. M. Schlesinger, "The Colonial Merchants and the American Revolution, 1763–1776." "Studies in History." Columbia University, 1918.

[33] Diary, December 17, 1773. Works, Vol. II, p. 323.

[34] Works, Vol. IX, p. 333.

his", Judge Oliver, who had become John Adams' *bêtes noires*.

This was little more than a passing mood. The destruction of the tea was necessary, "absolutely and indispensably so", but other means could be found to bring to reason "the Egyptian taskmasters." Adams had already discussed the tenure of judges in his letters to General Brattle. Since the judiciary was to be made dependent on the Crown, and the judges to receive their compensation, not from the General Court, but from the king, some means had to be found in the arsenal of laws to counteract this move of the governor. This could be done, Adams thought, by claiming for the House of Representatives the same power of impeachment as Parliament had in England. As Judge Trowbridge put it to Adams, the procedure to follow was to explore the constitution and bring to life all its dormant and latent powers "in defence of your liberties, as you understand them." Although nothing came of the articles of impeachment drawn against Chief Justice Oliver, the patriots signified once more their intention to leave no stone unturned and on every occasion to carry the war into the enemy's camp.

Meanwhile in London retaliatory measures had been passed: the Boston Port Bill, closing the port until the town should agree to pay for the tea destroyed; an act changing the Constitution of Massachusetts, putting an end to the free town meetings and placing the judiciary under the direct authority of the governor; a third act was intended to protect the soldiers, by which all persons accused of participating in riots were to be sent to Great Britain or some other colony to be judged. Finally, General Gage, Commander in Chief in America, was appointed to supersede Hutchinson, called back to England, with power to quarter the soldiers upon the people.

Until the blow fell, John Adams refused to take a tragic view of the situation. As late as April 9th he was writing to James Warren:

News we have none. Still! silent as midnight! The first vessels may bring us tidings which will erect the crests of the tories again, and depress the spirits of the whigs. For my own part, I am of the same opinion that I have been for many years, that there is not spirit enough on either side to bring the question to a complete decision, and that we shall oscillate like a pendulum, and fluctuate like the ocean, for many years to come, and never obtain a complete redress of American grievances, nor submit to an absolute establishment of parliamentary authority, but be trimming between both, as we have been for ten years past, for more years to come than you and I shall live. Our children may see revolutions, and be concerned and active in effecting them, of which we can form no conception.[35]

How far this was from Samuel Adams, who for more than a year had prophesied "the entire separation and independence of the colonies"![36] But more than ever John Adams seemed determined not to engage openly in activities which, in his opinion, could not produce any immediate results. At the beginning of the year he had bought from his brother the homestead and house in which he had been born; thirty-five acres of land and eighteen acres of pasture. He had acquired it somewhat out of sentimental motives, for he had always wanted the house and "that beautiful, winding, meandering brook" which delighted him; but he had to improve it and make it pay. The courts were practically closed and for months he had not received a shilling per week; there was no prospect that any business would come his way for a long time. He could no longer afford to keep up his Boston establishment and, when the ships bringing the fateful news arrived on May 10th, he decided at once to remove the family to Braintree, keeping only an office in Boston.

He was ready and willing to battle with his pen, to contribute to a newspaper planned by William Woodfall,[37] but he had "little connection with public affairs" and he hoped "to have less." While Samuel Adams was working with the Committee of Correspondence and the General Court had convened at Salem, John Adams in Boston was fretting and chafing, "his head empty and his heart full"; he should have been in Braintree with his wife and children, he felt lonesome and dull, and could not think of any other diversion but to engage in the

[35] Works, Vol. IX, p. 337.
[36] To Arthur Lee, July 10, 1773, in J. K. Hosmer, "Samuel Adams", p. 267.
[37] Works, Vol. IX, p. 337.

writing of "a history of the contest between Britain and America."

He was in Boston presiding as moderator at a meeting held in Faneuil Hall when, on the 17th of June, the General Court appointed a committee of five to meet with delegates from the other colonies on the first day of September following. The dramatic scene has often been described: the representatives deliberating behind locked doors while the messenger of the governor demanded admission in vain; the almost unanimous resolution (twelve members only dissenting) to select as delegates Mr. Bowdoin, who refused the appointment, Mr. Cushing, Mr. Samuel Adams, Mr. John Adams, and Mr. Robert Treat Paine. It was the last act of the Provincial Assembly; this time the die was really cast.

John Adams heard the news, for which he was probably prepared, with mixed feelings. Of his high qualifications as an outstanding lawyer he held no doubt: in his own opinion he stood head and shoulders above the other members of the Boston bar. He had a larger library than any of them, and, unlike Mr. Gridley, he was a reader, not simply a borrower of books. He had mastered the intricacies of legal procedure, had all the precedents at his fingers' end; he had gone deeply into the principles of the laws and had pondered them. More than any other man in the province he had paid particular attention to constitutional law; he knew all the charters and acts of Parliament on which rested the government of the colonies. In his investigation he had even gone abroad and perused Montesquieu, Beccaria and Rousseau. But the questions to be debated by the coming Congress dealt with unfamiliar matters. The resolutions to be taken would affect not only the New England colonies, but New York and Virginia, whose problems and conditions were certainly different. Could common resolves be adopted when the divergence of interests and grievances was so evident? How would it be possible to bring into some sort of unity a people whose "ideas were as various as the faces"?

The "morbid vanity" of John Adams has been so often emphasized that it is only just to call attention once more to the fundamental intellectual honesty of the man — to the hesitation, doubts, misgivings and anxiety that troubled his mind during the weeks following his appointment. He wandered alone, "pondered, moped and ruminated, lost in reveries and brown studies." How could America follow Samuel Adams and the patriots to the end, when her people were so inexperienced, "so deficient in genius, in education, in travel, in every thing"? And yet to submit was an unbearable thought; it would mean "infamy and ruin." But he was "at a loss, totally at a loss, what to do when we get there."

Advice was not lacking, however. John Adams consulted with friends and counsellors; with James Warren, who seems to have been instrumental in having him appointed; with Joseph Hawley of Northampton, a remarkably clear-headed and farsighted man; with Samuel Adams, who occasionally led out to the Common the boy Josiah Quincy, "to see with detestation the British troops, and with pleasure the Boston militia." [38] Meanwhile preparations were made for the solemn departure of the delegates. Samuel Adams, who had never paid attention to externals, was equipped by friends with a new suit of clothes, a new wig, a new hat, six pairs of the best silk hose and six pairs of shoes, while another gentleman presented him with a purse containing fifteen or twenty johannes. [39]

On the 10th of August the four delegates started from the house of Cushing. They drove past the Common in sight of the five regiments encamped there, in a coach preceded by two white servants well mounted and armed, with four blacks behind in livery. It was a "very respectable parade" and a brave show, but there was no joy in the heart of John Adams.

His was not an heroic mood, and he had no inkling that he was entering upon his national career. Behind him, in Braintree, he was leaving his wife and children with a very small store of cash, and no one knew when he would be able to resume his practice of the law. He was embarking upon a fateful and hazardous venture. No one could tell what measures would be

---

[38] To Samuel Adams, April 27, 1785. Works, Vol. IX, p. 532.
[39] Andrews to William Barrell, August 11, 1774. Massachusetts Historical Society Collections, 1865.

agreed upon, or to what extent the British Government was decided to use force. These were ugly reflections, and it was cold comfort to remember that "Brutus and Cassius were conquered and slain, Hampden died in the field, Sidney on the scaffold, Harrington in jail." [40] Truly, politics were "an ordeal path among red hot ploughshares." At most he had engaged upon a thankless task. The delegates had no instructions, no precise aims in view, no program, and they were going to face untold difficulties. Yet even at that time it did not enter Adams' mind that he could have refused the dangerous mandate. When designated by the freeholders of Braintree, he had dug ditches and built roads. No sensible man for the pleasure of holding office would select such a career. "Yet somebody must." The more unpleasant, the more imperious the duty; so with his old kinsman all primped up in his new regalia, the "steady" and "secretive" Cushing, and the fitful, witty, learned and conceited Bob Paine, John Adams started forth on his historic journey.

[40] To James Warren, June 25, 1774. Works, Vol. IX, p. 339.

CHAPTER IV

INDEPENDENCE

LEAVING Boston on the 10th of August, the "Committee for Congress traveled leisurely and arrived in Philadelphia on the evening of the 29th. The first part of the journey through Massachusetts and Connecticut was a continuous ovation — everywhere the delegates were dined, cordially entertained with punch, wine and coffee; salutes were fired; men, women and children crowded at the doors and windows "as if it was to see a coronation"; "no Governor of a Province, nor General of an army was ever treated with so much ceremony and assiduity." New York gave them a different welcome. It was a *terra incognita* inhabited by people of different stock, with different religious traditions, of different tempers and dispositions, and all their misgivings were soon confirmed.

They had been warned by Joseph Hawley of Northampton that they would find there "divers gentlemen of Dutch, or Scotch, or Irish extract" who might be offended by the "big and haughty airs" which the gentlemen from Boston were apt to assume from "an inward vanity and self conceit."[1] It was a timely warning, but there is some doubt that Adams heeded it carefully. He was flustered by the New York people; their way of talking "very loud, very fast, and altogether" shocked the New Englander, accustomed to the solemn and orderly procedure which in Boston passed for conversation, and he concluded that although the delegates had been treated with marked respect, he had not seen in town "one real gentleman, one well-bred man."[2] Some had Episcopalian prejudices against New England; others feared lest "the levelling spirit of New

[1] July 25, 1774. Works, Vol. IX, p. 344.
[2] Diary. Works, Vol. II, p. 353.

England should propagate itself into New York." Peter Vanbrugh Livingston, a retired merchant, even blustered that the Boston populace had acted as so many Goths and Vandals and, much to the surprise and indignation of John Adams, he had the bad taste to mention "our hanging the Quakers." [3]

Philadelphia was to prove more hospitable, but during their two-months' stay in the strange city the Massachusetts delegates never felt quite at ease. Mindful of their great responsibility, and coming not to prescribe and to dictate, but to consult and to ask for aid, they did not try to play openly any conspicuous part. Many were the orators in the First Continental Congress — gentlemen with a name for eloquence, eager to speak, with a wonderful flow of language at their command. The New Englanders listened to speeches and attended committees, but they did most of their work behind the scenes. "We have had numberless prejudices to remove here," wrote John Adams to William Tudor. "We have been obliged to keep ourselves out of sight, and to feel pulses, and to sound the depths; to insinuate our sentiments, designs, and desires, by means of other persons, sometimes of one province, and sometimes of another." [4] They soon despaired of accomplishing much, although they accomplished as much as could be expected under the circumstances; but this "Areopagus, Council of Amphictyons, conclave, or divan", was to the New England lawyer a real "University." To the moralist and portrait painter it provided a unique opportunity to observe new characters, new types of mind, new enigmas to decipher and new personalities to unveil. Adams would not have been true to himself if occasionally he had not fretted, had not expressed disgust and irritation at the unnecessary delays and exasperating procedures. It was his first long absence from home, and often he longed for the calm of Braintree, worried for his wife and children, for his dear books left unprotected in his Boston house, and even for his "poor cows." But, on the whole, he enjoyed himself immensely.

During the most important meetings of Congress he took

[3] Diary. Works, Vol. II, p. 351.
[4] Philadelphia, September 29, 1774. Works, Vol. IX, pp. 346, 348.

abundant notes, and his account supplements in the most vivid way the dry, matter-of-fact *Journals of Congress*. Back in his lodgings, in the house of Miss Jane Port, on Arch Street, about halfway between Front and Second streets, he filled page after page in his Diary; never before had life been so rich, so colorful and so fascinating. In comparison with Philadelphia, Boston seemed a village — everywhere elegant houses, "clever" libraries, bookshops, taverns, stores where one could talk while eating dried smoked sprats and drinking punch. Then there was the hospital where lunatics were kept in "rooms under ground", anatomical charts of Doctor Shippen, and the far more impressive skeletons and waxworks of Doctor Chovet. Entertainment was not only copious, but delicate; even the "plain Quakers" offered one "ducks, hams, chickens, beef, pig, tarts, creams, custards, jellies, fools, trifles, floating islands, beer, porter, punch, wine, and a long &c." [5]

The next day, it was "a most sinful feast again": turtle, flummery, jellies, sweetmeats of twenty sorts, almonds, raisins, melon "fine beyond description", and pears and peaches as excellent. As for the wines, nothing but the best of clarets, Madeira and Burgundy, of which Adams could drink at a great rate and find no inconvenience in it.

There was such a quick and constant succession of new scenes, characters, persons and events turning up before him, that he could not keep a regular account; but the diffidence he had felt on leaving Boston soon vanished; the New England lawyer was not to be awed by such a display.

Philadelphia, with all its trade and wealth and regularity, is not Boston. The morals of our people are much better; their manners are more polite and agreeable; they are purer English; our language is better, our taste is better, our persons are handsomer; our spirit is greater, our laws are wiser, our religion is superior, our education is better. We exceed in every thing but in a market, and in charitable, public foundations. [6]

This was the not unnatural reaction of a young provincial introduced for the first time to the life of a metropolis; it was

[5] September 7, 1774. Diary. Works, Vol. II, p. 369.
[6] October 9, 1774. *Ibid.*, p. 395.

also the Puritan in Adams trying to reassert himself by condemning the sinful pleasures thrust upon him from every quarter. If in conversation he had learned to exercise a certain discretion, his pen was never sharper, more alert and cruel. He had lost none of his talent for caustic delineation, and when he left Philadelphia, he had considerably enriched his gallery of moral portraits. There was Cæsar Rodney, "the oddest looking man in the world; he is tall, thin and slender as a reed, pale; his face is not bigger than a large apple, yet there is sense and fire, spirit, wit, and humor in his countenance." [7] Dickinson was subject to "hectic complaints"; he was "a shadow, tall, but slender as a reed; pale as ashes." [8] Young Ned Rutledge "a perfect Bob-o-Lincoln, — a swallow, a sparrow, a peacock; excessively vain, excessively weak, and excessively variable and unsteady; jejune, inane, and puerile." [9] Since he heard so many speeches on the way, he passed judgment on the orators: Galloway, Duane, and Johnson, "sensible, learned, but cold speakers"; Paca, a deliberator; Dyer and Sherman, speaking often and long, but very heavily and clumsily. Lee, Hooper and Henry were "the orators." On the whole, he was immensely pleased with his colleagues. He had never doubted the ability of New Englanders to shine in any circle, but he had not expected so much wit, sense, learning, acuteness, subtlety and eloquence among the fifty delegates meeting in Carpenters' Hall. In all sincerity he could write to Mrs. Adams: "The art and address of ambassadors from a dozen belligerent powers of Europe, nay, of a conclave of cardinals at the election of a Pope, or of the princes in Germany at the choice of an Emperor, would not exceed the specimens we have seen." [10]

He was not as well satisfied with the results obtained during these two long months. The record of the First Congress is not generally considered as one of great achievement. It certainly fell short of the expectations entertained by some of the delegates. In his opening speech, Patrick Henry proposed to start

[7] Diary. Works, Vol. II, p. 364.
[8] Ibid., p. 360.
[9] Ibid., p. 401.
[10] September 29, 1774. Ibid., p. 391 note.

from a *tabula rasa:* "Government is dissolved. Fleets and armies and the present state of things show that government is dissolved. Where are your landmarks, your boundaries of Colonies? We are in a state of nature, sir. . . . The distinctions between Virginians, Pennsylvanians, New Yorkers, and New Englanders, are no more. I am not a Virginian, but an American." [11] John Adams greatly enjoyed the discussion which followed and, even more, the contention of Colonel Lee that the rights of the British colonists "are built on a fourfold foundation; on nature, on the British constitution, on charters, and on immemorial usage." [12] These were propositions to delight the heart of a lawyer and political philosopher. His disappointment was great when, on September 24th, it was *"Resolved,* That the congress do confine themselves, at present, to the consideration of such rights only as have been infringed by acts of the British parliament since the year 1763, postponing the further consideration of the general state of American rights to a future day." [13] The text finally adopted after long wrangling was not, in fact, a real Declaration of Rights, but a mere reiteration of the protest made by the people of Boston in 1772. The addresses to the king, to the people of England, to the British American colonies, and to the people of Canada provided a better opportunity for a fine display of scholarship and eloquence. Most important of all was the plan of Association by which the delegates agreed to the nonimportation and the nonconsumption of British goods "on which duty has or shall be paid." The nonexportation was not to take effect until September, 1775. If this was not yet independence and the beginning of a new order, at least Massachusetts no longer stood alone against the British Government. No definite promise had been made, but when the false news came that Boston had been bombarded, the horror and indignation were such that the delegates felt reasonably certain that the colonies would rally to

[11] Diary. Works, Vol. II, pp. 366, 367.
[12] *Ibid.,* p. 370.
[13] "Journals of the Continental Congress, 1774–1789", edited from the original records in the Library of Congress by Worthington Chauncey Ford. Vol. I (1904), p. 42.

their assistance should any overt act be committed, and John Adams had carefully noted in his Diary "the most eloquent speech at the Virginia Convention that ever was made", for had not Colonel Washington declared, "I will raise one thousand men, subsist them at my own expense, and march myself at their head for the relief of Boston." [14]

Before adjourning, Congress had voted to convene again in the following year. To John Adams it had been a wonderful experience which he had no wish to renew. He had done his part and felt as when he had been chosen, — that these arduous duties ought to be discharged in rotation. "It is not very likely that I shall ever see this part of the world again," wrote he, on leaving Philadelphia, and public life seemed to him less alluring than ever. With great satisfaction he saw, on his way back, great military preparations being carried out everywhere in New England; the spirit of the people was aroused; young men were drilling on the green and young ladies sang the new Liberty Song — but at thirty-nine John Adams felt like an old man, weak and tired, his eyes so inflamed that he could hardly read or write. He needed the rest and calm of his country house.

Hardly was he back, however, when he was sent by the town of Braintree to the Provincial Congress, and soon he engaged in a new controversy, carried on in the columns of the *Boston Gazette*. He had not forgotten his old project to write a history of the conflict between Great Britain and the American colonies. When he read in the *Massachusetts Gazette* an obviously biased account of the period given by the talented "Massachusettensis", whom he suspected to be his old friend Sewall, he could not restrain his pen.[15] The "Novanglus" papers were published in the *Boston Gazette* from December 12, 1774, to April, 1775; their publication was stopped only by the Battle of Lexington, and in the confusion several articles already written and sent to the printer were irretrievably lost. Perhaps we should not mourn for them, as the "Novanglus" is a heavy, pedantic, ill-composed dissertation on the right of the Massachusetts people

[14] Diary, August 31, 1774. Works, Vol. II, p. 360.

[15] The author, as John Adams discovered much later, was really another friend of his, Daniel Leonard. Works, Vol. IV, p. 10 *note*.

to govern themselves without interference from Crown or Parliament. It is an attempt to prove that colonization, as such, has no legal status, and that the laws of England cannot extend beyond the sea. It is also a new recital of the abuses condoned, recommended and perpetrated by governors Hutchinson and Bernard. In his articles, Adams displayed an enormous erudition, a rare familiarity with all legal and historical authorities; he called on Aristotle and Plato, Livy and Cicero, Sidney, Harrington and Locke for his definition of the principles of nature and eternal reason. Unfortunately he was more occupied with the minute refutation of Massachusettensis' arguments than with his own thesis; he took the tone, not of the political philosopher, but of the theological controversialist, and neglected to emphasize the *fundamentals* on which the whole case rested.

Of the impression made upon him by Lexington and Concord, Adams has left no record. A few days after the event, he rode to Cambridge and saw the New England army. There was "great confusion and much distress." Everything was wanting, but "neither the officers nor men, . . . wanted spirits or resolution." [16] He felt that "the die was cast, the Rubicon passed, and, as Lord Mansfield expressed it in Parliament, if we did not defend ourselves, they would kill us." [17] This was not the time to remain idle or to avoid public duties. Once again he searched his heart and in all humility and all honesty saw that he could not help putting his hand to the pump, now that the ship was in a storm and the hold half full of water.

On his return home, he was seized with a violent fever, but the time was coming to repair to Philadelphia for the opening of Congress. In a sulky, with a servant on horseback, he proceeded on his journey, overtaking in New York, John Hancock, Thomas Cushing, Samuel Adams and Robert Treat Paine. This time the New Englanders had before them a grim business, and conviviality, rejoicing and feasts were decidedly out of order. Adams had particular reason to feel depressed. In Braintree he had left his wife with four little children, in a

[16] Diary. Works, Vol. II, p. 406.
[17] *Ibid.*

rather exposed situation; everything was to be feared from British raiders and particularly from the fleet. That such an apprehension was well justified appears in a very vivid letter written by Mrs. Adams, describing the great alarm of May, 1775, when "people, women, children from the iron works came flocking down this way", and the militia jumped on sloops "to prevent a landing of the British on Grape island." Soldiers passed through Braintree for lodging, supper and drink; refugees from Boston, "tired and fatigued", sought asylum for a day, a night, a week. The distress of the poor people was "beyond the power of language to describe." [18] War had not been declared, but, in fact, a state of war already existed in Massachusetts. Badly organized and badly equipped, the most irregular New England army, made up of farmers and militiamen, was already facing the regulars kept by Gage in Boston. A bloody conflict could occur at any time.

In Congress great sympathy for the poor people of Boston and great indignation at the conduct of the British troops were commonly expressed, but there was apparently a curious lack of unanimity on measures to be taken and policies to be adopted. From the very actions of Congress, more than from any expression of their sentiments, it appears clearly that a large number of delegates still clung to the hope that a complete and official break with Great Britain could be avoided, and no fatal and final step would have to be taken. Besides the few Loyalists, who were in a decided minority, there was a strong element made up of men honest and timid, but whose influence was undeniable. These had to be placated and conciliated in some manner, and the delegates during the first few weeks in Philadelphia had a unique opportunity to perfect their knowledge of parliamentary tactics and politics. Apparently there was little logic in one day recommending to receive and treat well British troops, if any were sent to the city, and the next day resolving that batteries be erected on each side of the Hudson River to prevent any vessel from passing that might harass the inhabitants.[19] The most curious resolutions on the state of America

---

[18] "Letters of Mrs. Adams", pp. 29, 32, 34.
[19] Journals of Congress, Vol. II, p. 60.

were offered by the committee and passed by Congress, recognizing on the one hand that hostilities had been "actually commenced in the Massachusetts bay", and on the other hand accepting that a petition be sent to the king "for a restoration of the harmony formerly subsisting between our Mother country and these colonies." [20]

With all these half-measures Adams was very impatient. He knew of the distress of the inhabitants in Boston; the letters from his wife increased his alarms for the safety of his family, his friends and all his people whom he had been sent to Congress to protect and defend. In his head he agitated schemes and plans, went from delegate to delegate to press his point and, in doing so, naturally ran against the moderates and the pacifists. He wished at once to secure hostages and to seize all the town officers, informing them that "hitherto we were free"; and, most of all, "to adopt" immediately the army in Cambridge as the Continental Army.

But Congress was a slow-moving body. First they felt very reluctant to go beyond an earnest recommendation "to the several Colonies of New Hampshire, Rhode Island, Connecticut and the interior towns of Massachusetts Bay, that they immediately furnish the American army before Boston with as much powder out of their town, and other publick stocks as they can possibly spare", [21] then that "six companies of expert rifflemen, be immediately raised in Pennsylvania, two in Maryland, and two in Virginia", [22] to be enlisted in the "Continental Army", and on the same day Mr. George Washington was appointed on a committee to bring in a "draft of Rules and regulations for the government of the army." On the next day it was "*Resolved*, That a General be appointed to command all the continental forces, raised, or to be raised, for the defence of American liberty." [23]

It is generally admitted that the choice of George Washington as commander in chief of the Continental forces is due to

[20] *Journals of Congress*, Vol. II, p. 65.
[21] June 10, 1775. *Ibid.*, p. 85.
[22] June 14, 1775. *Ibid.*, p. 89.
[23] June 15, 1775. *Ibid.*, p. 91.

John Adams. As a fact, this assertion rests largely, if not solely, on the account written many years later by Adams himself in a fragment of his "Autobiography." His account is too well known to be repeated here: how the New Englanders were naturally desirous to control the army before Boston; how the Virginians were reluctant to send to New England troops to be placed under the command of a New England general; how apparently a deadlock had developed and was broken only when Adams, unable to obtain the formal approval of his fellow delegates, in a dramatic speech from his seat, made a "motion in form" that Congress should adopt the army at Cambridge, adding that, although the proper time for nominating a general had not come, he had no hesitation to declare that there was but one gentleman in his mind for this important command. Thereupon Washington, who happened to sit near the door, "darted into the library room", and Mr. Hancock, who had ambitions of his own, expressed "mortification and resentment as forcibly as his face could exhibit them."

On the whole, there is no serious reason for questioning the correctness of this account, although John Adams' imagination and sense of picturesqueness may have induced him to dramatize somewhat the famous scene. It seems, however, that he was not the first to think of Washington, since as early as May 4th Elbridge Gerry, with the approval of Warren, wrote to the Massachusetts delegates that they would "rejoice to see this way the beloved Colonel Washington as generalissimo." [24] It will also be remembered that George Washington was nominated by Thomas Johnson of Maryland,[25] and Adams' speech, as well as his original motion, does not seem to have been mentioned by any contemporary. Writing two days later to Elbridge Gerry, Adams indicated his satisfaction at the choice of Congress, without claiming any credit for it, and he observed the same modesty in a letter to his wife.[26] This, however, may have been prudence as much as modesty, as letters

---

[24] "Life of Gerry", Vol. I, p. 79, in Winsor, "The Memorial History of Boston." Boston, 1880–1881, Vol. IV, p. 131.

[25] *Journals of Congress*, Vol. II, p. 91.

[26] Works, Vol. IX, p. 358; "Familiar Letters of John Adams", p. 65.

were frequently intercepted by the British, and Adams was not without qualms about the reception of this news by New England.

That he felt himself responsible for the choice of the commander in chief is shown rather indirectly in his repeated praise of the General in his insistence that there was "something charming" in the conduct of Washington. "A gentleman of one of the first fortunes upon the continent, leaving his delicious retirement, his family and friends, sacrificing his ease, and hazarding all in the cause of his country! His views are noble and disinterested. He declared, when he accepted the mighty trust, that he would lay before us an exact account of his expenses, and not accept a shilling for pay." [27]

Adams was one of the committee of three sent to wait on General Lee, to inform him of his appointment as major general — a rather difficult task since it was known that his ambition was to be *aut secundus, aut nullus,* and Artemas Ward had been chosen first major general. Then smaller appointments had to be made, and the pay for all the officers chosen by Congress had to be determined. This was not easily settled, as the Southern delegates insisted on a pay which seemed extravagant to the more parsimonious New Englanders. "They think," wrote Adams, "the Massachusetts establishment too high for the privates, and too low for the officers, and they would have their own way." All of it caused Adams more anxiety than he had ever suffered in all his lifetime, and it must be added that his health "quite infirm", and his "smarting eyes" which prevented him from reading and writing, contributed to depress his spirits. [28] Still, he was keeping about and attended Congress very constantly. It was trying work, and progress was very slow, "like a coach and six, the swiftest horses must be slackened, and the slowest quickened, that all may keep an even pace." [29]

A few days later a very distressing report reached Phila-

---

[27] To Elbridge Gerry, Philadelphia, June 18, 1775. Works, Vol. IX, p. 357. For the speech of Washington, see *Journals of Congress*, Vol. II, p. 92.
[28] June 10, 1775. "Familiar Letters", p. 61.
[29] June 17. *Ibid.*, p. 66.

delphia. "A battle at Bunker's Hill and Dorchester Point. Three colonels wounded, Gardner mortally." The next morning, June 23d, Washington, Lee and Schuyler started off on their journey to the American camp before Boston. Adams and all the Massachusetts delegates accompanied them a little way; a large troop of light horse in uniform was lined up behind the generals, the bands were playing, delegates followed in their carriages with liveried servants. It was war, or rather it was that eve of war when uniforms are bright with gay colors, swords flash in the sun, drum and bugle quicken the pulse of spectators, and young men think of glory and easily won victories. Who could have resisted such contagious enthusiasm? Adams was too human not to feel it, and he was also somewhat melancholy at the thought that he would remain behind, comparatively unknown, "scribbling for his bread and his liberty, low in spirits and low in health", while others would wear the laurels he had sown.[30] How could he have felt otherwise, when at that moment he had before his eyes a letter written by his wife, starting with the triumphant: "The day — perhaps the decisive day — is come, on which the fate of America depends. . . . How many have fallen, we know not. The constant roar of the cannon is so distressing that we cannot eat, drink or sleep." [31]

While his friends were engaged at Bunker's Hill and Doctor Warren died "fighting gloriously for his country, saying: 'Better to die honorably in the field, than ignominiously hang upon the gallows' ",[32] Adams had to go back to his inglorious and arduous but necessary tasks, attending committees, talking endlessly to timid delegates, representing to them "Charleston laid in ashes", the "groans and cries of the injured and oppressed", the inhabitants of Boston reduced to "the state of the most abject slaves, under the most cruel and despotic tyrants." This was not the time for theoretical discussions on principles of colonization; one could think only of action. To his friend Warren he unbosomed himself fully:

[30] June 23. "Familiar Letters", p. 70.
[31] Mrs. Adams to John Adams, June 18, 1775. *Ibid.*, p. 67.
[32] *Ibid.*

. . . A certain great fortune and piddling genius, whose fame has been trumpeted so loudly, has given a silly cast to our whole doings. We are between hawk and buzzard. We ought to have had in our hands, a month ago, the whole legislative, executive, and judicial of the whole continent, and have completely modelled a constitution; to have raised a naval power, and opened all our ports wide; to have arrested every friend of government on the continent, and held them as hostages for the poor victims in Boston; and then opened the door as wide as possible for peace and reconciliation. After this, they might have petitioned, negotiated, addressed, &c., if they would.[33]

Only one fault could be found with this letter, which reflected the logical mind of Adams: it became public six or eight months before the right time, when neither Congress nor the Philadelphia people were ready for such radical measures. Unfortunately for Adams, the letter, with a similar one addressed to his wife, fell into the hands of the British, who published them in Boston. The effect of the disclosure, however, was not felt until the fall, and when Adams went home for the short recess taken by Congress in August, he was unaware of the difficulties and unpleasantness in store for him.

At Braintree distressing news awaited him; his brother Elihu had just died, and an epidemic of dysentery threatened the whole coast of Massachusetts. Occupied by his duties with the Provincial Assembly, he could hardly see his family, and early in September he had to start, for the third time, on his way to Philadelphia, leaving his dear ones, including little Tommy, laid up with the disease. "The smallpox was not more mortal than this distemper has proved in this town," wrote Mrs. Adams; "four, three, and two funerals in a day, for many days." [34]

By September the letters written to Warren had become known in Philadelphia. Dickinson could not fail to recognize himself in the "piddling genius" and was more than cold to Adams. By the moderates he was considered as a dangerous and somewhat irresponsible person to keep away from, and for a whole month he and his New England colleagues were al-

[33] July 24, 1775. Works, Vol. I, p. 179.
[34] September 10, 1775. "Familiar Letters", p. 96.

most blacklisted, as their names do not appear on any important committee appointed in September. Adams, according to his wont, pretended that on the whole the publication of his letters had done much good, but he refrained from giving any real news in his correspondence with his wife, and on October 7th he could write, "Really, my dear, I have been more cautious than I used to be." But soon after, he admitted to another correspondent: "Zeal, and fire, and activity, and enterprise, strike my imagination too much. I am obliged to be constantly on my guard; yet the heat within will burst forth at times." [35]

Not fit to be a soldier and take his stand on the firing line, Adams, during the fall, gave all his energy to military matters. Two problems were uppermost in his mind. He had no practical experience of the sea, but a man born in Braintree and practicing law in Boston could not fail to realize the importance of communication by water. The colonies had little chance to wage a successful fight against Great Britain unless they were in a position to intercept ships laden with men, ammunition and provisions, and to deprive England of her uncontested mastery of the sea. There was no hope of improvising a great navy, but at least a beginning could be made. It seems that this view of Adams' was at first ridiculed, but he finally succeeded in having a committee appointed and, on October 13th, Congress ordered that two swift sailing vessels be fitted out; then on October 30th, that two more armed vessels, one of twenty guns, and the other of thirty-six guns, be armed for the protection of the colonies. The question paramount in his mind, however, was how to preserve what he already called "the Union." [36]

Among the many elements which prevented the colonies from coalescing was a clear-cut division between the North and the South. It was not a matter of principle, but a question of fact. The Southern gentlemen, accustomed to deal with slaves and a white population of servants and poor whites, could not understand the attitude of New England towards what they

[35] November 25, 1775. To Mrs. Mercy Warren. Works, Vol. IX, p. 369.
[36] Ibid.

called the common people. In New England the common people were either farmers, small merchants, or mechanics and artisans who had acquired wonderful dexterity and received a modicum of education in the grammar schools. They objected not only to the privileges necessarily granted to their officers, but even more to the low pay they were receiving; while the Southern delegates maintained that the pay of the officers was too low and that of the men too high. Such contentions, resulting from local conditions and social prejudices, could not be altered in one day; Adams dreaded "the consequences of this dissimilitude of character", and added, in a letter to Joseph Hawley, that "without the utmost caution on both sides, and the most considerate forbearance with one another, and prudent condescension on both sides, they will certainly be fatal." [37] On this mooted question there could be no hope of ever getting a unanimous vote, and, unfortunately, even among the New England delegates there was some division of opinion. Cushing seemed to be unable to make up his mind and refused to commit himself; truly it was "very hard to be linked and yoked eternally with people, who have either no opinions, or opposite opinions, and to be plagued with the opposition of our own colony to the most necessary measures, at the same time that you have all the monarchical superstition and the aristocratical domination of nine other colonies to contend with." [38]

A third point seems to have occupied him during the fall session of Congress. He alluded to it the following year in a letter to Chase: "Your motion last fall for sending ambassadors to France with conditional instructions, was murdered; terminating in a committee of secret correspondence, which came to nothing." [39] Much later in life John Adams claimed credit, not only for having originated the idea, but also for a speech in which he enunciated the cardinal principle of American foreign policy: "This principle was, that we should make no treaties of alliance with any European power; that we should consent to none but treaties of commerce; that we should separate our-

[37] November 25, 1775. Works, Vol. IX, p. 367.
[38] Ibid., p. 368.
[39] July 9, 1776. Ibid., p. 421.

selves, as far as possible and as long as possible, from all European politics and wars." [40] It is very doubtful that this principle appeared so clearly at the time to the mind of Adams, and unfortunately all traces of the deliberations of Congress on the matter seem to have disappeared. It will be noted, however, that the question of trade with France and Spain was introduced by Chase on October 20th.[41]

His "whole time engrossed with business", attending committees from seven to ten in the morning, then Congress from ten to four or five, then committees again from five to ten, Adams hardly found time to write home. He was soon offered an unexpected opportunity to resign honorably from this arduous charge when, during the short trip to New England which he took in December, 1775, he was appointed Chief Justice of Massachusetts. With great hesitation he accepted, with the proviso that he should take possession of his seat "as soon as the circumstances of the colonies will admit an adjournment of Congress." For the present, however, his duty was clear, and in spite of the promise he had made himself never to return to Philadelphia without his family, alone and determined he went back to his duties, only regretting that he was too old, too much worn with the fatigue of study in his youth "to engage in more active, gay and dangerous scenes." [42]

In New York he had picked up an anonymous pamphlet recently published in Philadelphia under the title of "Common Sense", and he liked it so much that he sent it at once to his wife. A few weeks later, however, when Mrs. Adams had expressed great admiration for the work, he thought it his duty to tell her exactly what to think of it. It is a good page of literary criticism, much better balanced than Adams' later opinion of Thomas Paine:

Sensible men think there are some whims, some sophisms, some artful addresses to superstitious notions, some keen attempts upon the passions, in this pamphlet. But all agree there is a great deal of good

[40] To Benjamin Rush, September 30, 1805. "Life of John Adams." Works, Vol. I, p. 200.

[41] "Debates", in Works, Vol. II, p. 474.

[42] February, 1776. "Familiar Letters", p. 133.

sense delivered in clear, simple, concise, and nervous style. His sentiments of the abilities of America, and of the difficulty of a reconciliation with Great Britain, are generally approved. But his notions and plans of continental government are not much applauded. Indeed, this writer has a better hand in pulling down than in building. It has been very generally propagated through the continent that I wrote this pamphlet. But although I could not have written anything in so manly and striking a style, I flatter myself I should have made a more respectable figure as an architect, if I had undertaken such a work. This writer seems to have very inadequate ideas of what is proper and necessary to be done in order to form constitutions for single colonies, as well as a great model of union for the whole.[43]

In fact, at that date, Adams had already undertaken to show that he could be a good architect, in a letter written after a conversation with George Wythe of Virginia, and soon printed anonymously, through Richard Henry Lee, under the title of "Thoughts on Government." With the breaking up of their long-established forms of government, and their refusal to recognize the acts of the British governors, the colonies found themselves confronted with a curious situation. Theoretically, they had no government at all and, as Patrick Henry had said, they were back to "a state of nature"; in fact, it must be remembered that particularly in New England the traditions of the town meeting corrected to a large degree this apparent anarchy. The need of some common bond and of some central organization was nevertheless keenly realized in certain colonies, and in October, 1775, the New Hampshire delegates had been instructed to obtain "the advice and direction of the Congress, with respect to a method for our administering Justice and regulating our civil police." [44] A committee made up of John Rutledge, John Adams, Samuel Ward, Richard Henry Lee, and Roger Sherman, was appointed and reported on November third. The resolution adopted by Congress on this occasion was a compromise, since it preserved the legal fiction that the present situation was only temporary, and that such measures had to be taken only "during the continuance of the present dispute

[43] March 19, 1776. "Familiar Letters", p. 146.
[44] October 18, 1775. *Journals of Congress*, Vol. III, p. 298.

between G[reat] Britain and the colonies." It recommended, however, "to call a full and free representation of the people", and consequently recognized the principle of a democratic form of government.

In his letter to George Wythe,[45] and in similar letters sent to John Penn of North Carolina, and Jonathan Dickinson Sergeant of New Jersey, Adams was much more explicit and for the first time elaborated upon ideas over which undoubtedly he had pondered for many months, if not for many years. It is remarkable that in none of his letters on the subject did John Adams at that time think it necessary to enunciate clearly and unequivocally any abstract principle or appeal to "the rights of man." He did not think so much of the individual as of the function of government, and agreed with "all speculative politicians" that "the happiness of society is the end of government, as all divines and all moral philosophers will agree that the happiness of the individual is the end of man." But "happiness", in John Adams' opinion, meant something far from the commonly accepted sense: "All sober inquirers after truth, ancient and modern, pagan and Christian, have declared that the happiness of man, as well as his dignity, consists in virtue. Confucius, Zoroaster, Socrates, Mahomet, not to mention authorities really sacred, have agreed in this."

Of all possible forms of government, the best, consequently, is that which rests on virtue, as Montesquieu had shown; namely, the republican form; in fact, it is the only one that is good at all. Having thus established his principles, Adams then outlined the essential organs of his ideal government: an assembly chosen by the people, this assembly to elect a more restricted body called the council, and the two bodies thus constituted to elect a governor by joint ballot; the governor assisted by the council to have a negative on the legislative; the judges to be chosen by the governor or the council were to hold office during good behavior and to receive a fixed salary. In addition Adams recommended a law requiring "all men" to be provided with arms and munition, laws for the education of youth, and even sumptuary laws.

[45] Works, Vol. IV, pp. 193–200.

The most curious feature of the plan, perhaps, was Adams' insistence upon the rotation of offices and annual election of officers, especially of representatives and councilors, "there not being in the whole circle of the sciences a maxim more infallible than this; 'where annual elections end, there slavery begins.'"

In none of these letters did Adams elaborate on the qualifications of the electorate. He certainly thought at the time that it was a very dangerous ground on which to tread and a question not affecting the main principles. From an unexpected quarter he was soon to be notified that he was greatly mistaken. Ever since the beginning of the colonies, and particularly in New England, the women had shared responsibilities with the men in the establishment of their homes. For many months now, while their men were in the army before Boston or discussing politics in the taverns, they had run the farms, woven homespun and fed the cattle. They had sacrificed just as much as the men, perhaps more, and Mrs. Adams thought that since new laws had to be made, some attention should be paid to the ladies by the legislators. Starting in a semi-jocose way, she ended with a very earnest plea:

"Why not put it out of the power of the vicious and the lawless to use us with cruelty and indignity, with impunity? Men of sense in all ages abhor those customs which treat us only as the vassals of your sex." [46]

The poor lady was properly and not too gently rebuked. Adams was not far from believing that her plea reflected some new and dark ecclesiastical plot. "A fine story, indeed! I begin to think the ministry as deep as they are wicked. After stirring up Tories, land-jobbers, trimmers, bigots, Canadians, Indians, negroes, Hanoverians, Hessians, Russians, Irish Roman Catholics, Scotch renegadoes, at last they have stimulated the —— to demand privileges and threaten to rebel." [47] Mrs. Adams accepted as gracefully as she could this uncomplimentary bouquet of epithets, simply reminding her husband "to remember that arbitrary power is, like most other things which are very

---

[46] March 31, 1776. "Familiar Letters", p. 150.
[47] April 14, 1776. *Ibid.*, p. 155.

hard, very liable to be broken." The incident, however, left a
permanent impression on John Adams' mind; it helped to convince him that if the republican government was to work, it was
necessary to put a stop immediately to the nonsense that could
not fail to circulate if the qualifications of the voters were not
defined once and for all.

A few weeks later he had a chance to express his views to
James Sullivan, who, through Elbridge Gerry, had asked him
for advice. The letter written in answer by Adams is as clear a
definition as can be found of the stand he was to maintain all his
life. It exhibited a scorn for pure theory, a sense of what was
practical, as distinguished from what was desirable, a deep distrust of the mob, his refusal to condone "ochlocracy" or government of the crowd, which constituted the main aspects of his
political creed during his later years. In theory "the only moral
foundation of government is, the consent of the people." But
who are the people? Certainly not "every individual of the
community, old and young, male and female, as well as rich
and poor." It is obvious that in any community certain people
cannot rightly and correctly participate in government; such
are children, women, and men who, having no property, are
"too dependent upon other men to have a will of their
own."

It is very doubtful that Adams at that time had heard of the
French physiocrats, whose influence on the political philosophers
of America has been greatly exaggerated. His authority on the
subject was simply Harrington, who has shown "that power
always follows property." This he believed to be "as infallible
a maxim in politics, as that action and reaction are equal, is in
mechanics." Advancing even one step farther, he affirmed that
"the balance of power in a society, accompanies the balance of
property in land." One of the most important functions of a
good government would consequently be to make the acquisi-
tion of land easy to every member of society; to make a division of the land into small areas, so that the multitude may be
possessed of landed estates. "If the multitude is possessed of
the balance of real estate, the multitude will have the balance
of power, and in that case the multitude will take care of the

liberty, virtue, and interest of the multitude, in all acts of government." [48]

This, as John Adams realized himself, was simply the rationalizing of the situation which had existed in Massachusetts Bay from the beginning. The two changes which might be introduced were equally undesirable and dangerous: to admit men who have no property to vote would tend to confound and destroy all distinction, and prostrate all ranks to one common level; to proportionate the vote of men to the property they hold would be utterly impracticable, as the fortune of each man is apt to change and fluctuate too rapidly. Adams little suspected, when he thus defined his theories of popular government, that a day would come when he would be accused of being a monocrat and an enemy of true republicanism. Already in 1776, as later in life, he was a firm republican, and also in some respects a "democrat"; but his brand of democracy was the one in which he had grown and from which he sprang, the democracy of a rural town in New England, the democracy of the town meetings, not of the large city with its lawless population, its rough and shiftless workers, and its rabble. This fundamental distinction between democracy — government by the people — and ochlocracy — government by the irresponsible mob — although often reiterated by Adams, seems to have been little understood even by his friends and, indeed, by some of his biographers.

No less important, and no less permanent, was the attitude he took early in 1776 on questions of foreign policy. At the beginning of March, John Adams, in a series of speeches before Congress, again took up a question which he had much at heart. In common with many delegates, he had for a long time felt that the colonies had little chance successfully to carry out hostilities against Great Britain, unless they were able to receive assistance from the outside. Deprived of their trade with England, the colonists thought of developing their commerce with the only two nations with which they could profitably exchange goods. Spain was considered because of her continental possessions, but France, with her very rich colonies of the West

[48] To James Sullivan, May 26, 1776. Works, Vol. IX, p. 377.

Indies, was evidently the most desirable commercial associate. It was fully expected, and on very plausible grounds, that France would see where her natural interest lay. There is some appearance that French emissaries, authorized or not, had conveyed to the New Englanders the impression that the French Government would look with favor upon a rebellion of the colonies.[49] In Great Britain the possibility of an alliance between France and the Americans was feared and announced, and as early as 1775 Hamilton had predicted that in case of an open breach between Great Britain and her colonies, the French would seize the opportunity "to aggrandize themselves" and triumph over their hereditary enemy.[50]

Curiously enough, Adams was both eager for and fearful of the assistance of France. He had not forgotten the exultation that had seized Massachusetts at the news of the fall of Quebec, and he had no desire to see Canada and the former continental possessions of France restored to a nation afflicted with absolute monarchy and "popery." On the other hand, he realized that it was to the interest of France to dismember the British Empire. In case of a reconciliation with Great Britain, the British fleet and army, united with an American fleet and army, would conquer all the French West Indies in less than six months, and little more time would be required "to destroy all their marine and commerce." [51] The difficulty, in his opinion, was not how to secure French assistance, since it was clearly to the advantage of the French to render it, but how to avoid furthering the interests and ambitions of France while receiving assistance from her. Such were the motives which led him at that time to make the following proposition:

Is any assistance attainable from France?

What connection may we safely form with her?

1. No political connection. Submit to none of her authority; re-

---

[49] See Bernard Faÿ, "L'Esprit révolutionnaire en France et aux Etats-Unis", Paris (1925), Chapters I and II.

[50] See Edward S. Corwin, "French Policy and the American Alliance", Princeton (1916), p. 52 *note*.

[51] "Debates", March 1, 1776. Works, Vol. II, p. 488.

ceive no governors or officers from her. 2. No military connection.
Receive no troops from her. 3. Only a commercial connection; that
is, make a treaty to receive her ships into our ports; let her engage
to receive our ships into her ports; furnish us with arms, cannon,
saltpetre, powder, duck, steel.[52]

If we remember that Silas Deane of Connecticut had been
selected in February, 1776, for the position of business agent
of Congress to Paris, and that his instructions, drawn up by
the Committee of Secret Correspondence, are dated March 3,
1776,[53] this document takes on a singular significance. Adams
did not have to fight in order to make his colleagues accept the
principle of a French alliance. In fact, many were ready to
throw themselves on the mercy of France and even to offer
the French Government territorial concessions to induce them
to side with the American colonies. Patrick Henry had a
panicky fear that England might offer France "half of our
Continent . . . to aid our destruction", and believed it of immense importance "to anticipate the enemy at the French
Court." [54]

Whether or not Adams shared this fear, he was fundamentally opposed to any connection with France that would
enable the French monarchy to regain a footing on the continent. As early as the spring of 1776, even before independence
had been proclaimed, he warned his fellow countrymen against
the danger of what has since been called "entangling alliances."
To secure the recognition of independence by foreign nations,
to conclude with them treaties of commerce enabling America
to obtain supplies necessary to carry on the war was one thing
— to permit a French army to land, to fight, to occupy territories that the king might wish to keep as compensation for his
assistance, was another, most dangerous and to be avoided at
any cost. In this respect, Adams may well be considered as the
announcer of the "doctrine" proclaimed half a century later;

[52] "Debates", March 1, 1776. Works, Vol. II, p. 448.
[53] Francis Wharton, "The Revolutionary Diplomatic Correspondence of
the United States", Vol. II (1889), p. 78.
[54] Patrick Henry to John Adams, May 20, 1776. Works, Vol. IV, p. 201.

for weal or for woe he formulated a policy which was to guide the United States in their relations with Europe for more than a century and a half.

Nothing could be done, however, so long as the colonies themselves had not recognized their independence from the mother country, and to this end Adams was bending all his efforts. The first step was to proclaim that British rule had come to an end in the colonies. This was not effected until the 15th of May, when it was solemnly declared that "it is necessary that the exercise of every kind of authority under the said crown should be totally suppressed, and all the powers of government exerted, under the authority of the people of the colonies." [55] This declaration, drawn up by a committee composed of John Adams, Edward Rutledge, and Richard Henry Lee, served as a preamble to a resolution of May 10th, recommending that the colonies "adopt such government as shall, in the opinion of the representatives of the people, best conduce to the happiness and safety of their constituents in particular, and America in general." [56]

To John Adams it was a day of triumph which marked the climax of his career in Congress. Being a New Englander, he could not openly show his elation to his associates, but there was at least one person before whom he could unreservedly express himself, and to his wife he wrote a letter full of legitimate pride and wonderment:

Is it not a saying of Moses, "Who am I, that I should go in and out before this great people?" When I consider the great events which are passed, and those greater which are rapidly advancing, and that I may have been instrumental in touching some springs and turning some small wheels, which have had and will have such effects, I feel an awe upon my mind which is not easily described. [57]

Great Britain had "at last driven America to the last step, a complete separation from her; a total, absolute independence, not only of her Parliament, but of her crown." The rest was to

[55] *Journals of Congress,* Vol. IV, p. 358.
[56] *Ibid.,* p. 342.
[57] May 17, 1776. "Familiar Letters", p. 173.

follow as a matter of course: "Confederation will be necessary for our internal concord, and alliances may be so for our external defense." Unanimity among the delegates had not yet been obtained, but one by one the colonies fell in line, and June 7, 1776, the following resolutions were presented to Congress:

That these United Colonies are, and of right ought to be, free and independent States, that they are absolved from all allegiance to the British Crown, and that all political connection between them and the State of Great Britain is, and ought to be, totally dissolved.

That it is expedient forthwith to take the most effectual measures for forming foreign Alliances.

That a plan of confederation be prepared and transmitted to the respective Colonies for their consideration and approbation.[58]

On the committee chosen to write a declaration of the first article were placed Thomas Jefferson, John Adams, Benjamin Franklin, Roger Sherman, and Robert R. Livingston. The committee "to prepare a plan of treaties to be proposed to foreign powers" consisted of John Dickinson, Benjamin Franklin, John Adams, Benjamin Harrison, and Robert Morris. On the third committee, composed of twelve members, one for each colony except New Jersey, Samuel Adams represented Massachusetts.

The story of the Declaration of Independence has been so often and so aptly written that a new account of it is quite unnecessary. To Jefferson, because of his "felicity of expression", was entrusted the care of writing it, and it does not seem that either Franklin or Adams materially contributed to it.[59] The Declaration was reported June 28th, discussed July 1st, and July 2d it was resolved, "That these United Colonies are, and, of right, ought to be, Free and Independent States." The final form of the Declaration was agreed to on July 4th.

To the philosophical and political principles enunciated in the preamble, Adams probably gave little thought. He had long been familiar with them, and they had been repeatedly

[58] *Journals of Congress*, Vol. V, p. 425.
[59] For emendations and additions suggested by them, see the *Journals of Congress*, Vol. V, p. 491 *ff*,

maintained by Samuel Adams after the ancient philosophers. They represented only a clear and lucid condensation and crystallization of the doctrines preached since 1761. He did not even hesitate to accept the eighteenth-century formula of "the pursuit of happiness", since for him "happiness" meant "virtue." Independence was the thing for which he and his associates had striven and contended in conversations, committees and meetings of Congress. The last resistance had been overcome, the day of victory had come. It seems that the task of presenting and defending the Declaration fell to John Adams. Jefferson had no taste for public debate, and a fierce battle had to be fought in Congress. Of the speeches made by Adams on the occasion, there is, unfortunately, no record. That he was in these days the "Colossus" and "Atlas of Independence" has to be taken for granted, but we find at least a faint echo of what may have been the peroration of one of his discourses in a letter to Mrs. Adams written on July 3d:

The second day of July, 1776, will be the most memorable epocha in the history of America. I am apt to believe that it will be celebrated by succeeding generations as the great anniversary festival. It ought to be commemorated as the day of deliverance, by solemn acts of devotion to God Almighty. It ought to be solemnized with pomp and parade, with shows, games, sports, guns, bells, bonfires, and illuminations, from one end of this continent to the other, from this time forward forevermore.[60]

What added to the elation of Adams was the feeling that he had at last accomplished the main part of the task for which he had been sent to Congress. There was still work to be done — to decide on the form of a "limited and defined Confederacy", and some other measures that he did not feel at liberty to mention to his wife. But he could already look forward to the time when he would be reunited to his family, and he was constantly yearning for the exercise and "bracing quality" of his "native air", so essential to his well-being. He was homesick, tired by the unremitting attention he had paid to the debates in Congress, exhausted by the suffocating heat of a

[60] "Familiar Letters", p. 193.

Philadelphia summer. He had no personal ambition and he sincerely thought at the time that his political career had come to an end.

Still there were two other matters deserving careful attention. Adams followed very closely the discussion of the "Articles of Confederation and Perpetual Union" between the newly formed States. Most of the articles were reported on July 12th, considered on July 22d, then at different times, and not adopted until November 15, 1777. However, "two knotty problems" perplexed and plagued him. The first: "If a confederation should take place, one great question is, how we shall vote. Whether each colony shall count one; or whether each shall have a weight in proportion to its number, or wealth, or exports and imports, or a compound of all." The other: "Whether Congress shall have authority to limit the dimensions of each colony, to prevent those, which claim by charter or proclamation, or commission to the south sea, from growing too great and powerful, so as to be dangerous to the rest." [61]

Adams engaged passionately in the discussion of the first problem, constituted by the seventeenth article of the proposed plan. The article had been inserted for obvious reasons, and with very few exceptions the delegates in Congress felt more as representatives of their respective provinces or States than as Americans. The spirit of decentralization, or, if one prefers, of provincialism, was naturally much stronger than the spirit of union. The delegates from the smaller States felt that their individuality would be lost, that they would become dependents of the larger States, unless each colony was permitted to retain its entity as a separate organism, and to have as much power in Congress as any other member of the Union. On the other hand, the delegates from the larger colonies, realizing that they represented more wealth and a larger number of inhabitants, were strenuously opposed to giving Rhode Island the same power as Massachusetts. In one case, as Franklin put it, the whale might swallow Jonah, but in the other case Jonah would swallow the whale. Thus even before the Confederacy was accepted, a rift never to be completely mended appeared

[61] July 29, 1776. "Familiar Letters", p. 205.

in it. Neither at that time nor after the adoption of the Constitution was the problem really solved; it involved the questions of State Rights and State Sovereignty, and the Union contained already germs of dissolution and secession.

Being a delegate from a large, wealthy and well-populated State, Adams could take but one position. The arguments he used, however, are well worth remembering, in view of his future conduct. He boldly advanced the theory that the individuality of the colonies was "a mere sound"; that "the confederacy is to make us one individual only; it is to form us, like separate parcels of metal, into one common mass. We shall no longer retain our separate individuality, but become a single individual as to all questions submitted to the confederacy." [62]

The only logical and fair solution, consequently, was to admit "the voting in proportion to numbers"; the delegates did not represent a certain colony, but a certain number of people, and "the interests within doors should be the mathematical representatives of the interests without doors." [63]

On this occasion Adams thought and spoke more as an American than as a New Englander. He thought of America as one great nation into which the different colonies would fuse and lose their identity. It was also as an American that he undertook to protect his country against any foreign encroachments.

Unpleasant as it was to admit it, Adams and most of his associates realized that independence could not be secured without assistance from the outside. A few months previous he had thought that a treaty of commerce with France and Spain might serve the purpose; he was now aware that some sort of military or naval aid was also necessary. He had no doubt that France would eagerly seize an opportunity to weaken Great Britain and, at the same time, to recover her lost American possessions; and he was firmly convinced that this last point had to be avoided at all cost. There was no possibility of the United States ever becoming a great nation if their future expansion were limited on the north by a French Canada, if the

[62] Notes of Debates in the Continental Congress, by Thomas Jefferson. *Journals of Congress*, Vol. VI, p. 1105.

[63] *Ibid.*, p. 1104.

French again occupied the Mississippi Valley, and, possibly the Floridas.

With this object in view and this fear in his mind, he wrote into the proposed Plan of Treaties an article safeguarding the territorial integrity of the United States and establishing their claim on any territory that might be conquered as a result of the war. He saw to it that no loophole was left the Most Christian King to evade any of the stipulations of the treaty or to claim an inch of the territory he might occupy as a result of the war. This time the principle to which Monroe was to give his name nearly half a century later was clearly enunciated:

ART. 8. In Case of any War between the most Christian King and the King of Great Britain, the most Christian King shall never invade, nor under any pretence attempt to possess himself of Labradore, New Britain, Nova Scotia, Accadia, Canada, Florida, nor any of the Countries, Cities, or Towns, on the Continent of North America, nor of the Islands of Newfoundland, Cape Breton, St. John's, Anticosti, nor of any other Island lying near to the said Continent, in the Seas, or in any Gulph, Bay, or River, it being the true Intent and meaning of this Treaty, that the said united States, shall have the sole, exclusive, undivided and perpetual Possession of all the Countries, Cities, and Towns, on the said Continent, and of all Islands near to it, which now are, or lately were under the Jurisdiction of or Subject to the King or Crown of Great Britain, whenever the . . . shall be united or confederated with the said united States.[64]

Could anything have been more definite and more brutal even? Was it possible to say more openly to the Most Christian King that he would be a most undesirable and untrustworthy neighbor? It was, indeed, highly undiplomatic language, and the form, if not the substance, would have been unacceptable to the French Court, but Adams had said exactly what he meant.[65] He expressed in it a distrust of France which had not to await his arrival in Paris to manifest itself, and was due to no injury suffered by his personal vanity. It was inborn, ingrained in him; since his early childhood he had been accustomed to

[64] July 18, 1776. *Journals of Congress*, Vol. V, p. 576 *ff.*

[65] The substance of this article was retained in the Treaty of Alliance of 1778 (Article 6), but the language was, naturally, more diplomatic.

look upon "the turbulent Gallicks" as dangerous neighbors; his was neither a forgiving nor a forgetful nature, and he was not suddenly to discard prejudices and fears that rested on a traditional foundation.

In his "Autobiography" Adams declared that when the plan of treaties came up for discussion, several representatives argued that it held out "no sufficient temptation to France" and they attempted to insert in it "articles of entangling alliance, of exclusive privilege, and of warranties of possessions." All these motions were fiercely fought by Adams, who, years later, could boast that "the treaty passed without one particle of alliance, exclusive privilege, or warranty." [66]

To these great problems, which involved the whole future course of the nation, Adams could not give his undivided attention. On June 13, 1776, he had been made chairman of the "Board of war and ordnance", a position as nearly equivalent to that of Minister of War as could be created under the circumstances. It was an arduous and thankless task, since no regular machinery was in existence and everything had to be improvised from day to day. These activities of Adams, which filled most of his time from July, 1776, to November, 1777, except for his short vacation at the end of 1776, cannot very well be discussed here; their importance, variety and difficulty may be gathered from the *Journals of Congress* and the "Autobiography", but it would take an expert in military matters to appreciate them with any degree of fairness. As chairman of the Board, Adams, with Franklin and Rutledge, was delegated to meet General Howe on Staten Island and listen to his so-called peace proposition. [67] This was a not altogether unwelcome intermission in the dreary, monotonous routine of the committee. Officers had to be appointed and placated; urgent appeals had to be made to the different States to take all possible measures to reinforce an army rapidly dwindling. Washington had just

[66] Works, Vol. II, p. 517; *Journals of Congress*, September 17, 1776. Vol. V, p. 768.

[67] *Journals of Congress*, September 6, 1776. Vol. V, p. 738, "Autobiography." Works, Vol. III, p. 74 *ff*. and letter to Samuel Adams, September 17, 1776. Works, Vol. IX, p. 443.

lost New York, and had only been able to save his ragged army through a "strategic retreat", to use a euphemism so frequently resorted to in the last war. Smallpox had killed hundreds of soldiers, and people in Philadelphia were taking the inoculation in a panic. These indeed were dark days, trying to the soul. The great enthusiasm that followed the Declaration of Independence had subsided; men were again thinking selfishly of their own interests, their petty ambitions; soldiers, when begged to remain in the army, consented reluctantly to reënlist for six weeks. It was rumored that at the battle of Long Island "a regiment of Yorkers behaved 'ill' ", and, worst of all, that "several regiments of Massachusetts behaved ill too." [68]

In Braintree Mrs. Adams, with sick children around her, but nothing daunted, hearing only lies, millions of lies, exclaimed in patriotic fervor: "If our army is in ever so critical a state I wish to know it, and the worst of it. If all America is to be ruined and undone by a pack of cowards and knaves, I wish to know it." And in Philadelphia, Adams could only grit his teeth or cry out in despair: "O Heaven! grant us one great soul! One leading mind would extricate the best cause from that ruin which seems to await it for the want of it. We have as good a cause as ever was fought for; we have great resources; the people are well tempered; one active, masterly capacity, would bring order out of this confusion, and save this country." [69]

For this deep feeling of patriotic distress and such fervent outbursts many petty faults and weaknesses must be forgiven Adams. Some may reproach him for not realizing that in Washington America had precisely that "one great soul" for which he was clamoring; but in these dark days Washington had not yet given any manifest evidence of his greatness. He had not, at any rate, succeeded in galvanizing the country, in inspiring his men with faith and enthusiasm, or in subduing the jealousies of his subordinates by the superiority of his military genius. In his passionate heart, filled with classical remi-

[68] October 8, 1776. "Familiar Letters", p. 232.
[69] Diary, September 21, 1777. Works, Vol. II, p. 439.

niscences, Adams was longing for a man of destiny — for a general who would end the war by a masterly stroke; an apostle who would weld the faltering, incoherent colonies into one great nation. The story of the Revolution was, however, to be different.

BOOK TWO

THE DISCOVERY OF EUROPE

CHAPTER I

AN AMERICAN LAWYER IN PARIS

By the fall of 1776, John Adams had become very tired, mentally and physically. To a great extent he had remained an outdoors man, and for months in Philadelphia he had been deprived of his favorite exercise, riding, for which walking was a poor substitute. On several occasions he had expressed his wish to be permitted to return home and petitioned the General Court for a leave of absence. When it came, at the beginning of October, he started in a hurry, riding only "thirty miles" on the first day, "as his tendons were delicate, not having been once on horseback since the eighth day of last February."[1] Soon he was again in the small house at Braintree, with his dear "Portia" and the children, who had successfully withstood the inoculation, proud of Johnny, only ten years old, but already quite a man, riding to Boston several times a week as a courier. It was not in John Adams to remain quiet and idle, so to Boston he also went, more than once, to look at his house, at the depredations committed by the redcoats, to acquaint the local people with news of the war, and to press them to organize the army. A man who had coöperated in the writing of the Declaration of Independence, who had been sent by Congress to discuss with Lord Howe, who was chairman of one of the most important committees of Congress, was not a negligible character. This realization of his own importance and the confirmation from authorized persons that he was playing a great part were exactly what Adams needed to brace him up; to him it was just as much a tonic as the invigorating air of Braintree. But there was also work to be done at home; there were chores that required a man, for help could not be had, and if

[1] October 13, 1776. Diary. Works, Vol. II, p. 433.

Mrs. Adams could gather corn and husk it, she made a "poor figure" at digging potatoes.

This too short stay with his family convinced him more than ever that he was not made for public life. He was loath to resume the heavy burden which required every moment of his days "from four o'clock in the morning until ten at night." He had accepted to serve another year in Congress, but it was to be the last time. He had vanity, to be sure, but no definite ambition; he might at times envy those who occupied eminent positions, but he had never made any effort to place himself in the foreground. He had served his turn, done his duty, taken his part of the dangers, and contributed what he had in him to the cause of independence; others now had to take charge and to step on the proscenium.

Such were some of the ever-recurrent thoughts passing through Adams' mind during his last year in Congress. At least there was a change of scene, for Congress had to abandon Philadelphia and move down to Baltimore. It was a new and charming city, where everything was "agreeable, except the monstrous price of things." But how could a man preserve his equanimity when Congress and country seemed lethargic? Nothing apparently could move them; there was talk of raising men for the standing army, but no army was raised and, in the meantime, occasions were lost, officers seemed to be quite reconciled to the idea of a "long and moderate war", instead of a "short and violent war." [2] Most of them were thinking only of promotion, but none of any "heroic deed of arms." [3] They quarreled "like cats and dogs"; they "worried one another like mastiffs, scrambling for rank and pay like apes for nuts." [4] If some people could forget the horrors of war, Adams, because of his official position as head of the War Board, had to hear continual accounts of "the barbarities, the cruel murders in cold blood even by the most tormenting ways of starving and freezing, committed by our enemies", and "continued accounts of the deaths and diseases contracted" by the imprudence

[2] September 2, 1776. "Familiar Letters", p. 305.
[3] February 21, 1776. *Ibid.*, p. 248.
[4] May 22, 1776. *Ibid.*, p. 276.

of the soldiers.[5] With him, on this point at least, was Washington, who had "hinted at the flagitious conduct of the two Howes towards their prisoners in so plain and clear a manner that he could not be misunderstood", and yet with "a delicacy and dignity" of which Adams felt himself incapable.[6] In his wrath he ranked the two detestable brothers "with Pizarro, with Borgia, with Alva, and with others in the annals of infamy, whose memories are entitled to the hisses and execrations of all virtuous men."

If ever Adams had thought of military glory and had been thrilled by a fine band thundering away at the head of a regiment, he now saw only the sordid aspects of war, the two thousand soldiers buried in long trenches "in the Potter's Field, between the new prison and the hospitals", men who had died needlessly for lack of food, lack of surgical care, lack of attention on the part of their officers — a spectacle "to make a heart of stone melt away." [7] Such suffering could not have been experienced in vain; if there was a divine law, it was inconceivable that divine vengeance should not some day overtake the culprits and vindicate the wrongs of offended nature! Slow-footed is the vengeance of God, and remote the judgment of history; in the meantime Adams thought of employing every effort to perpetuate the memory of the hateful deeds and to place in as strong a light as possible the barbarity and impiety of the Britons. All means were to be good to perform this office: painting, sculpture, poetry were to assist, medals of gold, silver and bronze ought to be struck in commemoration of such shocking cruelties. At times, Adams bitterly regretted his inability to gird on a sword and enter the field, but at least it was to be hoped that the treatment of prisoners would steel the hearts of officers and soldiers and make them follow the maxim which had never failed to bring victory, "*Conquer or die.*" [8]

After such outbursts of passion, Adams, like a "galley slave"

---

[5] February 17, 1777. "Familiar Letters", p. 247.
[6] April 13, 1777. *Ibid.*, p. 257.
[7] *Ibid.*, p. 259.
[8] May 4, 1776. *Ibid.*, p. 258.

bent on his oar, attended more committees, wrote more letters, recommended more measures to raise a decent army, and by August could report that, at last, the men were "extremely well armed, pretty well clothed, and tolerably disciplined." They had not yet "quite the air of soldiers"; "they don't step exactly in time", he wrote to his wife; "they don't hold up their heads quite erect, nor turn out their toes so exactly as they ought. They don't all of them cock their hats; and such as do, don't all wear them the same way." But it was an army, and discipline as necessary as "laws in a society" was at last recognized. Adams could look with legitimate pride on the work he had so well done.

Such a spectacle was especially comforting to the members of Congress who, after moving back from Baltimore to Philadelphia, were again threatened by Howe's army, just landed at the head of the Chesapeake Bay. Soon they would have to move again, for theirs was not the fortitude of the Roman senators who refused to flee from the Gauls. Irritated as he was by the behavior of his colleagues, Adams was too busy with too many things to indulge in any extensive criticism of their attitude. The work was despairingly slow, and the great task of confederation was dragging heavily on; financial matters were in a terrible condition and the evils of inflation were sadly felt. "The worst Enemy we have now is Poverty, real Poverty in the Shape of exuberant Wealth," he wrote to Jefferson. "Pray come and help us to raise the value of our Money, and lower the Prices of Things." The eternal problem! Financiers were as rare as soldiers, and diplomats were shortsighted. Instead of making every effort to mobilize and organize all the resources of America, Adams saw with disgust that Congress placed all their hopes in a French alliance. He felt keenly, and not unreasonably, that even with all the reservations introduced into the plan of treaties, French intervention would place the United States under obligation to the Most Christian King. "I do not love to be entangled in the quarrels of Europe," he wrote to James Warren, and added, "It is a cowardly spirit in our countrymen, which makes them pant with so much longing expectation after a French war. I have very often been ashamed to hear so many whigs groaning and sighing with despondency, and whining out their fears that we must be subdued, unless France should step in." [9]

In his patriotism, deep and sincere, there was no trace of that missionary spirit so evident in Patrick Henry, Jefferson, and Thomas Paine. His horizon was much narrower and his vision did not transcend the present. He had undoubtedly read many of the French effusions which were beginning to reach America, and he had been told that French liberals regarded the United States as "the hope of mankind." Magnificent as were such prospects, the New England farmer and lawyer kept his feet on the ground. This new Messianism was closed to him and he was not conscious that America was fighting for mankind. It had been hard enough to persuade the New England farmers, the Pennsylvania "Quakers", and the Virginia planters to enlist and to stay enlisted; it had taken them a long time to realize that they were fighting for themselves, for their ancestral rights, and for their children, *pro aris et pro focis*. These liberties which were their sacred inheritance, it was their sacred duty to preserve, themselves, for they were not "beholden to France" for them.[10]

Ardent though it was, Adams' patriotism had a distinctly parochial tinge. In the late summer of 1777, Howe's army had landed at the head of the Chesapeake and was slowly organizing to march on Philadelphia. To protect the city, Washington had finally succeeded in raising and training a decent force entirely made up of Southerners. On the other hand, in the North, Gates with "New England troops and New York troops" was opposing Burgoyne. When most of his colleagues were thinking of their safety and the possibility of abandoning Philadelphia, Adams had one thought only in mind: the New Englanders had to show their mettle: "Now is the time to strike. New England men strike home!" [11] He may at times have displayed some irritation at the "Fabian tactics" of the Commander in Chief: more than once he declared to his wife,

[9] April 27, 1777. Works, Vol. IX, p. 462.
[10] *Ibid.*
[11] August 26, 1777. "Familiar Letters", p. 299.

and certainly to his friends, that if he were in Washington's shoes he would "put more to risk", and would show that the Continental Army could "do something." This probably led to rumors being circulated at the time that he was antagonistic towards Washington and working against him. In his letters to Mrs. Adams, however, he shows that his respect for the ability of the General had in no way diminished. He knew that Washington was very prudent, and "would not unnecessarily hazard his army." Much would be gained by a great victory, and a drawn battle would have advantages, since Howe could not easily obtain reinforcements; even the loss of Philadelphia would not be a disaster, since Howe would have to use all his army to occupy the city. He refrained from criticism when Congress had to abandon Philadelphia, and the "great battle" was not fought, for he never expected a real victory. He realized better than most that Washington's army lacked training, discipline and numbers. Probably the best method of drilling the raw recruits was to keep them in the field and make them fight: "fighting will certainly answer the end, although we may be beaten every time for a great while." [12]

When the news of Burgoyne's surrender came, he let the cat out of the bag. As a New Englander, he would not have been overjoyed if a Southern general, with Southern troops, had won a decisive victory while New England remained without her due share of danger and glory. Already at the beginning of the year he had expressed his distress at seeing "some members of this house disposed to idolise an image which their own hands have molten." [13] On October 26th, he wrote to Mrs. Adams: "Congress will appoint a thanksgiving; and one cause of it ought to be that the glory of turning the tide of arms is not immediately due to the Commander in Chief nor to southern troops. If it had been, idolatry and adulation would have been unbounded; so excessive as to endanger our liberties, for what I know. Now, we can allow a certain citizen

[12] October 15, 1777. "Familiar Letters", p. 317.
[13] Benjamin Rush's Diary, February 19, 1777, in the "Letters of Members of the Continental Congress", edited by Edmund C. Burnett, Volume II (1923), p. 263.

to be wise, virtuous, and good, without thinking him a deity or a savior."[14]

This letter seems to vindicate Adams of the accusation that he would have deliberately engaged in a cabal to displace Washington, out of personal jealousy. That he was irritated more than once by the "Fabian system" of the Commander in Chief we have already shown, but, above all, he felt that in a democracy not well established in tradition there is always a danger when the people idolize the man on horseback. In a republic it is not well for one man to monopolize military glory, and Adams had learned in Montesquieu of the instability of governments and how easily they can pass from republic to tyrant. His fears were exaggerated but by no means unreasonable. No constitution had been adopted, and fundamental republicanism was as yet an unknown quantity. Adams on this occasion simply expressed the apprehensions that were to haunt Jefferson some years later. After Saratoga, however, he felt no hesitation in recognizing the rare qualities of the Commander in Chief. The success of Gates had reëstablished the desired equilibrium and given New England her modicum of military glory; for the time being no danger threatened the Republic.[15]

With the British army in Philadelphia, the American army going into winter quarters at Valley Forge, and Congress at York, Adams felt that his presence was no longer required. For almost four years he had devoted all of his energy to the public business and neglected his own. He now desired to go back to Boston, to resume his practice of the law, to collect loose accounts, and to look after the education of his children. This attitude was by no means uncommon among the members of Congress, and was less surprising than would seem at first. We can hardly conceive of a senator or a representative who, in the midst of a war, would resign his seat to look after his private affairs. Politics had not yet become a career, and even

[14] October 26, 1777. "Familiar Letters", p. 322.
[15] In his "Autobiography", Works, Vol. III, p. 93, Adams has protested with indignation against this accusation, which he traces to Paine; but it seems to have been widely circulated. The truth is that the agitation in favor of Gates did not start until 1778, when Adams had left Congress.

less a business; members of Congress served in the national assembly in the same spirit as soldiers enlisted for a certain number of months, and insisted on going home at the expiration of that period. None of them considered serving indefinitely or for "the duration of the war", particularly as it was felt that the war might continue for months and even years. No modern politician would dare admit what Adams confessed without hesitation: that he was sick of the war, wearied with the life he was leading, and longing for the joys of his family.[16]

At the beginning of November he asked leave of Congress to visit his family and constituents, and on the eleventh of the same month started with Samuel Adams on his homeward journey. His firm intention was to decline reëlection and to devote all his time to the practice of law. Soon after his arrival at Braintree he found that his old clients had not forgotten him; new ones were eager to engage his services; from all quarters he had "applications in the most important disputes." Once more, however, his plans for a studious and fruitful life as a lawyer were to be frustrated. While he was speaking in an admiralty case at Portsmouth, on December 15th, a gentleman just arrived from Philadelphia whispered to him that Deane had been recalled and that he had been appointed in his stead to go to France. At first he refused to take the news seriously, although he knew that the conduct of Deane had been so "intolerably bad as to disgrace himself and his country, and that Congress had no other way of retrieving the dishonor but by recalling him." [17]

On arriving at Braintree, Adams found confirmation of his appointment made on November 28th, almost a month earlier, as well as his official credentials and pleasant letters from Henry Laurens, President of Congress, from R. H. Lee and J. Lovell, of the Committee of Foreign Affairs. This last communication was particularly peremptory, for Lee and Lovell refused "to admit thought of your declining this important service", and they added the cheerful recommendation to bag all the dispatches "with weight proper for sinking them, on any imme-

[16] October 25, 1777. "Familiar Letters", p. 321.
[17] "Autobiography", Works, Vol. III, p. 90.

diate prospect of their otherwise falling into the enemy's hands." [18]

In his heart, Adams probably never really doubted his acceptance. The fact that he had everything to risk and nothing to gain could not deter him, but he perhaps spent a few uncomfortable hours before making his decision. Travel was far from safe, ships were frequently captured and, in that case, the new commissioner knew that he would probably be tried for high treason in England. On the other hand, there was a chance for him to defend in France the Plan of Treaties which he himself had written, and to see to it that American interests would be properly safeguarded.

Twenty-four hours after receiving notification of his appointment, Adams wrote his letter of acceptance to the President of Congress.[19] At first Mrs. Adams thought of sharing with her husband the dangers of the ocean voyage, but she soon gave up her plan, and it was decided that Adams would take with him only his older son, John Quincy. The following weeks were spent in preparations all too slow for the new commissioner. He was "almost out of patience" when the frigate *Boston* arrived at Moon Head on the 13th of February. The wind was high and the sea very rough, but the passengers embarked without mishap. For two days the ship lay at anchor, and only on the 15th Adams and his son bade farewell to their native land.[20]

February is by far the worst month for crossing the northern Atlantic, and to the inexperienced travelers it was quite an ordeal. The almost incessant storms, the stench of the vessel, the sailors' general neglect of the most elementary rules of decency, the nonchalance of the cook, calling them to meals when he was ready, the alarm when a sail was sighted, even the encounter of British ships, made the voyage a painful experience. Still there was some compensation; the few passengers

---

[18] "The Revolutionary Diplomatic Correspondence of the United States", edited under the direction of Congress by Francis Wharton, Vol. II (1889), p. 443.

[19] December 23, 1777. Works, Vol. VII, pp. 7–8.

[20] Diary. Works, Vol. III, p. 95.

were rather pleasant and treated the new commissioner with great respect, the captain had received orders to consult him on all occasions and, at times, Adams could fairly believe that he was in command of the ship. It was a long crossing, but he kept busy all the time; he made a thorough study of the armament and equipment of the ship, "constantly" gave "hints to the captain concerning order, economy, and regularity", looked on when the marines were drilled, studied French with Mr. Noël, the ship's surgeon, read Boileau, Molière's "Amphitryon", and Charlevoix' "Histoire du Paraguay", conducted regular classes for his son and the two boys who had been placed in his care, young Vernon and a nephew of Silas Deane. There was real excitement when the *Boston* captured an English ship, but on the whole it was a "dull scene"; he was unable to eat or drink "without nauseating", no spirit for conversation, "nothing but sky, clouds, and sea, and then sea, clouds, and sky." [21]

At the end of March they finally sighted the Spanish coast, and on the twenty-ninth a French pilot boarded the vessel and told Adams in his "Gascon gibberish" that war had been declared. The news was soon confirmed, when the *Boston* entered the estuary of the Gironde River. The treaty of amity and commerce, as well as a treaty of alliance, to become effective if Great Britain declared war on France, had been signed on the 6th of February, at the very time when Adams awaited at Mount Wollaston the ship that was to take him to France; and now the Court of Versailles could openly side with the insurgents. Adams was received in Bordeaux, not simply as the representative of a friendly nation, but as the envoy of a new ally, with speeches and gun salutes, with dinners and galas at the theater; his departure was signaled by thirteen shots, and he read in the gardens a beautifully illuminated inscription, "God save the Congress, Liberty and Adams." He had come prepared to negotiate and to plead for his country, but there was no great feat to be achieved, and Adams' joy must have been mixed with a certain sense of frustration.

Traveling at times a hundred miles a day with his son, young

[21]Diary. Works, Vol. III, p. 105.

Deane and Mr. Noël, the ship's surgeon who acted as interpreter, Adams arrived in Paris on the evening of the ninth, and after finding several hotels full, finally engaged lodgings at the Hôtel de Valois, rue de Richelieu. The next morning he went to Passy to pay his respects to Franklin, dined in the evening with Turgot, and was asked many questions which he answered in a clear and concise way. The next day was spent in making arrangements to take his lodgings under the same roof with Doctor Franklin; dinner was had at Monsieur Brillon's, with many ladies and gentlemen, and supper at Monsieur de Chaumont's. Apparently the new commissioner had entirely forgotten that his first duty should have been to apprise the French Secretary of Foreign Affairs of his arrival. M. de Vergennes, who had been informed of Adams' presence in Paris through his police, gently and gracefully made him aware of this breach of etiquette by sending him a "gentleman" who told Adams that the Secretary supposed he was waiting to get himself a French coat, but he should be glad to see him in his American coat. Although Adams was still unable to speak French, and understood hardly a word of the conversations, he went everywhere, was introduced to M. de Maurepas, the king's mentor, paid his respects to M. de Sartine, dined with Boulainvilliers, and also with "Philippe de Noailles, Maréchal Duc de Mouchy, Grand d'Espagne de la première Classe, Chevalier des Ordres du Roi et de la Toison d'Or, Grand-Croix de l'Orde de Malte, nommé Lieutenant-Général de Guienne en 1768, et Commandant-en-chef dans le Gouvernement de la dite Province en 1775." [22]

The joy of being welcomed by noblemen who "lived in the splendor and magnificence of a viceroy" was somewhat marred by the bad feelings existing between the commissioners. This was not news to Adams, since the situation had led to the recall of Silas Deane, but he was not prepared for the disclosures made by Franklin in the first interview with him. Deane's departure had somewhat improved conditions, but Lee often acted without consulting his colleague. Izard, who had been appointed as minister to the Grand Duke of Tuscany, remained

[22] Diary. Works, Vol. III, p. 148.

in Paris with his wife and children. William Lee, a brother of Arthur, was lingering in Germany and called upon the commissioners in Paris for considerable sums of money; and all about them a number of Americans were constantly "exciting disputes and propagating stories that made the service very disagreeable.[23] Moreover, adventurers appointed neither by Congress nor by the commissioners flocked around them. There is no war without war profiteers. The American commissioners in Paris, in their anxiety to procure arms, munitions and provisions, had not always been very wise in their choice of agents, and much money had been spent, for which no bonds, bills or vouchers could be shown. Even in America this state of affairs had not remained unknown, since Henry Laurens had deplored that the ambassadorial commissioners were not exempt from "those curses upon mankind, pride and covetousness, sources from whence all the evils of this life spring." [24]

Even more disquieting was the financial condition of the American mission. Each of the commissioners had appointed separate commercial agents, and each of them was drawing from whatever funds were available for his personal expenses. Deane and Lee had been living in great state; Franklin had settled down at Passy in the house put at his disposal by Le Ray de Chaumont, without inquiring about the rent; no discrimination seemed to be made between personal and public expenses; no duplicates of letters were kept, no books, no files, no accounts. As a good husbandman, Adams undertook at once to set things aright. The first move was to ascertain what rent had to be paid to Le Ray de Chaumont "for his house and furniture, both for the time past and to come", and Adams was pleasantly surprised and somewhat suspicious when the French financier answered that to have his house "immortalized . . . by receiving into it Dr. Franklin and his associates" was compensation enough for him.[25] To Franklin, Adams pro-

---

[23] Diary. Works, Vol. III, p. 123.
[24] To Washington, May 5, 1778. Wharton, "The Revolutionary Diplomatic Correspondence of the United States", Vol. II, p. 570.
[25] September 18, 1778. Works, Vol. VII, pp. 31–33.

posed a new plan of keeping account of their personal expenses concerning the *maître d'hôtel*, the cook, the servants, the coachman, the hire of horses, and even the washerwoman.[26]

These were only palliatives; more radical measures had to be taken if the commissioners were to acquit themselves of their mission. Officially nothing could be done, but the new envoy thought it his duty to acquaint his kinsman Samuel Adams with the situation. He wrote him a long letter in which he enumerated the dangers of the system and made specific recommendations.[27] There was no reason whatsoever for keeping three envoys in Paris; one with the title of minister plenipotentiary was enough. The new minister was to receive a fixed compensation and should not be authorized to draw at will from the public funds for his expenses. The duties of the minister were to be political or diplomatic, and special commercial agents should be appointed to assist him. In this Adams concurred with his colleagues. There was little doubt in his mind that if only one minister were kept, Franklin would be chosen, but, much as he enjoyed himself in Paris, he had no ambition and did not believe that under the circumstances his presence was necessary. He felt decidedly, on the contrary, that with the signing of the treaty of alliance and the departure of D'Estaing's fleet for America, the decisive steps had been taken, and he could write in all sincerity to Lovell, "You may depend upon it, although your agents in Europe were to plead with the tongues of men and angels, although they had the talents and the experience of Mazarin or the integrity of d'Asset, your army in America will have more success than they." [28]

Of the political or purely diplomatic activities of Adams during the year 1778, there is little evidence either in his correspondence or his Diary. The treaties of commerce and alliance had been signed and France was already at war, although no formal declaration had been passed to that effect. The com-

---

[26] September 22, 1778. Works, Vol. VII, p. 43.
[27] May 21, 1778. Wharton, *op. cit.*, Vol. II, pp. 591–593. See also a letter of Arthur Lee to the Committee of Foreign Affairs, June 1, 1778, *Ibid.*, p. 602.
[28] July 26, 1778. Wharton, *op. cit.*, Vol. II, pp. 664–665.

missioners were only vaguely acquainted with the negotiations between France and Spain; there was little for them to do except to raise money by every means and to set their house in order. On one occasion only did he treat in his letters of a purely political matter. At the end of July, Vergennes acquainted the American commissioners of the reported intention of Great Britain to recognize the independence of the United States on condition of their making a separate peace.[29] Adams and Franklin wrote immediately to Congress to communicate their firm opinion that although no declaration of war had yet been published, the treaty was fully and completely binding, and that no such proposition could be entertained. This was not enough for Adams, who feared lest his dear countrymen be lured to the rocks by the siren song of peace. He sharpened his best quill to send a solemn adjuration to the President of the Congress. This was a last effort to "seduce, deceive and divide. They know that every man of honor in America must receive this proposition with indignation." [30]

In a letter to Samuel Adams he was even more emphatic; the proposal to discuss a separate peace was simply "a modest invitation to a gross act of infidelity and breach of faith." [31] These were very strong and very honest words, and it is unfortunate that a few years later Adams was to forget the incident and his indignation. Self-interest as well as honor prevented the adoption of such a course; in Adams' opinion at that date, as long as Great Britain should retain any spot of ground on the continent of North America, there would be enmity between the two nations, and France would remain "the natural defense of the United States against the rapacious spirit of Great Britain." [32]

He had been touched more than he cared to confess by the welcome tendered him from every quarter, but he constantly reminded himself of the necessity of keeping on the watch

---

[29] Franklin and Adams to the President of Congress, July 23, 1778. Wharton, *op. cit.*, Vol. II, pp. 660–661.

[30] Adams to the President of Congress, July 27, 1778. *Ibid.*, p. 666.

[31] July 28, 1778. *Ibid.*, p. 667.

[32] Wharton, *op. cit.*, Vol. II, p. 668.

lest the young nation abandon some of her sovereign rights. The idea that French soldiers would fight on American soil was still repugnant to him. He entertained dark suspicions that a French commander with a French army might try to supersede the American commander in chief and, after meeting the Maréchal de Maillebois, who had "intrigued" with Deane "to be placed over the head of General Washington in the command in chief of our American army", he wrote somewhat melodramatically, "I will be buried in the ocean, or in any other manner sacrificed, before I will voluntarily put on the chains of France, when I am struggling to throw off those of Great Britain." [33]

This was by no means a passing mood. Izard, who was constantly dissatisfied with Franklin, and Lee had made advances to Adams and tried to convince him that the United States had endangered their right to the fisheries in signing the treaties. Curiously enough, it was at that time a question which left him more than indifferent. He still believed that agriculture was the primary interest of America and particularly of Massachusetts. The fisheries were a source of luxury and vanity, induced the people to engage in foreign trade (always a source of danger) and, altogether, it would be a good thing for Americans if they were "taught to dig in the ground instead of fishing in the sea for their bread." [34] Adams was convinced that Izard's fears were groundless, but he added in a sentence which explains his attitude, "I agree with you, however, that as we are young States, and not practised in the art of negotiation, it becomes us to look into all these things with as much caution and exactness as possible." [35]

Here we have the real cause for the so-called hostility of Adams towards the French Court; it was not grounded on petty jealousy of the "veneration" in which Franklin was held, nor on any personal resentment. Feeling himself entrusted with a tremendous responsibility, fearful of being unequal to the task, haunted by the traditional prejudices entertained for

[33] April 29, 1778. Diary. Works, Vol. III, p. 147.
[34] Ibid., pp. 729, 741, 743.
[35] October 2, 1778. Wharton, op. cit., Vol. II, p. 755.

generations in New England against the "turbulent Gallicks", Adams was never completely at ease or completely himself in his dealings with French diplomats. Being fundamentally honest, and having no serious ground for suspicion, realizing that "in spite of the obstacles of language, of customs, religion and government", France was the natural ally of the United States, he succeeded during his first mission in allaying his misgivings and instinctive apprehensions. But efficient and honest as he was, he was hardly a man to win friends for the United States.

Adams did, in fact, suffer in his vanity, and largely through his own fault. When he arrived in France, he was asked from every quarter whether he was the "*fameux* Adams" to whom was ascribed the authorship of "Common Sense", reprinted in France. Upon his repeated denials, the French soon concluded, according to his Diary, that he was "a man of whom nobody had ever heard before, — a perfect cipher; a man who did not understand a word of French; awkward in his figure, awkward in his dress; no abilities; a perfect bigot and fanatic." [36] Be that as it may, and with due regard for his rhetorical exaggeration, the short, fat, simply dressed and *gauche* Boston lawyer, suddenly transplanted from his native province to the Court of Versailles, must have cut a singular figure among courtiers so exquisitely trained that not a motion of their person could be criticized as ungraceful. When he found himself between bejewelled ladies, with ladies on the right, ladies on the left, and rows and ranks of ladies below him, he wished he could command as much power of face as a chief of the Six Nations. He gazed at the curtsies and bows of the courtiers with awe, in spite of a cheerful but assumed countenance. He felt ill at ease among these people whose gestures were so perfectly natural because they were so perfectly studied.

The "hardy republican" pretended to be shocked at such a display which philosophy condemns with great reason, but there were in all these ceremonies a perfection and an arrangement which immensely pleased the artist in Adams. He had lost none of his talent for portraying characters, none of his

[36] February 11, 1779. Diary. Works, Vol. III, p. 190.

acuity of vision, none of his biting acerbity of tongue and pen. His Diary, as well as the letters to his wife, presents the richest imaginable collection of etchings, portraits and scenes of life in Paris under the "inimitable days" of the Old Régime. One would vainly search the French memoirs of the period for such picturesque descriptions. Here was Condorcet, "a philosopher, with a face as pale, or rather as white, as a sheet of paper"; then the meeting of the Academy of Sciences, when the audience clamored to see Voltaire and Franklin "s'embrasser à la Françoise"; so "the two aged actors upon this great theater of philosophy and frivolity then embraced each other, by hugging one another in their arms, and kissing each other's cheeks." He described Vergennes, coming from one of the receptions given to the *cordons bleus*, stiff and aching from having kneeled for some hours on the marble pavement in church. There was a visit to Marly, "Lucienne", or Bellevue, built for Madame de Pompadour, where had been made "judges and counsellors, magistrates of all sorts, nobles and knights of every order, generals and admirals, ambassadors and other foreign ministers, bishops, archibishops, cardinals, and popes." One night he attended the public supper of the royal family and the *grand couvert*, and he did not miss a single gesture or expression of the king and queen. But he was too busy with his bookkeeping, his accounts and his study of French to roam about in Paris, as Jefferson did a few years later. He had decided to take his lodgings with Franklin in Paris, and as the venerable Doctor was quite a man about town, and used the only carriage at the disposal of the commissioners, Adams spent most of his time in Passy. Whenever he could escape, however, he went to the theater to see plays of Molière, a tragedy of Voltaire, or some "touching", philosophic drama.

Adams' friends were few, for he had not the marvelous adaptability of Doctor Franklin. He went everywhere, but besides Madame Helvétius and the two amusing abbés, De Chalut and Arnoux, he did not become acquainted with any French person of note. He was too self-conscious and too much aware of his imperfect knowledge of French to feel at ease in any society. There was nothing he could complain of;

the "climate and soil" agreed with him, and so did "the cookery" and even the manners of the people, "churlish republican" though he was called by some.[37] Yet he was not happy.
For Franklin he entertained no mean jealousy, but he felt
that he was playing a second or third fiddle to the Doctor and
that any good accountant could fill his place. Such a position
at best was only temporary; he expected either to be recalled
or to be sent to some other capital as a result of the letter in
which he had recommended that only one commissioner be
retained in Paris. When the news came, it brought Adams considerable disappointment. On September 14, 1778, Congress
had appointed Franklin minister plenipotentiary at the court
of France without indicating in any way what would be the
position of Adams.[38] He learned of this strange situation on
February 11th and vehemently complained that "Congress
had not taken the least notice" of him; "they never so much as
bid me come home, bid me stay, or told me I had done well
or done ill." [39] This statement was not absolutely correct, since
on October 28th the committee of foreign affairs had written
Adams, "Congress must and will speedily determine upon the
arrangement of their foreign affairs. This is become, so far
as regards you, peculiarly necessary, upon a new commission
being sent to Doctor Franklin. In the mean time we hope you
will exercise your whole extensive abilities on the subject of
our finances. The doctor will communicate to you our situation in that regard." [40]

This hint Adams refused to take, and without waiting for
further instructions, he wrote to Vergennes that having been
"restored to the character of a private citizen" he intended to
leave the kingdom without any further trouble than to take
an opportunity of paying his respects.[41] On the same day he
wrote to De Sartine to request passage on the first French
vessel leaving for America.[42] This hasty decision was probably

[37] To Mrs. Adams, February 13, 1778. "Familiar Letters", p. 358.
[38] Wharton, *op. cit.*, Vol. II, p. 709.
[39] "Familiar Letters", p. 356; Wharton, *op. cit.*, Vol. III, p. 51.
[40] Wharton, *op. cit.*, Vol. II, p. 815.
[41] *Ibid.*, Vol. III, p. 51.
[42] *Ibid.*, p. 71.

due to the irritation and real anxiety he felt on learning of the campaign conducted by Silas Deane in Philadelphia against his former colleagues. Apparently he had burned his bridges and made his decision, but it was a decision that he soon regretted. He was far less categorical in a letter written to his wife five days later: he had heard that he would be appointed to Holland or to Spain — rumors without real foundation; but what if orders came after his departure, orders that no one but he could execute? Perhaps it would be better to take a ride to Geneva or Amsterdam, and to wait. Everything was charming in Paris, and it was hard to leave; all the prejudices he had entertained against the French had vanished as he was about to depart, never, as he thought, to return to the enchanting city.

The weather is every day pleasant; soft, mild air; some foggy days, and about ten or twelve days in January were cold and icy. But we have had scarce three inches of snow the whole winter. The climate is more favorable to my constitution than ours. The cookery and manner of living here, which you know Americans were taught by their former absurd masters to dislike, is more agreeable to me than you can imagine. The manners of the people have an affectation in them that is very amiable. There is such a choice of elegant entertainments in the theatric way, of good company, and excellent books, that nothing would be wanting to me in this country but my family and peace to my country to make me one of the happiest of men. John Bull would growl and bellow at this description. Let him bellow if he will, for he is but a brute.[43]

The "churlish republican", the Gallophobe, had finally been conquered, and no American ever was sadder than John Adams on the eve of his departure. He spent his last days in paying his calls and in visiting Saint-Denis, Montmartre, in taking his own son, and Mr. Genêt's son to the Ménagerie, little thinking that fifteen years later he would again see the boy, become a man, as envoy from the French Republic. With Vergennes, he had a long talk, and found that his French had so much improved that he could speak as fast as he pleased. The minister was frank and open on every question except on the subject of Spain: *"Quant à l'Espagne, Monsieur. Ah! je ne puis pas dire."*

[43] February 21, 1779. "Familiar Letters", p. 358.

But he wrote Adams a letter which the American diplomat treasured, congratulating him "on the wise conduct you have held during the whole time of your commission, as well as the zeal you have constantly displayed both for the cause of your country and for the support of the alliance which attaches it to his Majesty." [44]

Having paid his calls and bidden farewell to Franklin, Adams regretfully took his way to Nantes. The pleasure of returning home was very great, but he admitted to himself that it was "a mortification" to leave France. He was just beginning to understand a conversation in French, to prattle with common people; he had even observed that the female shopkeepers are the chattiest in the world, "very complaisant, talk a great deal, speak pretty good French and are very entertaining." [45] He felt that had he stayed, he would have enjoyed the country and the people much more than during the first months; but the Congressional gods had decided otherwise. Indeed France was so pleasant that, contrary to his wont, he did not fret too much when told that he would probably not sail until June, and had to wait for the new minister to the United States, M. de la Luzerne. This delay gave him more time to renew acquaintance with his son, to help him with his Latin, to read with him Cicero's orations and, when he became tired of Cicero, the "Carmen Seculare", for there can be too much of a good thing and, as Henry IV used to say, "*Toujours Tully* is as bad as *toujours Perdreaux*, and infinitely worse than *toujours sa femme*." [46] Truly, Adams was becoming quite French, and Mrs. Adams would not have appreciated the finesse of this *bon mot*.

In the meantime he analyzed himself with that rage for introspection which was inborn in him. He knew that he had an inherent lack of strength, that he was fitful, more stubborn than resolute, and apt to flare up on provocation. "There is," he wrote, "a feebleness and a languor in my nature. My mind and body both partake of this weakness. By my physical consti-

[44] February 21, 1779. Wharton, *op. cit.*, Vol. III, p. 55.
[45] Diary. Works, Vol. III, p. 196.
[46] *Ibid*, p. 197.

tution I am but an ordinary man. The times alone have destined me to fame; and even these have not been able to give me much. When I look in the glass, my eye, my forehead, my brow, my cheeks, my lips, all betray this relaxation. Yet some great events, some cutting expressions, some mean hypocrisies, have, at times, thrown this assemblage of sloth, sleep, and littleness into rage a little like a lion. Yet it is not like the lion; there is extravagance and distraction in it that still betray the same weakness." [47]

From Nantes he had to go to Lorient, to embark on the French frigate the *Sensible*. There he met Captain Landais of the *Bonhomme Richard*, and Captain John Paul Jones, magnificently dressed up with golden buttonholes and two epaulettes, and his marines in red and white, instead of green — an eccentricity and irregularity most shocking! There were also pleasant gentlemen who had traveled all around the world and seen strange people, who could discuss politics, oratory, etymology and the use of oaths. The city itself was most fascinating and colorful, with its "beggars, servants, *garçons*, *filles*, *décrotteurs*, *blanchisseuses*; barges, *bateaux*, bargemen, coffee-houses, taverns, servants at the gates of woods and walks; fruit, cakes, ice-creams, *spectacles*, tailors for setting a stitch in clothes, waiters for running with errands, cards, &c.; cabin boys, coach hire, walking-canes, pamphlets, *ordonnances*, carts." [48]

At last the Chevalier de la Luzerne arrived, with Barbé-Marbois, the secretary of the commission, his staff of secretaries and *maître d'hôtel*, and after much ado about quarters on board the *Sensible*, the ship finally sailed on June 17, 1779. The return voyage of Adams was very unlike the first crossing. He was shown every honor by the royal envoys, complimented on his French, on the attainments of his son, and on his knowledge of literature, which he paraded. He beamed and expanded in this atmosphere of gentility and cordiality; he was consulted, asked for information and advice about his country and his countrymen. Adams on several occasions recog-

[47] Diary. Works, Vol. III, p. 197.
[48] June 12, 1779. *Ibid.*, p. 210.

nized that there was something of the teacher in him; he was always ready and eager to set people right and, as was to be expected, he spoke too much and too freely. He was shrewd enough to realize that he "was led on naturally by the chevalier and M. Marbois", but he was sure it was "his duty" as well as in "the interests" of his country that he should conceal none of his sentiments concerning some prominent Americans. Only Laurens found grace in his eyes, probably because he had recently resigned, but Mr. Jay, who had succeeded him, was not quite so solid as his predecessor; Gouverneur Morris was no governor at all, just a man of wit and of character *très léger*. When he came to Franklin, his gall bladder burst: the good Doctor never had any religion, he had in his train all the atheists, deists, libertines, as well as the philosophers and the ladies. He was probably a great philosopher, but was no legislator, and with a sort of fury Adams repeated: "He has done very little." To the American Constitution, to the confederation, even to the constitution of Pennsylvania, "bad as it is", he had contributed nothing. He had written neither the Bill of Rights nor the Declaration of Independence. Franklin had "great merit as a philosopher. His discoveries in electricity were very grand, and he certainly was a great genius", he had wit and irony, "but he agreed with Marbois that these were not the faculties of statesmen." The whole conversation ended with a more than nasty allusion to "Mr. F.'s natural son, and natural son of a natural son." [49] This was what Adams called doing "justice" to the merits of his former colleague, for "it would be worse than folly to conceal my opinion of his great faults." If discretion, if not dissimulation, is the first virtue of a diplomat, Mr. Adams belonged to a new school of diplomacy. The well-trained, refined and perfectly self-controlled French envoy who, while walking the deck of the *Sensible*, was thus "leading on" the American commissioner, displayed much more reserve, simply telling Adams that he had heard many of the honest people in France lament that he had left that country, and adding that should Mr. Adams return to France or some other part of Europe, "the Court

[49] Diary. Works, Vol. III, p. 221.

of France would have confidence in any gentleman that Congress should have confidence in." [50]

Adams was obviously incapable of appreciating this subtle irony and quite at a disadvantage in this sort of fencing. A revealing incident should have opened his eyes and made clear to him that he did not enjoy the full confidence of the French Court. The Chevalier de la Luzerne assured him that "there was no need of policy between France and the United States; they need only understand one another — *rien que s'entendre*." [51] Evidently La Luzerne thought that a complete knowledge of the situation was not indispensable for such an understanding. When Adams had paid his farewell call on Vergennes, the minister had refused to say a word about the Spanish situation. A few weeks later, on April 12th, the secret Convention of Aranjuez had been signed by Florida Blanca and Montmorin, [52] and when the *Sensible* sailed, the American plenipotentiary was still unacquainted with this new and important development. It was only on the third day out that La Luzerne entrusted Adams with news that he had "bound himself in honor not to communicate while he was in France." Without mentioning the treaty, he simply said that Spain had declared herself against England, "without saying anything about the independence of America." Adams at once suspected "some scheme." "The subtlety, the invention, the profound secrecy, the absolute silence of these European courts, will be too much for our hot, rash, fiery ministers, and for our indolent, inattentive ones, though as silent as they." Evidently Adams placed himself in neither class, but these suspicions did not make him more cautious or more prudent.

[50] Diary. Works, Vol. III, pp. 218–220.

[51] *Ibid.*, pp. 225–226.

[52] For negotiations leading up to the treaty, see Edward S. Corwin, "French Policy and the American Alliance", Princeton (1916), pp. 193–217, and Paul Christler Phillips, "The West in the Diplomacy of the American Revolution", University of Illinois Studies in the Social Sciences, October 1913, pp. 90–172. On June 13, 1779, Lovell had complained to Adams of not having received even a "hint" from the commissioners in Paris. Wharton, *op. cit.*, Vol. III, p. 220. Lee wrote a very brief note to the President of Congress on June 21st, to inform him that "Spain had declared against Great Britain." Wharton, *op. cit.*, Vol. III, p. 229.

Never had his self-satisfaction and complacency been greater. He had written to Warren that "a retreat infinitely less splendid than that of Pythagoras, at the head of a little school to teach a few children the elements of knowledge would be a kind of Heaven" to him.[53] Vainly he tried to model himself on President Jeannin, who could write to his king, "I am so accustomed to work hard, with little profit, that I have acquired a disposition which enables me to stand with patience the harshness of bad fortune, without complaining or murmuring";[54] he had neither the simplicity nor the *bonhomie* of the old French diplomat. He knew that he would seize the first occasion to relinquish "the honour to be reduced to a private citizen."

As the *Sensible* approached the American coast and the danger of encountering the enemy increased, a thick fog surrounded them, as if to conceal the ship from the British fleet.[55] With well-feigned modesty, Adams refused to flatter himself with the idea that these happy circumstances were all ordered for the preservation of the frigate, but, like the conqueror of old, he was conscious that the ship carried John Adams and his fortune.

---

[53] "Warren-Adams Letters", Vol. II, p. 91.
[54] July 20, 1779. Diary. Works, Vol. III, p. 227.
[55] July 31, 1779. *Ibid.*, pp. 227–228.

CHAPTER II

SHIRT–SLEEVE DIPLOMACY

JOHN ADAMS had left Mount Wollaston on a stormy afternoon, fearful of British cruisers; he was coming back on a French frigate, at the head of a small fleet, accompanied by a new French ambassador and elegant gentlemen in court dress.

He attended all the functions given in honor of the new envoy, who tarried in Boston, but most of Adams' time was spent in Braintree, where we may picture the family reunion through Mrs. Warren, who knew them so well:

. . . The Gladdened Mother can scarcely suppress the tear of Rapture, to listen and smile alternately at the Narration of her young traveler, and the simple tale, with which the two younger Masters (emulous for papahs Attention) strive to entertain him, while the observing Daughter silently watches every accent, and treasures up every article of inteligence for her future improvement. The Father thanks his Negligent Countrymen for suffering him so soon to Indulge in the Highest Joys of Life. But the Patriot must secretly chide the want of Decission, the Inattention to the Interests of the States, that has permited him thus early to leave Europe, when by a longer stay he might have rendered them such an essential service.[1]

He was not permitted to enjoy long "the still delights of domestic felicity." Hardly a week after his arrival, he was selected by the town meeting to represent the people of Braintree "in the Convention to be convened at Cambridge on the first day of September next, for the purpose of forming a Constitution." If Congress had apparently forgotten Adams, he still came first in the estimation of the people of his native village, and this was very pleasant. It was for him a splendid

[1] August 6, 1779. "Warren-Adams Letters", Vol. II, p. 116.

opportunity to defend some of the ideas he had already expressed in his letter to George Wythe, three years earlier, and to be of service to his native State. On several occasions Adams had manifested his regret that Massachusetts was lagging behind, and more than ever he felt the need of securing the future through the establishment of good constitutions reasserting the fundamental "rights of every state." [2]

In the convention he obtained further recognition. He was placed on the Committee of Thirty entrusted with the care of preparing a draft of the Constitution, and when the committee adjourned on September 7th, with James Bowdoin and Samuel Adams, he became a member of a subcommittee of three, which was really to do the work. Working with and for men of his native province, dealing with ideas long familiar, and having at hand not only his old library, but the precious books on government brought back from Paris, he set about his task with a will, and engaged in "the new trade of a Constitution monger." [3]

A detailed analysis of such a document can hardly be undertaken here, but some of its essential features must be indicated, since they correspond to the principle for which Adams entered the field a few years later. On the whole, the final draft, as presented to the convention, may be regarded as his work, although, as we shall see, the subcommittee refused to endorse one of his fundamental propositions.[4] To him was left the wording of the "Declaration of the Rights of the Inhabitants of the Commonwealth of Massachusetts", which reiterated the principles enunciated in the Declaration of Independence, with modifications suitable to the Massachusetts people. The Constitution was founded on the principle of popular sovereignty and it proclaimed that all men were born "free and independent" and had certain "natural, essential and unalienable rights", but duty to worship "THE SUPREME BEING" was solemnly affirmed, and the right of the legislature to provide "at the ex-

[2] To James Warren, April 27, 1777. Works, Vol. IX, p. 462.

[3] To Benjamin Rush, November 4, 1779. Ibid., p. 507.

[4] For a more detailed study, see Samuel E. Morison, "A History of the Constitution of Massachusetts", Boston, 1917; and for the text of Adams' draft, see Works, Vol. IV, pp. 213–264.

pense of the subject", if necessary, a suitable support "for the worship of God" was asserted. The rights of the newly created State were protected by the fourth article:

The people of this commonwealth have the sole and exclusive right of governing themselves, as a free, sovereign, and independent state; and do, and forever hereafter shall, exercise and enjoy every power, jurisdiction, and right, which are not, or may not hereafter be by them expressly delegated to the United States of America, in Congress assembled.

The sixth article was intended to prevent the formation of an hereditary aristocracy, for "the idea of a man born a magistrate, lawgiver, or judge, is absurd and unnatural."

When it came to the form of government, the principle of the separation of powers was proclaimed, and the preamble to the second part declared that "the legislative, executive and judicial power shall be placed in separate departments, to the end that it might be a government of law, and not of men." [5] But, much to his regret, Adams could not convince his colleagues that the legislature should "consist of three branches"; [6] and the establishment of two branches — a Senate and a House of Representatives — both elected annually, was recommended. The Senate was a somewhat aristocratic body, clearly intended to protect the rights of the property owners; the House of Representatives, on the contrary, was "founded in equality." A council of nine persons selected by the joint houses was to assist the governor, chosen annually by popular election. Adams had given the chief magistrate an absolute veto which, much to his regret, was considerably altered, since upon resubmission and approval by two thirds of both houses, a law could be passed over the head of the governor.

The chapter on the "judiciary power" insured the independence of the judges, who were to hold office "during good behavior", although providing for their removal by the governor, with the consent of his council, "upon the address of

[5] See letter to Wythe. Works, Vol. IV, p. 184.
[6] To Benjamin Rush, November 4, 1779. Works, Vol. IX, p. 507.

both houses." And thus another principle dear to Adams was asserted.

To a great extent the committee had kept, with important modifications, the frame of the colonial government to which Massachusetts had been accustomed for more than a century. A certain number of religious qualifications were retained; Harvard University was to enjoy in the commonwealth the same protection and privilege as under the old régime. But in a curious section, entirely due to Adams, it became the duty of legislators and magistrates "in all future periods of this commonwealth", not only "to cherish the interests of literature and the sciences" but "to countenance and inculcate the principles of humanity and general benevolence, public and private charity, industry and frugality, honesty and punctuality in their dealings, sincerity, good humor, and all social affections and generous sentiments among the people." [7] Truly Mr. Adams had not lived in vain in Paris and associated for a year with Doctor Franklin. He did not believe that his fellow countrymen were quite ready for such *"philanthropie"*; he was particularly apprehensive that the "good humor" would be stricken out. Much to his surprise, "the whole was received very kindly, and passed the convention unanimously, without amendment." [8]

That the draft and the Constitution as finally adopted reflected the chief tenets of Adams cannot be doubted. He could rightly boast that "There never was an example of such precautions as are taken by this wise and jealous people in the formation of their government. None was ever made so perfectly upon the principle of the people's rights and equality. It is Locke, Sidney, and Rousseau and De Mably reduced to practice, in the first instance." [9] It was, in his opinion, as wise a document as human ingenuity could devise. He placed too little faith in human nature to believe that it would make virtue prevail, and forever insure peace and happiness to the inhabitants of Massachusetts. But the "engineer" had done his

[7] Ch. V [VI], Sec. II, Works, Vol. IV, p. 259.
[8] Works, Vol. IV, p. 261 *note.*
[9] *Ibid.*, p. 216.

work well, and he could write with satisfaction, "If the people are as wise and honest in the choice of their rulers as they have been in framing the government, they will be happy, and I shall die content with the project for my children, who, if they cannot be well under such a form and administration, will not deserve to be at all." [10]

The business of the convention did not, however, take all of his time. After the plan was drafted, Adams went back to Braintree and attended to his private affairs, sadly neglected for a period of years. His duties as a convention delegate from Braintree provided him with a good excuse for not appearing before Congress. A more ambitious, or less wise man would have rushed to Philadelphia to find out for himself the reason for the apparent neglect of Congress. Whether he was sulking, or because he was well advised by his friends, or simply because he had no wish to undertake a long and unpleasant journey, Adams decided to stay at home and he reported by letter to the President of Congress. [11]

During the crossing he had prepared a long account of the situation in Europe. It was an excellent state paper, for Adams was always at his best when refraining from personalities. He showed the necessity for France "to preserve the faith of treaties inviolate, and to cultivate our friendship with sincerity and zeal" — a remark which was not amiss at a time when the French alliance was attacked in Congress. He predicted the approaching ruin of Great Britain: "She resembles the melancholy spectacle of a great widespreading tree that has been girdled at the root", [12] which was bad prophecy but good propaganda. He insisted on the chances of drawing Holland into an alliance, and on the desirability of sending a minister there: "It will be proper to give him a discretionary power to produce his commission or not, as he shall find it likely to succeed; to give him full powers and clear instructions concerning the borrowing of money; and the man himself, above all,

---

[10] To Edmund Jennings, September 23, 1780. Works, Vol. IX, p. 509.
[11] August 3, 1779. Wharton, "The Revolutionary Diplomatic Correspondence of the United States", Vol. III, p. 276.
[12] August 4, 1779. Works, Vol. VII, p. 103.

should have consummate prudence, and a caution and discretion that will be proof against every trial." [13] This was the nearest Adams ever came to making a bid for a new diplomatic position.

It took him a few weeks to get somewhat acquainted with the situation in Congress. He had heard only vaguely before leaving France of the scandal following the attempts of Deane to justify himself and his attacks against Lee, but he did not know that originally he had been included in a resolution to blame the French commissioners on the ground that "suspicions and animosities have arisen among the said commissioners which may be highly prejudicial to the honor and interests of these United States." [14] If he had read the record further, he would have discovered that his name had been excepted from this general censure by a formal vote. But he did not realize at first that the only result of this solemn Congressional investigation had been to stir up muddied waters and ill feelings, and finally to leave everything in much the same condition as before. Benjamin Franklin, Silas Deane, Arthur Lee, Ralph Izard and William Lee had been spanked like bad boys, on April 20th; thereupon Franklin had been maintained as plenipotentiary at the Court of France, and Arthur Lee, Ralph Izard and William Lee informed that they need not repair to America. [15]

On the other hand, ever since the coming of Gérard, Congress had been discussing the conditions of a "truce" and an eventual peace. On February 15, 1779, the French envoy had officially signified to Congress "the desire of his most Christian majesty that the United States would speedily put themselves in a condition to take that part in the negotiation for peace apparently about to take place which their dignity and interest required . . . by giving their plenipotentiary the most ample instructions and full powers." [16] Congress had promptly taken up the question and, on February 23d, a preliminary report

[13] Works, Vol. VII, p. 104.
[14] Journals of Congress, April 15, 1779. Vol. XIII, p. 456.
[15] Ibid., May 3 and June 8, 1779. Vol. XIV, pp. 542–543, 700–703.
[16] Wharton, op. cit., Vol. III, pp. 49–50.

was presented. It was not, however, until August 14th that "the Instructions for a treaty of peace with Great Britain" were finally drawn up for "the ministers to be appointed for negotiating a peace", and unanimously agreed upon. The discussion in Congress had been long and hard and involved many problems that will be indicated later. A fierce battle started again when Congress had to designate the minister to be entrusted with such a momentous mission. There was a great deal of jockeying until only two candidates remained, John Jay and John Adams, and a study of the debates fully justifies the exclamation of an old Congressman, "What d—d dirty work is this of politics!" Finally, on September 27th, John Adams was appointed minister plenipotentiary to negotiate the treaties with Great Britain, with Dana to be his secretary; Jay was to negotiate with Spain, with Carmichael as secretary, and Colonel John Laurens was to be secretary to Doctor Franklin.[17]

It does not appear from available evidence that John Adams took any direct or even indirect part in the proceedings. His published communications with Congress had been strictly on official business, and he had not openly expressed any wish to serve again abroad in any capacity. In a letter to Thomas McKean [18] he had stated his firm belief that "it would be better to employ a single man of sense, even although he should be as selfish and interested as is possible, consistent with fealty to his country, than three honest men, even of greater abilities, any two of whom should be at open variance with each other. It would be better to employ a single stockjobber or a single monopolizer." To the same correspondent he had presented Franklin in a very unfavorable light, reiterating in a slightly more polite form the criticisms of the Doctor made to Barbé-Marbois. Franklin was a wit and a humorist, but "not a sufficient statesman for all the business he is in." He was "too old, too infirm, too indolent and dissipated, to be sufficient for the discharge of all the important duties of ambassador, board of war, board of treasury, commissary of prisoners, &c., &c., &c." Such was his name, however, that perhaps it were better to

---

[17] Laurens declined the appointment. Wharton, *op. cit.*, Vol. III, p. 343 note.
[18] September 20, 1779. Works, Vol. IX, pp. 484–486.

leave him there, "but a secretary and consuls should be appointed to do the business, or it will not be done." This letter could hardly have reached Philadelphia in time to influence any one, but undoubtedly several of Adams' friends felt that some sort of vindication was due to him and to New England. It was also known that Adams would not be as pliant in the hands of Vergennes as the good Doctor, although he was on good terms with the Court and his friends had displayed to good advantage the letter of appreciation written him by the French minister of foreign affairs.[19]

From Lovell and Gerry, Adams received the most flattering letters; Barbé-Marbois openly rejoiced at the choice of Congress, and La Luzerne wrote to the new plenipotentiary one of those delightfully penned letters, the art of which has been lost since the Revolution.[20]

This time Adams did not even pretend to deliberate about the matter. Before receiving his commission and instructions, he signified that he would not hesitate to say that "notwithstanding the delicacy and danger of this commission, I suppose I shall accept it without delay and trust events to Heaven."[21] He had been offered passage on the *Sensible* by La Luzerne, and he had no intention of detaining the ship unnecessarily on his account. His bags were packed in short order and on November 13th he sailed again from Boston, with his sons John Quincy and Charles, and his servant, Joseph Stevens.

This hurry was both perfectly legitimate and most unfortunate. We can hardly conceive to-day of a plenipotentiary leaving his country to conclude a treaty of peace without having had an opportunity to confer with his government. Adams' only excuse was that there was no American Government worthy of the name. The glorious era of Congress had already passed, and he had no taste for the "dirty work of politics" conducted in Philadelphia. Besides the alleged dishonesty,

[19] Gérard, who had never met Adams, could write to Vergennes that "the presumption that he would be agreeable" to the French minister had influenced the opinions of some members of Congress. September 27, 1779. Wharton, *op. cit.*, Vol. III, pp. 337–338 *note*.

[20] *Ibid.*, pp. 339, 345, 349, 352.

[21] To Henry Laurens, October 25, 1779. Works, Vol. IX, p. 505.

more or less real, of some members of Congress, there was an obvious lack of consistency and unanimity which was most evident in matters of foreign policy. Had he gone to Philadelphia, Adams would have been besieged by representatives eager to promote sectional rather than national interests; but he would also have had a chance to ascertain the motives underlying his instructions; he could have conferred with Lovell and Laurens, and from Gérard and La Luzerne obtained some precious indications. Above all, he would have discovered that both of them were perfectly acquainted with his secret instructions and thus he would probably have avoided his first *faux pas* with Vergennes.

If any of these considerations passed through Adams' mind, as he was sailing from Boston, no trace of them is to be found in his correspondence. He paid no heed to the wise words of Henry Laurens,[22] who had warned him that he would not be "directly the object of negotiation" and that "for some time" he would have to "remain behind the curtain." To Elbridge Gerry, who had advised him to keep his appointment secret, he had pointedly answered that "it was public in Boston and in every body's mouth." [23] He intended to devote himself without reserve or loss of time to the discharge of the high honor done him by the appointment. No longer would he play second fiddle to Franklin; in the fullest sense of the term, he was to be the minister plenipotentiary of the United States.

The trip across was most unpleasant. The old *Sensible* was crowded with three hundred and fifty passengers and sailors, and soon sprung a leak. Instead of landing in a French port, with the proper ceremonies and salvos, they had to put up at Ferrol, on December 8th. After waiting a few days for the ship to be repaired, Adams decided to brave the horrors of a land journey in Spain, and with the two boys, Mr. Dana and Mr. Thaxter, started from Corunna. It was a very picaresque caravan, with three ancient calashes drawn by mules; the carriages were in disreputable condition, with their worn leather that had never seen oil, broken harness tied with cords and

[22] October 4, 1779. Works, Vol. IX, pp. 496–499.
[23] November 4, 1779. *Ibid.*, p. 506.

twine, the servants riding on the mules. They had to carry in
their saddlebags bread, cheese, meat, knives and forks, spoons,
apples and nuts. The inns were a nightmare, with the mules,
hogs, fowls and human inhabitants "pigging" it together.
Everywhere he saw only "signs of poverty and misery among
the people. A fertile country, not half cultivated, people ragged
and dirty, and the houses nothing but mire, smoke, fleas, and
lice. Nothing appears rich but the churches; nobody fat but the
clergy." [24]

It was no sentimental journey, and to Adams not even a
picturesque one. Although he tried to amuse himself as well
as he could, "never was a captive escaped from prison more
delighted" than he was, when, after crossing the frontier, he
arrived at St. Jean de Luz.[25] The weary travelers reached Paris
on the 9th of February and obtained lodgings at the Hôtel de
Valois, on the rue de Richelieu, where no less a person than
the Prince of Hesse Cassel had established his quarters. On the
next day Adams called at once on Franklin and with him
waited on Vergennes, Sartines and Maurepas, the French
ministers. His impressions were of the best: never had the
French ministry been "so frank, so explicit, so decided, as each
of these was in the course of this conversation, in his declarations to pursue the war with vigor, and to afford effectual aid
to the United States." [26]

An unfortunate incident, or rather a series of incidents, was
soon to change for the worse this happy situation. So much
importance has been attributed to the difficulties arising between John Adams and Vergennes in the spring of 1780, that
no passing notice of them would suffice. In themselves, they
were of little consequence, but they revealed the rift already
existing in the alliance, a radical difference between two schools
of diplomacy and two national psychologies. They also reveal
a fact very apparent, but little understood and too seldom taken
into consideration. In dealing with the United States, it was

[24] December 30, 1779. Diary. Works, Vol. III, p. 244.
[25] January 20, 1780. *Ibid*, p. 257.
[26] To the President of Congress, February 15, 1780. Works, Vol. VII,
p. 121.

impossible for European diplomats to use the same methods as with the nations of the Old World. Comparatively slow as were communications in the eighteenth century, it was only a matter of days, or at most of a few weeks, to obtain information from London, Madrid, Berlin or Vienna. With the United States, on the contrary, it was a matter of months rather than of weeks, and this impossibility for American plenipotentiaries to communicate satisfactorily and rapidly with their home government explains to a large extent one of the most disconcerting features of American diplomacy. In instructions to special envoys, it was manifestly impossible to provide for every eventuality and to foresee all the modalities which might be considered during the course of negotiations. While the European diplomats could easily refer to headquarters any new proposition and ask for advice and new instructions, the American diplomats, placed in a distinct position of inferiority, were forced to assume an appearance of fixed and uncompromising determination. They could not really negotiate, they could not participate in conversations, they could not play the old game of give and take, yield more than they had been authorized to do and accept any serious modifications of the terms they had been empowered to propose or accept. It is really the geographical remoteness of the United States rather than a national disposition which on so many occasions has led the United States to depart from the traditional rules of old-fashioned diplomacy, to insist that the game should be played in their own way, to present their propositions as ultimata and to adopt the so-called shirt-sleeve diplomacy, of which John Adams may well be considered the first exponent.

One of the objects of Gérard's mission to the United States had been to determine on what terms peace could be made, and at the time of his departure for America the prospect of a peace, or at least of a mediation, was in sight. Adams had been appointed more than a year after the arrival of the French minister in Philadelphia and had been sent as the bearer of a plan of peace, at a time when, on his own admission, the only policy to be considered was one of intensive war. There was every reason to believe and to fear that the arrival in Europe of an American plenipotentiary intrusted by Congress with a plan of peace and a project of a commercial treaty with Great Britain, would be interpreted as an indication that Congress had no strong will to war and that the peace party had gained the upper hand.

With all his vanity, Adams could not help but realize that he had been placed in a very awkward situation, and after paying a first formal call on Vergennes, he asked him:

1. Whether, in the present state of things, it is prudent in me to acquaint the British Ministry that I am arrived here, and that I shall be ready to treat, whenever the belligerent powers shall be inclined to treat?

2. Whether it is prudent in me to publish in any manner, more than the journals of Congress may have already done, the nature of my mission?

3. Or whether to remain on the reserve, as I have hitherto done since my arrival in Europe? [27]

He added that he would be pleased to communicate to Vergennes any proposition that should be made directly or indirectly by the British ministry and, as he was "the only person in Europe who had authority to treat of peace", he expected that the French minister would reciprocate.

Nothing could be more disturbing to the peace of mind of a man belonging to the traditional school of diplomacy, inasmuch as Adams declared that he was "not confined by commissions, nor instructions, nor by any intimations from Congress to reside in any one place in Europe more than another", and at the same time confessed that he could not inform Vergennes "of the rise and progress" of the plan of peace, since he "was not in Congress when this transaction took place." The prospect of having to deal with a plenipotentiary whose powers were at the same time so broad and so vague, and who could play the part of the bull in a china shop, was exceedingly distasteful to Vergennes.

At first the French minister tried to gain time by simply answering that for the present it would be prudent to conceal

[27] February 12, 1780. Diary. Works, Vol. III, pp. 259–261.

"the eventual character" of Adams, and "above all to take the necessary precautions, that the object of your commission may remain unknown to the Court of London." Then, making an allusion to the fact that Adams himself had acknowledged that he had had no recent contact with Congress, Vergennes added that in any case it would be better to await the arrival of M. Gérard, who was due to return from Philadelphia, "because he is probably the bearer of your instructions, and will certainly be able to make me better acquainted with the nature and extent of your commission." [28]

Vergennes was probably fundamentally right, but he could not have committed a worse psychological mistake than to refuse to accept the *pleins pouvoirs* of the American plenipotentiary without confirmation from the French envoy at Philadelphia. Adams was deeply hurt by what he considered a personal slight, and he insisted that he could not communicate further his instructions, except to assure the French minister that they contained nothing inconsistent with the letter and spirit of the treaty between His Majesty and the United States. [29] Thereupon, Vergennes answered politely that he was quite satisfied that Adams' instructions had for their certain and invariable basis the treaties subsisting between the king and the United States, but he again urged the American plenipotentiary to keep secret his powers "to negotiate a treaty of commerce with the Court of London." For the rest, he saw no objection to informing the public of the other part of Adams' mission. It soon became evident, however, that the French minister meant to avoid any undue publicity for the American envoy.

Adams was presented to the king on March 7th, with so little ado that even the official *Gazette de France* did not mention the event in the briefest paragraph. In spite of all Adams' protests, Vergennes only agreed to have a short notice, which he himself wrote, inserted in the unofficial *Mercure*. [30] The only quality recognized to the American plenipotentiary was to have been designated by Congress "to attend the peace conferences

[28] February 15, 1780. Diary. Works, Vol. III, p. 261.
[29] February 19, 1780. *Ibid.*, p. 263.
[30] Doniol, "Histoire de la Participation française", Vol. IV, p. 412 *note*.

whenever they may take place [*quand il y aura lieu*]." [31] Adams was to observe a policy of watchful waiting, but not to take any initiative and to remain as inconspicuous as possible. The situation in which he found himself was just as awkward as that of a year before. Such a rôle might have suited Franklin, but the passionate New Englander was the last person to play such a part or to keep his peace.

If he could not act, he could at least write and assume some of the duties which, in his opinion, Franklin had neglected. Having nothing else to do, he could at least inform Congress of the true situation of European affairs and distribute correct information on American affairs to the French public. He consequently wrote at once to his friend Genêt, who was acting as a sort of press agent for Vergennes, to ask correct data on certain rumors circulated by the British regarding a contingent of twelve ships and twenty thousand men to be sent over from Russia to serve in America under the British flag. It was his intention to transmit this intelligence "to Congress, where it is of importance that it should be known." [32] In order to answer authoritatively, Genêt submitted the letter to Vergennes, who denied the danger of the mythical Russians and asked Genêt to inform Adams "that on every occasion he will be very happy to have you address yourself directly to him, and that you will always find him eager to satisfy your inquiries." [33]

While undertaking to establish himself in Paris as a correspondent or propaganda agent, Adams had a worthier object in view. On several occasions he had called attention to the desirability of appointing a capable and honest minister to Holland; he had insisted to Vergennes that an article about his mission be published in the Dutch gazettes, and, as early as February 27th, he wrote to the President of Congress that "an American minister is much wished for, who, although he might not yet be publicly received, would be able to do as much good

---

[31] Wharton, *op. cit.*, Vol. III, p. 580, gives a rather unsatisfactory translation of this passage.

[32] February 18, 1780. Works, Vol. VII, p. 125.

[33] February 20, 1780. *Ibid.*, p. 126.

as if he was." [34] As an irresistible inducement, he added that "money might be borrowed there by such a minister directly sent by Congress, applying directly to solid Dutch houses."

Had he been as much of a philosopher as Franklin, Adams could have spent his time very pleasantly. Paris was calling to him with its "public walks and gardens", its "fine squares ornamented with magnificent statues." He could have filled volumes with descriptions of temples and palaces, paintings, sculptures, tapestry, porcelains; but he could not do this without neglecting his duty. An American of his generation had no right to listen to "the siren song of sloth." "I must study politics and war, that my sons may have liberty to study mathematics and philosophy," he wrote to his wife. "My sons ought to study mathematics and philosophy, geography, natural history, and naval architecture, navigation, commerce and agriculture, in order to give their children a right to study painting, poetry, music, architecture, statuary, tapestry, and porcelain." A not untrue prophecy of the future of the house of Adams! So he went grimly to his self-appointed task of setting everybody right about everything.

To the President of Congress and to Lovell he sent long reports on the political situation in Europe, dissertations on sea power; he cut and transcribed long articles from the gazettes; he carefully listed all the ships of the British fleet, with the number of guns for each vessel, and he urged Genêt to publish translations of the American constitutions. To Vergennes he wrote endlessly, informing him of the true state of American opinion and protesting with indignation against the peace feelers of the Dean of Gloucester. He engaged an agent in London to send him all the political pamphlets as they came out, and he carefully analyzed the English methods of influencing the public, a mighty matter, for "all governments depend upon the good will of the people." [35]

He was less fearful now of seeing "America beholden to

[34] Wharton, *op. cit.*, Vol. III, p. 526.

[35] To Genêt, May 15, 1780. Works, Vol. VII, p. 170; Wharton, *op. cit.*, Vol. III, p. 679.

France for her liberty", but his old prejudices appeared in his reluctance to place too much confidence in the French soldiers who were to fight on American soil. The war was to be won on the sea by the French fleet; and as for the British army, the American militias would prove fully equal to the task of surrounding it and rendering it powerless. Soon he considered himself the champion of the French alliance — an alliance which Lord Conway had dared to call "not natural." He procured Conway's speech and point by point answered all the arguments of the ignorant Britisher. Distance, differences in tradition, language and religion, considered by the English speakers as insuperable obstacles to a permanent friendship between France and America, counted very little, for there were more essential interests: America would never interfere with French commerce and marine, they would have no common frontiers, they would have a common enemy — particularly if Great Britain unfortunately retained Canada. Adams solemnly declared that "The people of America, . . . whose very farmers appear to have considered the interests of nations more profoundly than General Conway", knew that from the day independence was declared, America became the natural friend of France, and France the natural friend of the United States — powers naturally united against a common enemy.[36]

Vergennes received dissertations, recommendations and advice, if not gratefully, at least with equanimity. Mr. Adams' conduct contrasted strangely with the calm of Doctor Franklin, his *bonhomie*, mistakenly termed "indolence" by Adams, and his perpetual *Ça ira;* but as he had constituted himself a propaganda and information bureau, he could undoubtedly do some good, and when the minister plenipotentiary offered collaboration in the *Mercure de France*, both Vergennes and Genêt expressed their pleasure and approbation.[37]

All of his information, however, was not equally welcome. One fine day in June, Adams informed Vergennes that Massachusetts had ratified the decision of Congress to redeem "bills

---

[36] To Genêt, May 17, 1780. Works, Vol. VII, p. 172; Wharton, *op. cit.*, Vol. III, p. 685.

[37] May 17, 1780. Wharton, *op. cit.*, Vol. III, p. 685.

payable in silver and gold or in produce at the market price in hard money." He enclosed a portion of a letter from Gerry, fully explaining the operation by which "every dollar . . . is equal to forty dollars of the old emission",[38] and added that although some Europeans might have considerable sums of money in loan office certificates, he did not believe that they would be materially affected by this radical deflation.[39]

Adams fully approved of a measure by which the indebtedness of Congress would be reduced from two hundred million dollars to five million; not so Vergennes, who insisted that the French merchants who, in exchange for this merchandise, had received and were still holding American paper would be ruined by this measure. He added that the Chevalier de la Luzerne had been given orders to make the strongest representations to Congress on the subject.[40] The incident would have been closed had Adams not requested Vergennes to stop or delay his instructions to La Luzerne and had he not written a long and curious dissertation on international finance. The gist of it was that no distinction should be made between natives and foreigners, and no distinction between French merchants and other foreign merchants. There was no breach of faith in the matter, or rather the breach of faith came from those who were demanding more money for their labors or goods than they were worth in silver. Furthermore, all merchants were profiteers, and Adams, well-informed by his wife, gave a long list of the exorbitant prices paid in Boston for French goods.[41]

In his first communication, Adams had mentioned his intention to discuss the matter with Doctor Franklin, but this time he was speaking in his own name, "with that freedom which becomes a citizen of the United States intrusted by the public with some of its interests." Welcome or unwelcome, he felt it his duty to speak out, and writing to the President of Congress, he announced that he was determined to give his sentiments to

[38] June 20, 1780, enclosing extract of Gerry's letter of May 5th. Works, Vol. VII, pp. 188–190.

[39] June 20, 1780. Wharton, *op. cit.*, Vol. III, p. 805.

[40] June 21, 1780. *Ibid.*

[41] June 22, 1780. *Ibid.*, p. 809.

his Majesty's ministers "whenever they shall see cause to ask them", and to "go to court often enough to give them an opportunity to ask them, if they wish to know them." [42]

Franklin, urged by Adams to intervene, had acquiesced and written to Vergennes, requesting that the instructions given to La Luzerne "be revoked or at least suspended." This time Vergennes lost patience; [43] he had not found anything in "the long dissertation" of Mr. Adams that might induce him to change his opinion. It contained only "abstract reasonings, hypotheses, and calculations which have no real foundation . . . and in fine principles, than which nothing can be less analogous to the alliance subsisting between his majesty and the United States." Vergennes added that the king was so firmly persuaded that Franklin's opinion differed from Mr. Adams' that he requested Franklin to support the representations to be made to Congress by La Luzerne. To Adams himself, the French minister sent a very polite but very firm note, stating again the French position and maintaining that France deserved "a preference before other nations who have no treaty with America, and who even have not as yet acknowledged her independence."

The next day Adams answered that the depreciation of bills and certificates, "being more the act and fault of their possessors than of government, was neither a violation of the public faith nor an act of bankruptcy." He agreed with Vergennes that further discussion of these questions was unnecessary — the matter was in the hands of Congress.

The incident had had the advantage of keeping Adams' mind from more important and personal problems during a whole month. In his correspondence with Vergennes he had shown no real acrimony. In fact, he had enjoyed the discussion and had engaged in it as a lawyer would debate with a friend on a purely academic question to while away the time. The discussion being closed, Adams could not let sleeping dogs lie. A few days later, he placed before Vergennes a complete picture of the military and naval situation in America, admitting

[42] June 26, 1780. Wharton, op. cit., Vol. III, p. 819.
[43] Vergennes to Franklin, June 30, 1780. Ibid., p. 827.

at the same time that he had "no authority to make any demand", but presenting "some observations" [44] and naturally giving plenty of advice. Adams had made the great discovery that the war had already been won; only he alone seemed to be aware of the fact:

I am, however, clearly of opinion, and I know it to be the general sense of America, that the English, both in North America and in the West India islands, have been for these two years past absolutely in the power of their enemies, and they are so now, and will continue to be so in such a degree that nothing will be wanting but attention to their situation and a judicious application of the forces of the allies to accomplish the entire reduction of their power in America.

Then he proceeded to outline his plan. If the French could be persuaded to send a strong fleet to the coast of North America, thereby establishing a practical blockade, the English troops, cut off from their sources of supply, would be very easily brought "to such misery as to oblige them to surrender at discretion." He had "a moral certainty" that "in one year . . . the power of the English in North America" would thus be reduced "to absolute annihilation without striking a blow on land."

Whether this plan would have been practicable must be left to the naval and military experts. It was presented in a forceful manner, although some details are rather disquieting, as, for instance, when Adams, unable to ascertain the exact strength of the British troops in the West Indies, calmly declared that "the climate in the West Indies, and in Georgia and Carolina is making a rapid consumption of their men."

Adams did not wait for Vergennes' answer, which was courteous and uncompromising, simply stating that the Chevalier de Ternay and the Count de Rochambeau, who had been sent for the express purpose discussed by Adams, would concert with Congress and General Washington, and that the plan of operations had to be settled "between them and the American generals." [45] He was already thinking of a more personal mat-

---

[44] July 13, 1780. Wharton, *op. cit.*, Vol. III, p. 848.
[45] July 20, 1780. *Ibid.*, p. 870.

ter. He could not forget that he had been prevented by the French minister from announcing publicly that he was empowered to conclude a treaty of commerce with Great Britain. Having nothing else to do, he undertook to enumerate to Vergennes the eleven points which, in his opinion, made such a communication highly desirable, and he went so far as to ask the French minister to give the reasons which made it desirable to conceal the nature of his powers in their full extent from the Court of London.[46]

Vergennes was too accomplished a diplomat to lose patience; as Mr. Adams wished an answer and explanation, he should have them. Point by point he discussed Adams' argumentation, but he did not mince his words.[47] The reasons which had determined Vergennes were "so plain that they must appear at first view." The English ministry "would consider that communication as ridiculous", they would return no answer, "or if they did, it would be an insolent one." Vergennes could not believe that the bait of a treaty of commerce would be sufficient to make England recognize the independence of the United States, which was the main object in view. To end the discussion, the French minister finally prayed and requested Adams, on July 25th, "in the name of the King . . . to communicate your letter and my answer to the United States, and to suspend, until you shall receive orders from them, all measures with regard to the English ministry." [48]

Adams could not very well refuse. He had not been convinced by Vergennes' argument, but at least he recognized that it was far better to keep his instructions secret than to publish them against the wishes of the French Court. He was defeated but he was not discouraged. He had been so absorbed in the preparation and presentation of his case that he had not studied carefully Vergennes' answer to his military plans. He read it again and soon picked up in it another bone of contention. The French minister had had the audacity to maintain that the

[46] July 17, 1780. Wharton, *op. cit.*, Vol. III, p. 861.
[47] "Observations on Mr. J. Adams' Letter of July 17, 1780." *Ibid.*, Vol. IV, pp. 3–6.
[48] Wharton, *op. cit.*, Vol. III, pp. 882, 883.

king, "without having been solicited by Congress, has taken effectual measures to support the cause of America." [49] This would never do. Vergennes had to be set right and credit given where credit was due. The French Court had to be won to the idea of sending a fleet by the variety of arguments presented by the commissioners on January 1, 1779. They had originated the "true plan, which is finally to humble the English and give the combined powers the advantage." This advice had been so useful that Adams declared himself determined "to omit no opportunity of communicating my sentiments to your excellency upon everything that appears to me of importance to the common cause in which I can do it with propriety", [50] and he added, "the communications shall be direct in person or by letter to your Excellency, without the intervention of any third person."

This time Adams had succeeded in making himself an unmitigated nuisance and meddler, and Vergennes had to suppress what he mildly called "Mr. Adams' teasing, [*la taquinerie de M. Adams*]." [51] He pointedly reminded him that it was his duty to inform him that "Mr. Franklin being the sole person who has letters of credence to the king from the United States, it is with him only that I ought and can treat of matters which concern them, and particularly of that which is the subject of your observations." Furthermore, Adams was curtly told that "the King did not stand in need of your solicitations to induce him to interest himself in the affairs of the United States." [52]

To make thorough work of it, Vergennes wrote to Franklin, sending him the correspondence with Adams and asking him to transmit the letters to Congress, "that they may know the line of conduct which Mr. Adams pursues with regard to us, and that they may judge whether he is endowed, as Congress no doubt desires, with that conciliating spirit which is necessary for the important and delicate business with which he is in-

---

[49] July 20, 1780. Wharton, *op. cit.*, Vol. III, p. 871.
[50] July 27, 1780. *Ibid.*, Vol. IV, pp. 13, 14.
[51] To La Luzerne, August 7, 1780. Doniol, *op. cit.*, Vol. IV, p. 424 *note*.
[52] Vergennes to Adams, July 29, 1780. Wharton, *op. cit.*, Vol. IV, pp. 16–17.

trusted." [53] Without formally requesting that John Adams be recalled, the French minister could not have expressed more clearly that the American envoy was considered a real danger by the French Court.

The whole unpleasant affair appears to have been perfectly summed up in the letter written by Franklin in compliance with Vergennes' request, forwarding the correspondence that had passed between Adams and the French minister. The old philosopher pointed out that some inconveniences were bound to result from having more than one minister at the same court. "Mr. Adams' proper business is elsewhere; but the time not being come for that business, and having nothing else here wherewith to employ himself, he seems to have endeavored supplying what he may suppose my negotiations defective in." This was to put the case very mildly, but at the same time Franklin did not feel that he ought to omit mentioning the reason which lay at the bottom of the difference between him and his self-appointed colleague. Adams thought that "America has been too free in expressions of gratitude to France, for that she is more obliged to us than we to her, and that we should show spirit in our applications"; whereas Franklin maintained, on the contrary, that "this court is to be treated with decency and delicacy", and a different conduct seemed to him "what is not only improper and unbecoming, but what may be hurtful to us." It was for Congress to decide. [54]

In the meantime Adams had departed for Holland. For several months he had insisted that substantial financial assistance could be obtained if a proper person with powers to treat and to contract loans were sent by Congress to The Hague. On October 26, 1779, Henry Laurens, former President of Congress, had been appointed a commissioner to negotiate a treaty of amity and commerce "with the United Provinces of the low countries." [55] He did not sail, however, until the fall of 1780, so Adams, having nothing better to do, decided to act as a *pro*

---

[53] July 31, 1780. Wharton, *op. cit.*, Vol. IV, pp. 18–19.
[54] Franklin to the President of Congress, August 9, 1780. *Ibid.*, pp. 21–25.
[55] *Journals of Congress*, Vol. XV, p. 1210.

tempore appointee, and on July 27th, with his two sons, set off for Amsterdam. He needed a change of air. He was convinced that a treaty with Holland would make America "less dependent on France" and, above all, he himself would be more independent and much less under obligation to pay lip service to the Count de Vergennes and Doctor Franklin. He was going, as he thought, for a few months, little suspecting that his absence would be prolonged over two years, and that Holland would be the scene of what he was later pleased to call "the greatest triumph of my life."

The situation then existing in Holland is not easily described. As soon as he arrived, Adams saw that Amsterdam could become a center of communication between America and many other parts of Europe. It was also a center of diplomatic intrigue.[56] As early as April, 1776, Franklin had corresponded with a secret agent at The Hague, and in July of the same year Vergennes had appointed as minister the Duc de la Vauguyon, a chubby, jolly, shrewd French diplomat "of the right cut for this Embassy, being as squab as anything in Holland."[57] If this was a necessary qualification to be *persona grata* with the Dutch, Adams must have been welcomed at once. Franklin, on the other hand, had maintained at The Hague, as secret agent, a Swiss scholar of extraordinary ability and devotion to the American cause, Charles William Frederick Dumas, who deserves thorough and elaborate study by American historians and biographers.

The Dutch, unable to protect their merchant vessels against search by English cruisers, had for several years been subjected by force to many indignities and arbitrary procedure, both on the high seas and in their West India colonies, but they had never become reconciled to it. By the end of 1779, although nominally not yet at war with Great Britain, the United Provinces were commercially supporting her enemies. In the early

[56] The best and, I believe, the only extensive study in English of this phase will be found in Friedrich Edler, "The Dutch Republic and the American Revolution", Baltimore, 1911, Johns Hopkins University Studies in Historical and Political Science, Vol. XXIX, No. 2.

[57] Sir Joseph Yorke to Lord Eden, December 24, 1776, Edler, *op. cit.*, p. 20.

part of the year following, they learned of the plan of Catherine II to form a coalition of the northern neutrals to insure the liberty of commerce of neutral ships, and in March, John Adams had heard of a quintuple alliance between Russia, Sweden, Denmark, Prussia and the United Provinces to maintain the honor of their flags.[58] Holland, unfortunately, was far from being a homogeneous country; each of the provinces had to be consulted and to agree, and the English party was still very powerful. When Adams reached Amsterdam, nothing had been decided, and the American envoy found himself in a hotbed of intrigue. To him it was exceedingly stimulating. There was not in Europe "a better station to collect intelligence from France, Spain, England, Germany, and all the northern parts, nor a better situation from whence to circulate intelligence through all parts of Europe than this." [59] He was so much himself again that he wrote to Franklin that he was never more amused with political speculation than since his arrival in that country.[60]

Having little immediate responsibility, Adams had all the time he wanted to collect information, to go through the English papers, to have Dutch papers read to him, to write long dissertations on the state of Europe to the President of Congress, and even to lay out a plan "of an institution for refining, correcting, improving and ascertaining the English language." Such an academy, created by Congress, would do more than any other measure he could think of to promote a union of the different States by fixing a standard for the signification and pronunciation of English words, and to establish English as a world language.[61]

Almost day by day he kept his correspondents informed of all the rumors, either true or false, that troubled the formerly peaceful life of Amsterdam.[62] By the middle of September,

[58] Adams to the President of Congress, March 18, 1780. Wharton, *op. cit.*, Vol. III, p. 558.

[59] Adams to the President of Congress, August 14, 1780. Wharton, *op. cit.*, Vol. IV, p. 29.

[60] August 17, 1780. *Ibid.*, p. 34.

[61] September 5 and 25, 1780. *Ibid.*, pp. 45–47, 67.

[62] To the President of Congress, September 16, 1780. *Ibid.*, p. 57.

Dana brought him from Paris a special commission from Congress, authorizing him to negotiate a loan with the United Provinces, pending the arrival of Henry Laurens; but, confronted with a definite task to accomplish, Adams realized that perhaps he had been much mistaken in his information and had thought that "money was more plentier here than it is." [63]

At this juncture Adams found himself faced with a situation somewhat analogous to that which had confronted him when he arrived in France. Should he make his commission known to the States-General and to the public, or keep it secret? This time, after consulting some gentlemen "of the most knowledge and best judgment", he decided it would be best to keep his designs secret as long as possible.[64] At first he was disappointed in his expectations. Private banks refused to handle the loan; he could not express himself in the Dutch language; not being accredited as minister plenipotentiary to the Dutch Government, he had no prestige, and above all, he felt almost powerless against the swarms of British agents and well-organized British propaganda. There was nothing he could do except resume his duties as an observer, and send dissertations to Congress on the government of the seven provinces of the Low Countries, in the hope that Congress would fully realize the difficulties he had to overcome.[65]

So were spent the first months of Adams in Amsterdam, not at all unpleasantly, if not very fruitfully. By the middle of October he received news that Henry Laurens, on his way to Amsterdam, had been captured and taken to the Tower of London. A few days later he heard that, in some manner never satisfactorily explained, Laurens had failed to destroy all of his papers when the ship carrying him was seized; that among these papers was the old draft of a treaty drawn up by William Lee in 1778, and that this draft would finally bring about a formal state of war between Great Britain and the United Provinces. One thing, however, seemed to him quite clear; he

[63] To the President of Congress, September 19, 1780. Wharton, *op. cit.*, Vol. IV, p. 60.
[64] To the President of Congress, September 24, 1780. *Ibid.*, p. 66.
[65] To the President of Congress, October 11, 1780. *Ibid.*, p. 88.

must take steps immediately to settle down in Holland, procure a home, and now speak openly about his mission.[66]

During the weeks that followed, Adams ran the gamut of hope and despair. At times he did not see how Holland could comply with the demands made by Great Britain in an insolent memorandum; again, realizing how few were the individuals like Van der Capellen, who would wish to render service to the United States, he almost lost courage.[67] He was counting without British obstinacy and scorn for a small nation. When the States-General refused to answer the second memorial presented by Sir Joseph Yorke, and the British minister left The Hague, he realized that the crisis had at last come to a head.

The new year brought him a good piece of news: the English Government had ordered "that general reprisals be granted against the ships, goods, and subjects of the States-General of the United Provinces." [68] He would believe nothing until the event transpired, but he could perceive everywhere a general spirit of resentment against the English. He did not thoroughly understand Dutch character. Weeks passed and no decisive action had been taken; there seemed little likelihood of obtaining a loan. Adams lost patience. He felt deeply humiliated that the young nation he represented should have to wait on the good pleasure of Spain and Holland, begging for money reluctantly granted or refused, begging for soldiers and ships; and in his resentment he wrote Franklin that he felt inclined to abandon the whole undertaking. "If it does not suit their affairs to make a bargain with us, let them tell us so candidly and let us all go home, that at least we may not be under the necessity of calling up your excellency for water to drink, which had much better quench the thirst of our army." [69]

Adams did not seem to be aware of the distress that had made Congress send to Louis XVI a most touching message, in which they threw themselves on the generosity of the French Court; [70] nor did he know that Franklin had written to Ver-

[66] To Capellen, October 22, 1780. Wharton, *op. cit.*, Vol. IV, p. 102.
[67] To Capellen, December 9, 1780. *Ibid.*, p. 189.
[68] To the President of Congress, January 1, 1781. *Ibid.*, p. 219.
[69] February 20, 1781. *Ibid.*, p. 260.
[70] November 22, 1780. *Ibid.*, p. 157.

gennes a long letter, using every argument that might decide the French to make new sacrifices, "particularly in the article of money." [71] Above all, he was not endowed with the "two Christian graces — faith and hope", which upheld the old philosopher, who added, "but my faith is only that of which the apostle speaks, the evidence of things not seen." [72]

Faith and hope Adams did have, however, — not in support from foreign nations, but that "the glory of baffling, exhausting, beating, and taking them will finally be that of the American yeomanry", and that "the art, malice, skill, valor, and activity of the English and all their allies" would be of no avail.[73]

If America alone could defeat the British, Adams was no less eager to see America alone finance the war. The burdens of the American people were much lighter than those of their enemies and even of their allies. America could not hope to obtain credit abroad until she had credit at home. "If taxes could be laid by Congress upon exports and imports, and upon the consumption of articles of luxury, convenience, and necessity, as they are in Europe, America would be able to raise more every year in taxes than she has ever spent in one year," [74] for it was demonstrable that the people of America were able to lend to Congress every year more than enough money to carry on the war and pay all expenses.

In more than one way this was patriotic and sound advice, and one cannot help regretting at times that Adams did not stay at home among the people of his blood and tongue. In Congress he would probably have played a much more useful rôle. His ardent patriotism might have spurred on a lagging and dispirited assembly of men pinning all their hopes on foreign help. He felt it so strongly that he was determined to make every effort to go to Congress at Philadelphia on his return home.

---

[71] February 13, 1781. Wharton, *op. cit.*, Vol. IV, p. 255.
[72] Franklin to Adams, February 22, 1781. *Ibid.*, p. 266.
[73] To Jennings, March 12, 1781. *Ibid.*, p. 287.
[74] To the President of Congress, March 29, 1781. *Ibid.*, p. 338.

Zealous as he was as a "propagandist", he came to recognize during his stay in Holland what any wise propagandist is bound to admit: that letters, pamphlets, newspaper articles, preaching and exhorting have after all small influence on public opinion; the means of negotiating peace were entirely in the hands of generals Washington and Greene.[75]

Still, day by day and step by step, the diplomatic situation was improving. Dana had been appointed minister to St. Petersburg, and Adams, made wise by experience, advised him not to make his commission known before reaching Russia, and even then not to do anything without consulting the French minister. This was the procedure taken by Holland in her struggle against Spain, the method taken by Switzerland and Portugal in similar cases with great success, and Adams added, "Why it should be improper now I know not." [76] This was as far as Adams could go to make apologies for his conduct towards Vergennes, but at the same time he took steps to announce to the States-General that he had received full powers and instructions to conclude a treaty of amity and commerce with the United Provinces.[77] In so doing, he squarely opposed Vauguyon, the French minister, who did not think the moment favorable for the public recognition of Adams as accredited plenipotentiary to The Hague.[78]

Adams, however, did not heed Vauguyon's advice. Although all the Dutch officials, from the Grand Pensionary to the Prince of Orange, refused to receive him, he went ahead and published his memorial in English, French and Dutch.[79] Vauguyon did not conceal his disapproval of what he thought was a very untimely step, adding, however, that since it was done, he would support and promote Adams' plans to the utmost of his power.[80]

[75] December 2, 1781. "Familiar Letters", p. 397.
[76] To Dana, April 18, 1781. *Ibid.*, p. 368.
[77] April 19, 1781. *Ibid.*, p. 370.
[78] Vauguyon to Vergennes, April 21, 1781. Sparks MSS., in Edler, *op. cit.*, p. 219.
[79] To the President of Congress, May 7, 1781. Wharton, *op. cit.*, Vol. IV, p. 401.
[80] *Ibid.*, p. 403.

Apparently Adams once more had broken all diplomatic precedents. To receive him officially as minister plenipotentiary from the United States would have been to recognize the United States as an independent and sovereign power. This neither the States-General, nor the Grand Pensionary, and even less the Stadtholder, were ready to do. By going over their heads and addressing directly the people, Adams hoped to force the hand of the constituted authorities, to create in each province an agitation favorable to America, and thus force the hand of reluctant and hesitating officials. In Holland he could see only "faint feeble symptoms of life." This *vis inertiæ* was to him perfectly incomprehensible. America had been too long silent in Europe; the time had come to speak loudly and frankly.

He was soon disappointed in his expectations. The Dutch could well have adopted the motto of *festina lente*, "make haste slowly", which, according to Jay, was the motto of the Spaniards. There was talk of an alliance between France and Holland, but the offer by Russia of a mediation between the belligerents had first to be considered. Adams, called post-haste by Vergennes to Versailles, had received the proposal coldly and maintained that no proposition for a truce or a peace not recognizing first the independence of the United States could be considered. He would rather be "a fugitive from Malabar or China" than ever reassume the character of a British subject.[81]

In a long memorandum to Vergennes, he elaborated on his point in more diplomatic but clear language. The independence of the United States could not be the object of negotiation by mediators or a congress of diplomats; "their sovereignty, with submission only to Divine Providence, never can and never will be given up." [82]

Peace certainly was desirable, but in the offer of mediation and in the Russian proposal Adams could only see, and rightly so, a maneuver of Great Britain to relieve her credit, to dis-

[81] To Vergennes, July 7, 1781. Wharton, *op. cit.*, Vol. IV, pp. 550–551, and 560.
[82] July 13, 1781. *Ibid.*, p. 573.

concert the projects of the neutral powers, and to encourage a peace at any price.[83]

French historians, particularly Doniol, have passed very rapidly over this episode, simply contrasting the radicalism and outspoken ways of the American plenipotentiary with the more conciliatory views of the French minister. There is little doubt, however, that shirt-sleeve diplomacy was not out of place. Some hesitation could easily be perceived under the fine language of Vergennes. The king was more decided than ever to stand for the independence of the United States, and even to guarantee their independence for a long period of years. Why insist on a mere formula when the *de facto* sovereignty of the United States was acquired? Spain more than hesitated, the neutrals were more indecisive than ever. Congress seemed to be spineless and maneuvers would be attempted to introduce a scission among the States, such as to have each State represented by a special delegate in the proposed peace congress. Adams clearly saw the danger, ruthlessly cut through all the fine threads of diplomatic niceties and stated forcibly the *sine qua non* of a peace with Great Britain. Having delivered his ultimatum, he went back to Amsterdam, disgusted with British chicanery and tricks "that have been the derision of America for a number of years", but were still taken seriously in Europe. No sighing and longing for peace would obtain it. America must put an end to a foolish and disgraceful correspondence and brace up her laws and military discipline.[84] If he could only go home to wake up his countrymen "out of their reveries about peace"! His "talent" lay "in making war", not in negotiating, and there is little doubt that Adams' presence in Congress might have galvanized his colleagues and inspired them with a spirit such as, a hundred and fifty years later, a man like Clemenceau could instill into the French Parliament. As it was, he had to stay in Amsterdam and saw wood. Under the strain and restraint, he almost completely broke down, and until the beginning of October was reduced so low by a nervous fever

---

[83] July 16, 1781. Wharton, *op. cit.*, Vol. IV, p. 576.
[84] To the President of Congress, August 6, 1781. *Ibid.*, p. 624.

that he could not take "a pen in hand to write to anybody."[85] He was hardly beginning to recover when he received news that on June 15th there had been appointed to serve with him as peace commissioners, Benjamin Franklin, John Jay, Henry Laurens and Thomas Jefferson, with full powers to make and sign treaties relating to the establishment of peace.[86]

At the same time the commissioners were instructed very briefly that no treaty of peace should be concluded that did not effectually secure the independence and sovereignty of the United States. They were not tied up by absolute and peremptory directions with reference to boundaries, or other limitations. Furthermore, they were "to make the most candid and confidential communications upon all subjects to the ministers of our generous ally, the King of France; to undertake nothing in the negotiations for peace or truce without their knowledge and concurrence; and ultimately to govern yourselves by their advice and opinion."[87]

In the appointment of the commissioners, as well as in the instructions, the hand of Vergennes and of La Luzerne could easily be seen. Without asking openly for the recall of Adams, the French minister had never ceased to insist that His Majesty's Government should be "authorized to prevent him from committing any unwarranted acts to which he would surely be led by his too ardent imagination, and his stubbornness, *être autorisé à l'arrêter dans les écarts dans lesquels son imagination trop ardente, son entêtement, ne manqueront point de l'entraîner.*"[88]

Adams tried to receive the blow gallantly. He was not without some information from Philadelphia, and for some time had feared that he would have "nothing more to do with commissions of any sort."[89] But to Huntington he wrote more frankly, in the midst of a fit of despondency such as seized him so frequently. The English would not treat with the United States for many years, his commission for borrowing money

[85] To Franklin, October 4, 1781. Wharton, *op. cit.*, Vol. IV, p. 767.
[86] *Ibid.*, pp. 503–505.
[87] *Ibid.*, p. 505.
[88] April 19, 1781. Doniol, *op. cit.*, Vol. IV, p. 589.
[89] To Franklin, October 4, 1781. Wharton, *op. cit.*, Vol. IV, p. 767.

had been useless, his letters of credence had been accepted *ad referendum* and no one could tell when he would be admitted to an audience. It was possible that the Provinces might make peace with England and even join her. Under these circumstances, he doubted very much that he was of any service in Europe, and once again he offered his resignation: "my prospects both for the public and for myself are so dull, and the life I am likely to lead in Europe is likely to be so gloomy and melancholy and of so little use to the public, that I can not but wish it may suit with the views of Congress to recall me." [90]

The news of Cornwallis' surrender did not cure Adams of his melancholy. Quite graciously he congratulated Vauguyon on the "glorious news", but to him, as indeed to the best-informed people of Europe, it was not yet the decisive blow that would bring England to terms.[91] It nevertheless justified his very sensible contention that the war had to be fought and won in America, not in Europe. The triumph of the allied forces had the immediate effect of making new friends for America in Holland, as Saratoga had made new friends in France. The Dutch, however, were not more willing to lend their money to the United States, and it seemed as if "invisible fairies" were disconcerting in the night "all the operations of the patriots in the day." [92]

The following months were to put Adams' patience and patriotism to a hard test. Livingston had been appointed by Congress to take charge of foreign affairs and bring about some order in the accounts and some unity in the efforts of the American ministers abroad. He apparently treated Franklin with great respect and deference, but with Adams he was at times unnecessarily harsh and, it seems, somewhat unjust. Through La Luzerne he had heard that there was little prospect of an alliance with Holland "till after a peace shall have been concluded",[93] and he informed Adams to that effect, shortly after the powerless plenipotentiary had decided to go

[90] October 15, 1781. Wharton, *op. cit.*, Vol. IV, p. 779.
[91] November 24, 1781. *Ibid.*, p. 868.
[92] To Jay, November 28, 1781. *Ibid.*, Vol. V, p. 32.
[93] January 29, 1782. *Ibid.*, p. 138.

from province to province to present his memorial and enroll new friends of the American cause. He blamed Adams for his haste in making his mission known to the public; he reproved him for not mentioning the French ambassador in his letters, and asked petulantly, "Is there no intercourse between you? If not, to what is it to be attributed?" [94] Certain as he was that the situation was desperate, that France was "the only enemy of Great Britain, who is at the same time our ally, who will persevere in the war for the attainment of our independence", [95] he did not wish to see dissension introduced by any rash act of his somewhat brusque minister. Later in the year, he did not even hesitate to accuse Adams of negligence in his duties: "Near five months have elapsed since I have been favored with a line from you. . . . Let me entreat you, sir, to reflect on the disgrace and discredit it brings upon this department to be kept thus in the dark relative to matters of the utmost moment." [96]

Fortunately Adams found some compensation in Amsterdam. He had presented a new request to be recognized in his official capacity of minister plenipotentiary and on April 22d he had been formally introduced to "his Most Serene Highness the Prince of Orange." [97] He was not a little proud that on such a momentous occasion the Prince had consented to speak English to him. On the next day Vauguyon had offered a banquet to "the whole corps diplomatique" to introduce the new brother to all the old fraternity, and the duke had been particularly attentive to Adams. [98] The voice of the people having spoken at last, the American minister was able to submit a plan for a treaty of commerce which was accepted *ad referendum*, and after innumerable vexations, he had agreed with three well-esteemed houses for a loan. In July the transaction had been successfully completed and the terms were as moder-

[94] March 5, 1782. Wharton, *op. cit.*, Vol. V, p. 221; also Adams to Livingston, February 19, 1782, *ibid.*, p. 185.
[95] To the Governors of the States, February 19, 1781. *Ibid.*, p. 182.
[96] August 29, 1782. *Ibid.*, p. 677.
[97] To Livingston, April 22, 1782. *Ibid.*, p. 319.
[98] To Livingston, April 23, 1782. *Ibid.*, p. 326.

ate as could be wished.[99] He was so pleased with himself and with the French minister who was so gracious that he attempted to correct some of Jay's anti-French prejudices: "I do not know, however," he wrote, "that America and Holland are too much under the direction of France, and I do not believe they will be, but they must be dead to every generous feeling as men and to every wise view as statesmen if they were not much attached to France in the circumstances of the times."[100] Curiously enough, instead of resenting Livingston's criticisms, he saw in them a rare opportunity to write a long dissertation with a full gallery of portraits of all the Dutch officials and all the foreign ministers, including the French ambassador, "an amiable man, whom I esteem very much. He is able, attentive, and vigilant as a minister."

As to the question asked by Livingston, whether he had consulted him on every occasion, Adams answered that the Duc de la Vauguyon "has been under infinite obligations to the United States of America and her minister for the success he had in this country." It was Adams who had introduced him "to some leading men here", and if any one denied it, "it must be owing to ignorance or ingratitude."[101]

At last, after plowing an ungrateful field for so long, Adams was to reap the rich harvest. The treaty of commerce was to be signed, he had obtained a loan in cash for fifteen hundred thousand guilders and he could write to Dana: "The standard of the United States waves and flies at The Hague in triumph over Sir Joseph Yorke's insolence and British pride. When I go to heaven, I shall look down over the battlements with pleasure upon the Stripes and Stars wantoning in the wind at the Hague."[102]

For a few weeks Adams showed some disposition to rest on his oars and look with complacency at the work he had done so well. The Spanish minister had declared that "it was the greatest blow [*le plus grand coup*] that could have been struck in

---

[99] To Livingston, July 5, 1782. Wharton, *op. cit.*, Vol. V, p. 594.
[100] August 10, 1782. *Ibid.*, p. 654.
[101] To Livingston, September 4, 1782. *Ibid.*, pp. 685–693.
[102] September 17, 1782. *Ibid.*, p. 732.

all Europe." He was now situated as well as he "ever could be in Europe." "I have the honor to live upon agreeable terms of civility with the Ambassadors of France and Spain," he wrote to Lafayette, "and the ministers of all the other powers of Europe, whom I meet at the houses of the French and Spanish ministers, as well as at court, are complaisant and sociable." [103]

Sociable he had become to an unexpected degree; he could now "run on about the Panurge, Pantagruel, &c. of Rabelais, the Romeo and Juliet of Shakespeare, the Mandragore of Machiavel, the Tartuffe of Molière." The Count of Sarsfield had given him elementary lessons in court etiquette, dress, billets, ranks, and he wondered "how it is possible to reconcile these trifling contemplations of a master of ceremonies, with the vast knowledge of arts, science, history, government, etc., possessed by this nobleman." [104] On the other hand, Adams realized that he had obtained as much as could be expected from Holland. He had no hope of seeing the Dutch fleet co-operate either with the Spanish or French fleet, even in the West Indies; no vigorous, aggressive policy could ever be adopted by a nation "whose mainspring had been broken." The treaties were finally signed, sealed and sent to Congress on October 8th, when Adams had begun his preparations to leave for Paris, where Franklin and Jay had for some time been discussing the terms of a peace treaty with the British commissioners. He had very little hope that these negotiations would result in any definite agreement. He knew that two ministers from England and another from Holland were in Paris to make peace, that the Count d'Aranda was said to have powers to treat on the part of Spain. But Franklin never wrote him and Jay had not kept him well informed of the progress of the negotiations. Most of the information had come from Vergennes through La Vauguyon, and the French minister had not much faith in the sincerity of the British commissioners. [105] Adams was thoroughly convinced that Great Britain would not recognize the independence of the United States

[103] September 29, 1782. Wharton, *op. cit.*, Vol. V, p. 785.
[104] Diary. Works, Vol. III, pp. 276. 291.
[105] September 23, 1782. Wharton, *op. cit.*, Vol. V, p. 751.

until beaten to her knees. This was a *sine qua non*, not only to a peace treaty, but to any conversations to be entered into with British emissaries. It was only on the night of October 6th that he had a brief note from Jay, informing him that "Mr. Oswald received yesterday a commission to treat of a peace with *the commissioners of the United States of America.*" [106]

The whole matter suddenly assumed a very different aspect. Adams could not forget that at one time he had been appointed the only plenipotentiary to treat of peace. Jefferson was in America, and Laurens being unwilling to serve, there remained only Jay, Franklin and himself, and every one knew that Doctor Franklin was seventy-six and "infirm, — had the gout and gravel or strangury, and could not sleep." [107] It was necessary for Adams to go. He did not believe, however, that he should make undue haste. He had warned Jay that he had never been "remarkable for a quick traveller", and this time he traveled more leisurely than ever. He left Amsterdam on the seventeenth of October, touring Utrecht, Breda and Antwerp, where he visited the cathedral, looked at the paintings of Rubens, and admired the famous "Assumption." He duly noted that the church was very clean, "no dust on any of the figures." He had a pleasant time in Brussels with Mr. Jennings of Maryland and William Lee, saw Valenciennes and Cambrai, stopped at Chantilly and, from a distance, looked at Mademoiselle de Bourbon, "dressed in beautiful white, her hair uncombed, hanging and flowing about her shoulders", and finally reached Paris "in very good season" on the afternoon of the twenty-sixth, where he again put up at the old Hôtel de Valois, rue de Richelieu. Being in a frivolous city and having to deal with people who attached great importance to appearances, he did not even think of calling at once upon his colleagues, for "the first thing to be done in Paris is always to send for a tailor, a peruke-maker and a shoemaker." Matters of state had to wait until the morrow.

[106] Wharton, *op. cit.*, Vol. V, pp. 778 and 803.
[107] Diary. Works, Vol. III, p. 291.

CHAPTER III

THE CHAMPION OF AMERICAN RIGHTS

WHEN Adams arrived in Paris with "an olive branch in his mouth, in his heart, and in his head",[1] he found the peace negotiations far more advanced than he had been led to believe by the necessarily summary communications from Jay. Not only had Oswald received a commission to treat with the *United States* Commissioners, but terms had been discussed and practically agreed upon. On the whole, these terms were satisfactory, but very unpleasant was the news that Congress had again, and in the most formal way, reminded the commissioners that they were on every occasion to take advice from the French Court and keep Vergennes informed of their negotiations.

There is no doubt that this unusual procedure had been adopted on Vergennes' recommendation. The French minister felt that the peace negotiations would be long and complicated; that he not only would have to protect the interests of France, which were not directly involved, but also have to see to it that no terms were accepted by the Americans which would prove unacceptable to the Spanish Court. No indication has ever been produced that he deliberately intended to injure the interests of the United States or unduly to restrict their possibilities for future development. But the war had been long and costly, and he did not intend to pursue a course ruinous to France, should the American envoys prove obdurate and insist upon terms such as the extension of their territorial right to the Mississippi, or the right to take and cure fish in Newfoundland and Nova Scotia. Vergennes trusted entirely the spirit of conciliation and coöperation of Franklin,

[1] Diary. Works, Vol. III, p. 290.

but he did not believe that either Jay or Adams were equally qualified to engage in a diplomatic battle with the Court of St. James. The French minister, fully conscious of his great responsibility, suspecting the sincerity of Great Britain, and made very uneasy by the behavior of two of the American commissioners, wished to keep the conduct of the negotiations in his own hands.

If his intentions were good, and if there was no French plot to prevent the Americans from obtaining as favorable terms as they could, Vergennes made a serious psychological mistake. America was a small nation, so far as the number of her citizens went; she was a poor nation, fighting her battles on French loans and French gifts, but he counted without the proud spirit of Adams and Jay, both of whom had been deeply hurt in their national, as well as personal pride when told that nothing should be done without the consent of the French minister. Adams offered to resign and requested that another person be appointed in his stead, if such was really the meaning of Congress.[2]

But Congress was far away, and in the meantime negotiations had to be carried on. Adams fully endorsed the independence of Jay, who had taken it upon himself "to act without asking advice, or even communicating with the Count de Vergennes, and this even in opposition to an instruction."[3] Fearing the "cunning" of Franklin, who, Adams thought, would "provoke", would "insinuate", would "intrigue", would "manœuvre" to divide his two colleagues, he delayed for two days his visit to Passy. On this occasion he seized the opportunity to tell the old patriarch of liberty, at once and without reserve, his opinion of the French Court, and of the wisdom and firmness with which Mr. Jay had conducted the negotiations. "The Doctor heard me patiently but said nothing," wrote Adams in his Diary. Two days later, however, in the course of a conference with Oswald, "Dr. Franklin turned to Mr. Jay and said, I am of your opinion, and will go

[2] To Livingston, October 31, 1782. Wharton, "The Revolutionary Diplomatic Correspondence of the United States", Vol. V, p. 839.
[3] October 27, 1782. Diary. Works, Vol. III, p. 300.

on with these gentlemen in the business without consulting this court." [4]

During his first two weeks in Paris, Adams had been so immersed in the discussion and conversations with the British envoys that he had apparently forgotten the existence of Vergennes and had not paid his respects to the French minister. He waited for a direct invitation, transmitted by Franklin, to call on him at Versailles. He should have been pleased with the reception he had at Court, for in the antechamber French noblemen showered him with compliments upon his diplomatic success in Holland. These he carefully reproduced in French; the finishing stroke being, "*Monsieur, vous êtes le Washington de la négociation.*" It was impossible to exceed this! Vergennes himself was no less gracious; he kept Adams for dinner and introduced him to Madame la Comtesse, who gave him her hand with extraordinary condescension; and during the dinner the Count constantly called out to him, "to know what I would eat, and to offer me *petits gâteaux*, claret and Madeira." Never in his life had Adams been treated with "half this respect", and all would have been perfect if Vergennes had not asked his guest how they were getting on with the British. Adams was ready. He could truly answer that they were still divided on the question of the Penobscot, claimed by Massachusetts in virtue of an old grant, and the question of the Tories, whose property had been confiscated and who, according to the British thesis, were to be indemnified for their losses.

This apparently was a purely American matter, in which the French could not possibly be interested; yet the British commissioners knew it was considered a vital question by the Court of St. James, and the American commissioners were both unwilling and powerless to settle it. Their arguments, perfectly sound, but difficult for European diplomats to understand, were, above all, that as the property of the Tories had been confiscated by the different States, Congress had no authority in the matter, and that the Tories, particularly those who had taken refuge in England, would find life so unpleasant in the

[4] Diary. Works, Vol. III, p. 336.

United States that it was much better for them never to come back. This was the first time that in dealing with foreign matters the inability of Congress to influence the States was alleged, but it was to be a precedent often resorted to in difficult circumstances, and one which has always proved unacceptable and incomprehensible to countries with more centralized forms of government.[5]

Vergennes felt that there was in this situation a very serious danger for the success of the negotiations.[6] Through Rayneval he advised the British to yield on the point, or at least to delay its consideration until the conclusion of the definite treaty, and he tried to convince the Americans of the soundness of the British arguments.[7] Whatever were his intentions, he made a serious mistake in attempting to defend the British thesis, arguing that all precedents were in favor of it. Rayneval, who was present, made matters worse by talking about "national honor" and the obligations of the British "to support their adherents." Adams spoke out with great "latitude of expression", to the effect that it was up to Great Britain to indemnify her supporters, and certainly not up to the nation that had suffered almost irretrievable ruin at the hands of these people, who had brought about untold damage both to Great Britain and to America.[8]

Vergennes saw that nothing could move the Americans from the stand they had taken, and a few days later, in the instructions he wrote for Rayneval, who was again crossing the Channel, he clearly indicated that "England is in position to indemnify the Tories." [9] But Adams was not to forget the incident so easily. His suspicions were aroused at once, and he pondered in his mind the reasons which had made the French minister take that strange attitude. He could see but one: to keep up in America the existence of a party of men of mo-

---

[5] See Strachey to the Commissioners, November 5, 1782. Wharton, *op. cit.*, Vol. V, p. 850.
[6] To La Luzerne, November 23, 1782. Doniol, "Histoire de la Participation française", Vol. V, p. 178.
[7] *Ibid*, p. 175.
[8] November 10, 1782. Diary. Works, Vol. III, pp. 304–305.
[9] November 15, 1782. Doniol, *op. cit.*, Vol. V, p. 176.

narchical principles, or men of more ambition than principle, or men corrupted and of no principle, who could therefore be "more easily seduced to this purpose than virtuous Republicans." [10] These two parties would be kept alive in America, a French and an English party; thus would the nation be divided against itself and remain necessarily weak.

Whether or not Vergennes entertained such dark designs, Adams was entitled to his opinion. He was less justifiable, however, in communicating outright his suspicions to "Mr. Whitefoord, the Secretary of Mr. Oswald", who called on him the next day; and he added that the French "might have political wishes, which we were not bound by treaty nor in justice or gratitude to favor, and those we ought to be cautious of." [11] Had he wished to give the British commissioners the impression that there was a complete lack of harmony between the French and the Americans, he would not have acted otherwise. He ended his speech to Whitefoord with a declaration worth noting, for it sums up his views on Europe and his attitude towards the French at that date:

For my own part, I thought America had been long enough involved in the wars of Europe. She had been a foot-ball between contending nations from the beginning, and it was easy to foresee that France and England both would endeavor to involve us in their future wars. I thought it our interest and duty to avoid as much as possible, and to be completely independent, and have nothing to do, but in commerce, with either of them. That my thoughts had been from the beginning constantly employed to arrange all our European connections to this end, and that they would continue to be so employed, and I thought it so important to us, that if my poor labors, my little estate, or (smiling) sizy blood could effect it, it should be done. But I had many fears. [12]

Adams was so pleased with this effusion that he inserted it almost verbatim in the letter he wrote to Livingston on the same day. [13] To do him justice, it must be said that France was

---

[10] To Livingston, November 11, 1782. Wharton, *op. cit.*, Vol. V, p. 877.
[11] November 11, 1782. Diary. Works, Vol. III, p. 308.
[12] Diary. Works, Vol. III, p. 308.
[13] Wharton, *op. cit.*, Vol. V, p. 875.

not the only object of his fears. A few days later, in a conversation with Oswald, he expressed his universal distrust of all foreign nations:

"You are afraid," says Mr. Oswald to-day, "of being made the tools of the powers of Europe." "Indeed I am," says I. "What powers?" said he. "All of them," said I. "It is obvious that all the powers of Europe will be continually manœuvring with us, to work us into their real or imaginary balances of power. They will all wish to make of us a make-weight candle, when they are weighing out their pounds. Indeed, it is not surprising; for we shall very often, if not always, be able to turn the scale. But I think it ought to be our rule not to meddle; and that of all the powers of Europe, not to desire us, or, perhaps, even to permit us, to interfere, if they can help it.[14]

Strachey had left for London on the 5th of November, taking with him a draft including the articles on which the commissioners had so far agreed, but still unsatisfactory and vague on the two main points of contention. Meanwhile the commissioners met with Oswald to go over the treaty once more, to explain the different articles to Laurens, who had just arrived from London, and to thrash out the question of the Tories and the fisheries. Some of their leisure was occupied in writing long letters home. Jay sent Livingston a detailed history of the negotiations,[15] accusing Vergennes of contriving to prevent the westward development of the United States to the Mississippi, and to restrict their fishing rights in Newfoundland and Nova Scotia. His conclusion, after an impressive array of argument, was that the French "are interested in separating us from Great Britain, and on that point we may, I believe, depend upon them; but it is not their interest that we should become a great and formidable people, and therefore they will not help us to become so. It is not their interest that such a treaty should be formed between us and Britain as would produce cordiality and mutual confidence. They will therefore endeavor to plant such seeds of jealousy, discontent, and discord in it as may naturally and perpetually keep our eyes fixed on France for security. This consideration must induce

[14] November 18, 1782. Diary. Works, Vol. III, p. 316.
[15] November 17, 1782. Wharton, *op. cit.*, Vol. VI, pp. 11–49.

them to wish to render Britain formidable in our neighborhood, and to leave us as few resources of wealth and power as possible." [16]

Jay protested that the thought of concluding a separate peace had never entered his mind. "I mean only to say," he added, "that if we lean on her [France's] love of liberty, her affection for America, or her disinterested magnanimity, we shall lean on a broken reed, that will sooner or later pierce our hands, and Geneva as well as Corsica justifies this observation." [17]

Adams' letter was much shorter, but no less emphatic: he protested against the instructions sent by Congress to the commissioners, and pointed out the real reason for the aggressive attitude taken by Jay and himself under the circumstances. It is a true explanation of the methods to which American envoys have so often had to resort for self-protection, the underlying reason for the so-called shirt-sleeve diplomacy. Unable to communicate easily, rapidly and completely with their government, fearful of exceeding their instructions, uncertain of the reception awaiting them upon returning home, the American envoys are in a position of inferiority which they are apt to conceal under a certain brusqueness; they can give ultimata, rather than negotiate. This was keenly felt by Adams, who was just the man to resent such inferiority, and he described it in words that could be affixed to all histories of American foreign policy:

In ordinary cases the principal is so near the deputy as to be able to attend the whole progress of the business, and to be informed of every new fact and every sudden thought. Ambassadors in Europe can send expresses to their courts and give and receive intelligence in a few days with the utmost certainty. In such cases there is no room for mistake, misunderstanding, or surprise, but in our case it is very different. We are at an immense distance. Despatches are liable to foul play and vessels are subject to accidents. New scenes open, the time

[16] Wharton, *op. cit.*, Vol. VI, p. 48. Is it necessary to say that if the French had such a design, nothing of it appears in Vergennes' correspondence? Could he have foreseen the future, including the French Revolution, he might have thought of it, but, in fact, he did not.

[17] *Ibid.*, p. 49.

presses, various nations are in suspense, and necessity forces us to act. What can we do? [18]

On November 25th, Franklin, Jay and Adams met at Mr. Oswald's lodgings with Strachey, who had at last returned from London. On the whole, the American propositions were acceptable to the British Cabinet, with three restrictions, one not important, on the northern boundary; but the questions of the fisheries and the indemnities to be paid the Tories had not made any progress. Franklin, much to the surprise of Adams and Jay, took it upon himself to speak about the Tories, which he did with unaccustomed vehemence, and the memorandum to Oswald drawn up by him on the occasion, recalling the burning of Charlestown, of Falmouth, of Fairfield, of Norfolk, of Esopus, "many hundreds of farmers, with their wives and children, butchered and scalped", lacked nothing in vigor.[19] With the memory of these outrages still fresh and "the wounds still bleeding", it was best for England "to drop all mention of the refugees."

Adams took personal charge of the fisheries. He was convinced that, on the whole, it was bad for the people of Massachusetts to engage in fishing, and consequently in foreign commerce, since salted cod was their principal article of trade with the West Indies. But he had been commissioned to obtain certain definite advantages for New England, not to moralize, and he used all the resources of his legal training to win his point. To Fitzherbert, Oswald, Strachey, and his colleagues, he delivered an oration, when Strachey, as a last concession, had proposed in the treaty that *"right"* of fishing be stricken out, and *"liberty"* of fishing be substituted instead. Adams thereupon "rose up and said":

Gentlemen, is there or can there be a clearer right? In former treaties,—that of Utrecht and that of Paris,—France, and England have claimed the right, and used the word. When God almighty made the banks of Newfoundland, at three hundred leagues distance from

[18] November 18, 1782. Wharton, *op. cit.*, Vol. VI, p. 52. On this subject see also Franklin to Livingston, December 5, 1782. *Ibid.*, p. 110.

[19] November 26, 1782. *Ibid.*, pp. 77–80.

the people of America, and at six hundred leagues distance from those of France and England, did He not give as good a right to the former as to the latter? If Heaven in the creation gave a right, it is ours at least as much as yours. If acceptation, use, possession give a right, we have it as clearly as you. If war, and blood, and treasure give a right, ours is as good as yours.[20]

The British commissioners, fearing to yield more than they had been authorized, yet unwilling to send back to London for instructions and to lay everything before Parliament, finally made a concession, for Mr. Adams had declared that "he would never put his hand to any treaty, if the restraints regarding the three leagues and fifteen leagues were not dispensed with." [21]

On November 29th the American and British commissioners agreed on every article, and Franklin wrote at once to Vergennes, to inform him "that the commissioners of the United States have agreed with Mr. Oswald on the preliminary articles of peace between those States and Great Britain. To-morrow I hope I shall be able to communicate to your excellency a copy of them." [22]

The following day the texts were compared, Laurens suggested the addition of "a stipulation that the British troops should carry off no negroes or other American property", then signatures were exchanged and "all went to Passy to dine with Dr. Franklin." Adams was so elated that he forgot the "preliminary" character of the agreement, and wrote in his Diary that the "treaties were signed, sealed and delivered." [23] It had been clearly specified, however, that these articles should not be considered as a treaty "until terms of peace shall be agreed between Great Britain and France, and his Britannic majesty shall be ready to conclude such treaty accordingly."

As he had promised, on the next day Franklin sent the preliminary articles to Vergennes, omitting, however, to com-

---

[20] November 29, 1782. Diary. Works, Vol. III, pp. 333–334.
[21] Oswald to Townshend, November 30, 1782. Wharton, *op. cit.*, Vol. VI, p. 94.
[22] *Ibid.*, p. 90.
[23] November 30, 1782. Diary. Works, Vol. III, p. 334.

municate a separate article by which it was agreed that if, at the conclusion of the present war, Great Britain "shall recover or be put in possession of West Florida, the line of north boundary between the said Province and the United States shall be a line drawn from the mouth of the river Yazoo, where it unites with the Mississippi, due east to the river Apalachicola." This was certainly secret diplomacy and implied a complete lack of faith in the sincerity of the French Cabinet. Vergennes seems to have been at first both surprised and pleased, on reading the terms accepted by the British Government. He wrote at once to Rayneval, expressing his satisfaction at seeing the English "buy the peace", rather than make it, and grant concessions exceeding all that he should have thought possible.[24]

In his conversation with Franklin, the French minister had indeed suggested that "this abrupt signature of the articles had little in it, which could be agreeable to the King", and he added that it would be very inadvisable to send the news at once to America. The articles were only "provisional and dependent upon the fate of our [the French] negotiations, which was then very uncertain." To hold out this hope of peace to a people tired of war seemed to Vergennes exceedingly dangerous and embarrassing.[25] He was not then aware that the commissioners had already asked a passport for the *General Washington*, bound for Philadelphia.[26] Great was his surprise when, on December 15th, he received a note from Franklin, informing him that the vessel was about to sail and would carry whatever mail the French minister might wish to send to America; the "courier" was to set out the next day at ten o'clock. At the same time, the old philosopher expressed his hope that Vergennes could send "part of the aids" he had applied for, namely, a new loan of six million livres.

This time Vergennes was deeply wounded. He wrote to

[24] December 4, 1782. Doniol, *op. cit.*, Vol. V, p. 188; Wharton, *op. cit.*, Vol. VI, p. 107.

[25] To La Luzerne, December 19, 1782. Wharton, *op. cit.*, Vol. VI, p. 151.

[26] Oswald to Townshend, November 30, 1782. *Ibid.*, p. 95.

Franklin expressing strongly and emphatically his disapproval of the procedure, and entreated him to consider what disastrous effect this premature announcement might have. And he immediately acquainted La Luzerne with the situation, asking him to inform influential members of Congress, without complaining formally, of the American commissioners' strange disregard of their instructions. He concluded with some bitterness: "I accuse no person; I blame no one, not even Doctor Franklin. He has yielded too easily to the bias of his colleagues, who do not pretend to recognize the rules of courtesy in regard to us. All their attentions have been taken up by the English whom they have met in Paris. If we may judge of the future from what has passed here under our eyes, we shall be but poorly paid for all we have done for the United States and for securing to them a national existence." [27]

Vergennes said nothing further, being apparently placated by a letter in which Franklin apologized for having neglected a point of *"bienséance"*, and added, *"The English, I just now learn, flatter themselves they have already divided us.* I hope this little misunderstanding will therefore be kept a secret, and that they will find themselves totally mistaken." [28] A few days later part of the loan requested by Franklin — six million livres, instead of twenty million — was placed at the disposal of the American commissioners. Vergennes even agreed to the departure of the *George Washington,* simply requesting La Luzerne to warn Congress of the true state of the negotiations, so as to prevent "demonstrations which would lead to suspect the existence of a plan of defection" believed by him to be "contrary to the intentions of Congress." [29]

Here the matter would have rested, had not Livingston officially, formally and lengthily laid the whip on the commissioners for having signed the secret article that might "fully justify Spain in making a separate peace without the least regard to our interest"; for having entertained unwarranted suspicions of the French Court, and disregarding the old maxim

[27] December 19, 1782. Wharton, *op. cit.,* Vol. VI, pp. 150–152.
[28] December 17, 1782. *Ibid.,* pp. 143–144.
[29] December 21 and 24, 1782. Doniol, *op. cit.,* Vol. V, pp. 197, 198.

"Honesty is the best policy", which applied "with as much force to States as to individuals." [30]

We have no record of Adams' feelings when he received Livingston's communication. What could he say that he had not already said a few months earlier, when he took his Diary as a confidant of his indignation: "I have been injured, and my country has joined in the injury; it has basely prostituted its own honor by sacrificing mine. . . . Congress surrendered their own sovereignty into the hands of a French minister. Blush! blush! ye guilty records! blush and perish! It is glory to have broken such infamous orders. Infamous, I say, for so they will be to all posterity. How can such a stain be washed out? Can we cast a veil over it and forget?" [31]

There is no reason to magnify unduly this breach of *bienséance*, and something can be said for the action taken by the American commissioners. Nothing in the preliminary articles was directly contrary to French interests; France was expecting so little for herself that no difficulty was to be foreseen in this respect. On the other hand, the French Court was committed by her treaty with Spain to obtain Gibraltar for her rather unsatisfactory ally. Reluctant as Vergennes was to continue the war simply to obtain this for Spain, he thought the king bound by his word. It is a question of little more than academic interest whether the British Court was not encouraged to resist this demand by the attitude of the American commissioners. The fact is that in the final outcome, Spain herself gave up Gibraltar, and in compensation accepted Florida. Adams judged quite properly, "the two Floridas and Minorca are more than a *quantum meruit* for what this power has done", but it was not too high a price to pay to end a war that had become the more odious as it was now purposeless.

As soon as he realized that the preliminaries of peace were going to be signed, Adams cast all reserve to the wind and started on an undignified and personal campaign against Ver-

[30] To the President of Congress, March 18, 1783. Wharton, *op. cit.*, Vol. VI, pp. 313–316; and to the Commissioners, March 25, 1783. *Ibid.*, p. 338. See also "Debates in Congress, March 18, 1783." *Ibid.*, p. 317.

[31] January 18, 1783. Diary. Works, Vol. III, p. 359.

gennes, the French Court, and the house of Bourbon. He felt that it was his "indispensable duty" to communicate the facts "to some English gentleman, who might put their Government upon their guard." As a confidant he selected Vaughan, showed him his instructions, repeated that it was a "fixed principle" with him "to hurt Great Britain no farther than should be necessary to secure our independence, alliance, and other rights." He boasted of having defeated the designs of the French Court and that "no wrestler was ever so completely thrown upon his back as the Count de Vergennes." Finally, he showed his commission to conclude a treaty of commerce with Great Britain. It is no wonder that Vaughan declared, "This was very important information, and entirely new", that "he would write it to the Earl of Shelburne, and his Lordship would make great use of it" without naming Adams.[32]

Not satisfied with a single confidant, Adams repeated to Oswald the next day what he had told Vaughan. Fortunately the negotiations were too far advanced to be stopped by these disclosures; the preliminary articles of peace and armistice were signed on January 22d, at Versailles, in Vergennes' office, and on the day following Fitzherbert "had his first audience of the King and the royal family, and dined, for the first time, with the *Corps diplomatique*." [33]

The war was over, and Adams judged that he had completed his mission. He immediately sent Livingston his resignation as plenipotentiary to the States-General, and asked that some other person be sent at once, so he could "go home in the spring ships." In this Adams was quite sincere: he could not bear the thought that an attack had been made on him by Vergennes, and that Congress had paid undue attention to the accusations of the French minister. It was a disgrace he could not endure. The "wish of his heart" was to return to his wife and children.[34] He wrote to Dana that he did not intend "to decline taking a seat in Congress." "I am grown very ambitious of being a limb of that sovereign. I had rather be master than servant

[32] January 12 and 13, 1783. Diary. Works, Vol. III, pp. 355–357.
[33] *Ibid.*, p. 359.
[34] January 11, 1783. *Ibid.*, p. 355.

on the same principle that men swear at Highgate — never to kiss the maid when they can kiss the mistress." [35]

It would have been better for all concerned if he had been permitted to go home at once. The story of the following months does not make very pleasant reading. Vergennes might be on his back, but Adams was convinced more than ever that France entertained dark designs against the expansion and prosperity of the United States. He realized that his opinions sometimes ran "counter to those generally received", but he had lived long enough and "had experience enough of the conduct of governments and people, nations and courts, to be convinced that gratitude, friendship, unsuspecting confidence, and all the most amiable passions in human nature, are the most dangerous guides in politics." [36]

His attitude was not altogether unjustifiable. For Great Britain he felt more sympathy than he was willing to admit, and he sincerely believed it desirable for the United States to effect, as soon as possible, a complete reconciliation with the mother country. This had become the more imperative as between the United States and the British possessions in Canada there would be a large and practically unprotected frontier. The United States could not fully recover or fully develop unless they were assured of the friendship of their powerful neighbor. On the other hand, he was no less firmly convinced that the peace just signed between France and Great Britain was at best a temporary affair. Upon hearing the terms of the peace treaty, an abbé had exclaimed, *"Voilà la semence d'une autre guerre"*, and into such a war America must not be dragged.[37]

According to Adams, the French plot was quite transparent: to sow seeds of discord between the United States and Great Britain and, at the same time, to keep America weak enough to need the protection of France in case of difficulties with England. If such a policy were successfully carried out, and if the French put through their "wing-clipping" schemes, the United

[35] May 1, 1783. Wharton, *op. cit.*, Vol. VI, p. 399.
[36] To Livingston, January 23, 1783. *Ibid.*, p. 227.
[37] Diary. Works, Vol. III, p. 344.

States would remain dependent on the French alliance and could be used as a football in the complicated game of European politics.

To defeat the "sinister motives" attributed to Vergennes, it was only necessary to make Great Britain realize that her true interest lay in fostering the development of the United States, for she had nothing to fear from a powerful and really independent nation. Adams was decidedly of the opinion that two steps had to be taken at once in order to further such a policy: first, to appoint a plenipotentiary to the Court of St. James; then, to conclude a good treaty of commerce, eliminating all causes of friction between the two nations. Such a minister must, to be sure, be endowed with rare qualities: in the first place:

> . . . he should have an education in classical learning and in the knowledge of general history, ancient and modern, and particularly the history of France, England, Holland, and America. He should be well versed in the principles of ethics, of the law of nature and nations, of legislation and government, of the civil Roman law, of the laws of England and the United States, of the public law of Europe, and in the letters, memoirs, and histories of those great men who have heretofore shone in the diplomatic order and conducted the affairs of nations and the world. He should be of an age to possess a maturity of judgment, arising from experience in business. He should be active, attentive, and industrious, and, above all, he should possess an upright heart and an independent spirit, and should be one who decidedly makes the interest of his country, not the policy of any other nation nor his own private ambition or interest, or those of his family, friends, and connexions, the rule of his conduct.[38]

Thus was Franklin clearly ruled out, since his colleagues had accused him of unduly favoring his natural son, William Temple Franklin. Of the possible candidates answering all these qualifications, only two remained: John Jay and John Adams. With real or feigned modesty, Adams declared that should he be permitted to vote on the matter, he would not hesitate to designate his colleague. A letter from Jay to Livingston, written a few weeks later, casts some doubt, however,

[38] To Livingston, February 5, 1783. Wharton, *op. cit.*, Vol. VI, pp. 245–246.

upon Adams' complete lack of ambition in this respect: "I view the expectations of Mr. Adams on that head as founded in equity and reason and . . . I will not by any means stand in his way. . . . I do therefore in the most unequivocal manner decline and refuse to be a competitor with that faithful servant of the public for the place in question." [39]

In fact from that time on, Adams considered himself the proper man for the post and acted accordingly. It is unfortunate that his plans for a reconciliation of the two countries took the form of violent attacks on France. He appointed himself protector of Holland and urged Hartley to form an alliance with that country in order to prevent "annexation" of the Dutch provinces to France.[40] He saw everywhere schemers who talked "of discouraging the people of the United States and encouraging those of Canada and Nova Scotia in such manner as to increase the population of those two provinces even by migrations from the United States." [41] He fretted over the long delays and protracted negotiations before the final exchange of signatures. He felt he was useless in Europe; that Jay and himself were "in a state of annihilation." [42] He went to Holland for a short visit "to assist the loan, and to turn the speculations of the Dutch merchants, capitalists, and statesmen towards America." [43]

There, perhaps, he could be of some use, but in France he could no longer deal with Vergennes and his associates. "In plain English," he wrote to Livingston, "the Comte de Vergennes has no conception of the right way of negotiating with any free people or with any assembly, aristocratical or democratical. He can not enter into the motives which govern them; he never penetrates their real system, and never appears to comprehend their constitution. With empires, and monarchs, and their ministers of state, he negotiates aptly enough." [44]

Of these opinions, according to Franklin as well as from

[39] May 30, 1783. Wharton, *op. cit.*, Vol. VI, p. 457.
[40] May 20, 1783. Diary. Works, Vol. III, p. 369.
[41] To Livingston, June 23, 1783. Wharton, *op. cit.*, Vol. VI, p. 501.
[42] To Livingston, July 18, 1783. *Ibid.*, p. 562.
[43] *Ibid.*
[44] To Livingston, July 31, 1783. *Ibid.*, p. 624.

admission contained in his own Diary, Adams made no secret. He expressed them "publicly, sometimes in the presence of the English ministers. . . . I am persuaded, however," continued the old philosopher, "that he means well for his country, is always an honest man, often a wise one, but sometimes and in some things absolutely out of his senses." [45]

The prospect of returning to France and living there in absolute idleness was very disagreeable to Adams. He had no hope that the treaty would ever be concluded, for now the British themselves, expecting new developments in the north, seemed to have decided to postpone indefinitely the exchange of signatures. Then quite unexpectedly, in the middle of August, came the news that the British commissioners were ready to sign; but they maintained that no signatures were needed in the case of America. They were unwilling to admit the diplomatic fiction that peace had been procured as a result of the mediation of Russia and Austria, whose representatives were to sign the treaties at Versailles. The peace with America was to be considered entirely a separate matter, their doctrine being that "the provisional treaty was to be, and will be of itself, a definite treaty the instant the definitive treaty is signed with France." Vergennes was very reluctant to accept this strange theory and replied: "We must finish all together. [*Il faut que nous finissions tous ensemble.*]" The American commissioners were even more loath to submit to this unusual procedure, for they desired "the solemnities and forms of a definitive treaty." [46]

Both the French and the Americans yielded, and it was finally agreed that signatures would be exchanged between Hartley and the American commissioners in Paris, at Hartley's lodgings, and that upon due notification, the plenipotentiaries at Versailles would proceed with the accustomed ceremonial, to the signature of the treaties of peace between Great Britain, Spain, and France, in the absence of a representative of America.

Once more Adams could look with satisfaction to work well done. "The third of September," he wrote Gerry, "will be more remarkable for the signature of the definitive treaties

[45] To Livingston, July 22, 1783. Wharton, *op. cit.*, Vol. VI, p. 582.
[46] To Gerry, August 15, 1783. *Ibid.*, p. 651.

than for the battle of Naseby or Worcester, or the death of Oliver Cromwell." But he had many misgivings. The first object had been attained; it remained, however, "to maintain and strengthen the Confederation, . . . to purge the minds of our people of their fears, their diffidence of themselves, and admiration of strangers", and, above all, "to defend ourselves against the wiles of Europe." [47] He still avowed that his most earnest wish was to go home, but in his heart he hoped that some way would be found to keep him in Europe. A few days after the conclusion of the treaty, news arrived that, with Franklin and Jay, he had been commissioned to negotiate a treaty of commerce with Great Britain. [48]

Having a definite task to accomplish, he was himself again. He accepted the new commission without hesitation; he could "attend to this business", and at the same time bargain for a new loan with Holland; he could even secure treaties with "Vienna, Petersburgh, Copenhagen, and Lisbon", if for reasons of economy Congress should refuse to send ministers to so many countries. Meanwhile, and although all the business was to be transacted in Paris, he could not refrain from going to London in a strictly personal capacity. "We are told," he wrote to Livingston, "that such a visit would have a good effect at court and with the nation; at least it seems clear it would do no harm." [49]

As he was about to set off on his journey, Adams underwent a complete collapse. Much as he enjoyed the official receptions, he had remained an outdoors man. For several months he had been shut in, going from his hotel to that of the British commissioners, reading, studying, writing lengthy reports, engaging in fierce discussion; the grand Hôtel du Roi, Place du Carousel, where he had apartments, "was a sort of thoroughfare" and carriages passing by his windows on the old cobblestones made a "constant roar, like incessant rolls of thunder." He was advised by his physician to remove to Auteuil, far from the tainted atmosphere of Paris, and there he discovered

---

[47] To Gerry, September 3, 1783. Wharton, op. cit., Vol. VI, p. 669.
[48] The commission was dated May 1, 1783. Ibid., p. 681.
[49] September 8, 1783. Ibid., pp. 683–684.

the Bois de Boulogne. He took long walks in the wooded paths, explored every corner of the town, visited Boileau's house and, from the window of his chamber, enjoyed the panorama unfolding before his eyes, "the view of the village of Issy, of the castle royal of Meudon, of the palace of Bellevue, of the castle of the Duke of Orleans at St. Cloud, and of Mont Calvaire." [50]

Having somewhat recovered, he left for England with his son John, and his servant, Levêque. Traveling leisurely, he arrived in London October twenty-sixth, bringing with him a cordial message from Franklin to Hartley:

> What would you think of a proposition, if I should make it, of a compact between England, France and America? America would be as happy as the Sabine girls if she could be the means of uniting in perpetual peace her father and her husband. What repeated follies are those repeated wars! [51]

On the whole, however, the English journey was very disappointing. Adams had no chance to offer the olive branch to the English ministers. He was introduced by Hartley to the Duke of Portland, Fox and Burke, and by all received ceremoniously. Nothing of importance was said, and the treaty of commerce was not even alluded to; there was nothing left for him to do except to enjoy the sights as any ordinary tourist. He received permission to go through Buckingham House and took great pleasure in the king's library. He visited "Mr. Wedgwood's manufactory" of china, Westminster Abbey, St. Paul's, the Exchange; he went to Windsor and finally was sent to Bath by his physician. The climate was abominable, the ordinary people enjoyable enough, but the gentry cold and distant.

Adams was not a man to waste much time in sight-seeing; he quickly realized that he could achieve even less in London than in Paris. Fortunately there was a place in Europe where he had no competition to fear, no colleagues to placate, where he alone represented as plenipotentiary the young and ambitious United States. Early in January he left London and, after a rough

[50] Diary. Works, Vol. III, p. 383.
[51] October 16, 1783. Wharton, op. cit., Vol. VI, p. 711.

crossing that exhausted him physically, he arrived at Amsterdam.

He entertained no illusions on the prospect of procuring a new loan from the Dutch bankers. Van Berckel and Visscher had frankly told him that "there was no hope of obtaining the least assistance from the regency", and nothing could be done until Congress agreed on a method of repayment for the sums already obtained. In the words of Franklin, "the foundation of credit abroad must be laid at home." [52] However, he unexpectedly found pleasant occupation in discussing the terms of a treaty of commerce with "the Baron de Thulemeier, Envoy Extraordinary to their High Mightiness from the King of Prussia." It was particularly gratifying to Adams that the king had chosen to treat through him, instead of making overtures to Franklin and Jay in Paris, for "it is not every ambassador, however high his rank, or numerous his titles, or magnificent his appointments, who arrives at the honor of concluding any treaty." [53]

The letters written during the early months of 1784 are singularly short and few. No longer did Adams indulge in long dissertations, in portraits, political considerations relevant or irrelevant. He had preoccupations of a very different order. For almost five years now he had been separated from his family, and for almost five years he could have repeated with his dear Portia: "How lonely are my days! How solitary are my nights!" Many times Mrs. Adams had planned to join him in Europe; many times, in a singularly frank manner, she had confessed her "heartache", and repeated an old Scotch song:

> His very foot has music in't,
> As he comes up the stairs.

In the fall of 1784 it had been decided that, come what may, Mrs. Adams would not longer delay her departure for Europe, but it was the spring of the following year before she finally closed her house in Boston and took passage on the *Active*.

Any day now at The Hague, Adams was expecting news of

[52] February 10 and 11, 1784. Works, Vol. VIII, pp. 178, 179.
[53] To the President of Congress, June 7, 1784. *Ibid.*, p. 201.

her arrival in England. He had sent John Quincy to London to welcome his mother, but after a month the young man had returned without news. It was not until the end of July, 1785, that he heard that Mrs. Adams and his daughter Abigail, now a young woman, had safely reached London. The family was not to meet at once, however, Mrs. Adams remained for several weeks in England, then, although her husband was loath again to undertake the crossing, he changed his plans and the reunion took place at the Adelphi Hotel, in London. By this time Adams had heard from Franklin of the extent of his new commission. "You will see that a good deal of business is cut out for us, — treaties to be made with, I think, twenty powers in two years, — so that we are not likely to eat the bread of idleness."[54] Such, indeed, was the purport of the "Instructions to the Ministers Plenipotentiary appointed to negotiate treaties of Commerce with European Nations", drawn up by Jefferson, and adopted by Congress on the 7th of May. Jefferson himself had been appointed "in conjunction with Mr. John Adams and Dr. Franklin" to negotiate such treaties, and was hourly expected. Much less welcome was the news that Congress had seen fit to reduce the allowance granted to plenipotentiaries; "plain beef and pudding", if not "salt pork and pumpkin", would have to do for the future.

Adams could no longer think of settling down at The Hague, so on August 8th the whole family started from the Adelphi Hotel in a "wretchedly equipped" coach, sailed from Deal, and landed the next day in France.[55] He had fallen in love with Auteuil, and particularly with the Bois de Boulogne, which he called his park. He could live no more in the mephitic atmosphere of Paris, so he rented at a bargain the country house — "the folly" — of Count Rouault. It was not so pleasant as the Boston house, or even Braintree: red-tiled floors, which Mrs. Adams abhorred, stairs dirty as "a cow-yard", no furniture worth mentioning, everything had to be bought and cost dearly, a small army of parasitic, lazy and insolent servants, the

[54] Franklin to Adams, August 6, 1784. Works, Vol. VIII, p. 208.
[55] "Journal and Correspondence of Miss Adams [Abigail Adams Smith]." Edited by her daughter. New York (1841). Pp. 7–8.

maître d'hôtel, whose business it was "to purchase articles in the family, and oversee that nobody cheats but himself", the *valet de chambre,* the *femme de chambre,* the *coiffeuse,* — such was the dismal picture painted by the thrifty New England housewife in a mansion provided with every luxury and no comfort.[56]

Adams was far less critical; he had become accustomed to French ways and, on the whole, thought himself "better off than even Dr. Franklin . . . These hills of Auteuil, Passy, Chaillot, Meudon, Bellevue, St. Cloud, and even Mont Marte and Mont Calvaire, although they command the prospect of Paris and its neighborhood, that is, of every thing that is great, rich and proud, are not in my eyes to be compared to the hills of Penn and Neponset, either in the grandeur or the beauty of the prospects." [57] Nothing could make him forget his native hills, but while thinking of them he had to admit that the scene before his eyes was not entirely without charm.

In a general way, the following months constituted for the family a period of rest and comparative happiness. Adams still had worries — he was never without them — but he no longer had great responsibilities. He was harassed by financial problems and, first of all, personal problems, for on Jefferson's proposition, the allowance to ministers had been cut down by one fifth, and the Auteuil establishment cost much more than either Adams or Mrs. Adams had expected. Money was nowhere in sight, and there was no hope that even Doctor Franklin could obtain relief from the French Court. To all Adams' entreaties, the Dutch bankers answered that no further loans could be granted until Congress ratified the previous loan and took steps to meet the interest on it.[58] Of all the commercial treaties to be concluded, only two seemed likely to materialize within a reasonable time: one with Prussia, full of "platonic philosophy" which was to be a lesson to mankind,[59] and the other with Sweden. Negotiations might have been en-

---

[56] "Letters of Mrs. Adams", Boston, 1841, Vol. II, pp. 45–53.
[57] To James Warren, August 27, 1784. Works, Vol. IX, p. 525.
[58] To Jay, December 15, 1784. Works, Vol. VIII, p. 219.
[59] To Thulemeier, February 13, 1785. *Ibid.,* p. 225.

tered into with the Emperor of Morocco and the Barbary powers threatening American commerce in the Mediterranean, but, contrary to Jefferson's emphatic opinion, the only manner to deal with the "pirates" was to make them presents, and the commissioners had neither money nor authority to offer or promise anything.[60]

More than ever, Adams was convinced that "sending a minister to England" was "the corner stone of the true American system of politics in England." His plan was a very simple one: "Let us preserve the friendship of France, Holland, and Spain, if we can, and in case of a war between France and England, let us preserve our neutrality if possible." All his reasoning, he admitted, rested on the assumption that the United States were "independent of France, in point of moral and political obligation." [61]

During his trip to England, Adams had bought many books on government, good editions of the classics; in France he completed his library and gathered a collection of works not as numerous, but much more homogeneous than Jefferson's. Many hours were spent in M. Rouault's "folly", taking notes on the ancient and modern historians, culling from them all indications that might prove useful in establishing a new form of government in America. The result of this work and leisurely meditation was to appear later in his "Defence of the American Constitutions."

It had been decided that John Quincy, who had seen much of the world, but whose formal education had been necessarily neglected, should go back to America at the first opportunity, in order to register at Harvard. His father being a born schoolmaster, and also wishing to have Quincy make as good an impression as possible at the old college, decided to go over the whole program with him. Many evenings were thus passed with the young man, reading Roman and English history, translating Virgil, Suetonius, Sallust, Tacitus, a great part of Horace, some of Ovid, Cæsar, and Tully's orations. In Greek they took up "morals in Aristotle's Poetics, in Plutarch's Lives, and

[60] To Jay, December 15, 1784. Works, Vol. VIII, p. 217.
[61] To Jay, April 13, 1785. *Ibid.*, pp. 233–236.

Lucian's Dialogues", as well as several books in Homer's Iliad. The father even "attempted a sublime flight", and after the books of Euclid in Latin, plane trigonometry, algebra and conic sections, endeavored to give him "some idea of the differential method of calculation of the Marquis de L'Hôpital, and the method of fluxions and infinite series of Sir Isaac Newton." [62]

In the meantime, Adams found life in Paris very agreeable, and he had nothing but his "inutility" to disgust him "with a residence here." Mrs. Adams was becoming reconciled to French ways. Mme. Helvétius, of whom she drew an unforgettable portrait, had deeply shocked her at first. The old lady with her frizzled hair, her small straw hat with a dirty gauze half-handkerchief around it, a black gauze scarf thrown over her shoulders, her habit of giving Franklin double kisses, and of throwing her arm around the back of Adams' chair, had stirred in her an amusing puritanical indignation. [63] No less shocking was the opera: "girls, clothed in the thinnest silk and gauze, with their petticoats short, springing two feet from the floor, poising themselves in the air, with their feet flying, and as perfectly showing their garters and drawers as though no petticoats had been worn", was a sight altogether new to her. [64] In Paris she loathed, or affected to loathe, everything — the muddy streets, the dark, dirty, musty churches with their confessionals brought into her mind very uncharitable assumptions. She protested against the slavish conformity to the *mode de Paris*, against the French Sundays, when everything was "jollity, and mirth, and recreation." But of Paris she really saw very little, for French etiquette did not require the wives of ministers to be presented at Court, and Mrs. Adams, chiefly for economic reasons, availed herself of the privilege of staying away. Like the Roman matron of old, this New England housewife spent most of her time giving tasks to the servants, planning and saving for the necessary entertainments they had to offer. Her French was not improving, and her range of ac-

---

[62] To Benjamin Waterhouse, April 24, 1785. Works, Vol. IX, pp. 530–531.
[63] "Letters of Mrs. Adams", Vol. II, p. 55.
[64] February 20, 1785. *Ibid.*, p. 82.

quaintance was necessarily limited. Madame de Lafayette was the only French woman of whom she really approved, and she saw with pleasure Adams' friends, the abbés Mably, Chalut and Arnoux, Mr. and Mrs. Grant, and particularly Mr. Jefferson, the tall, lanky Virginian clad all in black, courteous and reserved, who had become her husband's colleague in Paris. But the days were desperately long, while Adams tramped in the Bois de Boulogne for his health, or went to Paris, and Quincy and Abby ran around the old city with the eagerness of youth. During those afternoons of Parisian winter, she had no company other than "a little bird" she had bought, and to which she felt more attached than to any object out of her own family, "animate or inanimate." [65] Her daughter enjoyed much more the months in Paris. With Quincy she went about town, visiting Notre-Dame, the foundlings' hospital, and the picture galleries, going to the opera, the Italian comedy, and the Comédie Française. The churches, with their magnificent ceremonial, offered her endless entertainment, but she was so "grave", according to Madame de Lafayette, that she only reluctantly yielded to the attractions of life in Paris, preferring rather to be instructed than amused.

Thus the Adams family passed the winter in a rather melancholy fashion. It was a great joy to be reunited, but their thoughts went constantly back to Braintree, to the friends they had left in America; "Mr. Adams in his easy-chair at one side of the table, reading Plato's Laws, Mrs. Adams at the other, reading Mr. St. John's [Crèvecœur] Letters; Abby, sitting at the left hand, in a low chair, in a pensive posture." This was how most of the envoy's evenings were spent at Auteuil, unless Quincy brought from Paris a package of letters from home; then the scene was such "as poets and painters wisely draw a veil over", and for a few hours they could think themselves transported to their native land.

And yet, unknown to them, the irresistible charm of Paris was working on the homesick family. The 5th of May, 1785, Adams heard great news: Congress had appointed him "to represent the United States of America at the Court of Great

[65] "Letters of Mrs. Adams", Vol. II, p. 93.

Britain", and Jay had sent him his "commission, instructions and letters of credence." There was no time to be lost in executing the instructions of Congress, and it was desired that Adams should be in London for the birthday of the king, at the beginning of June. Only when confronted with this sudden departure did the entire family realize the hold France had taken on them. Mrs. Adams had to abandon her "delightful and blooming garden"; the fishpond had just been put in order, the trees were in blossom — where could they find again such a charming place in the midst of a city? Quincy was to go back to America, and in London it was very doubtful that they would find such a good friend as Mr. Jefferson, "one of the choice ones of the earth." Even Mr. Adams had to admit that he was quitting "the situation in Europe the most to my taste and the most for my health, for one that will probably be agreeable to neither." This was as near as the New Englander could come to the famous "Give me my country . . . then France", but the sentiment was almost the same. From a note in his Diary we may even suspect that he would have preferred to be accredited to Versailles rather than to the Court of St. James, for when he paid his last call on Vergennes, he could not help expressing the thought that he merited "compassion more than felicitation", "Because, as you know, it is a species of degradation in the eyes of Europe, after having been accredited to the King of France, to be sent to any other Court." [66]

Young Abby did not conceal her regret "in the prospect of leaving France"; in spite of puritanical prejudices, she had become really attached to the good old abbés Chalut and Arnoux; "they are two such good old men that one feels for them the respect, veneration, and esteem, that we should for a relation." [67]

In a letter written to Jefferson from London, a few days after their arrival, Mrs. Adams spoke for the whole family: "I think I have somewhere met with the observation that nobody ever leaves Paris but with a degree of tristeness." The departure from Auteuil had been pathetic, with the servants all

[66] May 3, 1785. Diary. Works, Vol. III, p. 391.
[67] "Journal of Miss Adams", p. 73.

in tears, surrounding the carriage, and the little bird threatening to flutter itself to death in its cage, so that she had to leave the poor thing with her Parisian chambermaid.[68]

The Adams family were not given to an external show of their feelings, but as they left Auteuil they sincerely regretted a few dear friends, the quiet evenings devoted to study and reading, perhaps even some of the French people, so different in their customs, but so courteous and attentive, and, as they took their way to England, they "journeyed slowly and sometimes silently."

[68] To Jefferson, June 6, 1785. Jefferson MSS., Library of Congress.

CHAPTER IV

A NEW WORLD ARISTOCRAT IN ENGLAND

THE presentation of the Adams family to the Court of St. James was a very formal affair. Fond as the French were of court etiquette, they had been willing to make endless allowances in favor of the American ministers. Franklin had established a precedent, and the most sophisticated courtiers had marveled at the republican simplicity of the old philosopher. In England it was to be different. In Paris the Duke of Dorset had already coached John Adams and informed him of the exact protocol: he was to call first on Lord Carmarthen, Minister of Foreign Affairs, who would introduce him later to His Majesty; but he would do business with Mr. Pitt, the Prime Minister.[1] Mrs. and Miss Adams were to be presented and as dresses brought from Paris were out of the question, they had to go to the "mantuamaker" of the Court for dresses that could not be of use "anywhere else", a fact which the thrifty "Ambassadress" deplored at length in letters to her sister.[2]

The interview with the king was not such an ordeal as Adams had feared. He delivered his compliments in a very creditable manner and His Majesty, whose position was, to say the least, embarrassing, answered with some tremor and visible agitation that he had been "the last to consent to the separation", but that he would be the first "to meet the friendship of the United States as an independent power." Both of them were greatly affected, and the king rather undiplomatically referred to the fact that Adams was thought "not the most attached of all his countrymen to the manners of France" — to which the American envoy, with true republicanism, answered that he had no

[1] Diary. Works, Vol. III, p. 392.
[2] "Letters of Mrs. Adams", Vol. II, p. 100.

attachment except to his own country, thus ignoring the allusion just made by the king to "the circumstances of language, religion and blood", which united Great Britain and America.[3]

The presentation of Mrs. Adams and her daughter was a much more formal affair. His Majesty was gracious enough, and saluted Mrs. Adams on the left cheek, but the queen was evidently embarrassed, and the ambassadress had "disagreeable feelings too." On the whole, it was a most painful ordeal, and not even a good show, as the ladies of the Court were in general, "very plain, ill-shaped, and ugly." [4]

Nevertheless, it was important, for it counteracted in some way the unpleasant attacks of the British papers, and particularly of the *Public Advertiser*, which had published in honor of Adams this singular welcome:

An Ambassador from America! Good heavens what a sound! — The Gazette surely never announced anything so extraordinary before, nor once on a day so little expected. This will be such a phenomenon in the Corps Diplomatique that 'tis hard to say which can excite indignation most, the insolence of those who appoint the Character, or the meanness of those who receive it. Such a thing could never have happened in any former Administration, not even that of Lord North. It was reserved like some other humiliating circumstances to take place

Sub Jove, sed Jove nondum
Barbato.[5]

Even in those early days England had a "Thunderer", and no pains were spared to make the new minister feel that he was decidedly unwelcome, at least to a certain party.

Foreign ministers, secretaries of embassies, as well as some English earls and lords called on Adams, and were pleasant enough. But neither he nor Mrs. Adams was to be satisfied with the appearances, and the whole atmosphere decidedly lacked cordiality. "Whilst the coals are coverd the blaize will not burst," she wrote to Jefferson, "but the first wind which

[3] To Jay, June 2, and 10, 1785. Works, Vol. VIII, pp. 255, 265.

[4] "Letters of Mrs. Adams", Vol. II, p. 104.

[5] Mrs. Adams to Jefferson, June 6, 1785. Jefferson Papers, Library of Congress.

blows them into action will, I expect envelop all in flames. If the actors pass the ordeal without being burnt they may be considered in future of the Asbestos kind." [6]

London at first had proved to be much more unpleasant than Paris. The old Adelphi Hotel was full, and the Adams family had to take lodgings at the Bath Hotel, paying for four rooms a third more than for the whole house at Auteuil. Adams missed his "fine walks and pure air" of the Bois de Boulogne. To Jefferson, who during the years in England was to become the confidant of the family, he wrote early in June, "The smoke and damp of this city is ominous to me. London boasts of its trottoir, but there is a space between it and the houses through which all the air from the kitchens, cellars, stables and servants' appartments ascends into the street and pours directly on the passenger on foot. Such whiffs and puffs assault you every few steps as are enough to breed the plague if they do not suffocate you on the spot." [7]

Soon, however, a commodious house was found in Grosvenor Square, at a short distance from Hyde Park, so similar to Boston Common, only much larger and more beautiful, and the family prepared to settle down. Much to their dismay, they discovered that everything was even more expensive than in Paris. Tea and coffee were almost prohibitive in price, owing to the heavy duty upon them; clothes and silk, and even such feminine articles as corsets or silk stockings had to be procured from Paris through the patient and kind assistance of Mr. Jefferson. Adams fretted not unreasonably when he discovered that he could not bring duty free into England the fine store of Madeira, port and claret he had laid in at The Hague and Paris, and had to be satisfied with ale. Fortunately there was very little entertainment to offer, and after the duty calls had been paid and returned, the American family was practically ignored by the British officials. In October, Mrs. Adams had had only one feminine caller, a very tactless person who had assumed that Mrs. Adams undoubtedly preferred England to America, and had conclusively demonstrated to Miss Adams

[6] Jefferson Papers, Library of Congress.
[7] June 7, 1785. *Ibid.*

that "the culture" was carried to "a much greater degree of perfection here than in America." [8]

On arriving in London, John Adams had the great pleasure of finding already on the spot the secretary of the new American legation, Colonel William Stephens Smith, of New York, former aide to Washington and General Sullivan, "one of the most gallant and skillful officers of the Revolution." The brilliant colonel was not perhaps all that could be desired as a secretary and was somewhat lacking in diplomatic reserve, but he was fond of social life, a wit of a kind, who soon attracted Miss Adams' attention, and shortly was begun between the two young people a romance culminating a year later in their marriage.[9] But Adams had not accepted the London post for the honor of it, and simply because it was "a mark", as Louis XVI had kindly told him. He sincerely believed that his mission was the most important that could be intrusted to any American abroad. Doctor Franklin, quite an invalid now, was due to go back to America at any time, to become God only knew what, President of Congress, or perhaps even more. Jay had returned to New York and had been appointed Secretary of Foreign Affairs. Dana had left Russia. America was represented abroad by only two men, Mr. Jefferson in Paris, a most congenial soul, a pure American and a virtuous man, and Mr. Adams in England. The fact that Paris remained the center of diplomatic interest gave Jefferson some precedence over Adams, but the modest and wise Virginian had been careful to emphasize Mr. Adams' seniority on the point of age, his greater experience of foreign affairs, and had always shown due deference to the sensitive New Englander. For the first time since he had arrived in Europe, Adams felt that he was placed on his own responsibility and could show his mettle and capacity.

It is more than likely that he had come to London with great expectations. Both Oswald and Strachey in Paris had manifested their interest in a *rapprochement* between the

---

[8] "Journal of Miss Adams", p. 79.

[9] On W. Smith see "Colonel William Smith and Lady", by Katherine Metcalf Root (Boston), 1929.

United States and Great Britain and, in John Adams' opinion, it was clearly the best policy for the Court of St. James to strengthen America and make her position so secure that she would not have to lean on a French alliance. He had relented somewhat in his hostility to Vergennes and the Court of Versailles, and had no intention, secret or avowed, to be disloyal to the old treaty; but he remained convinced that France would not exert herself to avoid friction between the recent enemies, while the evident interest of the United States was to establish peaceable and, if possible, amicable relations with their northern neighbor.

It was a perfectly logical thesis, one that might have resulted in great benefit to both countries, if it had proved acceptable to Great Britain. Unfortunately Adams arrived in London at a time when "the public pulse was beating high against America", and there was "too much reason to believe that, if this nation had another hundred millions to spend, they would soon force the ministry into a war against us." [10] After making overtures which were received politely and coolly, Adams realized that he could entertain no expectation to see the "proposed treaty soon agreed", and he had to turn his activity into other channels. [11]

In appointing him Minister to the Court of St. James, Congress had not so much the intention to promote harmony between the two nations as to protect American interests, and to obtain redress for wrongs committed by the British after the conclusion of the peace treaty. By the instructions sent to him with his commission, Adams had been invited to insist "that the United States be put without further delay in possession of all the posts and territories . . . now held by British garrisons"; to remonstrate "against the infraction of the treaty of peace by the exportation of negroes and other American property"; to represent the tendency of the British restrictions on American trade to incapacitate American merchants; finally to "represent in strong terms the losses which many of our and also of their merchants will sustain, if the former be unseason-

[10] To Jay, July 19, 1785. Works, Vol. VIII, p. 282.
[11] Ibid., p. 289.

ably and immoderately pressed for the payment of debts contracted before the war." [12]

Adams had presented his protests with great gusto during an
early interview with the Marquis of Carmarthen, and followed
his oral representations with several written communications.[13]
For a few weeks he entertained the fond illusion that the
British would see the light and would not only live up to the
terms of the treaty but adopt "more liberal principles" towards
the United States. The day after he had written in such an
optimistic vein to Jefferson,[14] he had his first conference with
Pitt and all his hopes were destroyed at once. The minister
was willing enough to return the negro slaves that had been
captured and taken away by the British troops; he admitted
that some terms of the armistice treaty had been misconstrued
and some American ships illegally seized.

When Pitt came to the evacuation of the forts still held by
the British troops, his attitude suddenly changed. Granting
that Great Britain had not respected some specifications of the
treaty, it was no less true that several American legislatures
had "interposed impediments to the recovery of debts"; that
contrary to the opinion maintained by some American lawyers,
"wars never interrupted the interest nor principal of debts, and
that he did not see a difference between this war and any other,
and the lawyers here made none." On this point, in spite of
Adams' very specious argumentation, a deadlock was soon
reached, and although Pitt never ceased smiling through the
conversation, when Adams left him he was convinced that the
British would never evacuate the forts willingly and that they
would put every possible obstacle in the way of American commerce with the West Indies.[15]

When he wrote again to Jefferson he had almost given up
all plans for a treaty of commerce: "We must not, my Friend,
be the bubbles of our own liberal sentiments. If we cannot
obtain reciprocal liberality, we must adopt reciprocal prohibi-

[12] "Secret Journals of Congress", March 7, 1785. Vol. III, p. 535.
[13] June 17, July 14, 27 and 29, 1785. Works. Vol. VIII, pp. 268, 276,
284, 286.
[14] August 23, 1785. Jefferson Papers, Library of Congress.
[15] To Jay, August 25, 1785. Works, Vol. VIII, p. 302.

tions, exclusions, monopolies, and imposts. Our offers have been fair, more than fair. If they are rejected, we must not be the dupes." [16]

Curiously enough, Adams represented himself quite sincerely as an apostle of free trade. He could not applaud too much the *arrêt* of the 10th of July, in which the King of France had declared that "nothing could appear more desirable, or suitable to his own principles, than a general liberty which, freeing from all kinds of fetters the circulation of all productions and goods of different countries, would make all nations, as it were, but one, in point of trade." This was the doctrine of the United States as well as of the physiocrats, but if Great Britain refused to play the game, the only possible policy was to retaliate, to exclude from the United States "those foreign goods which would be hurtful to the United States and their manufactories, make the balance of trade to be against them, or annihilate or diminish their shipping or mariners." [17]

To the Marquis of Carmarthen he delivered a vehement oration; he showed how the commercial bond between France and the United States would be strengthened by the attitude of Great Britain, that it would result in a final alienation between England and America; "it would be a deeper stain, a blacker blot upon his administration, than the independence of the United States had been upon that of Lord North." [18]

To this the Marquis refused to give any positive answer; the members of the cabinet had gone away, nothing could be decided for several weeks, and Adams left with the correct impression that the conversation had been useless and the "reciprocity all on one side."

From that time on, Adams was convinced that this policy of obstruction would soon cause the ruin of England; the people were discouraged and dispirited, patriotism was no more. Pitt was "but a tool and an ostensible pageant, a nose of tender virgin wax"; Sidney and Carmarthen were ciphers, and this was "the naked truth." In his disgust Adams thought even of

[16] September 4, 1785. Jefferson Papers, Library of Congress.
[17] To Jay, August 10, 1785. Works, Vol. VIII, p. 299.
[18] To Jay, October 21, 1785. *Ibid.*, p. 331.

turning towards France. In comparison with the British ministers, Vergennes and his associates appeared very decent. If the
United States had to deal with a European nation, better France
than England, and he could see nothing to prevent the States
from "deliberating upon a new treaty of commerce with France,
or even a new alliance." [19]

While the negotiations were thus lagging, Adams found another field in which to employ his activity. As soon as the
armistice was proclaimed, American merchants had attempted
to resume trade with the Near East and the Mediterranean,
only to discover that their ships were subject to the attacks of
the "Barbary pirates." Unable to claim protection from any
European power, unable to maintain a navy in a distant part of
the world, they were placed at a distinct disadvantage, and
could not obtain redress for the outrages to which the American
flag was subjected. Ships were seized, sailors were captured
and enslaved, and in spite of Vergennes' vague promises, the
King of France had not undertaken to protect American interests against Morocco, Algiers, Tunis and Tripoli. It was comparatively easy to deal with Morocco, and the American commissioners in Paris had granted full powers to an agent, Thomas
Barclay, to conclude a treaty that was finally signed without
other stipulation than presents to the Sultan, amounting to about
thirty thousand dollars.

The other Barbary powers had proved more recalcitrant,
and Jefferson, deeply humiliated in his patriotic pride, had
stubbornly opposed the payment of a tribute which would
guarantee the safety of American ships in the Orient. Adams,
while agreeing with him that the only satisfactory way to deal
with the pirates was with force, was decidedly in favor of buying protection. He had several conversations in London with
the "Tripolitan ambassador", and described with great verve
his first interview with the "universal and perpetual" envoy of
the Sultan. He sat by the fire with him, smoked a pipe with a
stem more than two yards in length, exchanged whiff for whiff
with his Excellency, and behaved so well that the Moroccan
secretaries exclaimed in ecstasy, "*Monsieur, vous êtes un Turc.*"

[19] To Jay, November 24, 1785. Works, Vol. VIII, p. 347.

When it came to business, his Tripoline Excellency declared himself ready to sign, but nothing could be done immediately; the matter had to be referred to Congress, and George III for once justly estimated the situation when he told one of the foreign ministers that what the ambassador wanted was a present, and his expenses paid to another country.[20]

This unfortunate experience did not discourage Adams, who continued to maintain against Jefferson the contention that it would be much cheaper to pay a yearly tribute than to lose millions and have American citizens subjected to indignities of all sorts. On the whole, the letters exchanged between the two American ministers had a purely academic interest, since no money had been appropriated by Congress to make adequate presents to the pirates, and the so-called plenipotentiaries had no definite instructions to treat with them.[21] After thinking for a time of organizing an international expedition against Algiers, Jefferson finally decided to use whatever funds were available to redeem American captives through the Mathurin monks.

In July of the same year Adams married his daughter to the young secretary of the legation, Colonel William Smith. John Quincy Adams was now in Harvard and doing very well. Mr. Adams and his lady often remained alone in the big house in Grosvenor Square. They had plenty of leisure to read, to meditate, and also to take short trips around London. With Jefferson, who had come for a short visit, Adams went to "Stratford upon Avon" and Worcester, and grew indignant at the neglect of Shakespeare's resting place and the ignorance of the villagers, who had forgotten "the ground where liberty was fought for." Together they went to Stowe, Hagley and Blenheim, and Adams dutifully listed in his Diary the gentlemen's seats where they were entertained. He liked well enough the temples to Bacchus and Venus, Pope's pavilion and Thomson's seat; but nothing interested them as much as Viny's manufacture of patent wheels made of bent timber: This man had genius! As a duty rather than for pleasure they looked at the

---

[20] To Jefferson, February 17, 1786. Jefferson Papers, Library of Congress.
[21] Jefferson to Adams, July 11, 1786. "The Writings of Thomas Jefferson", Memorial Edition, Vol. V (1903), pp. 364–368.

collection of "antiques" in the house of Brand Hollis, and at Desenfan's collection of pictures. But Adams was not an artist and in his opinion "the story of the prince, who lost his own life in a bold attempt to save some of his subjects from a flood of waters", was worth "all the paintings that have been exhibited this year." With Mrs. Adams, having as their objects "fresh air, exercise, and the gratification of curiosity", they went to Hyde and thence to the market town of Braintree, but Adams was convinced that none of the American families had come from this village and failed to be moved.

This was pleasant enough, even if no official business could be transacted, but towards the end of the year Mr. Adams found an unexpected field for his activity. From several sources, and particularly from James Warren, he had received distressing reports of political conditions in America. Constitutional government had practically collapsed, several States neglecting to send delegates to Philadelphia, others passing resolutions that they would not comply with any future requisition of Congress.[22] Commerce was ruined, husbandry and manufactures could not be supported, no debts could be paid, "everything seemed verging to confusion and anarchy." Massachusetts herself, in Shays' Rebellion, had given the example, and a spirit of revolt far different from the revolutionary spirit was abroad in the land. At home, as well as in Europe, the great American experiment was in danger of being considered a failure; even in France, the wisdom of some provisions of the state constitutions had been questioned. No more patriotic undertaking could be planned than to remind the American people of the principles on which they had erected their state and federal governments, and to that task Adams feverishly applied himself during the last months of the year 1786, and early in January of the next year published the first volume of his "Defence of the Constitutions of Government of the United States of America, against the attack of M. Turgot, in his letter to Dr. Price, dated the twenty-second of March, 1778."

Like most of Adams' productions, it was an occasional work,

[22] Gorham to Warren, March 6, 1786. Warren to Adams, April 30, 1786. "Warren-Adams Letters", Vol. II, pp. 269, 271.

somewhat polemical in its presentation. Being a lawyer by instinct as well as by profession, and trained in an atmosphere of theological discussion, he had to take a text as a starting point, in order to present his own ideas. Turgot's letter to Price contained constructive criticism on free trade, commerce and peace. Turgot had particularly regretted the inclusion of religious tests for admission to the representative body — a provision found originally in the constitution of Pennsylvania and later incorporated in the constitution of Massachusetts; but his most irritating objection was that the American people, after agreeing with Montesquieu that "liberty consists in being subject to the law", had indulged in an "unreasonable imitation of the usages of England." They had established an elaborate and unnecessary array of checks and balances, and adopted in general a bicameral system of representation, as if they had to balance the authority of a king. On the whole, he thought that too much independence had been left to the respective States, and he did not see "in the general union of the States with one another, a coalition, a melting of all parts together, so as to make the body one and homogeneous: . . . It is only an aggregate of parts, always too separate, and which have a continual tendency to divide themselves, from the diversity of their laws, their manners, their opinions; from the inequality of their future progress."

Franklin had done some good work in publishing and circulating in Europe the text of the constitutions adopted by the respective States, but the old philosopher was neither a fighter nor a polemist. He had suffered many misconceptions on the origins of these constitutions to pass unchallenged, and Adams felt the need of convincing the European public, as well as the people at home, that the legislators had "adopted the method of a wise architect, in erecting a new palace for the residence of his sovereign. They determined to consult Vitruvius, Palladio, and all other writers of reputation in the art; to examine the most celebrated buildings, whether they remain entire or in ruins; to compare these with the principles of writers; and to inquire how far both the theories and models were founded in nature, or created by fancy; and when this was done, so far as the circumstances would allow, to adopt the advantages and reject the inconveniences of all."

It was also, to a large extent, a plea *pro domo sua* and essentially a defense of the main features of the constitution of Massachusetts. In France and in London, Adams had collected an important library of books on history and the science of government; he had written to George Wythe a letter which he thought had been taken as a guide by the inhabitants of several of the States in framing their government. He was the "engineer" of the constitution of Massachusetts, and he had probably read more on the subject than any other man of his time.

Thus equipped, he undertook to put together, not a systematic treatise on the science of government, but a collection of abstracts taken from the books he and his contemporaries had read, a documentary history of republican and federative governments, reducing to the minimum his own comments, but selecting his examples and illustrations with all the skill of a well-trained lawyer; for the "Defence of the American Constitutions of Government" is, above all, a lawyer's brief, looking for precedents, commenting on each case, piling up evidence and calling on the ancient and modern authorities, rather than the work of a political philosopher.

Neglecting all the secondary aspects of the subject, Adams limited himself to one point and against Turgot, who seemed to defend the theory that in a democracy a single assembly could be invested with all the functions of government; he stood as the champion of the doctrine of the balance of power, a doctrine well tried out in practice for many centuries, more or less exactly followed in ancient times, but brought to its perfection by England and, more recently, by the States of the American confederation. He attempted to demonstrate that no republican government can last unless three distinct powers are recognized: an executive (a king or a governor), a senate and a house of representatives. Such a government, if well organized, can be compared to a musical composition: "As the treble, the tenor and the bass exist in nature, they will be heard in the concert. If they are arranged by Handel, in a skillful composition, they produce rapture the most exquisite that harmony can excite; but if they are confused together, without order, they will rend with tremendous sound your ears asunder."

A careful scrutiny of Adams' great work would well repay a student of political institutions.[23] With all its faults and lack of composition, it contains a keen and most penetrating analysis of the democratic form of government. As representing a doctrine striving to correct some of the faults of the Jeffersonian system, while remaining essentially republican, it deserves more than passing attention.

Coming out boldly against Rousseau and using his own words against the philosopher of Geneva, Adams started out with the conviction that men are governed by their interests and their passions. A society of gods would govern themselves democratically, but "a simple and perfect democracy never yet existed among men." Adams had too much experience of the town meetings of Braintree and Boston, and he remembered too well the sessions of the Caucus Club to believe that even the highly praised New England institution was truly democratic. He was certain that neither in theory nor in experience was even a village of one hundred families capable of exercising all the legislative, executive and judicial powers by unanimous votes, or by majorities; some of the powers had to be delegated to the moderator, the town clerk and the constable, and on important occasions, committees would only be the counselors of both the former, and commanders of the latter.

This was not a mere assumption based solely on personal experience, but an undeniable fact which could be observed by whoever was willing to open his eyes. The republic of San Marino, so often mentioned by theorists of government, was, in fact, an aristocratic republic with a very elaborate system of checks and balances, and three branches of government; the same could be demonstrated of the so-called democratic cantons of Switzerland, while the others were clearly aristocratic

---

[23] A carefully documented study will be found in Mr. Correa Moylan Walsh, "The Political Science of John Adams", New York (1915), now, unfortunately, out of print.

republics, and Geneva itself offered a perfect example of the fatal effects of an imperfect balance. The same would be true of Genoa and Venice.

After briefly analyzing the government of England, almost perfect in theory although somewhat corrupted in practice, Adams came to the conclusion that, contrary to Turgot's contention, "among every people, and in every species of republics", one would find constantly *"a first magistrate, a head, a chief,* under various denominations, indeed, and with different degrees of authority, with the title of stadtholder, burgomaster, avoyer, doge, gonfaloniero, president, syndic, mayor, alcalde, capitaneo, governor, or king." He had not lost his old taste for these long enumerations and strings of picturesque words. In every form of government he had found also a senate and a larger assembly. He was ready to admit that in many governments the different attributions of these three branches were not in general well defined and that in no government except in England was there a distinct separation of the legislative from the executive powers, and of the judicial from both. In theory at least, the English constitution was "both for the adjustment of the balance and the prevention of its vibration, the most stupendous fabric of human invention."

Preserving in their institutions the essential features of the British constitution, and rejecting the few objectionable aspects of the Anglo-Saxon tradition, the American people had devised a form of government as nearly perfect as could be expected of human beings; and Adams ended the first part of his plea with an eloquent summation of his argument:

"Our people are undoubtedly sovereign; all the landed and other property is in the hands of the citizens; not only their representatives, but their senators and governors, are annually chosen; there are no hereditary titles, honors, offices, or distinctions; the legislative, executive, and judicial powers are carefully separated from each other; the powers of the one, the few, and the many are nicely balanced in the legislatures; trials by jury are preserved in all their glory, and there is no standing army; the *habeas corpus* is in full force; the press is the most free in the world. Where all these circumstances take place, it is unnecessary to add that the laws alone can govern."

The second part of the book, in which Adams reviewed the opinions of philosophers on government, is perhaps even more interesting, for it confirms what we already know of Adams' broad knowledge of ancient and modern literature, and in his criticisms of men he revealed once more curious aspects of his own character. He discussed in an order which was not exactly chronological, Doctor Swift, Doctor Franklin, Doctor Price, Machiavelli, Algernon Sidney, Montesquieu, Harrington, Polybius, Dionysus of Halicarnassus, Plato, Milton and Hume. He mentioned incidentally Aristotle, Livy, Hobbes, Mandeville, La Rochefoucauld, Delolme and Rousseau. He accumulated anecdotes, personal reflections and comments, but from the whole, two or three main ideas stand out quite clearly.

One of the most important, perhaps, which in his old days was to provide him with a bone of contention in his letters to Jefferson, was that, contrary to Turgot's opinion, it is almost universally agreed that there is no such thing as natural equality. Even in the society of Massachusetts, where a moral and political equality of rights and duties prevailed among all citizens, one had to admit that there existed inequalities of great moment because they had a natural and inevitable influence on society. Inequality of wealth, which made some people live in the employ and on the dependence of others; inequality of birth, which could not be denied and meant that the name of Andros and the name of Winthrop could not be heard with the same sensations in any village of New England; which resulted in the son of a wise father finding the world disposed to honor the memory of his father, and which required that some men, in order to obtain or to hold office, had to behave better and work harder than some others. There are in addition great inequalities of merits, talents, virtues or service, and often of pure reputation, deserved or undeserved. In the words of Harrington, there is "a *natural aristocracy*, diffused by God throughout the whole body of mankind." What shall be done about it? Shall they all be massacred? Would it not, on the contrary, be better to recognize the value of such men and, with due caution, enable them to be of service to the commonwealth by putting them in a special branch of the government, namely, the senate? It would be to all honest and useful intents an ostracism, but a dignified ostracism, "where the influence of such men would be counterbalanced by the influence of men of the same type, while in a house of representatives they might soon acquire too much power for simple honesty and plain sense."

It is somewhat amusing to remember that Adams, a short time later, was to preside over the first Senate of the United States. He probably felt at that time that he too had been ostracized, and he remembered the words of his favorite philosopher, Lord Bolingbroke, in his "Idea of a Patriot King": "It has pleased the Author of Nature to mingle, from time to time, among the societies of men a few, and but a few of those on whom he has been graciously pleased to confer a larger proportion of the ethereal spirit, than in the ordinary course of his providence he bestows on the sons of men. These are they who engross almost the whole reason of the species. Born to direct, to guide, and to preserve, if they retire from the world their splendor accompanies them, and enlightens even the darkness of their retreat."

Of all the ancient philosophers and historians discussed by Adams, Polybius seemed to be worthy of the first rank. He was the first to enunciate clearly and completely the doctrine of the balance of powers without which no truly republican government could exist; he was a man whose character was deservedly revered and "whose writings were in the contemplation of those who framed the American constitutions." This admission of Adams is most curious, as many various origins have been ascribed by historians to the famous doctrine. It was Polybius and none other who, in his sixth book, showed how "Lycurgus . . . formed his government not of one sort, but united in one all the advantages and properties of the best governments; to the end that no branch of it, by swelling beyond its due bounds, might degenerate into the vice which is congenial to it; and that, while each of them were mutually acted upon by *opposite powers*, no one part might incline any way, or *outweigh* the rest; but that the commonwealth being equally *poised* and *balanced*, like a *ship* 'or a *wagon*,' acted upon by *contrary powers*, might long remain in the same situation."

From this passage, which could be corroborated by many others, it will easily be perceived that in the case of Adams, as in that of Jefferson, the influence of the classical historians and philosophers was no less potent and fruitful than the undeniable influence of Locke and Montesquieu. Without entering into a detailed discussion of the origins of the American Constitution, we may be permitted to point out that the principles of government so often represented as the birthright of the Anglo-Saxon people were, at least in America, blended with the tradition of Greece and Rome. If, in the words of Adams, the constitutions of the several united States proved themselves "improvements both upon the Roman, the Spartan and the English commonwealths", it was largely because the American legislators were thoroughly acquainted with the efforts of their predecessors, and no complete study of the American Constitution can be rightly made without more than passing reference to the experiments in free government made by the old civilizations of the Western World.

Adams, more than Jefferson, had made a thorough study of the governments of the Greek cities; he reinforced his distrust of integral democracy by examples taken from the history of Athens. "Was this government, or the waves of the sea?" He repeated that although "every example of a government which has a large mixture of democratical powers, exhibits something to our view which is amiable, noble, and I had almost said, divine", nevertheless, "the people in a body cannot manage the executive power, and, therefore, a simple democracy is impracticable."

Contrary to most of his contemporaries, who placed unlimited faith in the possibilities of popular education, he did not believe that education alone could much increase the capacity of men for self-government. He maintained that,

. . . Experience has ever shown, that education, as well as religion, aristocracy, as well as democracy and monarchy, are, singly, totally inadequate to the business of restraining the passions of men, of preserving a steady government, and protecting the lives, liberties, and properties of the people. Nothing has ever effected it but three different orders of men, bound by their interests to watch over each other, and stand the guardians of the laws. Religion, superstition, oaths, education, laws, all give way before passions, interest, and power, which can be resisted only by passions, interest, and power.[24]

In his conclusion, hastily written, Adams briefly summed up his views on government — not as clearly as could be desired. He was convinced that, in the present state of manners in America, the people could "live and increase under almost any kind of government, or without any government at all." The colonial Congress had served its purpose very adequately and had been "not a legislative assembly, nor a representative assembly, but only a diplomatic assembly." He thought it desirable from his own experience to give to it full powers in foreign matters and foreign commerce, and some authority over the commerce of the States. He was not quite clear over the election of a governor or a president, but seemed to favor the choice of the chief executive by the people at large, in order to make the office independent of any coterie in the assembly. He was decidedly against a single assembly, for "a constitution consisting of an executive in one single assembly, and a legislative in another, is already composed of two armies in battle array; and nothing is wanting but the word of command to begin the combat." He did not seem to care particularly whether the executive was to be in the hands of a single person, assisted by a council, or in the hands of a committee, the only essential being to have an executive with clearly defined powers and properly checked by the legislative bodies, each of them having a negative. While admitting that the legislative functions, as well as most of the offices, would necessarily be in the hands of an aristocracy, for "the army, the navy, revenue, excise, customs, police, justice, and all foreign ministers must be gentlemen", he thought that the formation of an hereditary aristocracy ought to be discouraged by every possible means; hence his constant opposition to the Society of the Cincinnati. He did not even question the fact that the people were the

[24] Works, Vol. IV, pp. 557–558.

ultimate source of all government, but supported by history, he maintained that the people could not exercise, themselves, all the powers of government. Such a course would inevitably lead to anarchy and dictatorship, for even popular authority and political parties had to be checked in some ways; and there were only two ways, "either by a monarchy and standing army, or by a balance, in the constitution", for "where the people have a voice, and there is no balance, there will be everlasting fluctuations, revolutions, and horrors, until a standing army, with a general at its head, commands the peace, or the necessity of an equilibrium is made to appear to all, and is adopted by all."

Such was the very curious work hurriedly composed and hurried through the press, with which the American Minister at the Court of St. James occupied his leisure during the last months of 1786. To evaluate its influence on the members of the Federal Convention would necessitate a detailed analysis which can not be undertaken here. It may suffice to say that the first volume of the "Defence", printed in January, 1787, reached Paris early in February.[25] At the beginning of May, Jay had already found time to read it and announced to Adams that a "new edition" was being printed.[26] In several communications Jay, although refusing to accept Adams' indorsement of Congress, repeated his approval of it, adding that the book gave "many useful lessons" and would "tend to establish a thorough principle of government on which alone the United States can erect any political structure worth the trouble of erecting", and in July he repeated that the book was "circulating and doing good."[27] Even a casual glance at the records of the Federal Convention will show that Adams' book was used as a sort of repertory by many speakers, who found in it a confirmation of their views, and chiefly convenient historical illustrations and precedents.[28]

---

[25] Jefferson to Adams, February 6, 1787. "Writings of Jefferson", Memorial Edition, Vol. VI, p. 80.

[26] May 12, 1787. Jay's Correspondence, Vol. III, p. 247.

[27] *Ibid.*, pp. 249, 251.

[28] See particularly in Max Farrand's edition of the "Records of the Federal Convention", the speeches of Madison, June 6 (p. 135) and June 7 (pp. 152,

The plan finally adopted by the Convention greatly pleased Adams, who wrote to Jefferson, on receiving a copy of it: "It seems to be admirably calculated to preserve the Union, to increase affection, and to bring us all to the same mode of thinking . . . thank heaven they have adopted a third branch. . . . I think that senates and assemblies should have nothing to do with executive power." [29] Jefferson was much less pleased and found in it, "things which stagger all my dispositions to subscribe to what such an Assembly has proposed." The President, being eligible for election "from four years to four years, for life", seemed to him "a bad edition of a Polish King", and "once in office, and possessing the military force of the Union, without the aid or check of a council, he would not be easily dethroned, even if the people could be induced to withdraw their votes from him." [30]

It was on this occasion that, for the first time, appeared the signs of the rift which was shortly so radically to divide the two friends and place them in different camps. "You are afraid of the one," answered Adams, "I, of the few. We agree perfectly that the many should have a full, fair and perfect Representation. You are Apprehensive of Monarchy; I, of Aristocracy. I would therefore have given more Power to the President and less to the Senate. . . . Faction and Distraction are the sure and certain Consequences of giving to a Senate a vote in the distribution of office. You are apprehensive the President when once chosen, will be chosen again and again as long as he lives. So much the better as it appears to me. You are apprehensive of foreign Interference, Intrigue, Influence. So am I. — But, as often as Elections happen, the danger of foreign influence recurs. The less frequently they happen the less danger."

Encouraged by the success of his book, which Jefferson had undertaken to have translated into French, Adams wrote a

158); Patterson, June 16 (p. 251); Hamilton, June 16 (p. 272), June 18 (pp. 284, 307); Madison, June 19 (p. 326); Hamilton, June 26 (p. 432); Madison, June 28 (pp. 446, 448); King, June 27 (p. 450); Madison, June 29 (p. 472); Morris, July 2 (p. 517).

[29] November 10, 1787. Jefferson Papers, Library of Congress.
[30] November 13, 1787. "Writings of Jefferson", Vol. VI, p. 370.

second and a third volume, both of them of much less interest, but both containing more than one passage worthy of being collected in political anthologies. His description of the Italian republics in the second volume was largely a compilation of well-known authors like Machiavelli and Guicciardini, and lesser lights like Malavolti, Fioraventi, Campo, Equicola, and Spinello Benci; but here and there he inserted reflections, exploded with indignation at Portenari's contention that farmers, merchants and mechanics ought to be excluded from participation in the government of the city, and when discussing Montepulciano, launched out in a vehement denunciation of the Society of the Cincinnati and hereditary descents.[31]

Much more important was the third volume, entirely given to criticism of "The Excellency of a Free State, or the Right Constitution of the Commonwealth of Marchamont Nedham", published for the first time in 1656, and of which Thomas Hollis had given a new edition in January, 1767. Here was an adversary worthy of Adams' foil, a man who pretended to be a friend of self-government, the authority on which Mr. Turgot had built his system. Taking one after the other of the rules enunciated by poor Nedham, he used against him all the weapons he could find in the modern and ancient authorities, lambasted him, piled up sarcasms and denunciations, used against him every trick of a lawyer trying to convince a jury, and thoroughly deflated the balloon of democracy. In no less than thirteen propositions he demonstrated against Nedham and Montesquieu that "no democracy ever did exist or can exist", that "no such passion as a love of democracy, stronger than self-love, or superior to the love of private interest, ever did, or ever can prevail in the minds of the citizens in general", that "no love of equality, at least since Adam's fall, ever existed in human nature", and finally that "the democracy of Montesquieu and its principles of virtue, equality, frugality" are all "figments of the brain, delusive imaginations", and "delirious reveries." [32] Two years before the beginning of the French Revolution, Adams had already proclaimed

[31] Works, Vol. V, pp. 455, 488.
[32] Works, Vol. VI, p. 210.

his distrust of eighteenth-century optimism and philosophism. While Jefferson, more imaginative, trusted that a new order of things had been born to bring happiness, if not to mankind, at least to the chosen people, Adams clearly represented the Old World rationalism and traditionalism. Against those who placed their hopes in indefinite and infinite progress, he maintained that man had not changed and could not change "since the garden of Eden"; every man hating a superior and no one being willing to have an equal. He could exclaim: "A prospect into futurity is like contemplating the heavens through the telescopes of Herschell"; his mind may have melted "into reverence and awe", his conception of the prospect before him was more static than dynamic. Like an Old World statesman, he was more preoccupied with preserving, consolidating and maintaining the present order than in opening, developing and organizing new territories. In a New World and in spite of the virulence of his style, he could at most be considered as a liberal conservative, not as a pioneer or a prophet. His vision was too limited, his imagination too much checked by cold reason and moral pessimism, to inspire him with those magic formulas that fire popular passions and win popular support.

Studying, reading, copying and writing had taken the major part of his time during the year 1787. There was very little else he could do. There was no hope of concluding a treaty of commerce with Great Britain, or even of obtaining the evacuation of the forts on the Canadian borders. In the persistent refusal of the Court of St. James to send a full-fledged minister plenipotentiary to the United States he saw a clear indication that a complete reconciliation and coöperation were not to be contemplated. He would remain in England until the end of his mission, but not one day longer. In January he had already written officially to Jay that he wished to return to America at the expiration of his commission, in the early spring of 1787, and in a private letter he had confirmed his "unalterable decision to come home in all events." [33] A letter of the same date to the delegates of Massachusetts in Congress requested them to promote his recall, and not to expose him

[33] January 25, 1787. Works, Vol. VIII, p. 424.

to an odium, should he "come home against orders, or without permission."

No change sufficient to modify his decision took place during the course of the year. He had hopes for a time that he might succeed in transferring to Holland "the French debt, and all the domestic debt of the United States." [34] But nothing could be accomplished with Congress as it was then constituted.

France was in the throes of the approaching revolution, and the Assemblée des Notables, according to Jefferson, would not succeed in bringing order in the prevailing confusion. Holland had been unjustifiably attacked by Prussia. England was arming to the teeth, nobody knew against whom, and Montmorin, Vergennes' successor, was working on a new system of alliance. Adams became more convinced than ever that "neither Philosophy, nor Religion, nor Morality, nor Wisdom, nor Interest, will ever govern nations or Parties, against their Vanity, their Pride, their Resentment or Revenge, or their Avarice or Ambition. Nothing but Force and Power and Strength can restrain them." [35]

During the summer, and in order to escape "the pestilence of London", he took several short trips to the country. Mr. and Mrs. Adams, like so many American tourists to follow them, were eager to go on pilgrimage to the places where their forbears had dwelt for many centuries. They went to Winchester, where lived a Saer of Quincy, created earl by King John in 1224, and Mrs. Adams quite proudly deciphered his signature on the original of the Magna Charta in the British Museum. They visited Weymouth, merely for its name; Axminster, where they found a relative of Mr. Cranch, who had married Mrs. Adams' sister. On their pilgrimage they could not forget Plymouth, where they tarried several days; then returned through Bristol, Oxford and Woodstock, and ended their tour at Blenheim, the magnificent seat of the Duke of Marlborough. [36] None of these picturesque scenes, however, could compare with the simple charm of Penn's Hill; both

[34] To Jefferson, August 25, 1787. Jefferson Papers, Library of Congress.
[35] To Jefferson, October 9, 1787. *Ibid.*
[36] "Letters of Mrs. Adams", September 15, 1787, Vol. II, pp. 180–190.

Mrs. Adams and her husband failed to be deeply moved, and all their thoughts were already turned towards America.

At the beginning of December, Adams received a letter from Jay informing him that his resignation had been accepted, and transmitting the thanks of Congress for the important services he had rendered his country. But Congress had neglected to appoint a successor to Adams and to include any instructions concerning the American legation in London. Worse luck, they had even forgotten to recall Adams officially from his mission to Holland, and according to the protocol, he had to take formal leave from the States-General. For a time he had hopes that the business could be transacted by correspondence, and that he would be spared the fatigue of a journey to The Hague. But the memorials he had sent to the Prince of Orange and to the States-General were returned to him, and he felt obliged to go for the last time to Holland, where he had the pleasure of meeting Jefferson and of discussing with him and the Dutch bankers the possibilities of financing new loans. His leave-taking of the British Court was severe and frigid. Lord Carmarthen was noncommittal and oracular; everywhere he was "personally treated with the same uniform tenor of dry decency and cold civility which appears to have been the premeditated plan from the beginning. . . . Mr. Fox and Mr. Burke, Lord Camden and the Duke of Richmond, Lord Hawkesbury and Lord North and Lord Stormont have all behaved alike." [37] The king contented himself with saying, "Mr. Adams, you may, with great truth, assure the United States that, whenever they shall fulfill the treaty on their part, I, on my part will fulfill it in all its particulars." Nothing had been gained by Adams during his three-year mission, the situation was unchanged and the prospect for an entente or a reconciliation between the two countries seemed as remote in 1788 as in 1785.

The Adams family left England without any pangs, and if any tears were shed by the servants, they were unrecorded. With them, however, they were taking mementos of their stay in Europe: the fine pieces of furniture bought in Paris for the

[37] To Jay, February 14, 1788. Works, Vol. VIII, p. 476.

reception hall of the legation, the big-bellied chest of drawers bought by Adams in Holland, trunkfuls of cambrics, "double Florence", and books, twelve pairs of silk stockings specially obtained by Jefferson from the hermits of Mount Calvaire for Mrs. Adams.[38] They had no plans for the future and if Adams had any ambitions, he did not express them in writing. He was looking forward to a life of rest and study in his retreat of Braintree, from which he could continue to advise his countrymen in scholarly, leisurely written books. As for Mrs. Adams, she openly professed that feeding her poultry and improving her garden had more charms to her fancy than residing at the Court of St. James, where she had seldom met "characters so innofensive" as her "hens and chickings." In their joy to go home and to be "out of the Noise of all these Speculations in Europe", they forgot all their unpleasant impressions of Paris and London, and Adams himself, in a more mellow mood than was customary with him, sailed from England, leaving behind "the most fervent good wishes for the Safety and Prosperity of all who have the Cause of Humanity, Equity, Equality and Liberty at heart." [39]

[38] Mrs. Adams to Jefferson, December 5, 1787, and Jefferson's memorandum, January 9, 1788. Jefferson Papers, Library of Congress.

[39] To Jefferson, December 10, 1787. Jefferson Papers, Library of Congress.

BOOK THREE

A SCHOLAR IN POLITICS

CHAPTER I

THE "HEIR APPARENT"

ON his return home John Adams was given by the Massachusetts people a welcome worthy of a victorious general. Orders had been issued days in advance by the governor, and when the ship entered Boston Harbor in the early morning of June 17th, a discharge of cannon was heard from the Castle, followed by more salutes when the passengers appeared on deck. "Several thousand people" gathered along the water front repeatedly shouted the three ritual "huzzas." Received by the Secretary of State of Massachusetts, taken to the house of his Excellency the Governor in the gubernatorial coach, Mr. Adams spent several days receiving congratulations from distinguished citizens and from the Honorable Legislature.[1] For a short time, at least, he could believe that the old proverb was untrue, and that he was a prophet in his own country.

During the crossing, as well as in London, he had vainly attempted to deceive himself with visions of scholarly leisure in the house he had recently acquired in Quincy. While in London he had managed to purchase the old colonial dwelling built in the early eighteenth century by Major Leonard Vassall, a wealthy merchant with extensive connections in the West Indies, and he had already ordered that it be enlarged by building a new ell. There, in the dining room paneled with San Domingo mahogany, he would place the beautiful furniture bought in Paris and Holland. He would arrange in his study, with his old books, the works on law and government procured abroad, the translations of ancient writers. Comparatively small as the dwelling still was, it was a far cry from the farmhouse in which he was born. It would be a visible sign of his social

[1] *Boston Gazette,* June 23, 1788.

progress. A former ambassador, the co-signer of the treaty of peace, he would spend in ease the rest of his days, content to be first in his village, loved and respected by his neighbors. In these plans he was probably encouraged by Mrs. Adams, a home-loving person, who had suffered in Paris and in London, and whose only desire was to settle comfortably in Quincy, to enjoy the peace of her home, and to care for her garden. This was not shirking his duty; he had done his share. He could look back with satisfaction to the services he had rendered his country. Thirteen years of his life had been devoted to the public good; now he could think of himself, and with a naïve pleasure he clipped the eulogious articles daily appearing in the newspapers and sent them to his good friend Jefferson, who had them translated and published in France and Holland.[2]

At first he was able to resist successfully the efforts of his friends to make him reënter public life. Already on June 6th, with Nathaniel Gorham, Theodore Sedgwick, Samuel A. Otis and George Thatcher, he had been elected to represent the commonwealth in the Congress of the United States, commencing in November.[3] His name was added to the list of toasts at all public festivities; by his old friends he was looked upon as a leader, and soon he was given to understand that he would not be permitted to live in retirement. The Constitution had just been ratified by a majority of the States, but the new government had to be organized, and in Massachusetts no one seemed to be better qualified than Mr. Adams to represent the commonwealth in the new councils of the government. Early in the winter a strong movement was started to send him to New York, with the Honorable F. Dana and Samuel Adams, as a "Federal senator."[4] He probably would have been elected if before the election he had not announced his "unchangeable determination" to refuse the office.[5] To be "ostracized" to the

---

[2] Jefferson to Adams, August 2, 1788. "Writings of Jefferson", Memorial Edition, Vol. VIII, p. 101.

[3] *Boston Gazette*, June 9, 1788.

[4] *Ibid.*, November 3, 1788.

[5] To Theophilus Parsons, November 2, 1788. Works, Vol. VIII, pp. 483–484.

Senate, even if it was flattering, was not in his plans. He did not go to New York to take possession of his seat in Congress, but stayed in Braintree, apparently idle, unpacking his books, setting his house in order, and looking after his fields. For more than ten years he had lost contact with pure politics. The "old, stanch, firm patriots, who conducted the revolution in all the civil departments", had been discarded, and pilots much less skillful and much more selfish had been called to the helm. The patriots and Tories of old had disappeared, but new groupings were beginning to appear with the Federalists and the Antifederalists. Whether he would have a share in the new government seemed to him very doubtful at the beginning of December.[6] He was not entirely pleased with the Constitution recently adopted; on the whole, however, the government of the United States was a *balanced* government, and he took pleasure in thinking that he had helped to establish it and to secure its ratification by the publication of the "Defence."[7] On the other hand, in many quarters it had already appeared that Adams should "be in the government."

For President, none but George Washington could be considered, and since a Virginian was to become the chief executive, it seemed desirable that the position next in prestige should be occupied by a New Englander. As neither Hancock nor Samuel Adams had evidenced any hearty good will for the new Constitution, John Adams soon appeared as the outstanding and stanchest friend of the Federalists in Massachusetts, and Alexander Hamilton, somewhat reluctantly and not without misgivings, accepted rather than endorsed the efforts of Adams' friends to have him elected as the first Vice President of the United States. There is good evidence to show that, fearing Adams would receive too large a majority, he advised his partisans to scatter their votes.

According to the curious procedure then followed, the electors were left theoretically uninstructed, and the person receiving the largest number of votes in the electoral college

[6] To Thomas Brand-Hollis, December 3, 1788. Works, Vol. IX, pp. 557–558.

[7] To Benjamin Rush, December 2, 1788. *Ibid.*, p. 556.

became President, while he who received the next largest number became Vice President.

Hamilton's efforts to reduce to a minimum the votes cast for Adams may be attributed to some extent to his diffidence towards a man who had been known to oppose Washington during the Revolution. It is also possible that he believed that if a Vice President constitutionally without powers should obtain the endorsement of a large majority, he might try to rally his partisans to him and become a source of many difficulties to the President.

Whatever may have been the guiding motives of Washington's young lieutenant, when the college met, the General was elected unanimously, while Adams, receiving more votes than any other candidate (thirty-four out of sixty-nine), failed to obtain a majority. According to the Constitution, he was proclaimed Vice President, but if Washington was "first in the hearts of his countrymen", Adams had to recognize that only after a long interval could he be recognized as second to him.

Although Charles Francis Adams and many biographers date the hostility between Adams and Hamilton from this episode, it does not seem that at the time the former plenipotentiary to England felt any resentment against the young leader of the Federalists. The result was not unexpected, and a few days before the election he had announced to Jefferson that there would probably be a plurality, if not a majority "in favor of your Friend." He had taken no part in the campaign, and for "Six Months" had enjoyed a luxury which he had not tasted "for at least eight and twenty years" [8] — a complete rest, far from the agitation of political life; but now he felt quite refreshed and ready to enter the arena again.

All sorts of plans were already brewing in his head. Undoubtedly amendments to the Constitution would come up and would be discussed; the most important being to obtain a more complete separation between the executive and the legislative powers. The man who was, as a makeshift, given the chairmanship of the Senate, mistrusted the Senate, which he

[8] To Jefferson, January 2, 1789, and March 1, 1789. Jefferson Papers, Library of Congress.

already considered as a "Junto of Grandees", who probably would make every effort to obtain "the first chair." He had not yet a very clear understanding of his duties as a presiding officer, but his fixed intention was not to remain passive and to seize every opportunity to protect the independence of the executive.

In New England, however, he was second to none. There was no longer any question who was "the great Adams." Samuel Adams had been defeated by Fisher Ames as congressman from Suffolk, and was to become lieutenant governor, with Hancock as governor, of Massachusetts. For a few weeks at least John Adams tasted the strong wine of popularity. He left Braintree on the 13th of April with a military escort, the men on fine horses, in uniforms and fully equipped. He rode in a coach at the head of a real procession of no less than forty carriages.

He had no reason to complain of his reception in New York. He was waited on by every important Federalist. Fenno, the publisher who had recently started his *Gazette of the United States* to keep the public informed of the acts of the government, and to print state documents, published in his paper a poem in which the adoption of the Declaration of Independence was attributed to Adams:

> Lo! Adams rose! a giant in debate
> And turned the vote which fix'd our empire's fate.

He was even given credit for having concluded the treaty which "Gave us rank as a nation", and without any hesitation the bard concluded that he was,

> Columbia's Safeguard, Glory, Boast and Pride.

So exaggerated was the praise that the old *Boston Gazette* did not hesitate to print a protest from a faithful reader, *Philo justicia*, in which it was vehemently remonstrated that "flattery is the bane of freedom, the thief of liberty." [9]

It does not appear that "the great Adams", as Fenno liked to call him, was particularly offended by this adulation, for

[9] *Fenno's Gazette*, April 22, 1789; *Boston Gazette*, May 11, 1789.

at once he gave to the editor of the *Gazette* the voluminous letters he had written in Holland, to correct the false impressions that Europeans may have entertained of the United States.

Other labors, however, soon required his attention. His duties were not clearly defined by the Constitution, and the presidency of the Senate had been given to the Vice President, so as to provide him with a dignified and somewhat innocuous position. Adams took the matter very seriously. He soon undertook to lecture his audience on their duties and his prerogatives, and if we are to believe Maclay, the Pennsylvania Senator none too friendly towards him, the protocol to be followed in various circumstances seems to have been his chief preoccupation during the first session of the Senate.

From his experience in foreign courts, Adams had concluded that titles and dignities, futile as they may be, are nevertheless necessary even in a republic, duly to impress the crowd with the importance and dignity of the magistrates they have elected. In the first communication of the Senate to the House, he consequently proposed to address the Speaker as "Honorable", and suffered a first defeat. He then consulted the Senate on the procedure to be followed when the President addressed Congress. Should there be one chair or two chairs? He felt great difficulty in deciding how to act; for he declared, "I do not know whether the framers of the Constitution had in view the two kings of Sparta or the two consuls in Rome, when they formed it; one to have all the power while he held it, and the other to be nothing." Then he continued, "I am possessed of two separate powers: the one in *esse* and the other in *posse*. I am Vice President. In this I am nothing, but I may be everything." No wonder he was soon accused of having ambitions "to induce Washington to resign in his favor."

In spite of this uncertainty, the reception given Washington came off in a grand manner, even if everything was not done "with all the propriety that was proper", and Washington at times seemed to be most painfully embarrassed. Adams reminded him that "the eyes of the world were upon him" and thanked him for "his most gracious speech", — an unfortunate formula, since those were the very words used in addressing the King of England.[10] But this was no time for criticism. Everywhere in the city popular enthusiasm was at its height. There were great fireworks, the Spanish ambassador had adorned his house with transparent paintings, and the French minister's house was illuminated. Congressmen and townspeople went to bed persuaded they had witnessed the beginning of a new era.

Adams, however, was relentless in his efforts to adorn the presidential office with "dignity and splendor." He pointed out that since in England they had a throne, they could not do less than to have a seat "with a canopy", should the President wish to attend the sessions of the Senate. At any rate, there must be some title for him, and in this Adams was supported by Lee. For days the Senate wrangled over the choice of a proper qualification: his Electoral Highness, or more simply, as was proposed by the "Committee on Titles", *His Highness the President of the United States of America and Protector of the Rights of the Same.* These would have met with the full approval of Adams, who could not check his indignation when it was proposed to do away with all titles. Having still fresh in his memory the impressive ceremonial of Versailles and the Court of St. James, he rose to exclaim: "What will the common people of foreign countries, what will the sailors and the soldiers say: 'George Washington, President of the United States'? They will despise him *to all eternity.* This is all nonsense to the philosopher, but so is all government whatever." [11] This last remark, full of the bitter scorn of the old moralists, should have sufficed to define exactly Adams' position in the matter; but he already had enemies, and he was making new ones every day, and more and more the impression was established that Mr. Adams had returned from England a great admirer of the monarchy and kingly prerogatives.

In spite of the carefully selected evidence presented by Adams' enemies, and the fact that he could be damned by his own words, one will not easily believe that the son of the

---

[10] "The Journal of William Maclay, United States Senator from Pennsylvania, 1789–1791." New York (1927), p. 9; *Boston Gazette,* May 4, 1789.

[11] Maclay, *op. cit.,* p. 26.

Braintree farmer and the old friend of Samuel Adams had been so dazzled by the aristocratic trappings of the Old World and so intoxicated by his rapid rise as to lose all sense of republicanism. His true feelings had been very clearly expressed in his "Defence of the American Constitutions", and were soon to be reiterated no less clearly in another publication equally misunderstood. More likely, however, was the accusation that His "Rotundity" aspired to the Presidency. He made no great mystery of it. The second place in Rome was high enough for him, and he was not an ambitious man, but he was "forced" to look up to that goal, "and bound by duty to do so, because there is only the breath of one mortal between me and it." [12] Such an admission gave ample ground for rhymes which were later circulated:

TO A WOULD-BE GREAT MAN

> Daddy vice, Daddy vice
> One may see in a trice
> The drift of your fine publication,
> As sure as a gun
> The thing was done
> To secure you—a pretty station.

With a small Senate almost equally divided on many important questions, Adams had more than once occasion to cast the decisive vote. On tariff matters he naturally enough favored New England; the most important question he had to decide, however, was the organization of a Department of Foreign Affairs. As passed by the House, the bill provided that the chief clerk of the Department could be "removed from office by the President." On the 14th of July the bill went to the Senate, and was discussed for three days, raising fierce objections, and finally resulting in a tie. During the debates Adams took rather full notes of the arguments presented and finally sided with the twelve Senators who wished to grant to the President the power of removal without consultation with the Senate. The office in itself was of little importance, but it was the first open evidence of the conflict which so often in the future was to

[12] To James Lowell, September 1, 1789. Works, Vol. VIII, p. 494.

create severe difficulties between the President and the Senate. The attitude taken by Adams on this occasion made it apparent that he wished to increase the powers of the President on the supposed assumption that "the King can do no wrong", and Grayson went so far as to declare that "The matter predicted by Mr. Henry is now coming to pass: consolidation is the object of the new Government, and the first attempt will be to destroy the Senate, as they are the representative of the State Legislatures." [13]

In August, the situation became even more acute when Washington himself brought to the Senate a recommendation on treaties to be concluded between the Southern Indians and the United States and the States of Georgia, North Carolina, and South Carolina. When Adams attempted to put the question without any discussion, some protests were made, and the whole matter was adjourned to the next Monday, which put the President of the United States in "a violent fret" and made him hotly declare, "This defeats every purpose of my coming here." But the Senators were not to relinquish prerogatives. The President could not "bear down" their deliberations "with his personal authority and presence." This would not do with Americans! [14]

Thus the clouds began to gather over the head of Adams, for none dared attack openly the respected head of the new government, and Maclay, with some others, could already exclaim: "Ye Gods, with what indignation do I review the late attempt of some creatures among us to revive the vile machinery! O Adams, Adams, what a wretch art thou!" [15]

Apparently unaware of the threatening storm, the Vice President seemed to enjoy himself greatly. He had always been something of a pedagogue and had never forgotten the Worcester days when he presided over his microcosm of pupils, now frowning, now threatening, and always full of his self-importance. To the Senate he lectured as to a class of unruly scholars, to remind them of his superior knowledge of parlia-

[13] Maclay, *op. cit.*, pp. 107–114; Adams, Works, Vol. III, pp. 408–412.
[14] Maclay, *op. cit.*, p. 128.
[15] *Ibid.*, p. 151.

mentary procedure and proper "etiquette." With the House of Representatives he was less successful, and many of them did not behave while Adams was present, for they would spend their time "in lampooning him before his face, and in communicating the abortion of their Muses, and embryo witlings around the room." [16] But on the whole it was a very pleasant life. Dining with the President and his Lady, attending the presidential "levees" which aroused such indignant sentiments in the hearts of the pure republicans, and spending whole days of rest in the house he had rented on Richmond Hill. He had not left Quincy to live again in a dirty, dusty, smoky city; forest trees with plenty of shrubbery surrounded the house; in front the Hudson was rolling its "majestic waves", and in the distance could be seen "the fertile country of the Jerseys, covered with a golden harvest, and pouring forth plenty like the cornucopia of Ceres." [17] To the important problems discussed in the Senate he paid apparently but scant attention. Occasionally he was consulted by Washington, but he had soon realized that no man had influence with the President: "he seeks information from all quarters, and judges more independently than any man I ever knew." [18]

On the choice of the cabinet he made no comment. Hamilton was to be Secretary of the Treasury, and had not openly shown his distrust of Adams; Edmund Randolph, the Attorney-General, was a Virginian, but Henry Knox, the Secretary of War, was from Massachusetts. The office of Secretary of State was to be offered Thomas Jefferson, with whom he had never quarreled and who had treated him with the very essence of courtesy and deference. When Congress adjourned, the government machinery was slowly getting under way, and Adams had no reason to be displeased with the part he had played in the administration.

He was back in Massachusetts when Washington made his triumphal tour of New England. The President arrived in Boston on October 24th, passing through streets decorated with

---

[16] Maclay, *op. cit.*, p. 200.
[17] "Letters of Mrs. Adams", Vol. II, p. 201.
[18] To Silvanus Bourn, August 30, 1789. Works, Vol. IX, p. 561.

canopies, arches, flowers and inscriptions and lined with throngs of people.[19] Adams had dinner with Washington, showed him around the college at Cambridge, and basked in this reflected glory. He was still the "great Adams"; in his official conduct he had shown himself a friend of the new government and a supporter of Hamilton's policies, but he was too independent and too outspoken to be considered as the head of the Hamiltonian gladiators in the Senate. If he had been able to remain silent, he would probably have filled his term without great mishap, but Adams had a real passion for propaganda more than publicity. He sincerely believed that it was necessary to fight over again a battle which to all intents and purposes was already won. A mere politician would have let sleeping dogs lie; Adams thought it his duty to revive the old discussion of the unicameral system of checks and balances.

He had seen with horror that when the French changed their system of government they adopted the principle of a single assembly. This was bad enough, but not being a great admirer of the French, he never expected anything good to come out of their country. Unfortunately, the French had undertaken to prove the superiority of their system over the system recommended by Montesquieu as the ideal form of government, and among the many pamphlets and treatises written at the time, one at least had directly advised the Americans to modify their Constitution. It was the work of an old friend of Franklin, the Marquis de Condorcet, who had been honored with the title of "citizen" by the Town of New Haven, and it was entitled, "Quatre Lettres d'un Bourgeois de New Haven, sur l'Unité de la Législation." Adams took his best pen and wrote for Fenno's *Gazette of the United States* a series of thirty-one essays, forming the famous "Discourses on Davila."

Many years later he called it a "dull, heavy volume", a much too severe characterization. His most egregious mistake was to take as his starting point the work of a practically unknown and unimportant Italian writer, whose study had probably been

[19] *Boston Gazette*, October 25, 1789. "Diaries of G. Washington", Vol. IV, p. 35.

suggested to him by the commendation he had found in Lord Bolingbroke's fifth letter on the "Study of History." Although he possessed the Italian text, he used the French translation published in 1757, under the title of, "Histoire des Guerres civiles de France sous les règnes de François II, Charles IX, Henri III et Henri IV." As a moralist, not as a cabinet politician, he tried to present, not a system theoretically perfect, but a plan of government taking into consideration every weakness of the human heart, and making the best use of it. While so doing, he naturally attributed to the human species in general his own weaknesses and faults, and to some extent some of these essays may be considered a disguised or involuntary confession. At the bottom of the human heart he found, not the *amour propre* of La Rochefoucauld, but "the passion for distinction."

A desire to be observed, considered, esteemed, praised, beloved, and admired by his fellows, is one of the earliest, as well as keenest dispositions discovered in the heart of man. If any one should doubt the existence of this propensity, let him go and attentively observe the journeymen and apprentices in the first workshop, or the oarsmen in a cockboat, a family or a neighborhood, the inhabitants of a house or the crew of a ship, a school or a college, a city or a village, a savage or civilized people, a hospital or a church, the bar or the exchange, a camp or a court. Wherever men, women, or children, are to be found, whether they be old or young, rich or poor, high or low, wise or foolish, ignorant or learned, every individual is seen to be strongly actuated by a desire to be seen, heard, talked of, approved and respected, by the people about him, and within his knowledge.[20]

The first letters in which Adams develops this contention, with countless examples taken from history and from his own observations, would well repay an historian of American literature. A formidable array of poets and philosophers are called to the rescue: Epictetus, Plato, Homer, Shakespeare, Pope, Rousseau, Mably, Voltaire and Condorcet himself. To some degree certain passages remind one of Montaigne — a diluted Montaigne; but there is enough talent in some of the essays

[20] Works, Vol. VI, p. 232.

to claim for Adams a distinguished place among American essayists.

As in most essays, it would be dangerous to look for a very systematic presentation of a thesis; contradictions will be found in plenty, but from the whole can be obtained a full view of Adams' pessimistic philosophy of politics. He wished first of all to adjure the French to give up the fantastic idea that men are naturally good. "Frenchmen! Act and think like yourselves! The affectation of being exempted from passions is inhuman. The grave pretension to such singularity is solemn hypocrisy," and any government founded on these false principles will necessarily degenerate into "dangerous ambition, irregular rivalries, destructive factions, wasting seditions, and bloody civil wars." Convinced that "the essence of free government consists in an effectual control of rivalry", Adams started to follow the analysis made by Davila of the internal wars that tore France during the sixteenth century, to demonstrate both to the French and the Americans that the only possible remedy consisted in a well-balanced government. Since it is impossible and perhaps undesirable to think of a society without an aristocracy, it will be the function of the Constitution to check the evil of the aristocracy, or rather to encourage virtue, stimulating and directing it by generous applause and honorable rewards. It is no more difficult to preserve such a balance than to preserve liberty; but if such a balance is not preserved, liberty is lost forever. Adams concluded:

If the people have not understanding and public virtue enough, and will not be persuaded of the necessity of supporting an independent executive authority, an independent senate, and an independent judiciary power, as well as an independent house of representatives, all pretensions to a balance are lost, and with them all hopes of security to our dearest interests, all hopes of liberty.

The worst criticism that could be made of the "Discourses on Davila" was that it was a perfectly useless publication, having only a theoretical or academic importance. It did not contain an attack against any particular point of the American Constitution; it did not offer any practical amendment for bettering the existing and recently adopted system of government. It was far more "philosophical" than any publication of Jefferson, who in all circumstances showed himself a more practical politician than his former associate. Not only was it useless, it was dangerous. Perfectly innocuous if it had come from the pen of a cabinet politician or a college professor, it was represented at once as embodying the views of the party with which Adams was supposed to be connected — a party to which were attributed dark designs against the people. He was not in any manner the chief of the monocrats, but he could be considered as their spokesman and a host of ill-intentioned pamphleteers pounced upon him with eagerness.

It cannot be denied, however, that Adams was not perfectly satisfied with the Constitution as it existed. In a series of private letters to Samuel Adams and to Roger Sherman, and undoubtedly in many conversations, he had expressed himself quite frankly on several points. He made no mystery of the fact that he would have liked to increase the powers of the President and to give him "a decisive negative"; he would have taken from the Senate "the negative upon appointments" made by the President, for he was afraid of senatorial influences, coteries and even, as we would say, of senatorial courtesy. He was ready to admit that in propriety no other name could be given to the United States but that of "a monarchical republic, or if you will, a limited monarchy", for the powers of the President were much greater than those of "an avoyer, a consul, a podestà, a doge, a stadtholder; nay, than a king of Poland; nay, than a king of Sparta." In his opinion these powers ought to have been made still greater or much less, and he added: "The limitations upon them in the cases of war, treaties, and appointments of office, and especially the limitation on the president's independence as a branch of the legislative, will be the destruction of this constitution, and involve us in anarchy, if not amended." [21]

From such utterances it was easy for ill-intentioned critics to demonstrate that Mr. Adams would advocate or condone

[21] "Three Letters to Roger Sherman, on the Constitution of the United States." Works, Vol. VI, pp. 427–436.

the establishment of a monarchy in America, and that he would see without displeasure a real king as chief executive of the new government. He soon found it necessary to reassure his friends and to protest that he was "a mortal and irreconcilable enemy to monarchy", and "no friend to *hereditary limited monarchy* in America." He was, on the contrary, strongly in favor of "a balance between the legislative and executive powers." "I am," he wrote to Rush, "for having all three branches elected at stated periods, and these elections, I hope, will continue until the people shall be convinced that fortune, providence, or chance, call it which you will, is better than election." [22]

When Congress met again, the temporary seat of the government had been transferred to Philadelphia, much to the distress of Mrs. Adams, who had fallen in love with her New York house. They could not think of living in the city, and succeeded in finding a large, cold, gloomy house on Bush Hill. It was pleasantly located, but of difficult access, with mud up to the horses' knees in "open weather." Social activity was much more intensive than in New York, and the Adamses during their first winter led a life of "dissipation, with levees, receptions, attending the theater with the President" who never missed a performance, and countless official dinners. Politics, it seems, had not yet invaded Philadelphia society, for all parties met in the same companies. But more than this gayety, John Adams enjoyed the family fireside. He was now a grandfather, and little John, of whom they were growing every day fonder, could spend an hour "driving his grandpa round the room with a willow stick." [23]

This happy condition was not to last long, and soon Adams, who had enjoyed the temporary respite, was to be caught in a new storm.

In the early months of 1791, the first copies of Thomas Paine's "Rights of Man", written in answer to Burke's "Reflections on the Revolution in France", arrived in Philadelphia. The English edition, with a dedication to George Washington,

---

[22] April 18, 1790. Works, Vol. IX, p. 566.
[23] "Letters of Mrs. Adams", Vol. II, p. 214.

was loaned to Jefferson, who returned it to the owner with a note expressing his satisfaction that such a valuable work should be reprinted in America: "Something is at length to be publicly said against the political heresies which have sprung up among us. I have no doubt our citizens will rally a second time round the standard of 'Common Sense'." There is no indication that Jefferson intended the note for publication, but the printer thought it would help the success of the book if Jefferson's note were printed as a preface. When it came out, the Secretary of State was thunderstruck. Although disapproving of many views held by Adams, he had no intention of dissenting openly from his old friend. He suddenly realized the awkwardness of his position and wrote at once to Washington a long explanation which could be construed as an apology:

Mr. Adams will unquestionably take to himself the charge of political heresy, as conscious of his own views of drawing the present government to the form of the English constitution, and, I fear, will consider me as meaning to injure him in the public eye. I learn that some Anglomen have censured it in another point of view, as a sanction of Paine's principles tends to give offence to the British government. Their real fear, however, is that this popular and republican pamphlet, taking wonderfully, is likely at a single stroke, to wipe out all the unconstitutional doctrines which their bell-wether Davila has been preaching for a twelvemonth. I certainly never made a secret of my being anti-monarchical, and anti-aristocratical; but I am sincerely mortified to be thus brought forward on the public stage, where to remain, to advance or to retire, will be equally against my love of silence and quiet, and my abhorrence of dispute.[24]

At this juncture Jefferson decided to leave Philadelphia for a trip north, in company with Madison, hoping perhaps to avoid an unpleasant explanation with Adams. At the beginning of June, however, a series of articles signed "Publicola" began to appear in the *Columbian Centinel*. In the first article Jefferson was taken to task for advocating a political orthodoxy of which Thomas Paine would be the prophet or the pope. The writer maintained that a defense of monarchy or aristoc-

[24] May 8, 1791. "Writings of Jefferson", Memorial Edition, Vol. VIII, p. 192.

racy was no more in his intention than the defense of the Salic law of descent was in that of Mr. Paine, but as Adams had done on several occasions, he demonstrated the excellence of the British constitution, protested against the *artificial democracy* which the French had just established, and showed the dangers of a single National Assembly. The authorship of the letters was at once attributed to John Adams, although the printer denied it categorically. Madison had been rightly told that Publicola was "young Adams", but he inclined to believe that the materials had been furnished by the father. Thus, to the great delight of the newspaper editors, the difference between the Vice President and the Secretary of State was brought out publicly and the issue was joined.

It is much to the honor of the two men interested in the affair that they tried to minimize the scandal. On July 17th Jefferson wrote Adams a letter in which he frankly told the story of the note and declared "in presence of the Almighty" that nothing was further from his intentions or expectations than to have his own or Adams' name brought before the public on this occasion.[25] Adams answered quite at length, complaining that the publication of Paine's book had been the signal for unwarranted attacks against him from every quarter. Abandoned by his old friends, neglected by the Governor of Massachusetts and attacked by the Lieutenant Governor, "hunted like a hare" by his enemies, he foresaw that Mr. Paine's pamphlet would be used as an instrument to destroy him. He ended, however, with a fine declaration: "The friendship which has subsisted for fifteen years between us, without the smallest interruption, and until this occasion without the slightest suspicion, ever has been and still is, very dear to my heart. There is no office which I would not resign, rather than give a just occasion for one friend to forsake me." [26]

Jefferson's answer was much colder. He maintained that he never had in view any writing of Adams; the heresies he had

[25] July 17, 1791. "Writings of Jefferson", Memorial Edition, Vol. VIII, p. 213.
[26] Works, Vol. VIII, pp. 506–509, and Jefferson Papers, Library of Congress, slightly different.

alluded to, he wrote, "were principally those I had heard in common conversation from a sect aiming at the subversion of the present government to bring in their favorite form of a King, Lords, and commons." As he was perfectly aware that such opinions were commonly attributed to Adams, this denial was somewhat disingenuous. But the Virginian had no desire to continue the controversy and concluded rather dryly: "The business is now over, and I hope its effects are over, and that our friendship will never be suffered to be committed, whatever use others may think proper to make of our names." [27]

In fact, "the business" had just begun, and its "effects" were to be felt for many years. The first result of the controversy was to accentuate the distrust of Hamilton towards Adams. The Secretary of the Treasury had never felt that the Vice President was a strong supporter of the government. In a conversation with Jefferson, who had shown him Adams' letters, he declared it was his own opinion, although he did not publish it from Dan to Beersheba, "that the present government is not that which will answer the ends of society, by giving stability and protection to its rights, and that it will probably be found expedient to go into the British form." However, since the experiment had been undertaken, he was for giving it a "fair course", and thought other experiments might be tried before giving up "the republican form altogether." "Therefore," concluded Hamilton, "whoever by his writings disturbs the present order of things, is really blameable, however pure his intentions may be, and he was sure Mr. Adams's were pure." [28]

In other words, "Davila" was worse than a crime, it was a mistake. Adams had come out too openly, too soon, and too frankly; he had given confirmation to the misgivings of those who suspected some Federalists at least of dark designs against the Constitution, and he had certainly weakened their case. Quite involuntarily he had done worse. "Davila" was a direct attack against the French Revolution, which so many repre-

---

[27] August 30, 1791. "Writings of Jefferson", Memorial Edition, Vol. VIII, pp. 242–245.

[28] "Notes of a conversation between A. Hamilton and Thomas Jefferson", August 13, 1791. *Ibid.*, Vol. I, p. 284.

sented as a direct outcome of the principles of the American Revolution. Publicola had been even more outspoken in his pessimistic prophecies on the future of a movement based on the false doctrine of equality. On the other hand, with or without ulterior motives, Jefferson had openly and unequivocally endorsed the theories so enthusiastically preached by Paine in the "Rights of Man." Thus the French Revolution, which heretofore had aroused curiosity, sympathy and enthusiasm in some, and indignation, scorn and pity in others, ceased to be a matter of purely academic discussions, to become a domestic issue. At the same time, the real sentiments of both Jefferson and Adams began to be misrepresented. Jefferson, who had strongly urged his French friends to adopt a form of government similar to the British constitution, was portrayed by his enemies as the prophet of the French Revolution, simply because he approved of some of the principles enunciated by the French republicans. Adams, on the other hand, who had no particular reason to admire or love the British, who had maintained that England was doomed, stood out for the true republicans as the champion of Great Britain, because he had never concealed his admiration for the principles on which the British constitution rested. Both of them were, in fact, essentially American, but public opinion and partisan editors are fond of simplifications and generalizations, and both Adams and Jefferson were victims of the blind and irresponsible passions of their contemporaries.

At this juncture, however, Jefferson, disconcerted at the attitude of the two leading papers in Philadelphia, encouraged Philip Freneau, to whom he had offered the clerkship for foreign languages in the Department of State, to establish "a right vehicle of intelligence" for the true republicans. After a first unsuccessful attempt in Monmouth County, Freneau finally printed the first issue of the *National Gazette* in Philadelphia, in November, 1791. The first numbers of the *Gazette* were nonpartisan, and Freneau did not hesitate to publish attacks against Condorcet, "Thomas Payne", and the French Revolution.[29] Soon, however, he came out boldly as the cham-

[29] November 3, 1791.

pion of the doctrine of liberty, equality, fraternity, and through the mouth of "Aratus" proclaimed that "Whoever owns the principles of one revolution must cherish those of others — ; and the person who draws a distinction between them is either blinded by prejudice, or boldly denies what at the bar of reason, he cannot refute." [30]

The battle had begun, not on any real American issue, but, as is often the case in political campaigns, on a side issue which obscured much more important problems. Those who did not indorse unequivocally the principles of the French Revolution were soon represented as "the well-born, the first class, of high birth and good families", and laws should be passed to "discourage principles incompatible with the genius of the republican government." [31] Those who betrayed or avowed "the principles of monarchy and aristocracy, in opposition to the republican principles of the Union, and the republican spirit of the people", could not be the true friends of the Union. [32] Since orders and ranks were proposed, a fitting decoration for the new nobles would be a "Leech clinging to the bowels of an old soldier", and they should receive the title of "their Fulnesses." [33]

In the meantime extracts from the "Rights of Man" were printed in all the opposition papers. Adams was not represented as plotting a sudden overthrow of the government, but as favoring "the progressive administration of it into monarchy." [34] The tone became even more bitter when Jefferson was publicly accused of having given a government position and a government salary to the editor of a paper hostile to the government. Whether or not Jefferson was guilty of a lack of propriety on this occasion, Freneau, while defending himself, thought it his duty to stand for a man who was a true champion of the people, and had only advised "the adoption of the Constitution on the ground of expediency, not of perfection." To Jefferson he constantly opposed "poor John Adams" who, in

[30] November 14, 1791. Reprinted from the *American Daily Advertiser*.
[31] *National Gazette*, December 19, 1791.
[32] *Ibid.*, April 2, 1792.
[33] *Ibid.*, May, 1792.
[34] *Ibid.*, July 7, 1792.

his enthusiasm for political theories, had forgotten that the despised "lower order vote." [35] Even at home Adams was not without enemies. At many of the banquets given on the Fourth of July, the name of the Vice President had not been mentioned. The good people of Bennington had apparently forgotten him, and that he was toasted in Worcester County on the eastern shore of Maryland was slim consolation.[36]

When, at the beginning of September, the coming election began to be discussed in the papers, the attacks became more virulent. The editor of the *National Gazette* reminded his contradictors that

> For men
> I keep a pen,
> For dogs a cane.[37]

There was no possible discussion about the choice of the President. That Washington would be reëlected did not even present any question, but the *New York Journal*, listing the names of the candidates for the Vice Presidency, had enumerated Samuel Adams, George Clinton, John Jay, Thomas Mifflin, James Madison, and last of all John Adams, and had pointedly asked its readers to examine "who have endeavored to prepare the names of the people of America for a King and nobility." The allusion could not be mistaken.

When Congress convened on November 6th, Adams was still in Massachusetts. It had appeared very early in the campaign that the contest would be between John Adams, Esquire, and General Clinton: the one had been accused of being attached to a government of king, lords and commons, and nobody could "controvert that the accusation was true"; the other had been opposed to the Constitution before its adoption, but wanted "to modify the government, not to subvert it." [38] Then Franklin Bache, Franklin's grandson, came out openly in his paper against the "Discourses on Davila" and the "Defence of the American Constitutions", and the *Daily Advertiser* pro-

---

[35] *National Gazette*, September 12, 1792.
[36] *Ibid.*, August 11, 1792.
[37] *Ibid.*, August 29, 1792.
[38] Lucius in *American Daily Advertiser*.

claimed that "the question is no longer between federalism and anti-federalism, but between republicanism and anti-republicanism." The Constitution itself was firmly established, but there were some who called themselves Federalists, who were looking to it as a promising essay "towards an anti-republican system of anti-republican orders and artificial balances." The celebrated "Defence" was, in fact, "a total misnomer." [39] For the true patriots, the man who had signed the Declaration proclaiming the "equal rights of men" was no longer "the man he was from 1776 to the term of his mission to the British court"; he was a spurious patriot, and the French patriots of Charleston begged their American friends

"To chase all modern Tarquins from the throne." [40]

Adams' friends were no less virulent in their accusations. For them, "the Jackalls of Mobocracy were endeavoring to hunt down the character" of a man "who had simply expressed the reasonable opinions of a large body of sensible citizens." It was at this point that, curiously enough, Freneau pretended to enroll among his contributors "Mirabeau" and "Condorcet", who adjured their American friends to destroy every germ of aristocracy and monarchy in their Constitution. The letters could deceive no well-informed reader, but these were great names, and some naïve voters, at least, may have been misled by this evident fabrication. In spite of all these efforts, the editors failed to arouse popular passions. On the whole, the people were apathetic. In Pennsylvania forty thousand had voted in the congressional election, and four thousand only in the presidential contest. In Connecticut, in spite of many letters urging Clinton's election, Adams had been unanimously chosen. Georgia had voted against Adams particularly "not to let him too long at the head of the dark councils of the American Senate"; but South Carolina had simply voted "for the gentlemen in office." In Boston, none of the Antifederalists had been elected, much to the fury of the *Boston Independent Chronicle*, which predicted that they could not

---

[39] *Daily Advertiser*, and *National Gazette*, December 1, 1792.
[40] *National Gazette*, December 5, 1792.

forever be excluded from representation. The result was never doubtful; one by one the States sent in the results, and on March 1st, Jefferson, as Secretary of State, informed the Vice President that the list from Kentucky, the last State to report, had at last been received.[41] One hundred and thirty-two votes had been cast. Washington was reëlected unanimously; Adams had received seventy-seven votes, George Clinton fifty votes, Jefferson four, and Aaron Burr one.

The second inauguration took place without pomp or splendor, although "ladies were present." Momentous problems confronted Congress, but news from France had aroused popular passions to such a degree that purely domestic questions could not compare with the victory of the French against the monarchical coalition, and the beheading of Louis XVI. Adams had been deeply shocked by the political convulsions in France, but for a time he had attempted to maintain an Olympian calm. In October he had written to Rufus King: "There is such a complication of Tragedy, Comedy and Farce in all the accounts from France, that it is to me to the last degree disgusting to attend to them in detail. I read over the accounts in general and then endeavour to direct my own attention from any very serious, which must be very melancholy, reflections upon them." [42]

He soon heard, however, that in place of Ternant, the French had appointed as envoy young Genêt, whose father he had known so well in Paris, and whom he had once taken to the Ménagerie before leaving France. The execution of Louis XVI had found in America not a few outspoken apologies: by some it was to be regarded as a vindication of the rights of the people and as a warning to all monarchs; by others it was mildly blamed, and Bache did not fail to point out that the horror felt at the news came only from the old superstition that a king was the "Lord's annointed." Whatever might be said for him, "his life ought to be considered but as the life of one man." Meanwhile, after long discussions and consultations

---

[41] Jefferson Papers, Library of Congress.
[42] October 11, 1792. "Life and Correspondence of Rufus King", Vol. I, p. 432.

with the members of his cabinet, Washington had issued the famous proclamation declaring it the duty and the interest of the United States "to pursue a conduct friendly and impartial towards the belligerents" (April 22, 1793). The word "neutrality" had been avoided at Jefferson's request, but it was already clear that in the war waged between Great Britain and France the United States meant to remain absolutely neutral and the proclamation was, in fact, a denunciation of the treaty of 1778. As an apparent justification, it was advanced that the treaty was concluded with a régime now abolished and, consequently, it was no longer binding. In fact, this was but a reiteration of the doctrine so often maintained by Adams and taken up by Jefferson as well as Washington, — that America should carefully avoid embroilment in European affairs. At any rate, if Adams does not appear to have been officially consulted in the matter, some of his views were clearly reflected in a series of articles published by his son, John Quincy Adams, in the *Columbian Centinel*. Under the pseudonyms of "Marcellus" and "Columbus", the young Boston lawyer preached the doctrine of strict neutrality, and remembering his classical education, exclaimed: *"Non nostrum, tantas componere lites"*, to settle such mighty differences is not our province.[43] His father maintained several years later that John Quincy Adams' letters had "turned the tide." [44] At any rate the son had proved in his denunciation of the conduct of Genêt that he could wield an able pen, and would be a dangerous man to face in a controversy.

As Vice President of the United States, however, John Adams could not enter the arena, and during the year 1793 he remained aloof, observing an unwonted reserve. If he resented the violations of neutrality committed by both the French and the British fleet, the parading of the patriots in the streets of Philadelphia, he carefully refrained from committing his feelings to paper. During the summer, while the yellow fever was at its height, he had gone back to Braintree, to his books,

[43] "J. Q. Adams' Writings", Vol. I, pp. 135–176.
[44] John Adams to W. Cunningham, Jr., October 13, 1808. "Cunningham Correspondence", p. 35.

his farm and his family, and it almost looked as if he had succeeded in checking his irrepressible temper.

When he returned to Philadelphia to resume his duties as presiding officer of the Senate, the problem offered by foreign relations was more ominous than ever. During the whole year the neutrality of the United States had been constantly — almost systematically — violated by both the British and the French. American merchant vessels bound for and from the French West Indies had been captured by the British, their cargoes seized, their crews imprisoned and shamefully maltreated. On the other hand, privateers commissioned by Genêt and armed in American ports had captured British vessels. The case of the *Little Sarah*, a British prize taken to Philadelphia and refitted by Genêt's orders as a French privateer, had brought the matter to a head, and early in August Jefferson decided that Genêt's *"renvoi"* would have to be requested. Unfortunately for the French cause, "citizen" Genêt, a typical propagandist and the son of a propagandist, decided at this juncture to address himself directly to Congress, over the heads of the President and the Secretary of State.

Genêt had made no secret of his intentions of organizing the French patriots and launching from the territory of the United States an attack against the Floridas and New Orleans. In December Washington decided to lay "the whole budget of foreign affairs" before the Senate, and Adams gloomily foresaw, after a conversation with Jefferson, that, "It will require all the address, all the temper, and all the firmness of Congress and the States, to keep this people out of the war." [45] As Vice President there was little he could do, but that little would be "industriously employed", for Adams could not remain entirely passive in his decorative office.

Of the influence he exerted around him during the next two years there is little information. He had become fonder of reading than of writing; the newspapers, the political pamphlets, the study of Tacitus and of Homer employed all his spare time, but of his conversations with members of the Senate, and with his friends in Philadelphia, we have unfortu-

[45] December 5, 1793. Works, Vol. I, p. 459.

nately no record. Largely for reasons of economy, Mrs. Adams spent most of the time in Braintree, for the emolument of five thousand dollars received by the Vice President did not enable them to maintain a well-appointed establishment in Philadelphia, and, on the whole, Mr. Adams must have been, during these years, a rather solitary man. He apparently wrote few letters, but fortunately resumed his old habit of sending comments on recent events to his wife, and through this familiar correspondence we may obtain a glimpse of the workings of his mind during the next two years.

In this comparative obscurity he found at least one advantage. The newspaper editors had ceased to heap abuse upon him. Freneau's paper had been discontinued, and Bache, "almost as bad as Freneau", was editing the *Aurora;* but now the patriots "mauled the President for his drawing-rooms, levees", his supposed hostility to the French Revolution, and his monarchical tendencies. He had given Genêt "a bolt of thunder", but Genêt still had his advocates, and many desperate enemies had arisen against him in consequence of his best judgment against the French envoy.[46]

All these "Cabals, intrigues, manœuvres", ambition, greed, corruption, would have made "a pretty farce" for amusement had the times not been so tragic; and Adams had a unique position as an almost disinterested observer to watch the play of human passions and to indulge in moral reflections. Obliged to be punctual, confined to his seat "as in a prison, to see nothing done, hear nothing said, and to say and do nothing", he pretended to be "wearied to death with *ennui*."[47] It was real punishment to hear other men talk five hours every day and not be at liberty to talk at all; but as the Senate was nearly divided on all questions, the Vice President could occasionally cast the decisive vote, and Adams found great comfort in the thought that in some respects he could play a very important part in the destinies of his country. He derived further satisfaction from the polite and almost deferential attentions of

[46] January 2, 1794. Works, Vol. I, p. 460.
[47] February 8, 1794. *Ibid.*, p. 465.

Washington, who called on him at critical times, took him into his confidence, disclosed to him his anxieties, and "appeared in a very amiable and respectable light." [48]

At all costs neutrality must be maintained and war avoided; the *renvoi* of Genêt had encouraged pro-British sentiments and infuriated the patriots. It was not a pleasant prospect to imagine a French navy completely ruined, the West Indies in the hands of the British, and England ruling the seas, no more than to see "Brabant and Flanders in the power of Dumouriez." [49]

With the recall of Genêt and after his successor, Fauchet, had been officially received by the President, some of the animus against the French quieted down. Adams himself could not help feeling a little sympathy for the misguided envoy. "Bad as his conduct has been," he wrote to Mrs. Adams, "I cannot but pity him." [50] But the difficulties with England were more irritating than ever. Without any fleet to protect her merchant vessels on the high seas, or even to enforce ordinary police protection in her own harbors, America felt defenseless and humiliated, and at the mercy of British *"bon plaisir."* In a desperate attempt to avoid more incidents which could only result in war, it was then decided to proclaim a one-month embargo, soon extended for an equal period. It was in more than one way a measure indirectly favorable to the French, and caused great rejoicing among the patriots until it was discovered that the embargo had provided the speculators with a good excuse for raising prices. [51] Even this unfortunate result, however, did not quench the zeal of the patriots, contrary to Adams' expectations, and when the embargo was lifted, the war party was stronger than ever.

Adams himself had never felt friendly to the British, and being a New Englander, he could not help resenting British insults to the American flag. He had never been a pacifist at heart

---

[48] January 9, 1794. Works, Vol. I, p. 462.
[49] February 9, 1794. *Ibid.*, p. 466.
[50] February 23, 1794. *Ibid.*, p. 467.
[51] April 1, 1794. *Ibid.*, p. 469.

either, and would have favored going to war with England had this not meant coöperation "with allies the most dangerous that ever existed." [52]

War, however, seemed imminent, and in the House fiery speeches were made against the British violations of the treaty of peace, and their unwarranted retention of the posts along the northern border. Adams felt that the war spirit could not be curbed any longer, and although he struggled to maintain a judicial attitude, and felt that no good could result from a new war, he could not help thinking that Britain "deserves all that will fall thereon." When, as a last resort, Washington proposed to send John Jay as plenipotentiary to England, in order to make representations and to obtain redress, he entertained no sanguine hopes of his success. He would do better than any other man Adams could think of, and perhaps immortalize himself by keeping peace, but in fact the result of his negotiations depended largely on the valor of the French, for a defeat of the Revolutionary army in the field would surely add to the insolence of a "true game-cock" like Britain. [53]

At this juncture Adams felt thoroughly and genuinely nauseated by politics. As Vice President of the United States he had had unusual opportunities to watch the conduct of the legislators, and knew to what temptations they were exposed; he had never believed in the ultimate wisdom of the people, for the *vox populi* was "sometimes the voice of Mahomet, of Cæsar, of Catiline, the Pope, and the Devil." He entertained little hope now ever to reach the Presidency, for he expected Jay, if his mission was successful, to be in the eye of the public and considered the savior of the country. Corruption was as rampant in New England as in the South; among Republicans as among Federalists, and the Boston election was as good evidence of it as any could desire. The only excuse was that in a corrupted city, corruption is permitted, according to "Cato's principle: *In corrupta civitate corruptio est licita.*" But that was no justification, and in despair the uncompromising old patriot exclaimed: "O, liberty! O, my country! O, debt! And, O, sin!" [54]

Of his old friends very few if any remained with whom he could harmonize. Even Samuel Adams had become "a preacher of *égalité*", and was proclaiming the detestable doctrine of the French Revolution that "all men are created equal", and members of Congress in Philadelphia had no time or no taste for theoretical discussions. With Jefferson, who had retired to Monticello, far from "the din of politicks and the rumours of war", he felt perhaps more in sympathy than with any one else, and in the spring of 1794 he exchanged with him several philosophical letters. The Publicola affair had apparently left no ill feeling between the old associates, and Adams went as far as to declare that he "had always detested an aristocratical government." A war would only result in adding "two or three hundred millions of dollars to our debt; raise up a many headed and many bellied minister of an army to tyrannize over us; totally dissadjust our present Government, and accellerate the Advent of Monarchy and Aristocracy by at least fifty years." [55] On their common detestation of war at least, they could heartily agree, and commune thoroughly in their love for rural peace.

Amidst all these trials, however, Adams found that he had much to be grateful for: "good parents, an excellent wife, and promising children; tolerable health upon the whole and competent fortune." John Quincy was already promising to walk in his father's footsteps. He had become a successful lawyer in Boston and his measured articles on Genêt had attracted Washington's attention. When, in the spring, the question came up of sending a minister to Holland, Washington rightly thought that none was better qualified than this young man who had been partly educated in Holland, and knew the country and the people. On the 30th of May, John Adams had the joy of seeing the Senate ratify the nomination made by the President. Ten days later the Senate adjourned and the Vice President hurried back to Braintree.

[54] April 15, May 10, 1794. Works, Vol. I, pp. 471, 473.
[55] May 11, 1794. Jefferson Papers, Library of Congress.

During the following months he remained apparently in-different to the political controversies raging in the clubs and in the gazettes. Perhaps he had at last learned his lesson and resolved not to speak too much and not to write at all. For a man of his temperament, he had observed a singular discretion when subjected to the fiercest attacks. With the departure from America of John Quincy, who had made himself the champion of his father's ideas more than his mouthpiece, John Adams remained more isolated than ever.

The editors, it is true, had found another *"bête noire"*, and Jay had hardly sailed from New York Harbor when the Galli-can party took him as a target. When it was learned that he had kissed the queen's hand, he was accused of having "prostrated at the feet of majesty the sovereignty of the people." Abuse was heaped on him even before anything was known of the negotiations conducted with Grenville in London. Adams was not entirely forgotten, for when an effigy of John Jay was pilloried in Philadelphia during the summer, "hung from the neck by a hemp string was a copy of the 'Defence of the Con-stitutions'." [56]

When the Senate convened again, nothing was known of the treaty, which was signed on November 19, 1794. Adams apparently gave little attention to the changes introduced dur-ing the winter in the cabinet of Washington. Hamilton had ceased to be Secretary of the Treasury on January 31, 1795, and was succeeded by Oliver Wolcott, Jr., while Knox had resigned as Secretary of War, and Timothy Pickering had been appointed in his stead. As a disinterested observer, he followed the events in France, and predicted more than once that the efforts of the French to get rid of the nobility would prove futile, for nobility was founded in nature. [57] Congress had already adjourned, and Adams returned to Braintree, when early in March, 1795, the text of the treaty with Great Britain reached America. Adams presided over the special session of the Senate called at the beginning of June, to discuss and ratify the terms reached as a result of Jay's negotiations in London.

[56] *New York Journal*, August 2, 1784.   [57] Maclay, *op. cit.*, p. 339.

They were far from satisfactory, and the treaty could not be considered a triumph of diplomacy. Jay had obtained little and conceded much. According to his instructions, he had safeguarded the principle that there would be no deviation "from our treaties and engagements with France", obtained damages for the Caribbean spoliations, and secured limited admission of American ships into the West Indies trade. He had been unable, however, to secure recognition of the doctrine of "free goods, free ships"; he had accepted the British admiralty's definition of contraband; no article protecting American seamen had been inserted in the treaty, no satisfactory arrangement concerning the Indians had been reached; the forts still occupied by the British on the Canadian border were not to be evacuated immediately; and the question of the debts was to cause a great deal of discontent.[58] He had succeeded in avoiding an impending war, in removing at some sacrifice of the national *amour propre* causes of war; but it was generally felt that he had yielded too much and gained too little. As the Senate deliberated behind closed doors and in strict secrecy, little of this dissatisfaction transpired outside, but when it came to a vote, the treaty barely obtained the necessary majority of two thirds, being ratified by a vote of twenty to ten.

Adams had no occasion to express his opinion or to cast a vote, and even in his letters to his wife he was singularly reticent. The word "was mum-mum-mum", and he had reached the wise but for us unfortunate conclusion that "the least said the soonest mended." That he was not entirely pleased with the treaty can be read between the lines, for it was a matter of great importance not to be "rejected or adopted without a thorough examination." On the other hand, he was not entirely displeased to see that Mr. Jay had aroused a great deal of antagonism and that his chance to succeed Washington had been considerably lessened. Indeed, it was fortunate for the negotiator that he had been elected Governor of New York before the treaty was published.[59]

[58] For a judicious and well-documented estimate see Samuel Flagg Bemis, "Jay's Treaty. A study in commerce and diplomacy." New York, 1923.

[59] June 18, 1795. Works, Vol. I, p. 479.

When the Senate adjourned on June 25th, enjoining its members not to communicate to the "public" any copy of the treaty, Adams little suspected that another storm was brewing. From the safe retreat of Braintree he watched dispassionately the fury of the Republicans when the treaty was prematurely published in the *Aurora;* he read in the papers accounts of the indignation meetings held everywhere in the country against Jay and "the British tories", and the addresses sent to the President adjuring him not to sign. He was still away from Philadelphia when a dispatch of Fauchet (Genêt's successor) to the Directory was intercepted by the British and communicated to the American Government. It foretold of a revolution preparing in the West, pictured Washington as a man betrayed by his ministers, who "disguised truth from him", all of which was based upon conversations that had taken place between Secretary of State Randolph and the French minister. Randolph, forced to resign, wrote later in the year a feeble "Vindication of Mr. Randolph's Resignation", which did not come to the hand of Adams until he returned to Philadelphia.

On Randolph himself, he wasted no tears; happy was the country to be rid of him, but for Washington he expressed the most sincere admiration: "The President appears great in Randolph's vindication throughout, excepting that he wavered about signing the treaty, which he ought not to have done one moment." Evidently, if Adams had at first entertained some doubts about the advisability of ratifying the famous treaty, he had been thoroughly converted, not so much perhaps by the able "defence" of Jay presented by Hamilton during the summer, as by the attacks of the patriots. At the same time he realized that his chances to succeed Washington had been singularly enhanced. The treaty had been ratified as a matter of expediency, and Jay deserved some credit for having avoided an impending war with Great Britain, but it was no great diplomatic victory, and nothing to compare with that "red-letter day" when an armistice had been signed "between the United States and Great Britain in 1783." The treaty was now before the House, and the Representatives had demanded from the President that the papers connected with the negotiations be submitted to them, thus questioning the treaty-making power of the executive. Both Washington and Jay were pelted with abuse and insults by the patriots; no new Secretary of State had been appointed to succeed Randolph, and Washington, feeling discouraged and tired, had manifested his firm intention to retire.

Adams was too well informed of the political situation not to realize that his chance had finally come. As he had always done in similar circumstances, he weighed in his mind his personal preferences for a simple, dignified retirement with his wife and "children" against what he called the claims of his "country." This was just a formula which he had so often used that he probably did not remember at the time that with Abigail married to Colonel Smith, John Quincy a minister to Holland, and Charles become a self-supporting and independent young man, his children had now little claim on him. He had already resolved to do what "Providence shall point out" to be his duty, and "to watch the course of events with more critical attention" than he had done for some time.[60]

During the whole session of Congress, Adams was treated as the "heir apparent", and he became quite "a favorite" in the society circles of Philadelphia. The numerous attentions paid to him put some honey in the "bitter, nauseous, and unwholesome" cup of party malevolence.[61] In his letters to his wife, and undoubtedly in conversations with his friends he pretended to be still hesitating; he felt that perhaps he ought to retire with his file leader. But unconsciously he gave himself away when he deplored the fact that he was "too old" to continue "more than one, or, at most, more than two heats", and a single term was "scarcely time enough to form, conduct, and complete any very useful system." Real as his ambition was to round up his career on the presidential "throne", he had never felt "less anxiety when any considerable change" lay before him. It was a question of exchanging small cares for great cares, of living at Philadelphia or at Quincy, and both had distinct disadvantages, for quite sincerely Adams could say that he hated "speeches,

[60] January 7, 1796. Works, Vol. I, p. 483.
[61] January 20, 1796. Ibid., p. 485.

messages, addresses and answers, proclamations, and such affected, studied, constrained things." [62]

Not affiliated with any party, attacked as fiercely and feared as much by Hamilton's friends as by the Republicans, Adams maintained a curious and, for him, very unusual detachment, while the battle around the treaty was raging in the house and Washington became the most bitterly attacked and the most abused man in the nation. At times he felt that were he in the House, he could still make speeches, throw light on some questions, and castigate the mobocrats; but these were only passing whims. Not exerting himself in any way to make new friends or keep old ones, going openly to hear his old London acquaintance, Doctor Priestley, although Priestley was a deist and had been triumphantly received by the Republicans, reading Tacitus and Homer, Adams waited for Congress to adjourn, longing for his horse, his farm, his long walks, and his home. By a singular coincidence, Jefferson, in his hermitage of Monticello, seemed even more indifferent to the coming election, and apparently was entirely occupied in agricultural and scientific pursuits. The first presidential election to be disputed was to take place without any direct participation of the protagonists. No platform was issued by them; they made no flamboyant speeches, they promised nothing to their partisans. Apparently they wrote no letters, and, as in a modern battle, the two generals of the opposing armies established their headquarters far from the point where the rank and file were fighting their battles.

It had been suspected and even unofficially known that Washington would not accept a third term, but the campaign did not begin until September, when the President made public his "Farewell Address", and gave in this political testament his best advice to the American people. As Adams had foreseen, Jay's chances to succeed Washington had been utterly destroyed by the mission to England, and, in spite of the efforts of some New York friends, he was never seriously considered. An attempt was made by the Hamiltonians to press the candidacy of Thomas Pinckney of North Carolina, who was repre-

[62] March 1, 1796. Works, Vol. I, p. 487.

sented by Fenno's *Gazette of the United States* as a true Republican, and a stanch defender of the Constitution; but it soon appeared that the contest would be restricted to the two outstanding candidates, Jefferson and Adams.

In violence and scurrility the campaign of 1796–1797 has hardly been surpassed in the history of American politics. Adams was accused of entertaining dark designs against the Republic, of having no faith, no confidence in elective government. He was represented as a man who believed "with the jealous enemies of our Constitution abroad that a Monarchical Constitution is not only better than a Federal Constitution, but that a mixed Monarchy is the best of all possible governments." [63] His "Defence of the Constitutions" and the "Discourses on Davila" were scrutinized line by line, and every word extracted which could lend support to this opinion. He had discarded his sword and wig, but he still "prized *à la mode de noblesse*", and no title could better fit a man so much in love with nobility than "His Rotundity", for what he thought was his majestic appearance was just "sesquipedality of belly." [64] One had to admit that Mr. Adams was "an honest and moral man", and his religious sentiments were "his own", but since Jefferson was attacked for his reputed atheism, it was fit to remember that Mr. Adams was in communion with the Socinians, for "he was a disciple of Priestley and Priestley denies the divinity of Christ." The *Boston Chronicle* pointed out that if the Vice President were elected, the principle of hereditary succession would be established. It would mean at any rate that the errors of Washington's administration would be continued, that the new President would pursue the system of his predecessor; it was an expensive system, and it would result in a war with France.

No less fierce were the attacks against Jefferson, and Noah Webster in New York, as well as Fenno in Philadelphia, presented him as a friend of Genêt and the *Sans-culottes*, a rank atheist, a coward who had fled before Tarleton's cavalry during the war, a so-called philosopher interested in futile problems

[63] *Aurora*, November 11, 1796.
[64] *Aurora*, November 4, 1796.

of anatomy and the odoriferous glands of the Negroes, as clearly appeared in the "Notes on Virginia." As the campaign progressed, it became more and more evident that foreign politics would be exploited to the limit by the opposing parties. Jefferson, "friend of France", supported openly by the French minister Adet, who after being recalled, had just published in the papers notes and articles attacking the President, a man whose partisans were wearing the tricolor cockade of the French patriots, who would probably insist on an alliance with France which would necessarily entail war with Great Britain. On the other hand, Adams would insist on enforcing against France the humiliating clauses of the Jay treaty, would openly favor Great Britain, which could only result in a war with France. Never perhaps was the electorate more bewildered and, in the absence of any definite program from the candidates, the newspaper editors had a completely free field for their calumnious insinuations or direct insults.

Meanwhile both Adams and Jefferson maintained an Olympian detachment. At the beginning of December, the Vice President wrote to his wife: "John Adams must be an intrepid to encounter the open assaults of France, and the secret plots of England, in concert with all his treacherous friends and open enemies in his own country. Yet, I assure you, he never felt more serene in his life." [65] A few weeks later, Jefferson was moved to write his old friend that although the papers had been much occupied to place them "in a point of opposition to each other", he trusted that their personal feelings had not been affected. "It is possible," he added, "that you may be cheated of your succession by a trick worthy the subtlety of your arch-friend of New York [Hamilton] who has been able to make of your real friends tools to defeat their and your just wishes. Most probably he will be disappointed as to you; and my inclinations place me out of his reach." [66] As for him, he had no personal ambition, no sympathy for spies and sycophants, no desire for a painful and thankless office. Whether

[65] Works, Vol. I, pp. 494–495.
[66] December 28, 1796. "Writings of Jefferson", Memorial Edition, Vol. IX, p. 355.

the letter sent through Madison was ever delivered or not, it does honor both to Adams and Jefferson.

At that date, Adams already had reason to believe that "neither Jefferson will be President, nor Pinckney Vice President." Giles had said: "The V. P. will be President. He is undoubtedly chosen. The old man will make a good President, too." [67]

The day came when it was the official duty of the Vice President to proclaim the result of the election. On the 8th of February, "the tellers set down the votes", and the ballots of the electors were opened by John Adams. He had received seventy-one, Jefferson sixty-eight, Pinckney fifty-nine, Aaron Burr thirty, and Samuel Adams eleven. The election had been even closer than he expected; he was a "President by three votes", as he himself declared, and as his enemies were to remind him frequently during the next four years. On that day, however, there was no bitterness in him, and we may well assume that he shared the sentiments of his wife, who wrote that her feelings were "not those of pride or ostentation upon the occasion. They are solemnized by a sense of the obligations, the important trusts and numerous duties connected with it." [68]

In very handsome words he took leave of the Senate a week later. [69] He was even pleased to note "in that moiety of the senators from whose judgment I have been obliged to dissent", a disposition to allow him "the same freedom of deliberation and independence of judgment which they asserted for themselves." In his conclusion he availed himself of the opportunity to make his position clear and, indirectly, to protest against some of the accusations launched against him in the papers. He did not take back any of the principles enunciated in the "Defence of the American Constitutions"; he still had the same distrust of popular assemblies, and the same belief in the necessity of checks and balances — but he did feel that from his experience he could proclaim that there was a "consolatory hope (if the legislatures of the States are equally careful in

[67] December 12, 1796. Works, Vol. I, p. 495.
[68] February 8, 1797. Ibid., p. 496.
[69] February 15, 1797. Ibid., pp. 497–498.

their future selections, which there is no reason to distrust), that no council more permanent than this, as a branch of the legislature, will be necessary to defend the rights, liberties, and properties of the people, and to protect the Constitution of the United States, as well as the constitutions and rights of the individual States, against errors of judgment, irregularities of the passions, or other encroachments of human infirmity, or more reprehensible enterprise, in the Executive on the one hand, or the more immediate representatives of the people on the other hand."

This was no Fourth of July oration, and Adams was no Fourth of July speaker. There was little in his address that could please the editors and partisans who had fought the Federalist battle, there was even less that could please the Republicans, since Adams seemed none too certain of the permanency of the American system of government. But in these few words he expressed his very self better than on any other occasion and gave a perfect summary of his political philosophy.

CHAPTER II

FIGHTING FOR NEUTRALITY

On March 4, 1797, in the presence of the retiring President, "the great and good Washington", who had taken a seat as a private citizen, and before the members of the Senate and House of Representatives, the son of the Braintree farmer was inducted into office.[1] With mingled pleasure and surprise, the Republicans in Congress saw that he had discarded the little sword he had worn for a time, when presiding over the Senate. He had not devised any uniform or court dress to impress the common people with his new dignity. He wore a simple suit of light gray, with no jeweled buttons or buckles to adorn it; he had not permitted "the marshall and other officers to walk in procession before his carriage",[2] and he had sent back to their stables the four white horses of his predecessor. At one stroke, this supposed champion of monarchy had discarded all the trappings of gentry and of royalty. This was democracy, and his entire inaugural speech was full of the purest and most genuine republican spirit.

The address was as much a declaration of republican faith as a purely political speech. Adams had not been concerned with details of the previous administration; he had made no particular study of finance or commerce, had received no desiderata from any group, and had no precise measures to recommend to Congress for immediate attention. He knew, however, that his different publications on government had been variously interpreted, that his republicanism was much in doubt, and that he had been accused of favoring the establishment of a monarchy. It was his duty in taking office to abandon

[1] "Annals of Congress", p. 1582.
[2] *Aurora*, March 28, 1797.

all the theorizing in which he had heretofore indulged unreservedly and imprudently. He had not now to speculate on
the best form of government but to define his attitude towards
existing American institutions. This he did in such a manner as
to win the approval of even the Republicans, at least for a short
time, to the dismay of the Hamiltonians.

In the first part of his address Adams traced in a masterly
way the history of the last twenty-five years. He proclaimed
his faith in a form of government so well deserving the esteem
and love of all citizens; he derided "the robes and diamonds"
of the old governments and praised the people for their virtue
and the general dissemination of knowledge among them.
Never a party man, he could truthfully maintain that his only
preference was for "the principle of a free government formed
upon long and serious reflection, after a diligent and impartial
inquiry after truth." In alluding to foreign affairs, he declared
that he had "an inflexible determination to maintain peace and
inviolable faith with all nations, and that system of neutrality
and impartiality among the belligerent powers of Europe
which has been adopted by the government, and so solemnly
sanctioned by both Houses of Congress." But much to the delight of the Gallicans and the rage of the Anglomaniacs, he
added that he felt "a personal esteem for the French nation,
formed in a residence of seven years, chiefly among them, and
a sincere desire to preserve the friendship which has been so
much for the honor and integrity of the people of America."

Quite honestly and sincerely Adams was calling upon all
good citizens to put an end to the spirit of party and internal
dissensions — the only dangers threatening the country. For a
few days before and after his inauguration he could entertain
the optimistic illusion that he would succeed; he had underestimated the violence of professional agitators and the influence of rabid editors, who, sincerely or not, fed the fire with
passionate denunciations of the French or English parties. He
had also underestimated the stubbornness of the cabinet he inherited from Washington. "Ali Baba among his Forty Thieves
is no more deserving of sympathy than John Adams shut up
within the seclusion of his Cabinet room with his official fam-

ily of secret enemies" — such a characterization as this, given by Mr. Claude G. Bowers, is hardly too severe.[3]

Belonging to no group, having a few real friends whom he could take into his confidence and upon whom he could rely, Adams agreed to retain Washington's cabinet. Timothy Pickering, a Puritan office-seeker, was to remain as Secretary of State; Oliver Wolcott, a more genial but even less honest man, as Secretary of the Treasury, and James McHenry, a pleasant, worldly fellow with Irish charm and versatility, as Secretary of War. The three of them were Hamilton's creatures and devoted to their chief, who, from his retreat in New York, intended to direct the policy of the government. The Attorney-General, Charles Lee, was a good and honest lawyer, but without initiative or great political influence, and he could not counterbalance his colleagues. That Adams did not realize at once the true situation and did not clean the governmental house at one sweep seems inconceivable. Whether or not he had hopes of converting them to his views and harmonizing them, his retention of the old cabinet was the original mistake, from which most of his subsequent difficulties were to result.

That he intended to pursue a truly national policy and to remain above all party divisions had already appeared in his conversation with Jefferson two days before the inauguration. Relations with the French Republic remained the most dangerous problem of the new administration. Following Monroe's recall, it had been decided to send Pinckney as ambassador to the Directory, but in Adams' estimation Pinckney had not the necessary qualities to bring the negotiations to a successful conclusion. He consequently resolved to send a mission which "by its dignity should satisfy France, and by its selection from the three great divisions of the continent, should satisfy all parts of the United States." Jefferson, whom he had been urged by several advisers to appoint, was out of the question, for the "heir apparent" could not leave the country; but Madison could perhaps be prevailed upon to accept the mission, and would certainly be *persona grata* to the French.

On the morning of March 2d, Adams called alone on Jef-

[3] "Jefferson and Hamilton", Boston, 1925, p. 314.

ferson, to enlist his assistance, and had with him a very friendly talk. There was every indication that the President and the Vice President would work harmoniously, and that Adams' administration would be one of national union. Four days later, however, Adams had undergone a sudden change in disposition: when he saw Jefferson again, he refrained from mentioning the Paris mission and was cool and reserved, instead of open and friendly. Jefferson, not unwisely, surmised that in the meantime a meeting of the cabinet had taken place, and that Adams had been diverted from his original plan "to steer impartially between the parties" and had returned to his "former party views." [4]

For a few weeks it seemed that the President would be able to avoid further difficulties. Relations with England were far from satisfactory, but a compromise had been reached, and the Board of Commissioners established by the sixth article of Jay's treaty might enable the two nations to settle peaceably the questions still pending. The French situation was less satisfactory, but no news had yet been received of the mission of Monroe's successor, General C. C. Pinckney, and there was some hope that an arrangement might be concluded with the French Republic. Two weeks after Adams' inauguration, Knox could write him that his speech had given "general satisfaction", and that "the part relative to France was peculiarly pleasing." [5] The *Aurora* hailed Adams as a "real patriot" and a "practical republican." The country was undoubtedly in need of peace, and he had at least a chance to coalesce the more moderate elements of the population, and not only to keep the country out of war, but to develop a constructive national policy. This, however, was reckoning without the hot-headed editors and the stupidity of the Directory, explicable only by their lack of precise information on the real disposition of the new President.

News of the Jay treaty was received in France as a direct slap at the Republic, and it had taken all the diplomatic skill of Monroe, who was liked and esteemed by the French, to

[4] "Writings of Thomas Jefferson", Memorial Edition, Vol. I, p. 415.
[5] March 19, 1797. Works, Vol. VIII, p. 533.

avoid an open break. The Directory repeatedly presented formal protests regarding the "inexecution of the old treaties" and the departure, in favor of England, from the principles of neutrality established during the War of Independence.[6] At the time of Monroe's recall, the Directors had renewed their complaints in vehement terms, and the French consul in Philadelphia on several occasions had openly criticized the American Government and the President; but diplomatic relations had not been broken off between the two countries and, apparently, there was no reason why some arrangement could not be reached with France, as it had been with England.

Adams was too well informed of the European situation really to believe that the United States would not suffer in many ways, or that they would be able to maintain unobstructed commercial intercourse with Europe and the West Indies as long as Great Britain and France remained at war. However, he was no more desirous of siding with Great Britain than with France, but was thoroughly convinced that a declaration of war against either would necessarily embroil the United States in the most dangerous complications. To save at least the appearance of national honor, to reserve the rights of the United States, to support their claims for indemnity for the unwarranted seizure of their ships by the belligerents, to keep a stiff upper lip, and even to threaten retaliation, never to relinquish an iota of the principle of neutrality and the rights of neutrals, to do anything in his power short of an actual declaration of war — such seem to have been the main lines of the program that he followed during the four years of his administration as consistently as was in his character. At times he departed from it. Smarting under insults to the American flag, irked at the delays in negotiation, and yielding to the pressure exerted by Pickering and McHenry, he called the country to arms and made bellicose speeches; but on the whole, and in decisive circumstances, he did all he could to avoid an official recognition that a state of war existed between France and the United States, and exerted all his influence to preserve a neutrality which should be more than a mere diplomatic fiction.

[6] "American State Papers", March 9, 1796, Vol. II, p. 496.

Although he has received very little credit for it, and was damned equally by Gallomaniacs and Anglomaniacs, he nevertheless succeeded in keeping the only course which at that time the United States could possibly follow. The good husbandman would have delighted in setting in order the national house, in developing agriculture, and furthering national education. He had clear notions on these subjects and had expressed some of them in the constitution of Massachusetts; but by an ironic fate, for four years he had to wrestle with war problems, and his political horizon was never free from war clouds.

In the third week of March, disquieting news began to circulate; it was rumored that the Directory had refused to receive General Pinckney and that he had been ordered to leave French territory. Soon confirmation was received that the American envoy had crossed the frontier and taken up his abode at Amsterdam. It was not war, but war might be declared at any time; the issue was at the mercy of the least incident, and Adams, unwilling to assume further responsibility, decided to convene Congress in special session "to consult and determine on such measures as in their wisdom shall be deemed meet for the safety and welfare of the United States."

Congress was not to assemble until May 15th, but meanwhile the war was fought in advance in the papers. The *Gazette of the United States* declared that the country had been insulted by the Directory's refusal to receive Pinckney; the Republican papers, on the contrary, defended the action of the French Government and reaffirmed their friendship for France. Philadelphia celebrated the victories of the French Republic in Italy and the surrender of Mantua, while Hamilton was accused of trying to precipitate war, as he had tried to do more than once before. Two weeks prior to the reunion of Congress, the New York *Minerva* printed an alleged text of the letter written to Mazzei by Jefferson a year earlier, and new fuel was added to the controversy. But until the last minute the Republican organs made every effort to conciliate Adams, maintaining that war could be avoided and proclaiming their faith in the prudence of the President.

In the meantime Adams, following Washington's precedent,

had sent a questionnaire to the members of his cabinet, asking them particularly whether the refusal to receive Pinckney was a bar "to all further measures of negotiations" or whether "a fresh mission to Paris" would be "too great a humiliation of the American people." [7] Pickering was unequivocal in his answer and decidedly favored reopening negotiations without "fraternizing words"; McHenry was no less decidedly for further negotiations. Wolcott, in a long and ambiguous answer, seemed to oppose the sending of new envoys to the Directory.

On the whole there was no strong desire in the government to come to an open break with France, and there is no indication that Adams himself was eager to precipitate the issue; but the speech delivered by him on May 15th was to destroy the last illusions of the Gallicans. In fact, it was moderate enough. He made a perceptible effort to present the French situation in a judicial light, although he called attention to "the wound" that these recent incidents had "inflicted in the American breast." He resented not so much the refusal to receive Pinckney as the laudatory words of the Directory to Monroe on his taking leave of the French Government. In these words the President saw an effort to separate the people of the United States from the government, and thus to "produce divisions fatal to our peace." But being of the opinion that neither the honor nor the interest of the United States absolutely forbade a repetition of advances, he declared that he was ready "to institute a fresh attempt at negotiation." All of which would probably have been accepted without much protest, even by the champions of the French cause, if, in the second part of his address, he had not recommended a series of measures clearly indicating that, in his opinion, war was unavoidable. Not only did he advocate the establishment of a strong navy to protect American commerce against the abuses and insults of foreign nations, but he was no less positive in his recommendation that the regular artillery and cavalry be increased, and new laws passed for "organizing, arming, and disciplining the militia, to render that natural and safe defense of the country efficacious."

[7] To the Heads of Department, April 14, 1797. Works, Vol. VIII, p. 540.

This was simply intolerable! How could the man dare to speak for the people when he was just a "three votes President"? His address was not a state paper — it was a war song, or rather "a war-whoop!" Adams had feigned humility in order to be elected, but "if a man played the hypocrite for the purposes of the basest deception, the President by three votes was the man." [8] Unfortunately for Adams, one of the first actions of the Senate had been to ratify the nomination of John Quincy Adams as minister plenipotentiary to the Court of Berlin, and it was too easy for the *Aurora* to remark that "George Washington had never appointed to any station in government, even the most distant of his relations." [9] The whole argumentation was summed up in an appeal to the true patriots of America "to come forward in a manly tone of remonstrance to induce Mr. Adams to resign the helm to safer hands before it be too late to retrieve our deranged affairs." [10]

The Senate, without much debate, had acknowledged and indorsed in principle the President's declaration, but the House of Representatives had to provide the means to raise more revenue for the intended armament and militia. For several weeks the terms of the President's speech were discussed, and the answer was not delivered until the 3d of June. There has always been a natural unwillingness in the American people to increase armament and military expenditures. Only reluctantly, and not always adequately, had they consented during the Revolutionary War to make the necessary sacrifices. One could easily see that a strong navy would protect American trade, and the building and commissioning of three frigates passed without opposition; but it took a stronger effort of the imagination, and a more bellicose spirit, to vote large sums for the artillery, and to increase the militia to eighty thousand when no immediate danger threatened American territory. "Will they walk upon the sea, to protect American merchantmen?" asked the *Aurora*. Not only was this measure useless, it was dangerous, for in the bill (to which Hamilton had probably put his

[8] *Aurora*, May 18, 22 and June 6, 1797.
[9] *Ibid.*, May 22, 1797.
[10] *Ibid.*, June 19, 1797.

hand) could clearly be perceived the intention of creating a permanent and well-disciplined army. There was some hope that Europe would soon be pacified, and there was no strong reason to believe that America could not then conclude a satisfactory arrangement with France. Such was the plea of the pacifists, convinced that the enforcement of the President's recommendation could only promote a war spirit which sooner or later would draw America into that vortex which he pretended to be so anxious to avoid. Furthermore, one of the taxes proposed for the raising of new revenue bore a very unfelicitous name — it was to be a "stamp tax"; another consisted of an additional duty on salt, and neither the condition of the country nor the state of the public treasury warranted such an increase of a burden already too heavy, for there were in the Treasury "more than $90,000 in bills on which no interest had been paid." [11]

The atmosphere of Philadelphia in the early summer was not conducive to the promotion of judicial discussions in Congress. Monroe, who had just returned from France and thought he had been unjustly treated by Pickering, was asking for justification and the "blessings of an honest fame." Unable to obtain satisfactory explanations for his recall, he finally gave to the papers his correspondence with the Secretary of State. On the other hand, a member of the Senate, William Blount of Tennessee, implicated in a wild conspiracy to invade the territorial possession of Spain, was brought before the House and impeachment proceedings started. The *Aurora* did not fail to point out that although Sir Robert Liston, the English minister, had been aware of the conspiracy, the American Secretary of State in his communications to him employed "a canting, fawning style" which was ample evidence that there were "collusive proceedings between Timothy Pickering and his Majesty's minister." [12]

In this turmoil the President managed to keep a cool head. The Directory had refused to receive Pinckney as minister

[11] *Aurora*, June 19, 1797.
[12] *Ibid.*, July 10, 17 and August 18, 1797. "Annals of Congress", July 6, 7, 8, 1797.

plenipotentiary from the United States, but it had never said that the French Government would not welcome a new mission. In justice to Pinckney, he had to be reappointed as special envoy; the second member was to be John Marshall of Virginia, and for the third, Adams thought at first of Dana, who had worked under him at The Hague and whom he had advised when, still a young man, he had been sent to Russia. Upon Dana's refusal, he turned to an old friend whom he could trust and whose patriotism was beyond suspicion — Elbridge Gerry of Massachusetts. The fact that Gerry was counted a Republican did not deter him, but some of his ministers who had not the same broadness of mind could hardly conceal their disapproval of this nomination.[13] In the letters to Gerry urging him to accept the appointment, the President reiterated his "sincere desire that an accommodation may take place", and his wish for peace and friendship with the French.[14] He had but little hope that the mission would succeed, for he knew too well the methods of European diplomacy not to believe the negotiation would be "spun out into an immeasurable length", but this he carefully concealed from the negotiators, and the instructions they carried with them were distinctly conciliatory. They were authorized "to terminate our differences in such manner as without referring to the merits of our complaints and pretensions, might be best calculated to produce mutual satisfaction and good understanding." The "depredations on American commerce" were not to be treated by the envoys, but referred for settlement to a special commission. The desire of the new President to avoid further difficulties and to reach an agreement could not be questioned.

Congress had adjourned on July 10th, and the epidemic of yellow fever that seemed to be a regular occurrence had already started when Hamilton suddenly appeared in Philadelphia. It was suspected that he had not come for the benefit of the fresh air. Undoubtedly his purpose was to give instructions to "the wrong head of Timothy Pickering and the weak head of

[13] Gibbs, "Administrations of Washington and John Adams", Vol. I, p. 531.
[14] July 8 and 17, 1797. Works, Vol. VIII, pp. 547, 549.

John Adams." [15] Only two days later it was hinted that he had come on a much more personal matter, and shortly thereafter the letter exposing the sordid details of his love affair with Mrs. Reynolds and the blackmailing which followed, was made public — possibly by Monroe — much to the delight of the Republicans.

Adams had already left Philadelphia, and in his retreat at Quincy found a modicum of peace, while the press quarrels, unabated by the epidemic, raged in the temporary capital of the nation. It was a gloomy summer, and he felt that "a torpor, a despondency has seized all men in America as well as Europe." [16] The news that Talleyrand had succeeded Delacroix as Minister of Foreign Affairs gave a faint ray of hope, however, for he had been cordially received in America and had not the slightest reason for complaint. He could not be for war, and there was reason to believe that the Triumvirate would avoid "a measure so decided."

The President's message sent to Congress on November 23d was remarkably moderate in tone. Adams expressed some hope that the envoys extraordinary to the French Republic would succeed in obtaining terms compatible with the safety, honor, and interests of the United States; but the old pessimist could not pass this opportunity to express his views of human nature:

> The state of society has so long been disturbed, the sense of moral and religious obligations so much weakened, public faith and national honor have been so much impaired, respect to treaties has been so diminished, and the law of nations has lost so much of its force, while pride, ambition, avarice, and violence, have been so long unrestrained, there remains no reasonable ground on which to raise an expectation, that a commerce, without protection or defence, will not be plundered.

During the Revolution and his stay in Europe, Adams had often expressed his disapproval of the commercial bent of his fellow countrymen. He had clearly perceived that in the disturbed condition of Europe, foreign commerce would ultimately embroil the United States in foreign difficulties. On this

---

[15] *Aurora,* July 17, 1797.
[16] To O. Wolcott, Jr., October 27, 1797. Works, Vol. VIII, p. 559.

point he would have agreed perfectly with Jefferson, but like Jefferson he thought he had no right to force his personal philosophy of life on New Englanders and merchants of the seacoast, and in his message he spoke for the country more than for himself.

The commerce of the United States is essential, if not to their existence, at least to their comfort, their growth, prosperity, and happiness. The genius, character, and habits of the people are highly commercial. Their cities have been formed and exist upon commerce. Our agriculture, fisheries, arts and manufactures are connected with and depend upon it. In short, commerce has made this country what it is; it cannot be destroyed or neglected without involving the people in poverty and distress.

The American envoys, after staying in Holland, where they met Pinckney, had finally arrived in Paris on the 4th of October. On the 8th, they had a very short interview with Talleyrand, who refused to discuss any matter of importance with them. A few days later, however, the envoys received the visit of a mysterious emissary of the French minister, who indicated that there were serious obstacles to the official reception of the American envoys. Two of the Directors had been exceedingly irritated at some passages in the President's speech, and amends would have to be made. Furthermore, the French Government expected to obtain a loan from the United States, and it would be understood that from this loan should first be taken certain sums for the purpose of making the "customary distributions in diplomatic affairs." An interview between Gerry and Talleyrand failed to bring forward any proposition acceptable to the American envoys, the French minister insisting that if they had no power to negotiate a loan they could at least provide "a *douceur*" which would soften the feelings of the Directors and thus obtain permission to stay in Paris, pending new instructions from their government.[17] Talleyrand's emissary had used threatening language, expatiating on the danger of a breach with France, and on her power, which "nothing could resist."

[17] October 27, 1797. "American State Papers", Vol. III, p. 490.

It is generally admitted that the first dispatches of the American envoys sent by a vessel sailing November 28th were not received until March 4th of the following year. This does not mean, however, that Adams was completely unaware of the situation in Paris. He had been informed by Pinckney that at the beginning of November the envoys had not been received and, in his opinion, "would not be",[18] and we may surmise that Gerry would not have left him entirely without news. Whether he was particularly clear-sighted or had received private information that he did not divulge to the members of his cabinet, on January 24th he sent to the "Heads of Departments" a questionnaire asking them for expressions of opinions on the policy to be followed in case France should refuse an audience to the envoys extraordinary, or should order them to depart without accomplishing the objects of their mission.[19] The wording of the questionnaire itself shows clearly Adams' own preferences at an early date. He was evidently averse to an outright declaration of war, not so much out of a remnant of sympathy for France, as through his strong reluctance to favor England and, indirectly, to fight England's battles. He felt very strongly that it would be difficult to avoid some sort of connection with a nation which stood on the brink of a dangerous precipice and might drag America down in her fall.

McHenry pointed out that there was "a general aversion to war in the minds of the people of the United States, and a particular dislike, on the part of a portion of them, to a war with France"; consequently he recommended the pursuance of "a vigorous defensive plan", but, at the same time, the maintenance of the appearance of a disposition to negotiate, particularly if one or more of the commissioners should remain in Europe. Charles Lee, the Attorney-General, alone was for an immediate declaration of war, while Pickering, who had to be moderated by Hamilton, would have entered into an alliance offensive and defensive with Great Britain.

On the 5th of March the President informed Congress that

[18] Wolcott to Washington, January 30, 1798, in Gibbs, *op. cit.*, Vol. II, p. 12.
[19] Works, Vol. VIII, p. 561.

the first dispatches from the envoys extraordinary had been received. They were in cipher, except one of such importance that he thought it his duty to communicate it at once. It was the message of the Directory dated January 4, 1798, in which the French Government declared its intention to extend the provisions of the decree of 1794, that "the condition of vessels in what concerns their quality of neutral or enemy, shall be determined by their cargo, and that the cargo shall be no longer covered by the flag: in consequence, that every vessel found at sea, having on board English merchandise and commodities as her cargo, in whole or in part, shall be declared to be good prize, whosoever may be the proprietor of these commodities or merchandise." [20]

As the dispatches were deciphered, the whole intrigue was gradually revealed, with its characters worthy of Beaumarchais' pen: the two bankers, Hottinguer and Bellamy, Monsieur Hauteval, the mysterious lady and, behind the scene, the archplotter Talleyrand, haughty, distant and cynical, pulling the strings of his puppets. At first the envoys had manifested no moral indignation at the proposal to bribe the members of the Directory; they had simply considered that a loan to France would be a breach of neutrality and could not accept the French theory that this constituted a preliminary to further negotiations. The end of the story was to remain unknown for several months. Late in March, Marshall departed for home, Pinckney went to the south of France, and Gerry alone remained in Paris, to avoid a complete break of diplomatic relations.

Adams at first hesitated to communicate the text, or even the substance of the dispatches, to Congress. That such a communication might result in a declaration of war was a danger of which he was fully aware. On March 16th he sent to the "Gentlemen of the Senate" and of the "House of Representatives" a short message, dignified and moderate in tone, in which he apprised Congress that he could "perceive no ground of expectation that the objects of their mission can be accomplished on terms compatible with the safety, honor, or the essential interests of the nation." He added that he could see noth-

---

[20] "Annals of Congress", House of Representatives, March, 1798, p. 1202.

ing which had been omitted, nothing further which could be attempted. In conclusion, he simply reiterated the recommendation already made for putting the country in a state of defense, and proposed that American vessels be permitted to sail in an "armed condition." [21] This was a direct answer to the decree of the Directory, and a measure recognizing in fact the existence of a state of war, without resorting to a formal declaration of war.

Such was at once the interpretation placed upon the message by the *Aurora:* the Executive called on Americans to draw the sword on the side of England, and in fact the President had declared war without consulting Congress and the people. In the Senate, Humphrey Marshall of Kentucky, as a last measure to avoid open hostilities, proposed an embargo for a limited time "on all ships owned wholly or in part by the United States citizens",[22] but the proposition was voted down. In the House the discussion lasted much longer and was carried on with the usual virulence. The "war message" against France was vehemently denounced. "Gentlemen were willing to engage in a defensive, but not in an offensive war", and many were the Congressmen who expressed their opposition both to war and to the establishment of any connection with England.[23]

To silence opposition, as well as to obtain a favorable vote on measures he deemed essential for the defense of the country, Adams decided to comply with the request of the House, and to communicate in full the dispatches of the envoys, simply substituting the letters X Y Z for the names of Talleyrand's emissaries.

The Republicans made a weak effort to maintain their position and a judicial attitude, for the fact that some members of the French executive were corrupt was no reason for going to war, but their protests were unheeded, and the war spirit, or rather war hysteria, spread over the whole country.[24] It was quite seriously represented that if the French succeeded in de-

[21] "Annals of Congress", House of Representatives, March 19, 1798, p. 1271.

[22] *Ibid.,* Senate, March 27, 1798, p. 532.

[23] *Ibid.,* House of Representatives, March 27, 1798.

[24] *Aurora,* April 9, 1798.

feating the British fleet, or simply in making peace with England, it would be easy for them to land an expeditionary force
on the American continent. Without coast defenses, without a
fleet, without a trained army, America was at the mercy of sudden attack and, chimerical as these fears seem to-day, they undoubtedly were quite genuine. They were expressed not only
by Federalist editors, but by Congressmen, who admitted that
there was probably no immediate danger, but the time to
prepare against such an eventuality was before the enemy had
a chance to start on an expedition, for "it is a joke to talk of
raising a regular army to repel an invasion which has occurred,
or which is, as it were, at our door." [25]

Further uneasiness came from the fact that the number of
French refugees in Philadelphia was still considerable. Not all
of them would have supported the French Republic, but it was
felt that in case of war their allegiance to their country might
be stronger than their political prejudices. The Genêt affair
was still fresh in every one's memory. His successors, Adet
and Fauchet, had shown no restraint in their criticism of Washington and had aroused popular passions against the government. Foreigners had become more than a nuisance; in such an
emergency they constituted a serious danger, and measures had
to be taken to repress their turbulent dispositions.

At this distance it is almost impossible to determine to what
degree these considerations influenced the vote of the Representatives, or whether some deep minds did not see in the
situation a splendid opportunity to concentrate more power in
the hands of the Federal Government. At any rate, the measures recommended by the President in his January messages
were adopted, not without discussion, but with large majorities.
A separate Navy Department, distinct from the War Department, was established, and the fitting out of a fleet authorized;
a "provisional army" of ten thousand men enlisting for three
years was approved; money was appropriated for the manufacture of artillery, and the militia was reorganized under
federal supervision.

Four laws were passed against the enemies at home. On the

[25] Speech of Sitgreaves, May 11, 1798. "Annals of Congress", House of
Representatives.

motion of Sewall, it was decided to lengthen to fourteen years "the length of time necessary for an alien to reside here before he can be admitted a citizen." [26] By another bill the President was given full authority over alien enemies, who could be apprehended, restrained, secured, removed, and, with their goods and effects, be subject to a just retaliation for any unusual severities, restraints, and confiscations that might be suffered by citizens of the United States. This was supplemented with an act providing special penalties in case of treason by an alien. Finally, after a long and eloquent discussion, in which Edward Livingston distinguished himself, the famous Sedition Bill passed by forty-four votes to forty-one. It proclaimed a sort of martial law and provided a fine not exceeding five thousand dollars and imprisonment not exceeding five years for any person who "shall by writing, printing, or speaking, threaten any person holding an office under the government, with damage to his character, person or estate." "Any libellous attack by writing, printing, publishing or speaking against the Legislature of the United States or the President of the United States, or any court or Judge thereof", was only liable to a fine not exceeding two thousand dollars and imprisonment not exceeding two years.[27]

In a letter written ten years later to the *Boston Patriot*, Adams attempted a very weak defense of his attitude on the matter of the most detested legislation ever passed by an American Congress. The alien and sedition laws were really part of the whole system of instruction drawn up by Hamilton for the conduct of the President, the Senate, and the House of Representatives. According to Adams, "such was the influence of Mr. Hamilton in Congress, that, without any recommendation from the President, they passed a bill to raise an army, not a large one, indeed, but enough to overturn the then Federal Government. Nor did I adopt his idea of an alien or sedition law. I recommended no such thing in my speech. Congress, however, adopted both these measures." [28] Nevertheless, after attempting to throw the responsibility on Hamil-

---

[26] "Annals of Congress", House of Representatives, May 21, 1798.
[27] *Ibid.*, July 10, 1798.
[28] Works, Vol. IX, pp. 290–291.

ton, he admitted that, "I knew there was need enough of both, and therefore I consented to them. But as they were then considered as war measures, and intended altogether against the advocates of the French and peace with France, I was apprehensive that a hurricane of clamor would be raised against them, as in truth there was, even more fierce and violent than I had anticipated." A more unconvincing excuse could not be imagined, and Adams stands condemned by his own words. However, he had other preoccupations of a more absorbing nature and already realized that he would not find in his own cabinet the support and coöperation he was entitled to expect.

The last weeks Adams spent in Philadelphia and a large part of the summer were almost exclusively taken up by a question of pure politics, which must have reminded him of the worst days of the Revolutionary War. A new army was to be created, and the plain people as well as the militia were expected to do their duty. There was little doubt that in case of danger they would rally to the colors, as they had previously. The real problem was offered by the choice of officers to command that army of eighty thousand men, so far existing only on paper. No more glorious name than Washington's could be proposed, and although the General could not be prevailed upon to leave his "fig-tree", Adams, after asking him for advice and for the use of his name, instructed the Secretary of War to wait on General Washington with the commission of Lieutenant General and Commander in Chief of the Armies of the United States, which, with the advice and consent of the Senate, he had just signed.[29]

As it was realized that Washington could never take active charge of operations, it was of great importance to decide at once which officer should be "second in command." Washington had been requested to designate the men most suitable for inspector general, adjutant general, and quartermaster general, and suggested General Hamilton for inspector general with the rank of major general, and Charles Pinckney, Henry Knox

[29] June 22, 1798, Works, Vol. VIII, p. 573, and July 6, 1798, Ibid., p. 574.

and Henry Lee for major generals, with the correction that Henry Lee might be offered only a commission of brigadier general and, in that case, should be the ranking officer of that grade. The generals had no opportunity to "march with a quick step", or to use on the battlefield the tactics recommended by Adams, but they fought a mighty battle for precedence, and their quarrel revealed the lack of loyalty of the cabinet officers to the President.[30]

Adams was evidently reluctant to have Hamilton made second in command in name, and in fact commander in chief, and had thought that by making him inspector general he would be able to utilize his recognized talent for organization without placing him actually in command of the army. For this reason, if for no other, he supported against Hamilton the claims of General Knox, for whom he felt no great sympathy. The quarrel, in which Washington, Hamilton, Knox, McHenry and Wolcott were involved, lasted through the summer, and no less than thirteen lengthy documents were exchanged between July 25th and October 13th, on which date the cabinet officers decided that "it would not be respectful to the President to address him again on a subject which appears to have been attended with difficulties in his mind",[31] and urged Wolcott to transmit the commissions to the generals in the order indicated at first by General Washington, namely, Alexander Hamilton, Charles Cotesworth Pinckney, and Henry Knox.

The President took his defeat with unexpected meekness, for he had long since made up his mind to acquiesce in the opinion of Washington if the major generals could not come to some mutual agreement. He had reason to believe that the matter had not the importance the worthy officers attributed to it, and he devoutly hoped that the question of precedence in the field would never have to be settled.

To this quarrel may be attributed the curious change of heart undergone by John Adams during the fall of the year

---

[30] A good account of the battle is to be found in Channing, "A History of the United States", Vol. IV, pp. 191–200. See also, Adams, Works, Vol. VIII, pp. 577, 580, 587, 593, and Gibbs, op. cit., Vol. II, pp. 86–103.

[31] Gibbs, op. cit., Vol. II, p. 103.

1798. In the spring and early summer he had shown a bellicose spirit. He had received countless addresses of young Americans and patriotic organizations pledging their lives for the defense of the country in the warmest terms, and he answered in kind. "To arms! . . . my young friends, to arms!", he had written to the young men of Boston, and he had adjured the young men of New York to "beware of contaminating your country with the foul abominations of the French revolution." In a letter to the Legislature of Massachusetts, he denounced French imperialism, "aiming at dominion such as never has before prevailed in Europe", and he declared to the students of Dickinson College that "if there are any who still plead the cause of France, and attempt to paralyse the efforts of your government, I agree with you, they ought to be esteemed our greatest enemies." Towards the end of the summer, however, this ardor had calmed down considerably. In his retreat at Quincy, far from the feverish agitation of Philadelphia, he looked at things in a more disinterested and objective manner than his cabinet officers, and he felt no strong urge to sound the call to arms. "One thing I know," he wrote McHenry, "that regiments are costly articles everywhere, and more so in this country than any other under the sun. If this nation sees a great army to maintain, without an enemy to fight, there may arise an enthusiasm that seems to be little foreseen. At present there is no more prospect of seeing a French army here, than there is in Heaven." [32]

Adams was too well acquainted with the military mind not to realize that every effort would be made to keep as large a standing army as the country could afford. The danger of a French invasion was chimerical, but plans were already made to embark on a grandiose scheme favored by Hamilton, and of which the President had been apprised during the summer. Francisco de Miranda, a picturesque soldier of fortune, had submitted to Pitt, and then to Adams, a plan for the liberation of the Spanish colonies with the assistance of the British fleet and an American expeditionary corps. [33] Pickering and Hamil-

[32] October 22, 1798. Works, Vol. VIII, p. 613.
[33] To John Adams, March 24, 1798. *Ibid.*, p. 569.

ton favored such a plan, and Hamilton already saw himself marching at the head of an American army against the Floridas, taking possession of Louisiana and perhaps Mexico. Adams, apparently, was not informed of the details of the scheme, but knew enough about them to feel the danger. Not only would it mean war with Spain, but probably also war with France, with consequences no one could estimate. He had seen the letter sent from London by Rufus King to Pickering and Hamilton, and had no desire to favor the military ambitions of the inspector general.[34] He soon perceived that the United States had nothing to gain in such an adventure, or in the establishment of an *Ynca* on the Hispano-American continent. He wisely resolved not to answer, and for the time being the project had to be abandoned.

Thus, while in Philadelphia, Hamilton and the Federalists endeavored to provide new fuel for the war spirit, the old New Englander, back on his farm, felt reawaken in him the fundamental distrust of the man of law for the man of the sword. In his correspondence he never discussed the famous Kentucky resolutions framed by Jefferson during the fall of the year, which Madison was to bring before the Virginia Assembly. They were apparently a protest against the sedition law and the alien bill, but they showed above all that the federal bond was none too strong. There was no immediate peril for the Union, but this open protest against the Federal Government, the reassertion of state rights, the doctrine of nullification, and the proclamation that in the absence of a common judge the States had the right to decide for themselves the constitutionality of laws passed by Congress, were disquieting symptoms. The possibility of using the war peril as an opportunity to strengthen his power does not seem to have entered Adams' mind. Any fostering of military activities forebode evil for the Republic; the old-fashioned militia was good enough for him. During the summer he had frequently seen Gerry, the last of the envoys to return from France, and had succeeded in preventing him from publishing his report on the French mission. Adams wanted "all to be still and calm", and feared that the

[34] Works, Vol. VIII, pp. 583, 585.

publication of new documents might arouse controversies.[35]

When he asked the members of his cabinet for suggestions on the various matters to be discussed in his message, he clearly indicated that the President might say, "in order to keep open the channels of negotiation, it is his intention to nominate a minister to the French Republic, who may be ready to embark for France, as soon as he, or the President, shall receive from the Directory satisfactory assurances that he shall be received and entitled to all the prerogatives and privileges of the general laws of nations." [36] He even had in mind several persons who might be sent to France: Patrick Henry, Judge Patterson, Senator Ross, Senator Stockton, who, while they were stanch Americans, "have not been marked or obnoxious to the French."

However, the message read before Congress on December 8, 1798, did not reflect this conciliatory disposition. It was provocative, bellicose and cryptic. Adams mentioned the professed willingness of the French Government to receive a minister from the United States only to call attention to the fact that these declarations were expressed in terms inadmissible to the United States. He denounced the decree of the Directory as "an unequivocal act of war." He did not see anything in the conduct of France "which ought to change or relax our measures of defence"; on the contrary, he added, "to extend and invigorate them is our true policy." He concluded with a warlike declaration:

. . . Considering the late manifestations of her [France's] policy towards foreign nations, I deem it a duty deliberately and solemnly to declare my opinion, that whether we negotiate with her or not, vigorous preparations for war will be alike indispensable. These alone will give to us an equal treaty, and insure its observance.

On the other hand, he strenuously maintained the will to peace of the United States:

It is peace that we have uniformly and perseveringly cultivated; and harmony between us and France may be restored at her option. But

[35] December 15, 1798. Works, Vol. VIII, p. 617.
[36] To Pickering, October 20, 1798. Ibid., p. 609.

to send another minister without more determinate assurances that he would be received, would be an act of humiliation to which the United States ought not to submit. It must, therefore, be left to France, if she is indeed desirous of accommodation, to take the requisite steps.

Finally he added a mysterious sentence that might very well have been construed as an invitation to France to send a mission to America:

The United States will steadily observe the maxims by which they have hitherto been governed. They will respect the sacred rights of embassy.

It is unnecessary to search far for the explanation for this lack of definiteness and this wavering. Adams had followed a draft sent him early in November by Oliver Wolcott, probably on Hamilton's advice. He had been pressed by his cabinet to adhere to it, but unwilling to burn all of his bridges, he insisted upon inserting a few modifications which would leave the door open to negotiation, should the Directory recant and show a more conciliatory attitude.[37] But this explanation, offered by Charles Francis Adams, is no excuse for the President's unwillingness to assume full responsibility for the conduct of foreign affairs. On the whole, he had compromised, if he had not surrendered, to the demands of his cabinet, and against his better judgment had yielded to their opinion.

Soon after, however, Adams was to take the bit in his teeth and demonstrate his independence. While still at Quincy, he received several letters from William Vans Murray, American minister to The Hague, giving a full account of conversations with Pichon, secretary of the French Legation. Vans Murray was far from convinced of Talleyrand's sincerity, but he saw that under present circumstances it might be to the distinct interest of France to come to an understanding with America. Talleyrand's letters to Pichon, which were inclosed, proclaimed that the Directory never had any intention of severing diplomatic relations; negotiation had been made more difficult by

---

[37] See note giving parts of Adams' own draft, in Works, Vol. IX, p. 131, and for the text of Wolcott, see Gibbs, *op. cit.*, Vol. II, p. 168.

the publication, in Philadelphia, of the report of the envoys, but the French minister expressed the hope that the government of the United States would send to Paris "a plenipotentiary favorably known in France." [38] A letter from Talleyrand to Pichon dated the 7th Vendémiaire was even more explicit, requesting the French secretary at The Hague to inform Vans Murray "that any plenipotentiary sent by the government of the United States to France, to put an end to the difficulties which remain between the two countries would be undoubtedly received with the attentions suitable to the envoy of a free, independent and powerful nation." As Vans Murray remarked, this was not a direct declaration to the United States, but it was at least a declaration of intention. By Adams it was construed as sufficient for reopening diplomatic relations.

On January 15th he requested the Secretary of State "to prepare a project of a treaty and a consular convention, such as in his opinion might at this day be acceded to by the United States, if proposed by France." At the end of the month, he informed Congress that the French Directory had rescinded their edict concerning American vessels, and confirmed the news on February 15th, while remarking that a previous edict granting authority to "treat as pirates, American seamen found on board ships of the enemies of France" remained in force. Three days later, and without consulting the cabinet, Adams sent to the Senate a message nominating "William Vans Murray, our minister resident at The Hague, to be minister plenipotentiary of the United States to the French republic." His plan was not, however, to send Vans Murray to Paris at once, but to wait for "direct and unequivocal assurances from the French Government, signified by their minister of foreign relations, that he shall be received in character, shall enjoy the privileges attached to his character by the law of nations, and that a minister of equal rank, title, and powers, shall be appointed to treat with him, to discuss and conclude all controversies between the two republics by a new treaty."

This was the most courageous act of John Adams' political career. It required even more determination than to present the

[38] July 9, 1798. Works, Vol. VIII, p. 684.

defense of Captain Preston after the Boston Massacre. From the Republicans he could expect little gratitude, but he had no desire to placate them, and he had been too long in public life not to realize that the men of his own party would consider as a betrayal this last effort to avoid a war for which they had been several months preparing. He had everything to lose and nothing to gain but the satisfaction of doing his duty as he saw it, even against the judgment of his associates and so-called friends. The old New Englander, like the just man of the Latin poet, delighted in standing alone against friend and foe, with the sole comfort of his self-righteousness.

The House was discussing a bill "encouraging the capture of French armed vessels by armed ships or vessels owned by citizens of the United States", when Josiah Parker of Virginia announced that as the President had nominated a minister to go to France, he intended to vote against the passage of the bill. In spite of Otis, who maintained that "whilst we hold the olive branch in one hand, we ought to hold the sword in the other", the House adjourned without taking a vote, and two days later the bill was rejected.[39]

In the Senate the Federalists were thunderstruck, and the Republicans, unable to believe the evidence before their eyes, suspected a dark plot. For two days no action was taken; then it was decided to send to the President a committee of five members, of which Theodore Sedgwick was chairman, to ask for a voluntary withdrawal of his recommendation to avoid the necessity of acting upon it. Adams was adamant: "I have, on mature reflection," he said to them, "made up my mind, and I will neither withdraw nor modify the nomination."[40] He accepted a modification, however; realizing that Vans Murray, practically unknown in America and without long diplomatic training, might be unequal to the task, he agreed to send with him other envoys, and on February 25th proposed to the Senate that Oliver Ellsworth, Chief Justice of the United States, and Patrick Henry, late Governor of Virginia, be sent as "envoys extraordinary and ministers plenipotentiary" to the French

[39] "Annals of Congress", House of Representatives, February 18, 20, 1799.
[40] Life, in Works, Vol. I, p. 548.

Republic, with full powers to discuss and settle by treaty all controversies between the United States and France. As a last concession, he declared that it was not intended the mission should embark at once for Europe, but the envoys would await direct assurance sent by the French Directory that they would be received "in character." With these amendments and reservations the nominations were reluctantly approved by the Senate,[41] and on March 3d Congress adjourned *sine die* with the prospect that during the recess progress would be made towards a definite settlement of foreign difficulties.

Confident that he had asserted his authority, Adams gave his assent to three points to be embodied as ultimata in the instructions to the envoys: reparations and indemnities for the spoliations committed on American commerce by French armed vessels; that vessels of the United States were not bound to have on board a *rôle d'équipage;* that "the United States will not stipulate to guarantee any part of the dominions of France."

The most apparent result of the unexpected step taken by Adams was to widen the rift already existing between the President and his cabinet, and to provoke an incipient schism in the ranks of the Federalists. Had he been a popular leader and a political strategist, comparable to Hamilton or Jefferson, he would have seen his chance to appeal to the most reasonable element of the people and to form an independent party; but in neither of his messages to the Senate had he thought it necessary to elaborate on his political philosophy, or to rally to him those "friends of the country" whose ardent desire was "tranquillity upon just and honorable terms." He felt equally distrustful of the "babyish and womanly blubbering for peace" and of the fiery denouncers of the French. He knew that there was "not much sincerity in the cant about peace", for "those who snivel for it now, were hot for war against Britain a few months ago, and would be now, if they saw a chance." [42] He was convinced that "in elective governments, peace or war are

---

[41] Patrick Henry having refused the appointment because of his age and ill health, Adams appointed in his stead, during the recess of Congress, William Davie, Governor-elect of North Carolina. Works, Vol. VIII, p. 641.

[42] To Washington, February 19, 1799. Works, Vol. VIII, p. 625.

alike embraced by parties, when they think they can employ
either for electioneering purposes." All of which was probably
true, but this profound skepticism of human nature, this constant disbelief in the intentions of his fellow men, this distrust
of and scorn for popular opinion, would better have fitted a
philosopher like Montaigne than the head of a republican
government. On the other hand, he failed to realize that men
are more often weak than really dishonest, and that a leader
can raise them at least temporarily above their ordinary level.
The New England schoolmaster, trained in the school of self-
reliance and righteousness, forgot that the chief of the government must on occasion be a teacher.

At the same time he was almost naïve in the trust he placed
in his cabinet. Having agreed with them on the course to be
followed, he thought that he could leave them to their own
devices. In the midst of the battle he left the army and, quitting Philadelphia, repaired to Quincy. That he had many
personal reasons for so doing is no excuse. Mrs. Adams' health
had been very poor for several years, and she had been unable
to join her husband in Philadelphia. The summer climate,
with an ever-threatening epidemic of yellow fever and the
stifling atmosphere of the city, were particularly repugnant to
Adams. Finally, he had the precedent of Washington, who
spent weeks and months at Mount Vernon during his administration. But Adams already had reason to believe that some of
his cabinet were disloyal to him, and he should have suspected
that every effort would be made to scuttle the ship of peace.

Early in the spring of 1799, Uriah Forrest had warned him
of a possible plot, and frankly said:

I speak the truth, when I say that your real friends wish you to be
with your officers, because the public impression is, that the government
will be better conducted.[43]

But Adams was convinced that he could administer the government "here at Quincy, as really as I could do at Philadelphia. The Secretaries of State, Treasury, War, Navy, and
the Attorney-General, transmit me daily by the post all the

[43] April 28, 1799. Works, Vol. VIII, pp. 637–638.

business of consequence", and he entertained the fond illusion that "nothing is done without my advice and direction . . ." He little suspected that Pickering had deliberately delayed sending instructions to Vans Murray, who was not informed of the new developments in America until the 5th of May.

This retirement far from the madding crowd undoubtedly had some advantages. Once removed from the hectic atmosphere of Philadelphia, with his native hills before him, his feet solidly planted on ancestral fields, the President could be himself again. Since the beginning of the year, the back country of Pennsylvania had been in a state of riot. The new taxes levied by Congress in July, 1798, were particularly obnoxious to the farmers and in several counties the assessors had a very unpleasant time. No open resistance manifested itself until a country auctioneer, one John Fries by name, assumed leadership and undertook, at the head of a mob, to liberate some obstructionists who were kept in jail at Bethlehem. Fries, arrested and brought to trial, was adjudged guilty by the jury and, the crime being treason, he was sentenced to death. Both Pickering and Wolcott insisted that an example should be made of him, in order "to ensure future obedience to the laws", for, as Wolcott wrote, "in general the people are ignorant, strongly prejudiced against the measures of government, vindictive in their resentments, and I fear incapable of being influenced, except by their fears of punishment." [44] Adams, however, was too good a lawyer to yield to these invitations to institute a reign of terror. Before making up his mind, he had to be convinced that the culprit had really been guilty of "treason" under the law, for to permit a poor misguided country boor to be made the scapegoat was a "severe trial to his heart." [45] Doubtless he was glad when Fries was granted a new trial, and although the auctioneer was a second time sentenced to be hanged, Adams did not hesitate, a year later, to pardon him, against the advice of his cabinet officers. [46]

[44] May 10, 11, 1799. Works, Vol. VIII, pp. 643–645.
[45] To Pickering, May 17, 1799. Ibid., p. 649.
[46] Gibbs, op. cit., Vol. II, p. 361, and Pickering to Adams, September 9, 1799. Works, Vol. IX, p. 21.

This was neither weakness nor humanitarianism on Adams' part. For military offenders he felt no pity and was as ruthless in punishing deserters as Washington himself had been during the Revolutionary War. Without compunction he signed several death warrants, and in most cases followed the suggestions of Hamilton, simply recommending the limitation of executions to those necessary for the purposes of public justice.[47]

The organization of the navy brought him as many perplexities as the appointment of officers for the army. In several instances he had to overrule Stoddert, and spent days pondering over the rank to be granted to officers who had already served in the navy. The arming of the frigate *Constitution* "employed his thoughts by day and his dreams by night." [48]

Foreign affairs were not neglected, but pending definite assurances from the Directory, the French mission remained in the background. Recent developments in the West Indies caused the American Government some anxiety, and Adams feared that if the revolt spread to all the islands, the establishment of a new and unstable power at the gate of the United States would constitute a constant source of danger. Far better would it be to see the islands remain in parcels or divisions, as under the government of England, France, Spain or Holland. Even in fancy, he never entertained the plans of unlimited expansion which Jefferson at different times indulged in, nor did he dream of extending the dominion of the United States beyond its old historical limits. He received very coolly the overtures of England relative to the control of Santo Domingo by a joint commercial company. "It would be most prudent for us to have nothing to do in the business." It would also involve the United States in an enduring hostility with the European powers and "subject us more to the policy of Britain than will be consistent with our interest and honor." [49]

Meanwhile, Talleyrand's answer to Vans Murray had finally been received. It was dated May 12, 1799, and expressed the Directory's pleasure at being informed of the nomination of the

[47] Works, Vol. VIII, pp. 665, 667.
[48] *Ibid.*, pp. 664, 669.
[49] April 17 and June 15, 1799. *Ibid.*, pp. 634, 657.

special American envoys, and contained assurances that they would be received as befitted their character. Unfortunately, Talleyrand had been unable to refrain from expressing some impatience at the delay. "It was certainly unnecessary," he had written, "to suffer so many months to elapse for the mere confirmation of what I had already declared to Mr. Gerry, and which after his departure I caused to be declared to you at The Hague. I sincerely regret that your two colleagues await this answer at such great distance." [50] Aside from this rather undiplomatic passage, implying a sort of blame for the American Government, Talleyrand's letter was more than correct, and ended in a distinctly friendly manner, giving every desired assurance that the envoys would be received with all the honors and prerogatives attached to their quality. This being the case, it is difficult to explain why the President should see in it "the most authentic intelligence yet received in America of the successes of the coalition" and a distinct provocation. In an unexplainable fit of rage, he answered Pickering, who had called his attention to the ungraceful remark in Talleyrand's letter, that it was far below the dignity of the President to take any notice of Talleyrand's impertinent regrets. As long as he should be in office, the French would find "candor, integrity, and, as far as there can be any confidence or safety, a pacific and friendly disposition", and if the spirit of exterminating vengeance ever arose, it would be conjured up by them, not by him. After this display of temper came an unexpected conclusion. Governor Davie, who had been nominated after Patrick Henry's refusal to go to Europe, was to receive his commission at once; instructions were to be drafted, and members of the mission should be requested to "make immediate preparations for embarking." Adams had no confidence in the success of the mission, but he had resolved "to delay nothing, to omit nothing." In the meantime "operations and preparations by sea and land" were not to be relaxed "in the smallest degree"; on the contrary, he wished to have them "animated with fresh energy." [51]

---

[50] "American State Papers", Vol. III, p. 301.
[51] August 6, 1799. Works, Vol. IX, p. 11.

Making allowances for Adams' burst of temper, his intentions were clear, and his instructions definite, at least on one point — the envoys had to be sent on this mission with all possible dispatch. This plan, however, did not fit in with the policy of his cabinet. Without openly opposing the President, Pickering from the beginning used dilatory tactics. His disagreement with Adams was so plain that at the end of the month, Stoddert, the only member of the cabinet remaining faithful to the President, took it upon himself to urge Adams for the good of the country and for his own good to come to Trenton, where the cabinet had taken refuge during the summer, and to supervise, himself, the drafting of the instructions.[52]

Any man entertaining suspicions would have read between the lines, but Adams apparently trusted his cabinet as much as he distrusted the French, and he refused to leave Quincy in the midst of the summer. One consideration only could make him change his mind: sudden developments in the European situation might render it necessary to alter considerably the instructions to the envoys.[53]

In fact, such a change had taken place, for on August 26th, Pickering had received from Vans Murray news of the "very portentous" events about to take place in Paris — the reorganization of the Directory, the forced resignation of two Directors, and the impending "explosion." Even the warmest defenders of Adams must admit that under the circumstances there was some justification in Pickering's proposition to suspend the mission pending further developments.

In spite of Stoddert's entreaties, however, Adams refused to join the cabinet in Trenton. He was told that the situation was far more serious than he realized; that the British were now "soured and prejudiced" at the prospect of a peace with France and might insist on a quarrel. In guarded words, the Secretary of the Navy indicated that Pickering was "certainly too much occupied to find time to understand this subject." He finally warned Adams that instructions drawn in his absence could never "inspire the same confidence" and "wear the exact com-

[52] August 29, 1799. Works, Vol. IX, p. 19.
[53] September 4, 1799. Ibid.

plexion" as if the President had been on the spot.[54] Nothing could shake the President's complacency. He had no fear of England and was convinced that the popularity of the French had "so dwindled away, that no impression could be made to any great effect in their favor." He saw no reason why the business might not be as well conducted "by letter and the post", although the post made mistakes, and sent southward some of the letters intended for him. On September 21st, however, he decided to join his cabinet at Trenton, and fixed the departure of the envoys sometime between the 20th and 30th of October. Even then, he saw no need for great haste, and wrote to Pickering: "If our envoys are delayed so long at least, it will be no misfortune." [55] Meanwhile the instructions were to remain in abeyance. Of this, he gave confirmation to Ellsworth in equivocal terms, at one breath mentioning the convulsions in France and the prognostics of greater changes that might induce him to postpone for a longer or shorter time the mission to Paris, and in the next paragraph fixing the date of sailing between the 20th of October and November 1st. That Pickering, Wolcott and McHenry, before such indecision and apparent contradictions, thought they could influence the President's decision, was only natural.

When Adams reached Trenton, October 10th, after stopping at Windsor to see Ellsworth, his mind was apparently still open to suggestion. Much to his surprise, he found there not only the cabinet members, but also Hamilton and Wilkinson, who "by an accident" had arrived at the same time.[56] The President was unwell and "more fit for a chamber and bed of sickness than for much labour of the head or hands." If it was not yellow fever it was "something very like it, or at least almost as bad." [57] The town was in a turmoil — news of the landing of the British in Holland had been received, the Dutch fleet had surrendered and "the universal opinion appeared to be that the first arrivals from Europe would bring the glorious

---

[54] September 13, 1799. Works, Vol. IX, pp. 25–29.

[55] September 21, 1799. Ibid., p. 33.

[56] Gibbs, op. cit., Vol. II, p. 268.

[57] "Correspondence originally published in The Boston Patriot", Works, Vol. VIII.

news that Louis the Eighteenth was restored to the throne of France, and reigning triumphantly at Versailles." Such at least was the opinion propagated by the Hamiltonians.

At last Adams was confronted by such a situation in France as to make necessary the indefinite postponement of the mission, and even Ellsworth's opinion was similar to that of the heads of departments. For three days Adams held conferences, discussed paragraph after paragraph the instructions to the envoys, strenuously maintaining that the French Republic would last at least seven years, and that should England consider as unfriendly the sending of a mission to France, there was nothing in that prospect to frighten the United States. The secretaries were not convinced, and they persistently hoped that at the last minute the President would hesitate to antagonize almost his whole cabinet as well as the powerful Hamilton, whom they continued to look upon as their guide and master. After a session lasting until eleven o'clock at night, the draft of instructions was finally agreed upon. Not a word had been said by the President as to the date on which the mission would sail, and Pickering went to bed persuaded that no immediate decision would be reached in the matter.[58]

Old country people are early risers; the next morning Adams awoke earlier than usual and penned a short communication which the Secretary of State received before breakfast. He was requested to deliver fair copies of the instructions to the envoys and to notify them that they were desired to embark on the frigate *United States* (Captain Barry), now lying at Rhode Island, by November 1st or sooner. The President sent them his best wishes for their health and happiness, and, with a touch of New England humor in which he had not indulged in recent official communications, he added: "As their visit to France is at one of the most critical, important, and interesting moments that ever have occurred, it cannot fail to be highly entertaining and instructive to them, and useful to their country, whether it terminate in peace or reconciliation or not."

At last Adams had asserted himself. Pickering and McHenry

[58] Pickering to Hamilton, October 2, 1799. Gibbs, *op. cit.*, Vol. II, p. 277.

fumed and raged. They wrote indignantly to Washington that all good citizens deprecated the French mission "as fraught with irreparable mischief." The United States were humiliated, French principles would revive, the party opposed to the government would be strengthened, and, worst of all, wrote McHenry, "whether the President will think it expedient to dismiss any, or how many of us, is a problem." [59]

Never truly a politician, Adams probably did not realize that, according to Mr. Bowers' expression, he was "pulling down the pillars" of Federalism. Even the most rabid Federalists could perceive that this time the mission had a fair chance to succeed; it would be the end of the campaign against France and the Gallicans would triumph. If France accepted the conditions proposed, the difficulties with England would come to the fore; but the eventuality of a war was remote, and no reason would be left to raise and maintain a large army, for which Congress would certainly refuse appropriations. Even if these considerations had entered Adams' mind, they could not have stopped him. He had never felt that he was the head of a political party and had never exerted himself to lead clients and followers in a political battle. With all his personal and temperamental faults, he honestly attempted to be a national President and felt under no obligation to pay political debts. His duty, as he saw it, was to his country, and apparently unaware of the indignation and resentment of the Federalist leaders, he went on serenely with the preparation of his message for the opening session of Congress.

[59] November 10, 1799. Gibbs, *op. cit.*, Vol. II, p. 282.

CHAPTER III

THE LAST TRENCH

WITH the exception of his inaugural message, most of Adams' addresses to Congress had been warlike. The speech he delivered on December 3, 1799, to both houses was emphatically peaceful. Scorning mention of armament, of increasing the navy, of preparing the country against a dire eventuality, or of protecting American commerce and honor, the President emphasized the blessings of "a pacific and humane policy" and insisted upon the disposition of the French Government "to accommodate the existing differences between the two countries." On the other hand, he called attention to the difficulties that had arisen between the American and British commissioners dealing with the claims of British subjects residing at Philadelphia, and promised to endeavor to obtain explanations from London. Contrary to accusations of the Hamiltonians, Adams had not changed sides suddenly; neither pro-British nor pro-French, he was looking towards peace and reconstruction, the end of civil disturbances, and a better interpretation of the laws. Only at the end did he allude to the necessity of "maintaining our just rights", but in the same breath he preached severe economies and approved only of a "system of national defence, commensurate with our resources and the situation of our country."

Thus, quietly but very effectively, he put an end to militaristic dreams. The death of Washington (December 14, 1799), nominally at least Commander in Chief of the Army, and whose name alone was "worth a host", brought further discouragement to the camp of the Federalists. In his noble and sober message to the Senate, Adams emphasized the civil and republican qualities of America's "most esteemed, beloved and admired citizen" for "the attributes and decorations of royalty could have only served to eclipse the majesty of those virtues which made him, from being a modest citizen, a more resplendent luminary." If at any time Adams had entertained jealousy of Washington, if he had considered as a danger the worship of the crowd for a national hero, he had been cleansed of any feeling unworthy of himself and Washington. In his official eulogy he could not refrain from introducing a personal note, and with a melancholy unusual in a public document, Adams, tired of the political strife, felt that this death was a warning to him and to the men of his generation: "With a constitution more enfeebled than his at an age when he thought it necessary to prepare for retirement, I feel myself alone, bereaved of my last brother." [1]

Thus in less than two weeks Adams had given unequivocal indications that the time had come for him to retire. His address to Congress and this significant passage had all the earmarks of a farewell message and a political testament. It was also a program containing many parts which the Republicans could accept without coercion. Washington was hardly buried when Nicholas pointed out the desirability of "lopping off all unnecessary expenses in the army establishment" and proposed the repeal of the act of July 16, 1798, authorizing the appointment of a commander of the army "and raising twelve additional regiments of infantry." [2] The resolution was laid on the table for the time being, but it was already evident that with the passing of the Commander in Chief and the reluctance of the President to appoint Hamilton as his successor, the war party had lost its prestige and much of its appeal. The war fury had already subsided. The newspapers could advertise the opening of "military laboratories" for the sale of naval and military supplies for the merchantmen, popular passions had ceased to be aroused by the reports of French outrages. There was a momentary flare-up when the Philadelphia people heard the glorious news that Captain Truxtun of the American frigate *Constellation* had successfully withstood

[1] December 23, 1799. Works, Vol. IX, p. 142.
[2] "Annals of Congress", House of Representatives, January 1, 1800.

the attack of the French warship *La Vengeance*, and Adams heartily approved the resolution of Congress presenting a gold medal to the captain; but his heart was not in the war, and he was far more interested in forming an adequate library on naval subjects.[3]

The general tenor of the discussion prolonged in the House during the whole spring was that war was a costly business and that a permanent army would constitute a ruinous charge for the budget. The fear of a French invasion was just "a *bugbear*", maintained Nicholas, supported by Gallatin. There was more readiness to equip an adequate navy to protect American commerce, but even those who resented the insults offered America in the persons of the commissioners "could not agree to carry their resentment as far as to keep up such extraordinary expenses and systems when there was no real danger." [4]

As the Republicans became more conscious of their strength and popular support, they took up one by one the war measures adopted during the war hysteria of 1798. George Cabot had to admit regretfully that "popular passions had already evaporated." He could point out that "the whole world was becoming military", but good American common sense had asserted itself again.[5] It was not a question of national honor, but one of security and self-defense, and in the middle of February, much to the distress of the Federalists, an act was passed suspending further enlistments. It was to be followed with a supplementary act authorizing the discharge of officers and men already enlisted, and at the end of the session the military appropriation was reduced from over four to three million dollars.

To the distress of his cabinet, Adams seemed to have changed sides entirely. At the end of December, Wolcott, puzzled and bewildered, wrote to Fisher Ames:

The President's mind is in a state which renders it difficult to determine what prudence and duty require from those about him. He con-

[3] To Stoddert, March 31, 1800. Works, Vol. IX, p. 47.

[4] "Annals of Congress", House of Representatives, January 9.

[5] January 16, 1800. Gibbs, "Administrations of Washington and John Adams", Vol. II, p. 322.

siders Col. Pickering, Mr. McHenry, and myself as his enemies; his resentments against General Hamilton are excessive; he declares his belief of the existence of a British faction in the United States.[6]

Ames, who was still at Dedham, was even more pessimistic than the Secretary of the Treasury. He could already perceive "a want of accordance between our system and the state of our public opinion. *The Government is Republican; opinion is essentially Democratic.*" Factions were bold and powerful, and the old Federalist leader saw "within the United States, Jefferson and C°" at the head of a stronger faction "than any government can struggle with long, or prevail against at last, unless by military force." Both Ames and Wolcott, however, thought that the President had somewhat ingratiated himself with a large part of the public by "showing such respect for the voice of the people." Such an opinion was not shared by the Republicans. The *Aurora*, early in February, had called attention to the evident split among the Federalists: "the President's party" was formed by "the New England party, the Connecticut illuminati, the office-hunting party", while the Hamiltonian party was composed of "the old Tory or refugee party, the Army and Navy, the profit-hunting party, the funding, banking and loan party, the British agency and, finally, the monarchists and anti-Gallican party." [7]

As far as Adams was concerned, both the Hamiltonians and the Republicans entertained an exaggerated idea of his strength. Far from having the support of the New England party, he counted among them some of his fiercest enemies, and it nowhere appears that the Federalists placed more confidence in him now than in the past. On the other hand, the Republicans were relentless in their attacks and, in spite of Adams' apparent change of heart and the evidence he had given of his conciliatory disposition, they refused to lay down any of their old weapons. Many were the reasons why Mr. Adams should not be elected. He was anti-French and anti-Republican, he was openly pro-British, he had abridged the rights of the people, he was for a

[6] December 20, 1799. Gibbs, *op. cit.*, Vol. II, p. 314.
[7] February 17, 1800.

standing army and a standing navy, and he had encroached upon the constitutional authority of the other branches of government.[8] The Federalists, not averse to using similar arguments, did not fail to enumerate the reasons which made Mr. Jefferson equally unfit for the Presidency: he was a deist, he had opposed measures of the government, he was head of a party opposed to laws, his ability as a legislator was more than doubtful, his household was French, he associated with French people, his library was French, and the whole combination was most "unpalatable to the American people." [9]

Prosecutions and sentences only infuriated the editors; packed juries, heavy fines and terms in jail failed to suppress them. The hand of the law was laid heavily on Jefferson's friends: Benjamin Franklin Bache, the editor of the *Aurora*, would have been sentenced if his death had not closed the suit. Matthew Lyon was sent to jail and so was Anthony Haswell, the printer of the *Vermont Gazette*. Thomas Cooper, a friend of Priestley and an ardent Gallican, was sentenced to six months in prison for supporting the Republican Party. Thomas Callender, who for several years had reviled the President, was arrested in Richmond for the publication of a scurrilous pamphlet, "The Prospect before us", but neither prison nor fine could silence him.

There is no evidence that Adams ever encouraged prosecuting any of them except Callender; but it is equally certain that he highly approved of the conduct of Judge Chase, whose attitude was as unjudicial and as reprehensible as that of the offenders. He suffered intensely not only in his personal feelings, but his patriotism and sense of justice. He had less confidence than Jefferson in the ultimate justice of the people, and without entering the public forum, thought that the electorate ought to be kept informed of the acts of the government, and that public speeches and documents ought to be placed in their hands. None of the existing papers could be depended upon for such a purpose, and he proposed to his cabinet the establishment of a really national gazette similar to the *Gazette*

[8] *Aurora*, March 3, 1800.
[9] *Ibid.*, March 31, 1800.

de France or the *London Gazette;* apparently the secretaries did not share his view and the proposal was dropped.[10]

By the beginning of May the situation in the cabinet had become intolerable; Stoddert and Lee remained loyal to the President, but each day increased Adams' suspicions of McHenry, Pickering and Wolcott, whose allegiance to Hamilton had at last become plain. When a caucus of the Federal members of Congress decided to have "Mr. Adams and Major General Charles Cotesworth Pinckney run for President, without giving one a preference to the other", Adams felt that he was betrayed.[11] He was too well aware of the situation not to realize that he would not be able to draw a single Republican vote, while Pinckney, by his attitude in the House and his declarations on free speech, had won the approval of the Republicans.[12] At this juncture he decided to take the matter in his own hands, and on May 6th requested McHenry to see him. If Adams could not restrain his pen, he could even less control his tongue and temper. It was an unpleasant scene, in which McHenry, accused of having done nothing right, was finally permitted to resign. It was given out at the same time that Pickering would not proceed to the Federal City and that Marshall would be offered McHenry's place, but would not accept; at last "the Hydra was dying!" [13]

With Pickering, Adams was more high-handed. On the 10th of May he informed him that as a change in the administration of the office of state had become necessary, he had "the opportunity of resigning, if he chose", but that he might name the day on which the resignation would become effective.[14] Pickering's answer was both piteous and insolent, and does little credit to a man represented as "a Puritan who gloried in belonging to the chosen people of God." [15] He had expected to remain in office until Jefferson's inauguration — an event which he considered certain, from a conversation with Adams; he had

[10] April 23, 1800. Works, Vol. IX, p. 50.
[11] James McHenry, May 20, 1800. Gibbs, *op. cit.*, Vol. II, p. 347.
[12] *Aurora*, March 28, 1800.
[13] *Ibid.*, May 9, 1800.
[14] Works, Vol. IX, p. 53.
[15] H. C. Lodge, "Studies in History", Boston, 1884, p. 219.

not saved enough to remove his family into the woods, where he had land. The upshot of it was that he flatly refused to resign and was no less flatly informed that he was "hereby discharged from any further service as Secretary of State." [16]

"If ever a man went out of a public situation loaded with the universal execration of an injured country, it is Mr. Timothy Pickering," wrote Duane in the *Aurora*. "Let him be watched, for men never come out of office loaded with infamy, who do not take care to be loaded with plunder to counterbalance it." [17] The man who, more than Adams, was held responsible for the enforcement of the sedition law had been ignominiously dismissed; at last "the voice of the people" had been heard! But if the Republican editors exulted, they showed no gratitude to Adams. In this domestic *coup d'état* they pretended to see only an electoral maneuver and Thomas Cooper, from his prison in Philadelphia, declared that he would refuse a pardon should it be offered to him by the President, being unwilling to become "the voluntary cats-paw of electioneering clemency!" [18]

The fury of the Hamiltonians on the other hand was unbounded; they went so far as to decide in a caucus that C. C. Pinckney and Pickering should be the presidential candidates. Open war was declared. Adams had given aid and comfort to the enemy, betrayed his own party, and should be discarded. Undaunted by the raging criticism, Adams proceeded to reprieve Fries and his companions and, on May 21st, proclaimed an absolute pardon to all persons concerned in the Pennsylvania insurrection, on whose punishment Pickering had insisted to the last minute, and the *Aurora* at last grudgingly admitted that the President had acted in conformity with his principles against sanguinary punishment, and also "as a good lawyer." [19]

Congress had adjourned May 14th, and was to convene for its second session November 17th, in the new capital, Federal

[16] May 12, 1800. Works, Vol. IX, pp. 54, 55.
[17] *Aurora*, May 9, 1800.
[18] *Ibid.*, May 17, 1800.
[19] *Ibid.*, May 22, 1800.

City, which had been named after the first President of the United States. Before repairing to Quincy for the summer, Adams decided to visit the new seat of government and left Philadelphia "in a coach drawn by four horses, with the blinds up, as if he tried to conceal himself from the people." He was officially received, however, at York, with a civil procession, military escort, and the ringing of bells.[20] He visited the Federal City, with its presidential residence still in the hands of the workers, its unpaved streets hardly laid out, with unreclaimed wood and farm lots all about.

In Alexandria he took the citizens of Virginia into his confidence and confessed the "inexpressible grief and unutterable indignation" he had felt at times at the injustice and indignities which had wantonly heaped on his innocent, virtuous, peaceable, and unoffending country. These days were past, however, and America now enjoyed "an enviable tranquillity and uncommon prosperity." Had he been younger, or more willing to address the people directly and explain his policies, Adams would still have had a chance to go before the country as the man who had kept America out of war and who, between French and British intrigues, had steered a strictly national course. That the country wanted peace was admitted by both Republicans and Federalists; foreign conditions looked better than they had in years, the pardon granted to Fries had shown the government capable of generosity and clemency and reluctant to shed a single drop of American blood for revenge. But he was too much an aristocrat to go out and deal with the electorate on such a democratic basis. He was also too much a schoolmaster to think it necessary to justify his conduct. What he had done was a public record, with his faults and his achievements, his sterling patriotism, his eagerness to serve; shy and proud, he stood before his fellow citizens to elect or to reject — a pathetic, distant and somewhat incomprehensible figure.

His short excursion in Virginia appeared to some as a mark of his willingness to join hands with the Republicans. It was rumored that Jefferson had called on him to propose such

[20] *Boston Centinel*, June 14, 1800.

a combination, and the *Trenton Federalist* could affirm that Mr. Adams' conduct was evidently the result of a political arrangement with Mr. Jefferson. The details of the plan were given: on the one hand "to put down the *oligarchy* of the present counsels, and on the other effectually to disappoint the ambitious and disorganizing views of the *Demagogues* and *Democrats,* so as to produce a neutralization of the contending parties." "The people would never submit to such a bargain and sale." [21] Whether the editor was too suspicious, or the Hamiltonians had a hand in the propagation of such rumors, the clear result was to detach Adams more and more from the Federalist Party, without gaining for him a single vote from the Republicans.

While he was still in Virginia, Major General Hamilton, "the favourite of Washington, recommended by him as second in command", was touring New England, apparently in order to put the last touch to the disbanding of the army. It was easy enough, he found, to detach the Federalist leaders from the President, but the masses remained loyal to the old leader, and at the banquet held in Hamilton's honor on his election as President General of the Cincinnati, with C. C. Pinckney as Vice President, the following significant toast was offered: "The President of the United States — May he turn the Flank of his Enemies, press down their Center, throw their whole Line into Confusion, capture their Standards, military chest and Artillery, and burn their Baggage." [22]

While Boston was acclaiming Hamilton, the President had leisurely returned to Quincy. On his way he had received military honors, but he had avoided Brookline, where the citizens had prepared a reception for him, and the Bostonians could not pay their respects to "the First Magistrate of the Union." [23] It may be supposed that he desired chiefly to avoid Hamilton, and not to lend his presence to the reception given to his archenemy. He was to spend the whole summer in Massachusetts, receiving "company at his seat, on Tuesdays as formerly", at-

[21] Quoted by the *Boston Centinel,* June 11, 1800.
[22] *Ibid.,* July 5, 1800.
[23] *Ibid.*

tending Commencement at Cambridge, where he listened with patience to no less than twelve discourses and one Greek dialogue, and transacting by correspondence the business of the government.

In spite of this scholarly detachment, Adams could not enjoy much rest even at Quincy. In Marshall he had at last found a Secretary of State whom he could trust, a man well aware of all the pitfalls and traps of diplomatic negotiations. But the situation in France was far from satisfactory, and Adams, suspecting in the dilatory tactics of the French Government a repetition of their attitude towards the previous mission, considered at one time the possibility of declaring war. If a state of war continued to exist between the two countries, would it not be better "to take off all the restrictions and limitations" and put an end to the continual conflict of parties which "will continually rise up, until we have either peace or war." [24] But this was more a hypothetical question than a definite proposition; all possible eventualities had to be considered. There were hopes, however, of receiving at least assurances from the French that privateering would soon come to an end, and, unpleasant and irritating as the present situation was, it had to be remembered that the famous principle of *"free ships, free goods"* would never be honestly observed, "the dominant power on the ocean will forever trample on it." [25] This was as sensible an opinion as had ever been expressed on the matter, but hardly one which would have appealed to the electorate.

He was far from displeased by the patriotic declaration of some South Carolinians, who assured him that "if we should be reduced to the sad necessity of having recourse to arms for the defense of our country, its constitution or laws, either from foreign invasion or domestic commotion, the Jacobins of the day shall not have us among the number to demonstrate the truth of their calculation." [26] This was good campaign material to be communicated to the press, but in his answer Adams, more moderate in tone than his admirers, maintained that he

[24] To John Marshall, September 4, 1800. Works, Vol. IX, p. 81.
[25] To John Marshall, October 3, 1800. *Ibid.*, p. 86.
[26] *Boston Centinel*, August 30, 1800.

could perceive "no disposition in the American people to go to war with each other." He had really reached as much of a philosophical detachment as was in his nature. Cobbett, the British propagandist, and Fenno, the Federalist polemist, filled him with the same disgust as Callender, who had just been sentenced by Judge Chase in Richmond. The Federalist pamphleteers, "aided, countenanced, and encouraged by *soi-disant* Federalists in Boston, New York, and Philadelphia, have done more to shuffle the cards into the hands of the Jacobin leaders, than all the acts of administration, and all the policy of opposition, from the commencement of the government." [27]

Of the acts of his administration, or at least, those he had been responsible for, he regretted none. Proudly and quite justifiably he could declare to the North Carolinians: "I will be bold to say, no man ever served this country with purer intentions or from more disinterested motives." Few among his fiercest enemies would have gainsaid him, but many of his former friends and associates felt unable to share this satisfaction. Their support of Adams was no more than lukewarm. Already in July the *Centinel* had published a letter to Fisher Ames, maintaining that there was a wide difference "between saving the country and saving the government . . . *one* administration could succeed to *another* and the Constitution remain for ages the unchanged object of confidence and respect." [28] Hamilton, in New York, growing more and more irritated, gave clear indications that he intended to fight Adams' candidacy openly, and had to be restrained by old Fisher Ames who, from Dedham, kept writing letters urging the Federalists to unite on Adams and Pinckney. Granting that "Mr. Adams had conducted strangely and unaccountably and that his reëlection would be very inauspicious to the United States", it was nevertheless the only chance left to the Federalists. [29]

At this juncture further confusion was thrown into the camp of the Adamites by the publication in the *Aurora* of an old letter written by Adams to Tench Coxe, in which the "Duke of

[27] To John Trumbull, September 10, 1800. Works, Vol. IX, p. 83.
[28] July 12, 1800.
[29] August 26, 1800. "Works of Fisher Ames", Boston, 1854, Vol. I, p. 250.

Braintree", as he playfully called himself, had expressed his suspicion that Pinckney was favorable to British interests and that his nomination as plenipotentiary to Great Britain in May, 1792, was due to British influence.[30] The letter had all the earmarks of Adams' style, and was soon acknowledged to have come from his hand, although the *Centinel* at first denounced it as a forgery;[31] but Adams himself admitted the authorship in a letter to Pinckney.[32] As "the hardest thing for the federalists to bear" was "the charge of British influence", according to Fisher Ames himself,[33] the Republicans did not miss their chance to renew the old accusations and to tar both the Adamites and the Pickeronians with the same brush. A worse blow was soon to befall the Federalists.

As early as the beginning of July, Hamilton had thought of writing the President to protest against the constant allusions coming from Adams that the former Secretary of the Treasury belonged to the pro-British faction.[34] A month later, writing directly to Adams, he had requested the President to make good this accusation and to produce his evidence, without obtaining any answer.[35] Smarting under the slight, Hamilton then decided to draw up a letter to be sent to influential individuals in the New England States for the avowed purpose of "promoting Mr. Pinckney's election" and vindicating himself.[36] Goaded by McHenry, who had approved the draft of the letter and who insisted that "Mr. Adams ought, by all fair and honourable means to be deprived of votes",[37] held back by Fisher Ames, who insisted that Hamilton should not write anything that could be traced to him,[38] Hamilton, unable to keep his peace, had finally printed a limited number of copies which were supposed to remain in the hands of a select few. Whether or not such was

[30] *Aurora*, August 18, 1800.
[31] *Centinel*, October 8 and 11, 1800.
[32] October 27, 1800. Gibbs, *op. cit.*, Vol. II, p. 425.
[33] To Christopher Gore, December 28, 1800. "Works of Fisher Ames", Vol. II, p. 287.
[34] To Wolcott Gibbs, *op. cit.*, Vol. II, p. 376.
[35] Hamilton's "Works", Lodge's Edition, Vol. V, p. 444.
[36] To Wolcott, September 26, 1800. Gibbs, *op. cit.*, Vol. II, p. 421.
[37] *Ibid.*, p. 430.
[38] "Works of Fisher Ames", Vol. I, p. 282.

really the expectation of the author, extracts were promptly published by the *Aurora* and the New London *Bee*, and the amazing document was soon circulated, reprinted and analyzed throughout the country.

In "The Public Conduct and Character of John Adams, Esq., President of the United States", the disappointed politician developed at length the thesis that, without denying Mr. Adams' patriotism and integrity, he thought it his duty not to conceal the conviction that "he does not possess the talents adapted to the *administration* of government, and that there are great and intrinsic defects in his character, which unfit him for the office of chief magistrate." Then followed a scorching castigation of the man who had himself elected under false pretenses, who had refused, contrary to General Washington's recommendation, to favor a permanent army, who had a vanity without bounds, a jealousy capable of dissolving every object, and who had humiliated the country by sending ministers to France. Finally came the charges resulting from the dismissals of Pickering and McHenry, represented as martyrs to their patriotism, a protest against the pardon of Fries, and the failure to make Hamilton second in command against the *express stipulation* of General Washington. The conclusion was even more amazing than this long enumeration of Adams' sins. Although the President had so undermined the government that there was real cause to fear it might totter if not fall under his future auspices, the magnanimous Hamilton finally "resolved not to advise the withholding from him of a single vote." If Adams may have been accused of being at times "a little insane", one wonders what qualificative would apply to the man who, on the eve of a presidential election, had printed and circulated this strange document. In the words of Fisher Ames, the book, although one of Hamilton's "best written performances", could not fail to be considered "insidious, unfair, and deeply, rancorously hostile." [39]

The Republicans made the most of their opportunity. The "Duke of Braintree" was condemned in the words of the Republican Party leader. All their accusations were amply justi-

[39] "Works of Fisher Ames", Vol. I, p. 285.

fied. John Adams, Alexander Hamilton and Pinckney were now fairly before the public, and Mr. Jefferson was the only suitable candidate for President.

Adams himself must have been aware of the publication of the pamphlet early in October, but it was not until the beginning of December that he discussed it in writing on receiving a copy of an answer to "Major-General Hamilton by a Citizen." Although his vanity must have been deeply hurt, he had refused to take notice of it while he remained in office, and he wrote of Hamilton with singular equanimity: "I am not his enemy, and never was. I have not adored him, like his idolaters, and have had great cause to disapprove of some of his policies. He has talents, if he would correct himself, which might be useful. There is more burnish, however, on the outside, than sterling silver in the substance." [40]

On Monday, October 15th, the President of the United States left his Quincy seat to wend his way towards Washington, accompanied by his lady, who contemplated with apprehension the trials of starting housekeeping in a new and partly unfinished house. The journey was uneventful, but after leaving Baltimore the travelers, who had not been provided with a proper escort, lost their way in the wilderness and were "extricated from the woods" by a negro slave met by chance. The city itself was pretty enough, and the presidential residence pleasantly located, with a distant view of the river, and vessels passing and repassing. Six rooms had been made comfortable, but how to keep an establishment needing thirty servants with the President's salary was a problem. The weather was chilly, and although there were forests all around, no wood was to be had; the great unfinished audience room had to be converted into a drying room "to hang up the clothes in", and "the principal stairs were not up, and would not be this winter." [41]

The President and his secretary occupied two rooms, and Adams started gathering the loose strands of official business and preparing his message, while Congressmen slowly drifted into town, scrambling for lodgings in the few boarding houses set

[40] To Doctor Ogden, December 3, 1800. Works, Vol. IX, p. 576.
[41] "Mrs. Adams' Letters", Vol. II, p. 239.

up in the new capital city. On the eve of the presidential election, he would have been justified in summing up the achievements of his administration and in claiming some credit for himself and his party. Now was the time to sound the clarion call and to rally his troops, but Adams was no party chief, and if privately he indulged in his vanity, he was singularly free of boasting in his official expressions. Unmindful of the past, unwilling to justify his conduct, he simply acquainted Congress with the most recent developments and enumerated the tasks to be accomplished. The temporary army had been discharged, a treaty of amity and commerce with Prussia had been concluded and ratified, negotiations with Great Britain were still pending, the negotiations with France had not yet been concluded but the envoys had been received by the First Consul and there was hope that their efforts would be successful. He insisted, however, that efforts to build a navy adapted to defensive war ought to be continued, and left it to Congress to decide whether further appropriation ought to be made for the fortification of some of "the principal seaports and harbors."

Against all odds, the Federalists struggled to keep up their courage; they filled their papers with forecasts of the election, more optimistic as the campaign came to a close: Adams would have seventy-two votes to sixty-six for Jefferson. While the electors assembled in the different States, the *Centinel* exclaimed: "We shall have a Federal President. God be praised!" There could be no doubt of the result of the great election: Mr. Adams and General Pinckney would each have seventy-three votes; the House would choose Mr. Adams President, and General Pinckney would be Vice President. Messrs. Jefferson and Burr would each have fifty-five votes.[42] In Washington, however, well-informed people had no such illusions. General Pinckney had written that South Carolina would go to Burr.[43] It was a consoling reflection that New England had no share in the ignominy to which the nation was doomed for the ensuing four years. The probable result indicated by the

[42] *Centinel*, December 13, 1800.
[43] Letter dated Washington, December 10, 1800. *Centinel*, December 20, 1800.

popular election was: Adams, 65; Pinckney, 63; Jefferson, 73; Burr, 73. Adams was defeated and the House would have to decide between Jefferson and Burr.

In the presidential mansion, Adams received the returns listlessly. At the end of November he had suffered "the melancholy death of a once beloved son." Charles, who gave every promise of fulfilling the literary ambitions of his father, had died, leaving a wife and two very young children with their grandparents.[44] Adams had borne his grief with New England fortitude; neither moaning nor complaining, with Abigail he repeated: "There is nothing more to be said, but let the Eternal will be done." He would leave Washington without regret and without rancor, with a calm conscience and the unshakable conviction that he had done his full duty to his country. The reports of the envoys and the text of the convention at last signed with France had recently arrived, and this was ample justification of his conduct. He would leave the State "with its coffers full, and the fair prospects of a peace with all the world smiling in its face, its commerce flourishing, its navy glorious, its agriculture uncommonly productive and lucrative",[45] and he could go back to his books and farm and be again a private citizen and a farmer. In Jefferson's success he saw "nothing wonderful", but the unexpected good fortune of Mr. Burr provoked in him a last spark of his sarcastic humor: "All the old patriots, all the splendid talents, the long experience, both of federalists and antifederalists, must be subjected to the humiliation of seeing this dexterous gentleman rise, like a balloon, filled with inflammable air, over their heads."[46]

With less than four months separating him from retirement, the defeated President could now contemplate the political scene with a philosophical eye. Alone in the presidential mansion (for Mrs. Adams had early gone back to Quincy) he witnessed the bewilderment of the Federalist leaders who had unloosened the democratic tempest. The battle was not yet

[44] To Vandercamp, December 28, 1800. Works, Vol. IX, p. 577.
[45] Ibid.
[46] To Elbridge Gerry, December 30, 1800. Ibid., p. 578.

over, for the choice of the President would finally rest with the Federalist representatives in Congress.

On this occasion Adams might have played a decisive part. His influence was still real and his prestige intact; he could have been the arbiter between Jefferson and Burr and used his influence to defeat the efforts of Aaron Burr's friends. He could have played the part which was finally left to Hamilton to perform, and probably the famous and painful contest in the House between the partisans of the two candidates would have been avoided; perhaps he could even have effected this reconciliation of parties, which was the aim of Jefferson during the first months of his administration, and saved what could be saved of the Federalist Party. The stricken chief had no such political wisdom. "What course is it we steer, and to what harbor are we bound?" was all he could write to Gerry, and he confessed that he was "wholly at a loss." [47]

It was no longer his battle. Certain that there was no danger of a political convulsion, if either candidate were chosen in the House, or if a President *pro tempore* had to be appointed in case of a tie, he kept aloof, wrapped in the dignity of his office, and attended to his remaining tasks. Some of these were trivial, several were to be of great consequence. Unaware of the perfidious conduct of Wolcott, who for many months had betrayed cabinet secrets to Hamilton, Adams accepted with genuine regret the resignation of the Secretary of the Treasury, to take place on the last of December. [48] Much more important was the resignation of Ellsworth as Chief Justice. Quite conscious of the part that the Supreme Court could play in the government, he thought at first of nominating Jay to an office "as independent of the inconstancy of the people, as it is of the will of a President." In the court and in a solid judiciary, wrote Adams to Jay, will reside "the firmest security we can have against the effects of visionary schemes or fluctuating theories." [49]

When Jay refused to accept the nomination, some of Adams'

[47] To Elbridge Gerry, December 30, 1800. Works, Vol. IX, p. 578.
[48] November 10, 1800. Works, Vol. IX, p. 89.
[49] December 19, 1800. *Ibid.*, p. 91.

friends suggested that the office of Chief Justice might possibly be filled "by the present Chief Magistrate after the month of March next." This singular idea evidently could not have been entertained by Adams, who would have had difficulties in nominating himself. He answered one of his correspondents that he had already taken the matter out of his own hands by "the nomination of a gentleman in the full vigor of middle age, in the full habits of business, and whose reading in the science is fresh in his head." [50] Although Adams had not been long acquainted with his Secretary of State, he had probably recognized him as a man who would, as Jay, stand firm against "visionary schemes or fluctuating theories", and a few days previously, without even consulting the nominee, he had sent to the Senate the name of John Marshall, to be appointed Chief Justice of the United States.

More effectually than by fighting in the arena, and without compromising the prestige of the presidential office, Adams had thus provided a bulwark against attacks which the Democrats could not fail to launch against the Constitution. If Marshall's nomination seems to have been due to a sudden inspiration, it was nevertheless part of a plan dear to Adams' heart. He had never forgotten that he had been a lawyer, that he had fought for the independence of the judiciary, and one of the recommendations of his last message was the organization of the judiciary system of the United States. The bill presented by Griswold of Connecticut on December 19th was finally passed on January 20th, by a vote of fifty-three to forty-three.[51] It created many new judgeships, relieved the justices of the Supreme Court of the tedious work of sitting as circuit judges, and provided for three circuit judges to assume these duties. As the appointments were to be made for life, Adams had thus, by extending the influence of the judiciary, strengthened the control and check that this branch of the government was to exercise in the next administration. This step was perfectly con-

[50] To Elias Boudinot, January 26, 1801. Works, Vol. IX, p. 94.
[51] "Annals of Congress", House of Representatives, January 20, 1801. See also, Beveridge's "Life of John Marshall", Vol. II, pp. 547–559.

sistent with Adams' general theory of government; defeated as he was, he could still fight a defensive battle.

Foreign affairs were no less important. At last, the mission for which Adams had been so criticized had met with comparative success. After long-drawn-out negotiation, the plenipotentiaries, unable to agree fully on all articles, had, on September 30, 1800, signed a "convention" in place of a treaty. The French insisted to the last minute upon keeping some of the provisions and guarantees of the treaty of alliance of 1778, and the article had finally been reserved, pending further negotiations; but a working agreement had been reached on other points, and the convention, while leaving several questions unsettled, permitted the resumption of regular intercourse between the two nations. On January 21st, Adams sent to the Senate the report of the Secretary of State, and later the official correspondence of the envoys. He added to it a letter from Rufus King, American minister in London, relating a conversation with His Majesty and Lord Grenville, who had expressed the opinion that they saw nothing in the convention inconsistent with the Jay treaty. Thus the adversaries of Adams, who had so often predicted that an accord with France would result in a war with Great Britain, were deprived of their last argument and, with ill-concealed satisfaction, the President could write in his message to the Senate: "Although our right is very clear to negotiate treaties according to our own ideas of right and justice, honor and good faith, yet it must always be a satisfaction to know that the judgment of other nations, with whom we have connection, coincides with ours." [52]

Much to the disappointment of the President, the Senators made a last effort to defeat the early resumption of negotiations on the disputed questions by substituting for the second article an amendment by which the convention was to be in force "for the term of eight years from the time of the exchange of the ratification." [53] So serious was the matter in Adams' opinion that he seemed to have considered the possibility of vetoing the

[52] Works, Vol. IX, p. 166.
[53] "Annals of Congress", Senate, January 23, 1801.

conditional ratification of the convention. After long consideration, he decided that "it was better to ratify it under the conditions prescribed, than not at all", and nominated Bayard
minister plenipotentiary to the French Republic, to negotiate
the exchange of ratifications. As Bayard declined the appointment, Adams had to leave the documents in the hands of his
successor, "to proceed with them according to his wisdom." [54]
Thus he was partly deprived of the credit due him for keeping
the United States out of war, resuming peaceful relations with
a country which counted many partisans among the American
people, and making possible the work of national reconstruction
and expansion that Jefferson was to undertake. Then as later,
however, he was fully aware that it was the most remarkable
achievement of his administration, and not without reason could
he write fifteen years later: "I desire no other inscription over
my gravestone than: 'Here lies John Adams, who took upon
himself the responsibility of the peace with France in the year
1800'."

Although still in Washington, he had already passed out
of the scene. He had instructed Marshall to prepare letters
recalling John Quincy Adams from the Court of Prussia, to
avoid the humiliation of having his son dismissed by his successor. He had no longer any personal interest in the play and
watched it with as much detachment as was in his nature. The
electors' votes were counted on Wednesday, February 11th,
and upon proclamation of the results, unofficially known for
almost two months prior, the House proceeded to balloting
by States, after the Speaker had announced that "the vote of
nine States shall be necessary to constitute a choice of President
of the United States." On the first ballot Jefferson received
the vote of eight States, six declared for Aaron Burr and two
were divided. When the House adjourned over Sunday, thirty-
three ballots had been taken without appreciable change, the
Republican and Federalist parties remaining immovable in their
original vote for President, and the *National Intelligencer*
adjured the representatives to realize that "the unanimous and
firm decision of the people throughout the United States in

[54] Works, Vol. X, p. 113.

favor of Mr. Jefferson will be irresistible." During Sunday, conferences and caucuses were held by the Republicans and the "conspirators" — as the friends of Burr were called — but no agreement was reached. Only one ballot was taken on Monday, and the House adjourned after adopting the motion that the ballot be repeated on the morrow at twelve o'clock and not before. The next day the thirty-fifth ballot was taken without result; at one o'clock, on the thirty-sixth ballot, the votes of ten States having been given to Thomas Jefferson, while Aaron Burr had only four, and the votes of two States being blank, Jefferson was declared elected, and a committee of three, consisting of Mr. Pinckney, Mr. Tazewell, and Mr. Bayard, was appointed to wait on the President and notify him.[55] The "conspirators hurried to their lodgings under strong apprehensions of suffering from the just indignation of their fellow citizens." [56]

During these hectic days Adams remained distant, shut up in the presidential mansion, apparently unconcerned, and attending to routine business. An inventory had to be made of the furniture, accounts of sums spent rendered to the House, judges had to be appointed to the newly established courts. There is no record of his interview with the committee, which must have been cold and very formal. As a last courtesy to the departing President, the House extended him franking privileges.[57] There was very little he could do now except provide judges for the recently appointed courts. During the last days of his administration, Adams proceeded to send nominations to the Senate and to fill the judgeships with good Federalists. With an almost unbelievable lack of perspicacity, he then remembered Oliver Wolcott, who apparently had succeeded to the last minute in deceiving his chief, and nominated him a district judge. The fact that Marshall took the initiative in proposing Wolcott hardly seems a justification or an excuse. Adams endorsed it heartily, claimed credit for it, and presented

[55] "Annals of Congress", House of Representatives, February 17, 1801.
[56] Mrs. S. H. Smith, in "The First Forty Years of Washington Society", edited by Gaillard Hunt, New York, 1906, p. 25.
[57] "Annals of Congress", House of Representatives, February 18, 1801.

it as a reward for "twenty years of able and faithful service." [58] Until nine o'clock of the night before Jefferson's inauguration, Adams continued to send nominations which were ratified without debate by the Senate, while Marshall signed and sealed the appointments. Indignant as the Republicans were, there was nothing they could do, and the legend that Levi Lincoln, the incoming Attorney-General, stepped into Marshall's room, Jefferson's watch in his hand, has been satisfactorily disproved.[59]

That night Adams did not go to bed, however, but packed his last books and gathered his last papers — he was too tired, too bruised, to find courage to attend the inauguration of his successor and to witness Jefferson's triumph. Some years later, writing to the *Boston Patriot*, he compared himself to a poor animal he had once seen in a circus, which, after taking hold of a rope with its teeth, "was drawn slowly up by pullies through a storm of squibs, crackers and rockets, flaming and blazing round him every moment; and though the scorching flames made him groan and moan and roar, he would not let go his hold till he had reached the ceiling of a lofty theatre, where he hung some time, still suffering a flight of rockets, and at last descended through another storm of burning powder, and never let go till his four feet safely landed on the floor."

At last Adams felt his feet on solid ground. He had never had any taste for official functions, and although it might have been the gracious thing to do, at the moment he felt no desire to be gracious to Jefferson. Very early on the morning of March 4th, while the city was still asleep, he called for his coach. He "trotted five hundred miles through the bogs", and a few minutes after his arrival at Quincy was welcomed with a violent equinoctial gale of wind, accompanied with a flood of rain that confined him to his house for almost two weeks. It was a good "old-fashioned storm", such as he had so often seen in his boyhood, and it heralded in a tempestuous way the approach of an old-fashioned New England spring.

[58] Beveridge's "Life of John Marshall", Vol. II, p. 559, and Gibbs, *op. cit.*, Vol. II, pp. 495–498.

[59] Beveridge's "Life of Marshall", Vol. II, p. 561 *note* 1.

The weary traveler was home at last with his books and his family. He had found a hundred loads of seaweed in his barnyard — a God-sent boon for his fields. Not a rich man, still with enough slowly and painfully gathered not to be in need, he was like the field mouse of the old fable so delightfully told by Horace. Adams was returning to the land and in his country house he would feast on the humble productions of his farm.[60]

[60] To Samuel Dexter, March 23, 1801. Works, Vol. IX, pp. 580–581.

CHAPTER IV

THE PATRIARCH OF QUINCY

AFTER spending more than a quarter of a century in the service of his country, John Adams was again and at last a private citizen. This long political career had not been without its compensations. The son of the Quincy farmer who had started in life as a schoolmaster had reached the highest office in the government, and with just pride could recall the Independence, the Revolutionary War, the missions to France and Holland, the signature of the peace treaty, the mission to the Court of St. James, the four years during which he had basked in Washington's glory, his own administration, his efforts to maintain peace without sacrificing national prestige, and the not unmixed satisfaction that he had been right against the hot-headed leaders of his party.

He really never had much taste for the business and had never thrown himself whole-heartedly into it. It was pleasant to be the captain of the ship, to steer its course between the rocks, and to take responsibility. It was no less gratifying to associate with characters who would go down in history, to meet kings, lords, grand seigneurs, as the representative and spokesman of a new country which yielded to none in national pride and ambition. But a man in public life can never be himself, can never express himself unreservedly; the sense of responsibility rests heavily on the shoulders of the honest magistrate who has no reliable advisers to inform him and who sometimes has to act against the apparent trend of public opinion.

At sixty-five Adams felt he had done his work, and the disappointment at his last and, in his opinion, undeserved failure to be reëlected, did not rankle in him. A family man, for twenty-five years he had been most of the time separated from his family, and had not even been able to supervise, as he wished, the education of his children. John Quincy alone he had kept near him for some years, but the two others had grown up without his supervision. A practical farmer, he had to neglect the family acres, adding a piece of land here and there whenever he had saved on his salary, but having to trust hired men to cut the meadows, dig the ditches and gather the seaweed. A book lover, he had to steal time that belonged to the public to read his dear classics and recent productions which in his lifetime were accomplishing a revolution in literature. To his wife, his children grown up and scattered, to his grandchildren, and chiefly to the two little ones recently orphaned, to his books and his farm, he would now give his undivided attention. He would be able to accomplish the thousand little tasks, to enjoy the thousand little pleasures of which he had been deprived for so long; and far from being bitter and resentful, John Adams felt more at peace with the world and with himself than he had since he entered public life.

The old fighting spirit had not died in him, however; his tongue had lost none of its sharpness, and his pen could not long remain idle. A John Adams who would have submissively accepted the opinions of old and modern writers, and who would not have felt that it was his sacred right to be against something, would not have been true to his type and to himself. Age was not able to tame him completely, and to his last days he remained an American representative of that curious class of men both critical and conservative, skeptical and rationalist, to which belong Montaigne, Swift, Voltaire, Doctor Johnson and probably Clemenceau. But age had subdued him somewhat, and manifestations of his fiery temper became rarer and rarer.

He could never forget that he had been overthrown by Philip Freneau, Duane, Callender and Lyon; neither could he ever forgive them.[1] Against Jefferson, whose administration he dreaded and whose friends and supporters he despised, he felt and expressed no such resentment except when specially provoked. Grief opens the "cockles of the heart", and when Jefferson had sent him "accounts" of the funeral of "the son who

[1] To B. Stoddert, March 31, 1801. Works, Vol. IX, p. 582.

was once the delight of his eyes and the darling of his heart",
he had politely and heartily wished him "a quiet and prosperous administration." [2] He had failed to be reëlected, but Boston received him with honors such as are granted to a returning
general. Addresses were coming every day, and from every
town in Massachusetts, and the Senate and House had expressed for him their warmest admiration.[3] He was not a man
without honor in his own country, and his native State had to
the last remained faithful to him. No less flattering was the
realization that if he had ceased to be the first citizen of the
land, he was still the first citizen of Quincy.

He now had the best and one of the oldest houses in the
town. The large dining room built by Major Vassall in 1730
was still paneled with old mahogany from Santo Domingo,
which Adams or Mrs. Adams had painted all white, according
to the curious old custom. He had built a large addition to it,
with a "long room" in which were placed the beautiful chairs
brought back from Paris, and upstairs a study or library, with
shelf after shelf of old and new books on literature, history
and government. The owner of three houses in Quincy (for
he had retained his birthplace and the first house of his married
life, in which his eldest son was born), with comparatively
large landholdings, John Adams was not a rich man in the
modern sense of the word, for he had no money; but he was
comfortably situated. The larder was well stocked, Mrs.
Adams had "eight or nine barrels of good late-made cider put
in the cellar for his own particular use." [4] The crops promised
to be abundant and that year thirty tons of hay were cut where
eight years before Adams had obtained only six. The farmer
of Stonyfield could be quite proud of his little *chaumière*, and
commune with Lafayette, who in a distant land enjoyed similar
rural pleasures.[5]

[2] March 24, 1801. Works, Vol. IX, p. 581.

[3] March 26, 1801. *Ibid*.

[4] C. F. Adams, "Three Episodes of Massachusetts History", Boston, 1892,
p. 687.

[5] April 6, 1801. Works, Vol. IX, p. 583.

Early in the field to supervise the haymakers, he gave his afternoons to literary pursuits. In the study on the upper floor, in a comfortable armchair such as Voltaire had in his old days, his long pipe near him, and his old dog Juno wagging her tail whenever a visitor appeared, Adams leisurely read again his old books and many new ones. He went back to the old classics, never completely abandoned, and found in Horace a perfect picture of his own life and ideal of a moderate comfort. He read the moderns also, and having no one with whom he could discuss them, covered the margins with pithy annotations. Rousseau's "La Nouvelle Héloïse" held his attention, and he did not disapprove of the moral remarks of the Geneva philosopher. A "vain woman", whose father he had known in Paris, had recently published a treatise on "The Influence of Passions on the Happiness of Individuals and Nations." Madame de Staël had all the faults of her sex, but there were profound thoughts on the human heart in her little book, and many of her maxims on ambition, revenge, and glory applied very aptly to the present situation. "Sentenced to be famous, without being able to make one's self known" — was not this a perfect description of his own case? With her he agreed that "the one thing needful" was "to constitute a great nation with order and liberty." On details he dissented sharply from the "inexperienced woman"; wondered how she had forgotten to mention "Emulation, the Father of the Family of Pride, Vanity, Ambition, Love of Glory" among the human passions, and protested: "disappointed ambition breeds resentment. Often true, not always!" It was "possible to be ambitious and honest", and unknowingly Adams confessed himself while turning the pages of the book.

No less meaty was Voltaire's "Introduction to the Philosophy of History", and particularly his "Traité de la Tolérance"; it was both informative and provocative, a supreme quality in a book! Poor Voltaire, whom he had seen in Paris witnessing his own triumph and who died without realizing that "he would have been guillotined for Aristocracy in the last ten years of the 18th Century!" Blind philosopher who had proclaimed that philosophy had disarmed hands so long covered with blood! Was it "possible to read this with patience in 1801"? [6]

Only one regret remained: not to be able to return to the bar. At sixty-five Adams could not think of resuming his practice of the law, but he dreaded the long New England winters, for "ennui when it rains on a man in large drops is worse than one of our north-east storms", and he was still too active mentally not to feel the need of engaging in some occupation. To live the life of a dormouse was no life at all. The meetings of the Academy held in Boston were pleasant but rare occurrences, and Quincy was too much out of the way to permit many travelers to pay their respects to the former President. Soon Adams felt himself buried and forgotten at Mount Wollaston; there was "nothing but the plough" between himself and the grave, and he was too unaccustomed to comfort to accept his present existence with only gratitude and calmness. He had been solicited several times to write the memoirs of his administration, and the temptation was great, for attacks had not immediately ceased upon his retiring from office; but he was unwilling to engage in politics, unwilling to discuss the past. He did it, however, on a very unfortunate occasion.

In 1803, a remote cousin of his, William Cunningham, who had not given up the fight and intended to give a full view of the character of Jefferson, attempted to obtain from Adams information and materials that would enable him to wage his newspaper war against the President. At first Adams refused to encourage Cunningham. He maintained that he knew very little about Jefferson, there was no close intimacy between them in Paris, and he had had "little intercourse with him except in common civilities" while in Philadelphia. But Adams had not yet reached the point where he could really control his pen or his tongue, and he soon added that Jefferson had always professed great friendship for him, although countenancing Freneau, Bache and Callender. Then came one of those scorching characterizations in which Adams had so often indulged:

[6] Some of these annotations have been given in "More Books", the Bulletin of the Boston Public Library by Mr. Zoltán Haraszti, and I published some myself. Many more, and very important ones, remain to be published.

"I wish him no ill. I envy him not. I shudder at the calam.
which I fear his conduct is preparing for his country: from
mean thirst of popularity, an inordinate ambition, and a wa.
of sincerity." [7] The whole situation could be summed up in a
sharp, pungent sentence: "Democracy is Lovelace and the people is Clarissa. The artful villain will pursue the innocent
lovely girl to her ruin and death." [8]

For this unexpected burst of animosity there was an explanation, if not an excuse. Adams had never forgiven Jefferson for
pardoning, soon after taking office, "the vilest of his slander-
ers", Thomas Callender of Richmond, "a wretch who was
suffering the just punishment of his crimes for publishing the
basest libel, the lowest and vilest slander which malice could
invent or calumny exhibit, against the reputation of his predecessor." [9] This had been interpreted both by Adams and his
wife as an indorsement of Callender's campaign and a personal
insult. There was worse, however, for Jefferson had shown
his private resentment against the Adams family in depriving
John Quincy Adams of the modest position of commissioner in
cases of bankruptcy, to which he had been appointed by the
Judge of the Federal Court of Massachusetts, on his return
from Russia. When, early in 1802, the law made this charge a
permanent office and placed the appointment in the power of
the President, Jefferson had removed John Quincy and appointed a new incumbent in his stead. "This looked so particularly pointed that some Republicans in Boston had expressed their regret that the President had done so." [10] Adams
himself had not openly expressed his opinion on the matter, but
he was too prone to transmute a personal wrong into a public
danger, and several years were to elapse before he could think
of resuming personal relations with his former friend.

On the whole, however, the letters to Cunningham exhibited

[7] "Correspondence between the Hon. John Adams, late President of the
United States, and the late Wm. Cunningham, Esq., beginning in 1803, and
ending in 1813." Boston, E. M. Cunningham, 1823.

[8] March, 1804.

[9] Mrs. Adams to Thomas Jefferson, July 1, 1804. "Letters", Vol. II,
p. 252.

[10] *Ibid.*, p. 256.

animosity against Jefferson than might have been ex-
cted. Not written in any consecutive way and not meant to be
ublished, they did not answer the purpose of the wily Cunningham, who attempted in vain to elicit from Adams specific
accusations against Jefferson. They reveal nothing new on
Adams' vanity, acerbity of language, and inability to forgive
Hamilton and Pickering for their hostility. Nowhere, perhaps,
has he revealed himself more completely than in his project
for his tomb: [11]

No higher ambition remains with me than to build a tomb upon
the summit of the hill before my door, covered with a six foot cube
of Quincy granite, with an inscription like this:

Siste, Viator.
With much delight these pleasing hills you view,
Where Adams from an envious world withdrew,
Where sick of glory, faction, power, and pride,
Sure judge how empty all, who had all tried,
Beneath his shades the weary chief repos'd,
And life's great scene in quiet virtue clos'd.

Of "Hamilton's lubricity", he drew an "odious picture", denouncing it with a vividness of language borrowed from the
village smith. He disapproved of the repeal of the judiciary
law, of the omission to build a strong fleet, of the removal of
so many of the best men and the appointment of so many of
the worst. He had kept silent and quiet, but his silence should
not be misinterpreted. "Do they believe that I approve of
twenty other things, too many to be enumerated?" [12] He denounced the Federalists as the "calves of John Bull", and his
Republican enemy, Matthew Lyon, as "a mixture of monk
and monkey." But for Pickering he reserved his choicest shafts:
"He is, for anything I know, a good son, husband, father,
grandfather, brother, uncle, and cousin; but he is a man in a
mask, sometimes of silk, sometimes of iron, and sometimes of
brass. And he changes them very suddenly and with some dexterity." [13]

[11] November 25, 1808.
[12] September 27, 1808.
[13] November 7, 1808.

Thus striking right and left, sparing neither friend nor foe, once again the "old chief" gave himself the illusion that with undiminished strength he was back in the strife. Once more, also, the old moralist asserted himself. Politics and party system were definitely established in the heart of things, and there was no hope of ever forming a truly national government:

How long such a maxim can be maintained consistently with any civil government at all, time will determine. While it lasts all we can hope is, that in the game at leap frog, once in eight or twelve years, the party of the OUTS will leap over the heads and shoulders of the INS; for I own to you, I have so little confidence in the wisdom, prudence or virtue of either party, that I should be nearly as willing that one should be absolute and unchecked as the other.[14]

There was little in these letters to give aid and comfort to the surviving Federalists, and even if Adams had not made Cunningham solemnly promise they would never be published during his lifetime, they would have caused much more embarrassment to the Federalists than to the Republicans.

Far different in character, but no less devastating for the old guard, were the letters he sent to the *Boston Patriot* from 1808 to 1813. Soon after retiring from office, he thought of preparing the justification of his administration for later, if not for immediate, use. He had never kept a regular diary, except in his younger years, but while his memory was still fresh and documents readily available, he undertook to defend at least two acts of his Presidency for which he was willing to stand as long as he had an eye to direct his hand or a finger to hold his pen: the dismissal of Pickering and the missions to France. For various reasons which he has never expressed, he refrained from publishing his memoir at once. He may have felt too tired to engage in a controversy with Hamilton, who would not have failed to answer, and it is equally possible that he thought too much of the presidential dignity still clung to him to render such an apologia desirable.

The old patriot could hardly restrain himself, however, when England, resuming her attitude on neutral rights, re-

[14] To W. Cunningham, September 27, 1808.

vived her practice of impressing British subjects found aboard American ships sailing on the high seas. After the English frigate *Leopard* had fired on the *Chesapeake* in sight of the American coast, the issue was joined. John Quincy Adams, then in the Senate, although elected by the Federalists, had never been a party man and had proved as unmanageable as his father. Out of a sense of duty, he had slowly drifted to the side of the administration, much to the rage of the old Junto, and had been fiercely attacked in Boston by the Federalists, who, on this occasion, unearthed accusations launched against John Adams at the time of the French mission. After the efforts of the Essex Junto had succeeded in preventing the reëlection of his son as United States Senator, Adams felt it his duty to come out of his retirement and carry the war into the camp of the enemy. It was not only his own justification, but also that of his son, undertaken by him in a series of letters to the *Boston Patriot*, where he vigorously denounced the British party, which had never ceased to exist as a dangerous and anti-national faction in America. The first letters, in which he dealt with Pickering's efforts to prevent the sending of a mission to France and justified himself against the accusations contained in Hamilton's pamphlet, were soon reprinted in Baltimore as a campaign document.[15]

Soon forgetting his original purpose, he reviewed most of his career, from his mission to France and his difficulties with Franklin, to the organization of the navy and the Hamiltonian plots against him. He was still incompletely informed of the extent of the treachery of Pickering and Wolcott, and represented himself as better acquainted with the state of public opinion than he really had been. The letters were hastily written and not always well documented, but they still remain a mine of information for the historian of that period. Unfortunately, they have never been entirely extracted from the files of

[15] "The correspondence of John Adams, Esquire, Late President of the United States of America; concerning the British Doctrine of Impressment . . ." Baltimore, September 15, 1809. A more extensive collection was published in Boston, in a series of pamphlets including sixty-three letters: "Correspondence of the Late President Adams. Originally published in the *Boston Patriot*." Boston, Everett and Munroe, 1809–1810.

the *Boston Patriot,* and the editor of "The Life and Works of John Adams" has reprinted only a part of the available material. They are not the best of Adams' productions, but they are among the most characteristic.

With undiminished vigor and talent for sarcastic portrayal, Adams explained how he had been shackled by his cabinet, and "unable to name a man who was not devoted to Hamilton without kindling a fire." He enumerated the difficulties he had to overcome, with an almost naïve and disarming self-admiration. From the day he sailed back from his first French mission, he had never ceased to consider himself as intrusted with the destinies of the nation. His vanity took at times the guise of Puritanical pride, and he marveled how the John Adams he knew had so often been chosen to be the special instrument of a wonder-working Providence. Such was clearly the moral he drew from the history of his administration:

I have now finished all I had to say on the negotiations and peace with France in 1800.

In the meantime, when I look back on the opposition and embarrassments I had to overcome, from the faction of British subjects, from that large body of Americans who revere the English and abhor the French, from some of the heads of departments, from so many gentlemen in the Senate, and so many more in the House of Representatives, and from the insidious and dark intrigues as well as open remonstrances of Mr. Hamilton, I am astonished at the event.[16]

But the old spirit of the Revolution was rekindled in him when he reminded his fellow citizens that if the right of impressment were once conceded, "every British seaman will say to every American seaman, as the six nations of Indians said to the Southern tribes, whom they had conquered, 'we have put petticoats on you'."

Curiously enough, John Adams had never formulated his political and moral creeds. Trained as a lawyer, he had to start from a fact and a text, and apparently could not soar with the facility of Jefferson. His most extensive works had been commentaries and discussions; for mere theories he had little use

---

[16] *Works,* Vol. IX, p. 310.

and little taste. In vain Doctor Rush repeatedly urged him to write a sort of political testament for the use of future generations and to spend his last years on a work that would contain the essence of his wisdom and experience. This he strenuously refused to do. What could he say that would differ from the views of any liberal New Englander? He had been "a church-going animal for seventy-six years, from the cradle", and agreed that "religion and virtue are the only foundations, not only of republicanism and all free governments, but of social felicity under all governments and in all the combinations of human society." He believed in "free schools, and all schools, colleges, academies and seminaries of learning", but would not have limited suffrage to those who can read and write. He was strong for national, social and domestic virtues, including fidelity to the marriage bed, and to his friends could confide that he could not recollect "a single insinuation against me of any amorous intrigue, or irregular or immoral connection with women, single or married, myself a bachelor or a married man." [17]

He was as radically opposed as a half a century before, to the multiplication of taverns, retailers, dramshops and tippling houses, and would have favored prohibitive taxes on spirituous liquors. There was nothing new in these simple beliefs, but if he proclaimed them in his dying will,

Every one of your brother republicans and nine tenths of the federalists would say that I was a canting Puritan, a profound hypocrite, setting up standards of morality, frugality, economy, temperance, simplicity, and sobriety, that I knew the age was incapable of.

In finance, his ideas were equally obsolete. His opinion was that,

. . . a circulating medium of gold and silver only ought to be introduced and established; that a national bank of deposit only, with a branch in each State, should be allowed; that every bank in the Union ought to be annihilated, and every bank of discount prohibited to all eternity. Not one farthing of profit should ever be allowed on any money deposited in the bank.

[17] To Benjamin Rush, August 28, 1811. Works, Vol. IX, p. 637.

But he knew only too well that if he should talk in this strain, the people of America would pronounce him mad; so, much to the regret of Doctor Rush, the testament of Adams to the American nation was never written.

Besides the reasons advanced by Adams, there were others, much more personal, that were not given. With all his vanity, which at times was almost morbid, he had more reticence and modesty than he is generally credited with. To reveal to the public his opinion on morality would have seemed too much like an indecent exposure. He felt no such qualms in discussing public questions and official acts of his administration, and sometimes (particularly in the letters to the *Boston Patriot*) spoke of himself as "Mr. Adams", as though his personality as President or a public official were entirely distinct from and superior to his real self. No such detachment could be observed in dealing with matters of everyday life. Franklin had done it quite successfully, but Adams still retained so little respect for the private life of the old philosopher that he could hardly mention his name. He was also conscious of his limitations as a writer; much to his regret, he had never been able to put his name to any long, consecutive, well-balanced literary production, and his diffidence appeared clearly in a paragraph of his answer to Rush:

If I could persuade my friend Rush, or my friend Jay, my friend Trumbull, or my friend Humphreys, or perhaps my friend Jefferson, to write such a thing for me, I know not why I might not transcribe it, as Washington did so often. Borrowed eloquence, if it contains as good stuff, is as good as own eloquence.[18]

"My friend Jefferson", Adams had truly written to Rush, for between them remained few differences of opinion obscured by the memory of so many battles fought together. He agreed with Jefferson on the Constitution and on forms of government in general. He still differed on matters of administration; but both his and Jefferson's administrations were now so far in the past as to be of no more importance than that of the old Congress of 1774 and 1775. Even the irritation he had felt

[18] Works, Vol. IX, p. 639.

when John Quincy Adams had been deprived of his small position by Jefferson was now forgotten. John Quincy Adams himself had supported in the Senate several measures recommended by Jefferson and had been appointed by Jefferson's successor plenipotentiary to St. Petersburg. Rush thought the moment had come to bring the two retired Presidents together, and he invited Adams to resume correspondence with his old associate. This Adams at first refused to do. He could not see that it would be of any use to exchange letters with Jefferson: "I have nothing to say to him, but to wish him an easy journey to heaven, when he goes, which I wish may be delayed, as long as life shall be agreeable to him. And he can have nothing to say to me, but to bid me make haste and be ready."

Then, a week later, just to demonstrate that he had not changed from his younger days, he took his best pen to send to Jefferson "by the post a packet containing two pieces of homespun lately produced in this quarter by one who was honoured in his youth with some attention, and much of your kindness." [19] Amusingly enough, Jefferson fell into the trap, and even before receiving the package favored Adams with his views on "merino sheep" and "the spinning Jenny", discovering only later that the "homespun" was nothing but a book containing the lectures delivered by John Quincy Adams when he occupied the chair of belles-lettres at Harvard. But his response was even more cordial than Adams could have expected. With his accustomed gracefulness and felicity of expression, Jefferson recalled the days when they were "fellow laborers in the same cause, struggling for what is most valuable to man, his right of self-government, laboring always at the same oar, with some wave ever ahead, threatening to overwhelm us, yet passing harmless under our bark we knew not how, we rode through the storm with heart & hand, and made a happy port." He could not quite refrain from discussing politics; but how different he was from the man who had been represented as a champion of the French Revolution and the defender of the Jacobins, when he wrote:

[19] January 1, 1812. Jefferson Papers, Library of Congress.

As for France & England, with all their preëminence in science, the one is a den of robbers, & the other of pirates, and if science produces no better fruits than tyranny, murder, rapine and destitution of national morality, I would rather wish our country to be ignorant, honest & estimable as our neighboring savages are.[20]

Thus, after an estrangement of ten years and more, the two friends marveled that the bonds which united them had grown stronger with the passing years. Their old differences were now matters of history; it was for others to shoulder the burden, for others to fight, and strive, and suffer. For themselves, it was far more important to know what each other was doing, how they spent their days of retirement, to receive letters full of egotisms. To their curiosity we owe delightful pictures of the late lives of the two old philosophers. Both were hale and strong — Adams, already past seventy-five, walked "every day, sometimes three or four miles", and still rode "now and then, but very rarely more than ten or fifteen miles"; and Jefferson, ten years younger, was on a horse three or four hours every day, and three or four times a year went on horseback to Poplar Forest, a journey of some ninety miles. Statesmen of those days were truly husky men. Both of them felt as mentally alert as they had ever been, and Adams made the astonishing admission, not only that he was not weary of living, but that he had never seen a day when he had not had more pleasure than pain. Over Jefferson, he had the great superiority of having a large family — he had no less than thirteen grandchildren and soon expected to see his great-grandchildren.[21] This expectation was not an idle boast, since three years later he could write to another friend:

I have four pretty little creatures, who, though they disarrange my writing-table, give me much of my enjoyment. Why, you seem to know nothing about me. I have grandchildren and great grandchildren, multiplying like the seed of Abraham. You have no idea of the prolific quality of the New England Adamses. Why, we have contributed more to the population of North America, and cut down more trees, than any other race.[22]

[20] January 21, 1812. Jefferson Papers, Library of Congress.
[21] To Jefferson, February 3, 1812. *Ibid.*
[22] To Vanderkamp, July 13, 1815. Works, Vol. IX, p. 169.

Amusingly enough, one of the first subjects they discussed dealt with the early history of Braintree. In his youth, Adams had heard whispered and shocked allusions to the shameful conduct of Thomas Morton at Merry Mount, and of the revels of his company around the May Pole "till Bacchus and Venus were satisfied", but the relation of Morton had been so carefully suppressed that he had never been able to see a copy of the "New England Canaan." Quite by chance, John Quincy Adams, while in Berlin, had purchased at auction a volume containing three pamphlets bound together, written by "Thomas Morton of Cliffords Inne Gentleman." It was "whimsical" that this book, so long lost, should be brought to him, for the very hill that had been called Mount Dagon by the horrified Puritans was now on Adams' farm. It was no less curious that he had to write to Jefferson for a complement of information on the gay scamp,[23] and even more amusing that poor Thomas Morton was judged much more severely by the Virginian than by the New Englander. For men who sold arms to the Indians, for lawless fellows and "unclean birds", Jefferson had no sympathy and shared entirely the opinion of old Nathaniel Morton in his "New England Memorials", of which he sent copious extracts to Adams. Not so with Adams, who, acknowledging that the fellow "was not worth much", maintained that "the Character of the Miscreant, however, is not wholly contemptible. It marks the Complexion of the Age in which he lived", and, better still, "Morton was not wholly destitute of learning." [24]

Soon, however, while steering clear of contemporary politics, from which both friends seemed to be singularly detached, they took up much more serious questions, and wrote not merely to satisfy a "selfish, personal and local curiosity."

In spite of his trials and tribulations, Jefferson had not departed an iota from the optimistic tenets of the eighteenth century. Doctrines that had failed in the Old World would succeed in America; where the old nations could have only government

<hr>

[23] Adams to Jefferson, October 12, 1812. Jefferson Papers, Library of Congress.

[24] January 26, 1813. *Ibid.*

of the *canaille*, America's experience during the last twenty-five, nay, during the last two hundred years, showed that the people could safely be trusted with the control of their public affairs. A first experiment had failed with the French Revolution, but a time would come when even in Europe, with the regular progress of science, men would cease to be debased by ignorance, poverty and vice. "The American example had kindled feelings of right in the people", and a new revolution was on the way. Never, in any case, would the people again accept "a tinsel-aristocracy of rank and birth" — a new era had dawned for the peoples of the earth.[25]

Not so with Adams, who had always maintained that no real democracy could ever exist, and who refused to accept the idea that men could be made much better by education, or even by religion, as it is generally understood and practised. His was the philosophy of Montaigne and of Pope, not of Condorcet. He considered "the folly, the pride, the vanity, the selfishness, the artifice, the low craft & mean cunning, the want of principle, the avarice, the unbounded ambition, the unfeeling cruelty of a majority of those (in all nations) who are allowed an aristocratical influence, and on the other hand the stupidity with which the more numerous multitude not only become their dupes, but even love to be taken in by their tricks." How could Jefferson forget that Aaron Burr had received a hundred thousand votes simply because he was descended from President Burr and President Edwards? How could he refuse to see that the fine words, "aristocracy of talents", were only a lure, for "education, wealth, strength, beauty, stature, birth, marriage, graceful attitudes & motions, gait, air, complexion, physiognomy are talents as well as genius, science, & learning." Then came the delightful piece which long ago should have become a classic:

A daughter of. a green-grocer walks the streets in London daily, with a basket of cabbage, sprouts, dandelions & spinage on her head. She is observed by the painters to have a beautiful face, an elegant figure, a graceful step and a debonair air. They hire her to sit. She complies & is

[25] October 28, 1813. "Writings of Jefferson", Memorial Edition, Vol. XIII, pp. 394-404.

painted, by 40. artists in a circle around her. The scientific S^r· W^m· Hamilton outbids the painters, sends her to schools for a genteel education and marries her. This lady not only causes the triumphs of the Nile, Copenhagen & Trafalgar, but separates Naples from France, & finally banishes the King & Queen from Sicily. Such is the aristocracy of the natural talent of beauty. Millions of examples might be quoted from history sacred & profane, from Eve, Hannah, Deborah, Susanna, Abigail, Judith, Ruth down to Helen, M^{de}. de Maintenon & Mrs. Fitzherbert.[26]

Thus bit by bit, stone by stone, Adams proceeded to demolish Jefferson's supposedly democratic theories. Pushed to his last trench, the Sage of Monticello finally had to recognize that some inequality was unavoidable, and that even in the most primitive societies some sort of an aristocracy always establishes itself. In a last effort to save what he could of the fundamental principle proclaimed by the Declaration of Independence and reaffirmed by the Déclaration des Droits de l'Homme, he attempted to distinguish between a natural aristocracy and an artificial aristocracy — the one moral, and the other immoral. But not so with Adams, who retorted that no difference could be distinguished between them, that the one was as corrupt as the other, and that Americans themselves had to admit that in the most popular governments, "the elections will generally go in favour of the most antient families." In Rhode Island "the Wantons, Watsons, Greens, Whipples, Malbones, etc." were certain to command more respect and more votes than the newcomers, and so it was in Massachusetts, where the tribes of the old families were sure to carry all before them." [27] So it was probably in Virginia — which Jefferson indignantly denied. Family distinction, he maintained, "is so totally extinguished, that not a spark of it is to be found but lurking in the hearts of some of our old tories . . . Here youth, beauty, mind and manners, are more valued than a pedigree." [28] But the old realist stuck to his guns, and with cruel clear-sightedness concluded, after pointing to the love of Americans for for-

[26] November 15, 1813. "Writings of Jefferson", Memorial Edition, Vol. XIV, p. 3.

[27] November 15, 1813. *Ibid.*, p. 7.

[28] January 24, 1814. Jefferson Papers, Library of Congress.

eign titles, "An hundred other foreign Aristocracies have Sown and are Sowing their seeds in this Country; and We have an Abundance of them Springing up in this Country not from Virtues and Talents so much as from Banks and Land Jobbing." [29] The old *enfant terrible* had not changed; he continued to hit right and left the democrats and the pseudo-aristocrats, making fun of the family traditions and ancestor worship exhibited by the "Eliots, the Channings, the Ellerys and the Bowdoins of Massachusetts", or the "Livingstons, Van Rensselaers and Philips" of New York. His experience of more than fifty years had only confirmed him in his original views: no true democracy could be established on a permanent and secure foundation, even in America. Lucky and prosperous merchants would always obtain more consideration and have more weight than the wise and modest philosophers; the son of a rich father would always enjoy a prestige denied to the children of a poor farmer. Men would always be fooled, because they liked to fool themselves, and how to curb these ever-rising aristocracies, to prevent them from obtaining undue influence in public affairs, was the fundamental problem of self-government. Objectionable to the descendants of the old families of Massachusetts or Virginia who could only meet it with a supercilious disapproval and silence, this theory of Adams could not be indorsed by a people who had put their faith in the dogma of equal opportunities. But how eagerly it would have been discussed and approved by the Voltairian bourgeois of France, and what profit De Tocqueville could have derived from the letters of John Adams when he wrote his famous book on "American Democracy"!

After almost half a century of disagreement, the two old friends had at last reached rock-bottom. In their letters they finally enunciated the fundamental principles of two entirely different and antagonistic theories of life which have divided the American people ever since the establishment of the Plymouth settlement. No other documents throw so much light on the main conceptions that have directed the course of the American people, and there exists no better explanation of

[29] December 19, 1813. Jefferson Papers, Library of Congress.

the strange contradictions so noticeable in the history of the last hundred and fifty years. And curiously enough, it was the epicurean and materialistic philosopher of Monticello who had become the heir of the messianic or providential tradition of the Pilgrims. It was Jefferson who maintained that the Americans were a chosen people, set apart to demonstrate to the world by their example that it was possible to establish on this earth an entirely new order of things — a new form of government, a new political gospel offering hope and consolation to the oppressed peoples of the world. After so many centuries of suffering, the time had at last come when, breaking with traditions, a new people had discovered a new and unobstructed way to happiness. As Jefferson's French friends had so often proclaimed, America was still the example and the hope of the world. It was this unexpected combination of the messianic and the pioneer spirit, expressed later in the doctrine of manifest destiny, which was to inspire the builders of the American empire, and which has made of the American people a nation of dreamers and builders whose psychology and actions remain a mystery to the people of the Old World.

In sharp contrast with it stands the philosophy of life of which Adams has been the best American exponent. It is not the philosophy of the Puritans, but rather the doctrine and conclusions of the humanists and historians of the Old World. Adams would have strenuously denied and, in fact, did deny, that Americans were in any way different from the older peoples of Europe. Studying man as a moralist, he recognized in him everywhere the same passions, the same vices, the same appetites and the same prejudices. Given an opportunity, American politicians would be just as ambitious, corrupt and unscrupulous as diplomats of the old régime; New England priests just as intolerant as the Jesuits. If France had a Bonaparte, America had had a Hamilton and a Burr; and American institutions were as precarious as any established by the will of man. The development of the United States would be no different from the growth of so many nations that had fallen, for the Republic would become rich, and there was no means to prevent luxury from producing effeminacy, intemperance, extravagance, vice and folly. Perhaps it was treason to express a doubt of "the perpetual duration of our vast American Empire, and our free institutions", but even such an empire would not be more lasting than that of Rome; the day would probably come when the mighty fabric would be rent in twain, and "as many nations produced in North America as there are in Europe." This was the wise and bitter philosophy of a man who, by his culture, his temperament and his prejudices, still belonged to the Old World — the philosophy of one who could not detach himself from the past, whose feet rested upon ancestral ground, and who felt that man was shackled by historical fatalities and natural limitations from which he could never liberate himself.

Adams was not a reactionary, however, but was always ready to admit that "the eighteenth century, notwithstanding all its errors and vices, has been, of all that are past, the most honorable to human nature. Knowledge and virtues were increased and diffused. Arts, sciences useful to men, ameliorating their condition, were improved more than in any former equal period." [30] For this reason alone, he almost regretted the fall of Napoleon, which resulted in the return of the Bourbons, and, with them, of the Knights-errant of St. Ignatius of Loyola. But with singular detachment he looked at contemporary events.

Even the War of 1812 does not seem to have retained his interest. He was unmoved when Hull and Decatur came to breakfast at Quincy, and the fleet of Rodgers entered Boston Harbor; neither did he share the alarms of his fellow citizens when the militia was called to arms to protect the city against an imaginary landing of the British. [31] To the government which had given an important diplomatic post to John Quincy and had sent him to St. Petersburg, he was ready and willing to give the most loyal support, thus opposing the majority of his fellow citizens. Of the issue there was little doubt; it was just an episode in a long series of events, and he had seen so many

[30] November 13, 1815. "Writings of Jefferson", Memorial Edition, Vol. XIV, p. 359.
[31] C. F. Adams, "Three Episodes of Massachusetts History", p. 912.

horrors in the past forty years that he could only see more catastrophies ahead. In time, perhaps, out of it all would result some advancement in civil and religious liberties, but slow was the pace of mankind, and narrow the way, and neither he nor Jefferson would live to see the course which the wonders of the day would take.

What a contrast with Jefferson, steering with Hope ahead and leaving all fears astern, with an invincible optimism and faith in mankind! Such an optimism belongs only to the incredulous who, having lost all hope of dwelling in the celestial mansions, endeavor to build an almost divine city on earth, and set up a religion of mankind, or a religion of progress as a substitute for older forms of worship.

Although a "church-going animal", Adams had very early liberated himself from all the dogmas and teachings of revealed religion, but the mystery of life and death had always exerted on him an irresistible fascination. From his early education he had retained a taste for metaphysical discussion, although affecting the greatest contempt for metaphysicians. Church histories and the works of theologians occupied many shelves of his library, and in the silence of his study, which he liked to call his "boudoir", he spent long hours trying to solve the old enigma of the universe. He was too respectful of the beliefs of others, and too convinced of the moral value of religion, ever to broach the subject in the family circle, and Mrs. Adams probably would not have permitted such discussion. He may have tried more than once to embarrass the village preacher with searching questions, but this was a poor game. It was much better to discuss freely and without restraint with a more worthy opponent, with a true disciple of the materialistic philosophers of the eighteenth century, with the old friend of Priestley — Thomas Jefferson of Monticello.

To such a controversy Jefferson lent himself with great reluctance. He had been too often scorched to venture again into the fire; he had already written too much on the subject, and had been too often misinterpreted and misrepresented to take new risks and run against new enemies. He could trust John Adams, however, and both of them joined in denouncing the ecclesiastical usurpations and the legends and errors that had corrupted true religion. He communicated the only copy of his famous Bible to Adams, who approved it, and wished for more. As in politics, they agreed on unimportant and disagreed on the fundamental questions. They joined on matters of morality, but their metaphysical beliefs were basically different.

Adams' appetite for such information was not easily satisfied. He regretted his inability to procure the "Acta Sanctorum, in forty-seven volumes in folio" and "to possess in one immense mass, one stupendous draught, all the legends, true, doubtful, and false." [32] In lieu of the Bollandists, he did the best he could, and spent a whole winter reading the seven volumes of Dupuis' "Origine de tous les cultes." It was a tough diet for an old man, and no wonder his gorge rose at the end:

> The vast prospect of mankind, which these books have passed in review before me, from the most ancient records, histories, traditions and fables, that remain to us to the present day, has sickened my very soul, and almost reconciled me to Swift's travels among the Yahoos. [33]

While such a contemplation would, in his young days, have filled him with disgust for his fellow men, old age had mellowed him to a point where he almost felt some sympathy for even the most stupid of them:

> . . . I never can be a misanthrope — *Homo sum*. I must hate myself before I can hate my fellow men; and that I cannot, and will not do. No! I will not hate any of them, base, brutal, and devilish as some of them have been to me.
>
> From the bottom of my soul, I pity my fellow men. Fears and terrors appear to have produced an universal credulity. Fears of calamities of life, and punishments after death, seem to have possessed the souls of all men. But fear of pain and death, here, do not seem to have been so unconquerable, as fear of what is to come hereafter. Priests, Hierophants, Popes, Despots, Emperors, Kings, Princes, Nobles, have been as credulous as shoeblacks, boots and kitchen scullions. The former seem to have believed in their divine rights as sincerely as the latter.

[32] February [March 14?], 1814. Works, Vol. X, p. 89.
[33] April 19, 1817. "Writings of Jefferson", Memorial Edition, Vol. XV, p. 106.

It is true that the thought of death was ever present in the minds of these two men, and in this respect also their correspondence is almost unique, at least in America, for the thought of death seems to have been ignored or dismissed by the American people. With the calm resignation of the sages of old — Jefferson bolstered with opinions of ancient philosophers and modern physiologists, and Adams upheld by a strong faith in personal immortality — they faced death unafraid and, contrary to Pascal's saying, without qualms. Had the growing infirmities of old age not warned them, the fate of the dearest members of their families would have reminded them of the unavoidable end.

At first death was a subject for semi-playful discussion; Adams had mellowed enough with age to believe he could "get over all my Objections to meeting Alex Hamilton and Tim Pick, if I could perceive a Symptom of Sincere Penitence in either",[34] and he had the firm hope of meeting his "Wife and Friends, Ancestors and Posterity, Sages ancient and modern."

It is a sad ransom to be paid by men who reach an old age that they often see their children die. Twice already Adams had suffered such a loss. Early in 1812, Abigail Adams Smith had been operated on for cancer of the breast. At first, some hope was entertained for her recovery, but by the summer of 1813 she realized that the end was coming, and late in August came back to Quincy "to close her days under the parental roof." [35]

Adams was writing a learned dissertation to Jefferson, when he was called to his daughter's deathbed. The next day he added a pathetic postscript to the interrupted letter:

I can proceed no farther with this letter, as I intended.

Your friend, my only daughter, expired yesterday morning in the arms of her husband, her son, her daughter, her father and mother, her husband's two sisters, and two of her nieces, in the 49th year of her age, 46 of which she was the healthiest and firmest of us all: since which, she has been a monument to suffering and to patience.[36]

---

[34] May 29, 1818. Jefferson Papers, Library of Congress.
[35] Mrs. Adams to Jefferson, September 20, 1813. *Ibid*.
[36] August 16, 1813. Works, Vol. X, p. 60.

Four years later, Adams again wrote Jefferson a curious letter which he tried to make simply polite and friendly, until he came to the distressing part:

Now Sir, for my Griefs! The dear Partner of my Life for fifty four Years as a Wife and for many Years more as a Lover now lyes, in extremis, forbidden to Speak or be Spoken to.[37]

The most that philosophy can do is to reconcile us to the prospect of our own death — it is impotent to console us in the death of those who are dear to us; so the Epicurean and materialistic philosopher, feeling powerless, tried to evoke in the heart of his friend the picture of a future life of which he was himself more than doubtful:

The public papers, my dear friend, announce the fatal event of which your letter of October the 20th had given me ominous foreboding. . . . It is of some comfort to us both, that the term is not very distant, at which we are to deposit in the same cerement, our sorrows and suffering bodies, and to ascend in essence to an ecstatic meeting with the friends we have loved and lost, and whom we shall still love and never lose again.[38]

And Adams pathetically clutched at the branch extended to him. He was unable to prove physically that he would again meet Abigail, in a future state; even "Revelation" did not contain positive assurance of such felicity. His reasons for believing it were purely moral and divine:

I believe in God and in his Wisdom and Benevolence; and I cannot conceive that Such a Being could make such a Species as the human merely to live and die on this Earth. If I did not believe in a future State I should believe in no God. This Universe, this all; this $\tau\acute{o}\ \Pi\tilde{a}\nu$ would appear with all its Swelling Pomp, a boyish Fire Work. And if there be a future State Why Should the Almighty dissolve forever all the tender ties which Unite Us So delightfully in this World and Forbid Us to See each other in the next? [39]

[37] October 20, 1818. Jefferson Papers, Library of Congress.
[38] November 13, 1818. "Writings of Jefferson", Memorial Edition, Vol. XV, p. 174.
[39] December 8, 1818. Jefferson Papers, Library of Congress.

This was a most consoling belief, which Jefferson, for the time being, pretended to share, but which he fought with all his might as soon as he thought that Adams was able again to look at the question rationally instead of emotionally. He could not forget the reasonings, comparisons and experiments of Locke, Destutt de Tracy, and Cabanis, the "materialisms" of the Church Fathers, the theories of Dugald Stewart, and to his doubts and questions he thought he had at last definitely set an end when he discovered, through Lafayette, the experiments of Flourens on the nervous system.[40] But even then, Adams refused to be shaken in his consoling belief, for "incision knives will never discover the distinction between matter and spirit, or whether there is any or not; that there is an active principle of power in the Universe is apparent — but in what substance that active principle of power resides, is past our investigation. The faculties of our understanding are not adequate to penetrate the Universe." [41] After this long excursion and divagation through the works of modern and ancient philosophers, and in spite of the fine reasonings of Dupuis, Gebelin, Cudworth, Le Clerc, Leibnitz, Berkeley, Hume, Bolingbroke and Priestley, "and a million other volumes in all ages", he had come back to his original proposition and the counsel of wisdom once formulated for Jefferson's benefit:

Vain man! Mind your own business! Do no wrong! Do all the good you can! Eat your canvas-back ducks! drink your Burgundy! Sleep your siesta, when necessary, and TRUST IN GOD.[42]

After all, there was still some enjoyment to be extracted from life for the man who, having a calm conscience, could step into his tomb without fear of a severe judge. Jefferson had taken the building of a university as his hobby in his old days, and it was a fine undertaking. Adams himself had been much flattered when, in 1821, he had been sent as a delegate to revise the constitution of Massachusetts, which he had helped to frame almost half a century earlier. He had been received with

[40] March 14, 1820, "Writings of Jefferson", Memorial Edition, Vol. XV, pp. 239–241, January 8, 1825; *ibid.*, Vol. XVI, pp. 89–92.

[41] January 22, 1825. Jefferson Papers, Library of Congress.

[42] May 26, 1817. *Ibid.*

the most touching demonstrations of respect by the other delegates and was offered the presidency of the convention. To
assume such a task was too strenuous an undertaking at his age,
but he attended the meetings and even made speeches, "bog-
gling and blundering more than a young fellow just rising to
speak at the bar." [43] He was more pleased with himself than he
dared admit, for he proposed that the third article of the Bill
of Rights be amended so as to do away with the recognition of
distinct modes of religious faith by the State. It was to some
extent a parallel of the bill for religious freedom proposed by
Jefferson some fifty years before. Massachusetts had not yet
reached a stage of religious toleration that would have permitted the passage of the motion, and it was, as Adams' grandson expressed it, "gently put aside." The old fighter was not
so ready to admit defeat, and four years later still grew indignant at the thought that in most States of Europe, and certainly
in Massachusetts, "blasphemers upon any book of the Old
Testament or New" were still punished by fine and imprisonment. [44]

This was Adams' last expression on public matters. He could
have taken as his motto the words in which he had described
France — "always Protestant if not reformed." The man who
had been pilloried and hated for the sedition law had come
back to the old principles of his youth in his vehement denunciation of laws restricting free speech and retarding toleration
for, "as long as they continue in force as laws, the human mind
must make an awkward and clumsy progress in its investiga-
tions." [45]

On this point as on so many others, Adams had finally come
to agree completely with Jefferson. He had nothing to regret,
for he had always acted according to his best judgment, but he
was willing to admit, in his own words, that he had "an immense load of errors, weaknesses, follies, and sins to mourn
over and repent of." [46] One by one he had seen his old com-

[43] See his speech in Life, Works, Vol. I, p. 626.
[44] January 23, 1825. Ibid., Vol. X, p. 415.
[45] Ibid.
[46] To Rush, May 1, 1807. Ibid., Vol. IX, p. 593.

panions drop by the wayside and disappear. He was the oldest
survivor of the statesmen of his generation, and with Jefferson
and Carroll, one of the few survivors of the signers of the
Declaration of Independence. Much as he loved his children,
they belonged to another age, and the torch had already passed
from his hands to theirs. Jefferson was the remaining witness
of an heroic age, the only one with whom he could evoke anew
the days of 1776, the Declaration of Independence, and the
years in Paris. Such a friendship was a gift of the gods — a rare
and precious thing to be preserved at all cost. When, therefore, in the fall of 1823, E. Cunningham, to demonstrate the
danger that John Quincy Adams presented to the country, published the old letters now forgotten, addressed by John Adams
to his father, the old chief at Braintree, for the first time in his
life, perhaps, trembled with apprehension.[47] It was a clear
breach of faith, since the letters were written in strict confidence; but in the political battle waged around the Presidency
in 1823, as in 1801, editors little cared to distinguish between
foul and fair means. Pretending to justify Jefferson against
"the torrent of defamation which could be traced with un-
erring certainty to the prolific fountain at Quincy", Cunningham had but one aim: to kill effectively the candidacy of John
Quincy Adams.

Before publishing the letters in book form, Cunningham had
communicated to the papers their juiciest and choicest bits. It
was the last and most trying test to which this almost unique
friendship was to be submitted, and the letter that Jefferson
wrote on this occasion to the solitary of Quincy was perhaps the
noblest act of his whole career. His only feeling was one of
indignation at the author of this outrage on private confidence,
and in the whole transaction he saw only a last and desperate
effort of the contemptible editors who had so often in years
past endeavored "to instill into our minds things concerning
each other the most destitute of truth." Then came a passage
which should be inserted in all American histories as a fitting

---

[47] "Correspondence between the Hon. John Adams, late President of the
United States, and the late Wm. Cunningham, Esq. beginning in 1803 and
ending in 1813." Boston, E. M. Cunningham, 1823.

conclusion to the recital of the rivalry between Adams and Jefferson:

And if there has been, at any time, a moment when we were off our guard, and in a temper to let the whispers of these people make us forget what we had known of each other for so many years, and years of so much trial, yet all men who have attended to the workings of the human mind, who have seen the false colours under which passion sometimes dresses the actions and motives of others, have seen also those passions subsiding with time and reflection, dissipating, like mists before the rising sun, and restoring to us the sight of all things in their true shape and colours. It would be strange indeed if, at our years, we were to go an age back to hunt up imaginary or forgotten facts to disturb the repose of affections so sweetening to the evening of our lives.[48]

A few weeks later, when Henry Dearborn visited John Adams, the "aged and grossly outraged patriot, trembling on the brink of the grave", and read Jefferson's letter, he could recognize in it "the spontaneous development in all the ardour and vigour of youth, of that lofty friendship, formed in the times of our greatest perils, but which subsequent political dissensions, it was supposed, had obliterated." It was "Epaminondas extending his shield over the assailed Pelopidas", and "two of the only three surviving signers of the Declaration of Independence" would not be sent "to their tombs, as implacable enemies."[49] At Adams' urgent request, the letter of Jefferson was printed and circulated, and exerted some influence on the election of the man who, in Jefferson's opinion, was more qualified than any one else to perpetuate with zeal and fidelity the sacred principles of the Declaration.[50]

In congratulating himself on his son's election to the Presidency, John Adams could truly write of him as "our John." "I call him our John," he added, "because when you was [sic] at Culdesac at Paris, he appeared to me to be almost as much

[48] October 12, 1823. "Writings of Jefferson", Memorial Edition, Vol. XV, pp. 474–476.
[49] H. A. S. Dearborn to Jefferson, November 24, 1823. Jefferson Papers, Library of Congress.
[50] Jefferson to John Quincy Adams, July 18, 1824. *Ibid.*

your boy as mine." [51] No less truly could he say a few weeks later, "The little strength of mind and the considerable strength of body that I once possessed appear to be all gone — but while I breathe I shall be your friend." [52] This was no mere formula of epistolary politeness, and this last prophecy of Adams was to come amazingly true.

In the last years of his life he had kept remarkably healthy. He complained at times of sciatica and rheumatism, and his eyesight troubled him somewhat, but except for a "quiveration of the hands" which he painfully controlled in order to write to Jefferson, he retained for a long time the use of his limbs, and at eighty-five his short legs still carried him over four or five miles of rocky hills in his walks around Quincy. A time came, however, when he had to resort to the hand of an amanuensis to write his letters, and during the last years of her life Mrs. Adams often acted as his secretary. After her death, the grandchildren in turn rendered him the same service and read aloud to him when his eyesight had become so impaired that he could hardly use any book himself. But this was most unsatisfactory, and many things had to be left unsaid when the secretary was a young female, many books had to be left unread, particularly French books, for French, when read aloud, became almost unintelligible; so it was a rare treat to find such a book as Algernon Sidney's "On Government" in "as splendid an edition of it as the art of printing can produce", and with such good type that it could be read without assistance. [53]

At the beginning of 1826 he had to give up his walks even in the garden, and spent long afternoons sitting erect, supported by cushions in the big armchair near the window of his study, surrounded with his papers and familiar books. Although he breathed with great difficulty, he suffered with no particular disease, and his head remained clear; at least he would be spared a last affliction, for he dreaded nothing so much as "dying at top" and expiring like Dean Swift, "a driveller and a show", or like Sam Adams, "a grief and distress to his family,

[51] January 22, 1825. Jefferson Papers, Library of Congress.
[52] February 25, 1825. *Ibid.*
[53] To Jefferson, September 18, 1823. *Ibid.*

a weeping helpless object of compassion for years." He could not agree with Jefferson, who wished "to tread the ground over again", if he could recover his health. He had accomplished his term, he now had nothing to live for, and, after receiving the visit of Jefferson's granddaughter, who had just married Mr. Coolidge of Boston (a symbolical marriage, which reunited the two sister States of the Revolution) he wrote to his old friend: "I had rather go forward and meet whatever is to come — I have met in this life with great trials — I have had a father and lost him — I have had a mother and lost her — I have had a wife and lost her — I have had children and lost them — I have had honorable and worthy friends and lost them — and instead of suffering these griefs again, I had rather go forward and meet my destiny." [54]

He had nothing more to expect from life, and like the old French philosopher, he found it increasingly difficult to exist. He had lived in an "heroic age", and had been one of the Argonauts; now, after weathering many storms, the Argosy had reached the "halcyon calms." [55] But the inhabitants of Quincy thought he still had a last public duty to perform. The town was preparing to celebrate the fiftieth anniversary of the Declaration of Independence. If not the last, John Adams was the oldest of the surviving signers. Delegation after delegation was sent to him, urging him to make a last public appearance, a last speech. Finally they were satisfied with a toast which would be presented as coming from him. "I will give you," said he, *"Independence Forever"*, and, when asked if he would add anything to it, "Not a word", answered the old man, with true New England brevity.

On the morning of July 4th, as the town was preparing for the celebration, Adams' physician, Doctor Holbrook, predicted that his patient would not last beyond sunset. The opening salvos, the strains of the military bands, the huzzas of the crowd, did not penetrate the dimming consciousness of the patriot. All day he remained in his big armchair, attended by the doctor and his grandchildren, sometimes struggling to utter

[54] December 1, 1825. Jefferson Papers, Library of Congress.
[55] Jefferson to Adams, March 25, 1826. *Ibid.*

words hardly intelligible, but among which some of the at-
tendants could recognize a last thought and a last farewell to
his old friend: "Thomas Jefferson still survives." The inhabitants of Quincy had not yet heard the news that Jefferson had
expired at one o'clock on the same day, and this strange coincidence, when it became known, filled the country with awe
and wonder.

Adams, in the absence of his son, who reached Quincy on the
seventh, was laid to rest by the side of his wife. Four years
before his death he had left to the inhabitants of Quincy the
fragments of his library still in his possession, excepting those
which he reserved for his consolation in the few days remaining to him, and at the same time he had presented the town
with a portion of his lands, to make a foundation for a school
of the highest class and a library, forever to remain open for
the use of future generations.

When the Stone Temple, as it was called, was erected with
funds bequeathed by his father, John Quincy Adams prepared
for his parents an eloquent inscription, which one would like to
be shorter, to be placed in the church, and had their remains
transferred to the new building. Thus John Adams was deprived of part of the wish he had once expressed, — to rest
under a massive block of granite, on the top of the hill he had
so often climbed, and around which floated the spirit of
Thomas Morton, the gay pettifogger and adventurer. At least,
in the roughly hewn granite crypt where, by the side of his
"beloved wife" he was finally laid to rest, the granite sarcopha-
gus remained unadorned. To the cold, conventional First
Church, he would perhaps have preferred a more intimate
communion with the soil his ancestors had reclaimed from the
wilderness, and a simple New England burial in the family
plot on the farm, under the trees he had planted. But it would
not have displeased him to think that the grandson of the village brewer, the son of the Braintree farmer, had arisen above
the humble condition of his forbears to establish a new line;
for he was the founder of a dynasty and belonged to his descendants rather than to his ancestors.

INDEX

INDEX

ADAMS, ABIGAIL, daughter of John, 186, 191, 192; presented at Court, 195; marriage to Colonel Smith, 197, 202. *See also* Adams, Abigail Smith

Adams, Charles, son of John, 58; accompanies father abroad, 138; death, 308

Adams, Charles Francis, his picture of life in Braintree, 10; reference to, 224

Adams, Elihu, son of first John, 7; death, 85

Adams, Henry, progenitor of Adams family, 4, 5

Adams, John, son of Joseph, Jr., 7, 8; death, 39

Adams, Mrs. John (Susanna Boylston), wife of first John, 7, 8

Adams, John, a man of honesty and courage, v; education of, vi; designed for the ministry, vi; practices law, vii; his philosophy of life and government, vii–ix; his "Defence of the American Constitutions of Government", ix, x; his correspondence with Jefferson, xi; character of, xi, xii.

Birth, 3, 7; boyhood, 9, 10; schooling, 9; enters Harvard College, 12; in Harvard College, 12–19; his Diary, 17; his religious development, 17, 18, 25, 26; teaches school at Worcester, 19–28; his reading, 20, 21, 27, 28, 37, 40; forms ideal of society, 21; "turned politician", 23–25; studies law, 27, 28; begins practice at the bar, 30; his life in Boston and Braintree, 30, 31, 34–37, 54, 63;

his power of characterization, 32; his vocabulary, 32, 33; his literary style, 33; his talent for satire, 33, 34; tries to define duties of attorney, 38; fights taverns and licensed houses, 38, 39; sworn before Superior Court, 39; chosen "surveyor of highways", 39; his social pessimism, 40; on independence of judgment, 40, 41; draws picture of democracy, 41; on Otis's speech against writs of assistance, 41, 42; on speech of George III, 42; his ambition and patriotism for Great Britain, 42, 43; marriage, 44–46; joins Sodalitas Club, 46, 47; his "On Private Revenge", 47; his "Dissertation on the Canon and Feudal Law", 47, 48; attitude toward Stamp Act, 50, 52; his "Instructions of the Town of Braintree to Their Representative", 51, 52; chosen as town counsel, 53; his acquaintance increased, 53; in local politics, 54; becomes discontented with lawyer's profession, 55; removes to Boston, 55; refuses position of Advocate General in the Court of Admiralty, 55; protests against presence of troops in Boston and extension of jurisdiction of Admiralty Court, 56; increasing importance of, 56; and Otis, 56, 57, 63; acts as counsel of Capt. Preston, 59–62; representative to the General Court, 60–62; avoids politics, 63, 64; anger at Great Britain, 64, 65; his share in preparation of document declaring